The Story

of

THE

LONG MYND

The Story

of

THE

LONG MYND

told

through its

rights of way

by

Kate Thorne

First published in 1994 by Kate Thorne

ISBN 0 9524719 0 6

Printed in England by Livesey Ltd., Shrewsbury.

Kate Thorne

Churton House, Church Pulverbatch, Shropshire

CONTENTS

PREFACE

Rights of way in the English countryside are often ancient and are part of our heritage. To walk them is a pleasant way of enjoying the countryside and helps fulfil our common need to 'get back to our roots'. Unfortunately their use can be a source of friction between the landowner over whose land they pass and walkers and riders who enjoy them. Landowners should appreciate the need that so many people feel, in our increasingly urbanized lives, to walk or ride in our beautiful countryside and must acknowledge, and if possible welcome, their right to be there. Equally riders and walkers, while conscious of their rights, must not forget that the paths they use were all originally created by local people and belong to them in spirit. Property adjoining paths should always be respected and the country code upheld. If a set of rules is difficult to remember the golden rule should apply: imagine that the land and animals are yours, that they are your livelihood, then leave them as you would have them left by visitors - gates secured, crops undamaged and animals undisturbed.

Inevitably an obstruction will occasionally occur along one or other of the routes, although this is becoming an increasingly infrequent problem, thanks to the effort of the Shropshire Leisure Services, in my experience. Most such obstructions have arisen from prolonged disuse of the paths and not by deliberate intent; there is nearly always a way round them without the need to resort to the climbing of hedges and fences.

The maps in this book should help to keep you on course and the information on the history and natural history of the neighbourhood may make the walks and rides more interesting. If directions are all that are required, read the bold print only. Maps are only very approximately to scale.

If the description of the routes in this book in any way enhances the reader's enjoyment, helps to clarify his/her path or promotes understanding between the various interested parties in the use of the countryside then the writer's undertaking will have been worthwhile.

ACKNOWLEDGEMENTS

So many people have been kind enough to furnish me with local information and advice in the preparation of this book that it is impossible to acknowledge them all individually but I should like to express my special thanks to the following:

John Thorne	Editing/ornithology/languages
Mr.J.Downes	Minton
Mr.J.Evans	All Stretton
Rev.F.Carlos, Mrs.A.Cooke and Mrs.P.Carey	Wentnor
Mrs.M.Prince	Little Stretton/Asterton/Minton Batch
Mr. and Mrs.Randall	Medlicott/Wentnor/Ratlinghope
Robert Thorne	Fish/fishing
Mr.Howells	Asterton
Miss.E.Duckett	Little and Church Stretton
The Tyldesley family	Little Stretton/the Mynd
Mrs.P.Oliver	Smethcott
Mrs.Hone	Woolstaston/Lower Wood
Mr. and Mrs. Bib Williams	All Stretton/the Mynd
Mr.H.Stevens	Ponies/clogs/Cothercott
Mr.K.Feldmesser	Advice on photography

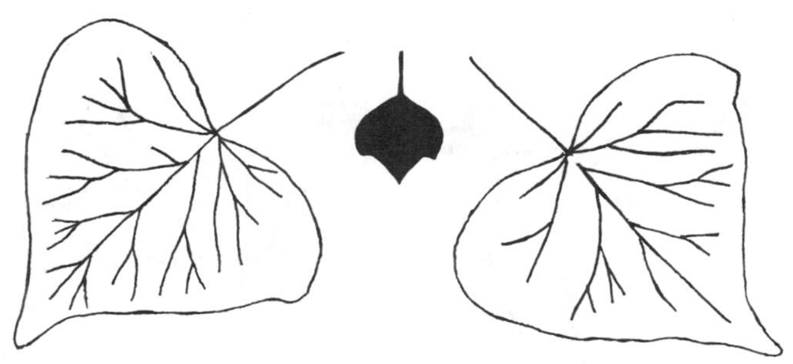

INTRODUCTION

AND

BACKGROUND

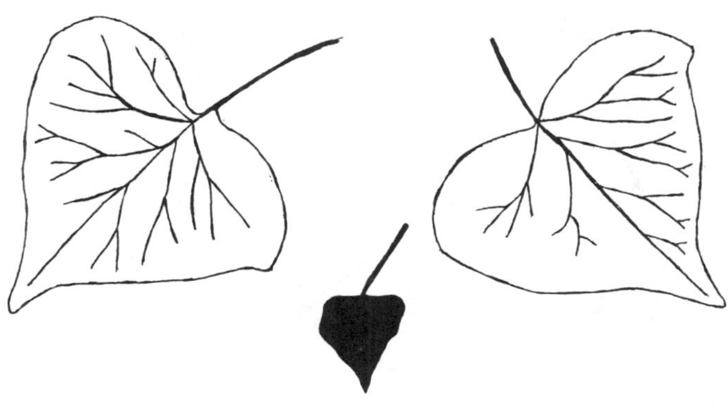

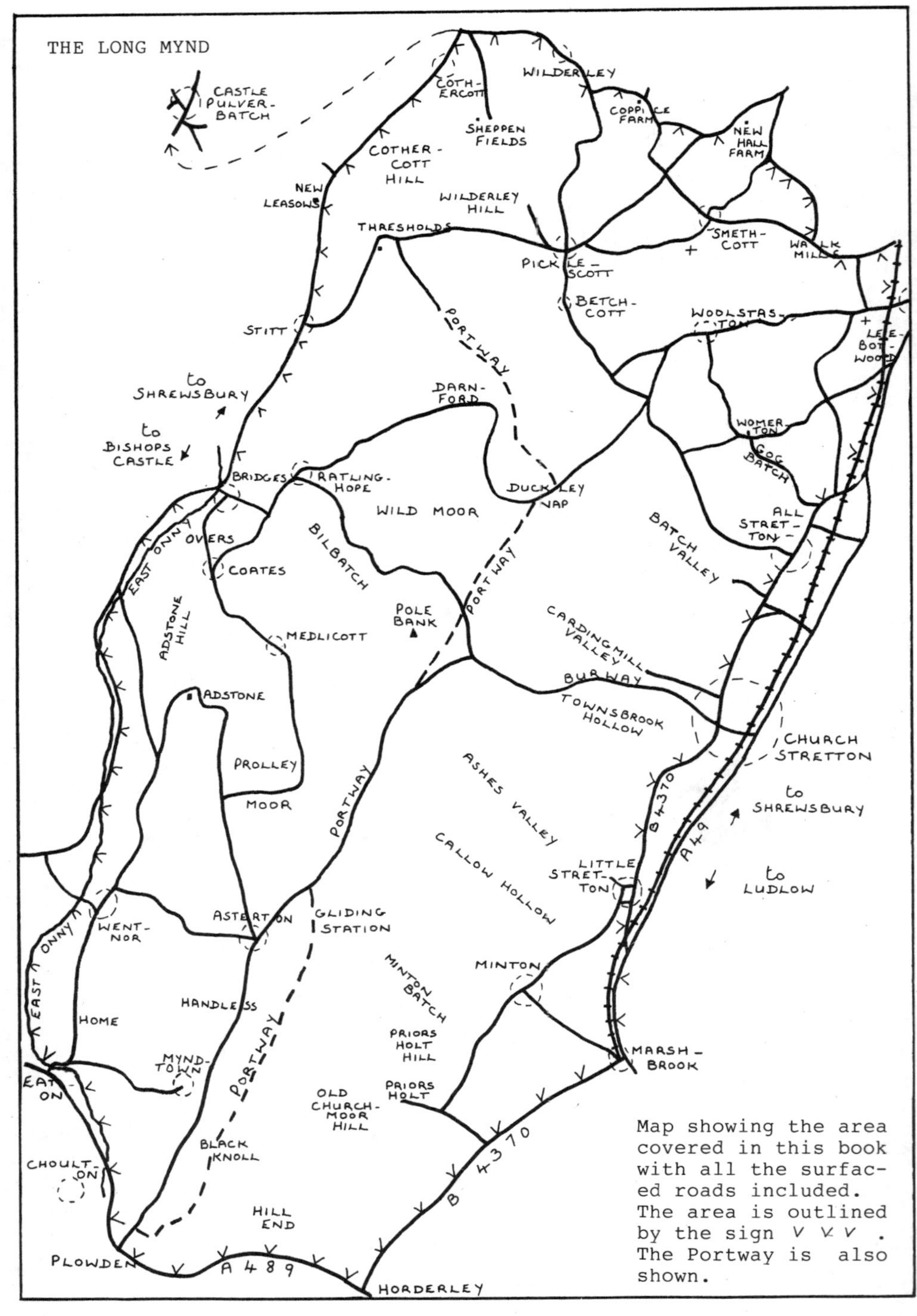

Map showing the area covered in this book with all the surfaced roads included. The area is outlined by the sign V V V. The Portway is also shown.

INTRODUCTION

The area chosen for this book covers the Long Mynd as an entity and not just the open hill which has already been included in several walking guides. The area is outlined on the map (see facing page) bounded on the north and west by the minor road from Shrewsbury to Bishops Castle and by the River East Onny, on the north-east by lanes, on the east by the A49, B4370 and the railway and on the south by the B4370 from Marshbrook to Horderley and the A489. It includes all rights of way within this area and consequently includes many of the rights of way in the villages of Pulverbatch, Smethcott, Woolstaston, the Strettons, Myndtown, Wentnor and Ratlinghope. The northward projection of the Long Mynd which comprises much of Pulverbatch is dealt with in a separate booklet. A few rights of way are difficult to use but have been included in this book. It is hoped that all rights of way will have been opened up in the near future.

There is a history to every right of way. Some of this history has been obtained from books and maps or simply from people who have lived in the area for a long time. By covering this whole area of the Long Mynd, some sort of story of the hill emerges. The rights of way that have become surfaced roads are all shown on the area map (see facing page) and no further descriptions are given of them. This book concentrates on the rights of way that have remained unsurfaced and those which are now bridleways or footpaths, all providing a rich heritage for us. Each right of way is described individually, as such ways usually arose. However, Church Stretton has grown more than the other villages and, although some of the paths and tracks were and a few still are utilitarian, many little paths have been created on the east side of the Mynd by an increasing population, and an increasing number of visitors simply walking for pleasure. To cover all these paths on the east in this book is an impossible task, but to record just those routes that were designated public rights of way in the 1950s, is insufficient. I have therefore included all public rights of way and several clear paths.

The first section of the book, following the Background, deals with two long-distance routes which, if combined, form a long circuit from south to north along the top of the Long Mynd, returning from north to south along lower ground to the west. The first route is the Portway, an ancient long-distance route, that can be used by walkers and cyclists and, for most of its length, by horse riders. The Portway maps in this book are marked at intervals by letters, each letter marking a point where another right of way joins it. This system of lettering is for the use of parts of the Portway in circuit routes (see Circuit Maps). The second long distance route I have devised to return to the start of the Portway by a different route, and is made up of several rights of way, each one numbered and described in the third section (The Villages). This return route, running down the west side of the Mynd, has had to differ for cyclists and riders from that taken by walkers.

The second section comprises circuit maps with numerous circuit routes suggested. The distances of these circuits are given and several heights above sea level have been specified as a rough guide to the amount of climbing involved. The heights are in metres so if you still think only in feet, remember to multiply by three. Flat routes are a rarity; the Portway after initial ascent being perhaps the best example. The circuit maps are arranged according to the order in which the villages are set around the hill, working clockwise from the north down the east side of the Mynd, round the south end and back up the west side to Ratlinghope. Some of the longer circuits are particularly designed for horse riders and cyclists. Each circuit, like the second long-distance circuit route, consists of several rights of way which are each labelled and described in the Villages section.

The third section concerns the villages, with a description of each one that includes information about such amenities as bus services, campsites, pony trekking, shops, pubs and refreshments. Maps and descriptions of every right of way are arranged around their villages, each way having been labelled according to which village most of it lies in; e.g. a way in Woolstaston, or mostly lying within it, is labelled WL together with a number, there being 8 rights of way in Woolstaston. The villages are arranged in alphabetical order.

Having explained the circuit maps and village rights of way to a certain extent, I hope that the following example clarifies it more fully. If, from the Woolstaston circuit map you decide to walk circuit number 3, (that is; start Woolstaston Church/WL 3/lane to Walkmills/WL 8/lane to Leebotwood Church/WL 7/Bog Lane/WL 5(in reverse) C to B/WL 6/lane back to Woolstaston Church) you will immediately find out that this covers 6¼ Km/nearly 4 miles. From the heights given on the map you should be able to work out that this is a descending route initially that levels out and finally reascends. By turning through the listed routes one by one, (that is; WL 3,WL 8,WL 7,WL 5(in reverse) C to B,WL 6) circuit number 3 can be completed. You will notice that WL 5 is 'in reverse'. This is one final concept; some of the ways are used in opposite directions for different circuits and to avoid confusion caused by trying to read maps and text in reverse, some ways have an 'in reverse' text and map as well. Some of the routes that are walked either way (particularly ones that go onto the open hill and have few stile or hedge features) have been drawn horizontally so that one drawing serves in whichever direction it is used.

I hope by this method to have provided an enormous amount of possible circuits, far more than if set circuits had been drawn. This method also helps to explain how the ways arose, and this was most certainly not in circuits.

The text for each route provides essential directions in bold print. Maps are only very approximately to scale.

Finally it should be pointed out that the starting points for the circuits usually have some space for parking although this is often very limited, the only large parking areas being in Church Stretton and Cardingmill Valley. There is overall a large amount of space for parking on the hilltop but this should be limited to parking near the surfaced roads, particularly in areas outlined by ditches.

The Long Mynd does suffer from an erosion problem. Sensitive parking and keeping to the clear paths are ways we can all help to preserve it. It would also help if a few people could be persuaded to forego the pleasures of the hilltop and use the ways lower down. These very underused ways offer wooded dingles, small hidden old fields, local character, good views and plenty of shelter. A major factor to consider is that spring starts earlier off the hill and it is probably at this time of year that these paths excel. Happy rambling.

THE BACKGROUND

A simplified geological history.

Earth is thought to be 4600 million years old. The oldest rocks in Shropshire were formed 700 million years ago, and the oldest in the Church Stretton area 650-600 million years ago, when volcanic lavas and ashes formed Lawley, Caradoc and Ragleth. 590-575 million years ago a shallow sea covered Shropshire. It was a cold lifeless sea in which sand and mud were laid down. These became sedimentary rocks. They contain no fossils, but ripple marks and marks from raindrops have been left trapped between the layers. Examples of these can be seen at Rowley's House Museum in its geological display. Most of Britain at this time is thought to have been part of a supercontinent in the southern hemisphere at 60 degrees latitude. At some stage, an area of these sedimentary rocks was folded up (the Church Stretton valley being a line of violent earthquakes for many millions of years) to form the Long Mynd and the small hills extending from it to the north. The centre of this fold runs approximately north to south passing through Bridges, and consequently the original layers of sediment have become almost vertical. These sedimentary rocks exist over a much wider area than the Long Mynd but, as is often the case, they have subsequently been overlaid by further rock formations. On the Long Mynd itself however, a large proportion of these ancient sedimentary 'Precambrian' rocks have remained uncovered, except for vegetation and soil, to the present day.

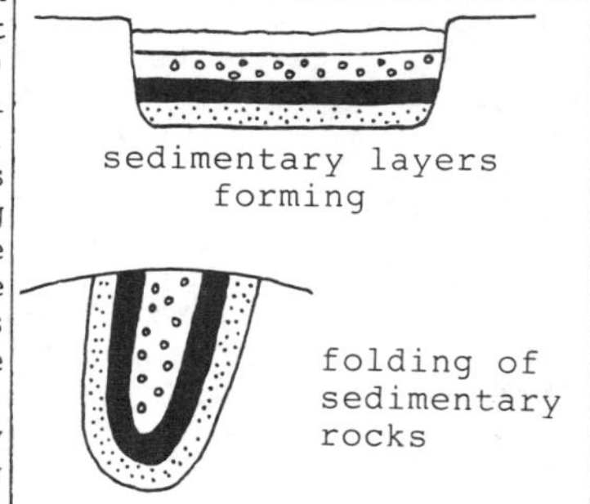

If man had existed, he would have seen many seas come and go over the ensuing millions of years. Depths varied, and sometimes the Long Mynd became an island. These became seas with life in them and the creatures and plants they supported became fossils, left in layer upon layer of different deposits that later became rocks. For nearly 200 million years, after the folding up of the Longmyndian rocks, Shropshire lay almost continually under the sea whose waters had meanwhile become tropical as Britain, forming part of a microcontinent, had broken away from its supercontinent and moved slowly northwards to the equator. Thus between 435 and 405 million years ago we can imagine Britain at the equator, and sedimentary layers formed during this time can be found in the floor of the Church Stretton valley and around the south end of the Long Mynd. The old shore line, with cliffs and sea stacks, has apparently been mapped. At about the end of this period, that part of Britain which had moved north to the equator is thought to have joined what is now Scotland (north of the Great Glen) and most of Ireland to form the British Isles (still as part of a much larger continent). Soon the whole of Shropshire surfaced, but between 355 and 290 million years ago most of it was again covered by sea whose waters were shallow and invaded by deltas bearing tropical vegetation. The fossilisation of this vegetation formed thin seams of coal between layers of sediment and some was deposited on the lower north-east slopes of the Long Mynd (barely in the area covered in this book).

No more deposits occurred on the Long Mynd and it would

seem that it remained little changed for millions more years although many events, including volcanic activity, were taking place elsewhere in Shropshire. About 50 million years ago Britain, with Europe, may have become separated from Greenland and North America and drifted northwards until it arrived at its present position about 2 million years ago. This was a time of global cooling and the Ice Age had begun that was to affect the areas adjacent to the polar regions. The Ice Age was a period of many cold times with warmer interglacials. Some, maybe not all, cold periods caused glaciation over Britain but there is evidence for the last few only. The last glaciation began about 80,000 years ago and has left abundant deposits as relatively loose clays, sand and gravel (known as glacial drift) which have not become rocks. A frozen Irish Sea spread south to Little Stretton while ice from the Welsh mountains spread east to meet it, with a tongue coming round south of the Long Mynd to Marshbrook. The Long Mynd itself, although it protruded above the ice, was affected by the climate. When the ice melted, the appearance would have been of ice fronts in retreat and the old rivers flowing once more. The Onny however, once flowing again, could not join the Camlad as it had done previously, since ice extending from Wales had not retreated sufficiently. It therefore pooled south of the Long Mynd and eventually cut eastwards between Plowden and Horderley as it flows today. Ice had disappeared from the Church Stretton valley by 13000 years ago but glacial deposits were left on the northern Long Mynd and on the sides of the Church Stretton valley up to 300 metres. Periods of high rainfall that followed the last glaciation for a few thousand years, speeded up the downcutting of the batches that exist mainly on the east side of the Mynd.

Man and the Long Mynd.

THE ICE AGE

By the time of the Ice Age man was already in existence and, while Britain would have seemed an inhospitable place, people may have come here especially in the warmer periods. If they came, it is likely that the evidence has become hidden under later glacial deposits.

As the Ice Age drew to a close the Long Mynd must have looked a desolate place. Soon it would have been covered by tundra, a landscape of stunted bushes of birch and willow with ground cover of bilberry, cowberry, lichens and mosses that had come from continental Europe. Slowly over a few thousand years as the climate improved, although not always continually, trees began to grow and man came to hunt in the forests. The Long Mynd may have been covered by birch trees initially and later by pine trees with willows in the water-logged valleys. There man would have hunted for wild deer, oxen and pig and for wild fowl living in the marshes. The forests were forever changing as more species came and were able to establish themselves. Hazel was followed by such trees as oak, elm and alder and later by ash and others, but as the climate became wetter the pines would have disappeared. The Long Mynd therefore, in about 5000 BC, may have been a forest predominantly of oak with willows and alders in the boggy valleys. This would have been typical of much of Britain at this time when it had become separated from the continent. Man, the hunter, has left little trace of himself here, but a few tools have been found relatively close to our area along the Clun-Clee Ridgeway (see below).

THE NEW STONE AGE

The New Stone Age (3500 BC-2500 BC) saw the introduction of agriculture and the beginning of the gradual destruction of Britain's forests. The people of this time, Neolithic Man, left behind tombs and implements but no evidence of settlement in the Marches. Numerous implements of this period made from flint have been found along the Clun-Clee Ridgeway, which suggests at least that this may have been an old trading route; from around 2500 BC it appears to have gained in importance as a link between the west and the south-east. On the basis of archaeological finds in the area, early trading of implements may have included the taking of axe heads made of picrite rock eastwards from a possible factory on Corndon, and perhaps a corresponding westward trade in stone implements of more easterly or even continental origin. Given the evidence for such use of the Clun-Clee Ridgeway in ancient times, a similar though less well documented significance as an ancient trade route has been suggested for the Portway, as there too a few scattered implements have been found. Ridgeway and hilltop routes developed because the valleys were wooded and boggy and lent themselves to ambush.

THE BRONZE AGE

With advances in knowledge and technology stone tools became replaced by copper ones, and from about 2000 BC by bronze. Ideas for change may have come with the arrival of different people in large numbers or from traders. This, the Bronze Age, has been attributed to the coming of the Celts, hence the use of the name 'Celtic' for monuments etc. of the Bronze Age. The Bronze Age peoples must have had a much more dramatic effect on the Long Mynd than their predecessors; wherever these peoples lived they would have been busy clearing the forest with their more efficient metal tools so that their animals had grazing and they could plant corn. Trees were not always felled, but by cutting a ring in the bark around their trunks to make them die more land could be made available for use. It is uncertain how much the Long Mynd was being farmed but the numerous tumuli on the plateau are thought to be early Bronze Age and indicate that Bronze Age man was here. Each tumulus is a burial ground for one person, together with things that were thought to be needed by him in afterlife. Apparently all the tumuli have been robbed and this may explain why so many of them are sunken in the middle. The burial of their dead on the hill may be because it was a revered place and would have given their dead proximity to the sky. It does not necessarily mean that Bronze Age man lived on the hill.

Tumuli or barrows are thought in some cases to act as signposts along ancient ridgeway routes. Although it is not felt that this is the case on the Long Mynd, it is not outside the bounds of possibility. As you walk along the Portway, notice how often a tumulus is passed, and at Duckley Nap the way past the tumuli (Robin Hoods Butts) is much more practical than the present day through route which dips into an already developing dingle. There are tumuli to lead you all the way from near Black Knoll at the south end, to Cothercott at the north end. Tumuli well clear of this route may have been on branch routes, as they all lie near practical travelling routes.

THE IRON AGE

Towards the end of the Bronze Age it is thought that the first 'hillforts' appeared. These may have begun as settlements but became well-defended sites and continued into the Iron Age (600 BC). It is not known if these were permanent settlements or refuges, but Caradoc's is thought to have been the former as hut platforms can be seen outlined within the fort.

Bodbury Ring is a hillfort above Cardingmill Valley. The two rings above Ratlinghope are now thought to have been enclosures for animals, that may have been Bronze Age. The upper one is referred to as Castle Ring.

More evidence is being found that man of the Bronze and Iron Ages was farming on the Long Mynd. Patterns of fields on the south end were discovered in 1938 possibly dating from circa 75-380 AD. On the higher land there is likely to have been more activity in the Bronze Age, since our climate deteriorated and became wetter around 800 BC. If the forests on the hill had been destroyed by then the land would have been leached of minerals, and the combination of poor and water-logged land would have resulted in the formation of peat. Perhaps this is when the moorland that we know today began - 3000 years ago.

THE ROMANS

By the time of the birth of Christ, there may have been a large expanse of man-made moorland on the higher ground of the Mynd with man-made tumuli and hillforts. The valleys and lower ground would have been woodland. The people are thought to have left the hillforts (why they left and where they went seems unclear) before the arrival of the Romans. The invasion by the Romans was the first of many which were to drive the British, as they were now known, further and further west. The Romans made little impact on the Mynd itself but the road that they built along the east side - the Watling Street - was to persist for centuries (at least until the present day) and would give Stretton its name - 'settlement by the street'. They mined for lead west of the Long Mynd and may well have traversed the hill to reach this road, but the routes they took remain a mystery. The Romans' stay in Britain lasted nearly 400 years.

THE ANGLES AND SAXONS

The next peoples to invade Britain were the Angles and Saxons who eventually reached this area. With their arrival, the countryside underwent major changes. Single fortified farms surrounded by fields, which had become a feature, were superseded and settlements began to appear in groups as villages and hamlets surrounded by common fields.

THE NORMANS

Little is known about the Dark Ages but when the Normans invaded Britain and after twenty years had compiled the Domesday Book, this pre-existing pattern of management of the countryside was shown. Although the Normans rearranged the ownership of land, the pattern of land divided into manors belonging to or 'held' by a 'lord', continued for several more centuries. In the Domesday Book, many of the hamlets as we know them today, each with its surrounding land, was recorded as a manor while other, perhaps smaller, hamlets were included in these manors. Some of the Domesday manors have dwindled to few or even only one dwelling e.g. Overs and Womerton. Some of the Domesday hamlets or areas rose to become manors later e.g. Medlicott, or at least to have their own common fields e.g. Betchcott and Picklescott.

There had been strife with the Welsh prior to the Domesday Book (and there would be more to come) and this explains in part some manors' being described as waste e.g. Ratlinghope. William the Conqueror granted much of Shropshire to Earl Roger de Montgomery (his cousin) whose duty it was to defend the Middle Marches. Mottes and baileys were built along the north and east sides of the Long Mynd (all to be vacated by 1300), and most of the manors were held of the Earl by other Normans while the Earl himself held Stretton. Few of the previous 'holders' remained but the place names that already existed, and were largely therefore Anglo-Saxon, have continued to the present day in some form. Many of the place names incorporated past 'holders' names together with a suffix that might mean something like cottage or settlement e.g. Woolstaston is thought to have been Wulfstan's tun, meaning Wulfstan's settlement. The Normans did not lend their names so readily but instead adopted the old names of their manors e.g. Richard de Wilderley, Roger de Pulverbatch, Llewellyn de Medlicott and Hugh atta Home. By the dropping of the prepositions, many of the surnames we know today were created and some of these names still feature in the area e.g. Medlicott, Minton and Home.

THE MONASTERIES The pattern of ownership would have influenced the use of routes on the Long Mynd. The same lord often held several manors e.g. Roger, son of Corbet, held Choulton, Ratlinghope, Woolstaston and Womerton. From the 12th century, Haughmond Abbey, by gifts and purchases, began to acquire land on the Mynd resulting in the linking of Leebotwood, Betchcott, Cothercott, Wilderley and Picklescott on the east and Stitt, Medlicott, Adstone and Gatten on the west, into the manor of Boveria. Some of the ways across the hill may have been used for collecting rent or goods in lieu of rent or for getting to meetings at the Manor Court, latterly at Sheppen Fields on Cothercott Hill. Ratlinghope and some of Choulton were given to Wigmore Abbey in Herefordshire and travel between these places is likely to have been by the ridgeway route over Adstone Hill to Wentnor (Wn 3 and 5). Shrewsbury Abbey was given the advowson of Wentnor Church, and Buildwas Abbey Wentnor Mill. These monastic links were abruptly severed in the 16th century with the dissolution of the monasteries.

PARISH AND DISTRICT The church and parish however, continued. Their story had begun in the Dark Ages but in this area records of the presence of any of the churches are unclear much before the Norman Conquest. The Domesday Book records a church at Stretton, but the other churches and the parishes as we know them today began to appear between the 11th century (Wentnor) and the 14th (Smethcott), each parish taking its name from a manor lying within it. Some parishes incorporated more than one manor, and some manors gave their names to townships (areas within a parish). Woolstaston is an example of one manor, one parish. Pulverbatch is an example of several manors - Pulverbatch, Wrentnall, Wilderley and Cothercott - all of which have given their names to townships, and one of which has given its name to the parish. Historically the parish and township boundaries were not necessarily the same as the manor boundaries but may have been so initially and later diverged as land ownership changed and old boundaries were crossed e.g. Leebotwood manor extended into Church Stretton parish and Wilderley manor into Smethcott. Many of the parish boundaries are centuries old, the most modern ones (200 years old)) being on the northern end of the hilltop and marked by very firmly embedded and inscribed stones! The parishes shown on the O/S Pathfinder maps are civil parishes, created to relieve the church of increasing civil duties and mostly, in this area, equating with the ancient ecclesiastical parishes. One exception is Myndtown ecclesiastical parish which appears to be the same as the civil parish today but which did not include the township of Asterton until 1894. Asterton township is ecclesiastically linked with Norbury and Norbury was a chapelry to the parish of Lydbury North until 1894 when it became a chapelry to the parish of Myndtown. It is therefore only indirectly that Asterton has been part of Myndtown parish for the past 100 years;

this explains why so many Asterton people, including a family from Handless stifled by snow in their cottage in 1814, are buried at Norbury.

The Portway, being an ancient landmark, forms parts of several parish boundaries (see figure 1) but has also, along with some other ancient walls on the Mynd, played a part in forming district boundaries. The ancient districts known as hundreds had been formed before the time of the Domesday Book and although altered later, the Portway from the south of the Mynd to Duckley Nap has probably always been a dividing line between the old and newer hundreds (see figures 2 and 3).

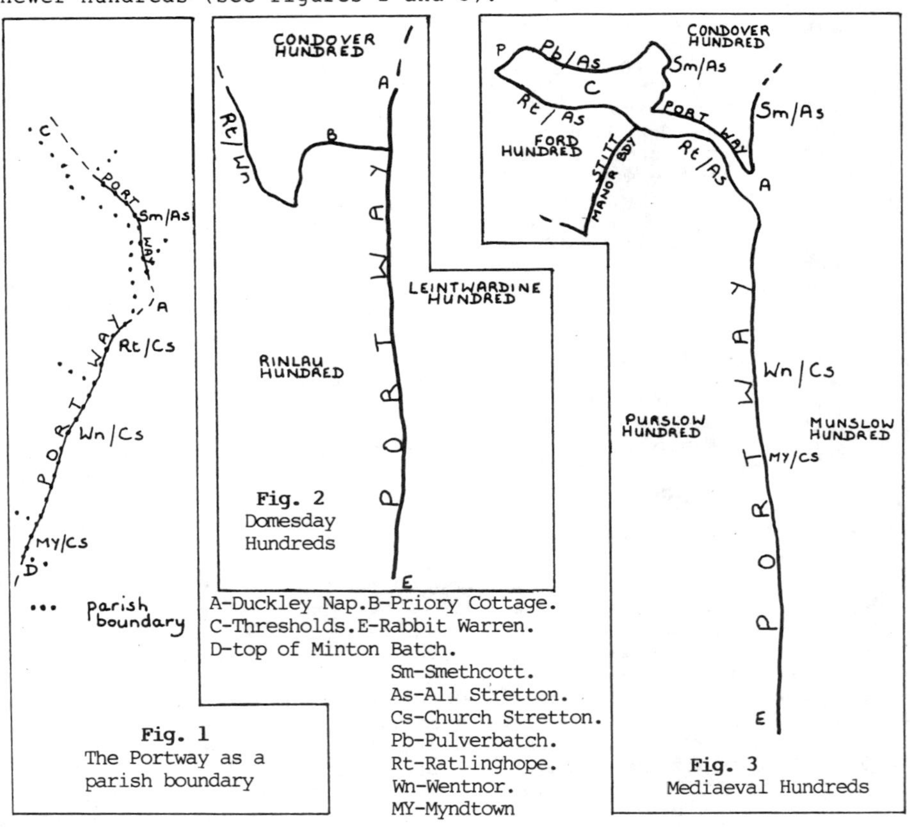

Fig. 1
The Portway as a parish boundary

Fig. 2
Domesday Hundreds

Fig. 3
Mediaeval Hundreds

In the 18th century, parochial unions were created for the purpose of administering the Poor Law and the Union boundaries on the Mynd used most of the hundred boundaries. In the 19th century these boundaries were adopted by the government, the newly designated districts then replacing the ancient hundreds (see figure 4). With some modification these boundaries became the boundaries of modern rural districts (see figure 5).

Apart from the Portway, the most striking boundary that served many of the above purposes is the present day Ratlinghope boundary, best seen from north of Henley Nap, stretching north in a long line of stunted trees undulating with the landscape. It is the Ratlinghope boundary and not the Portway, that at present serves as a district boundary.

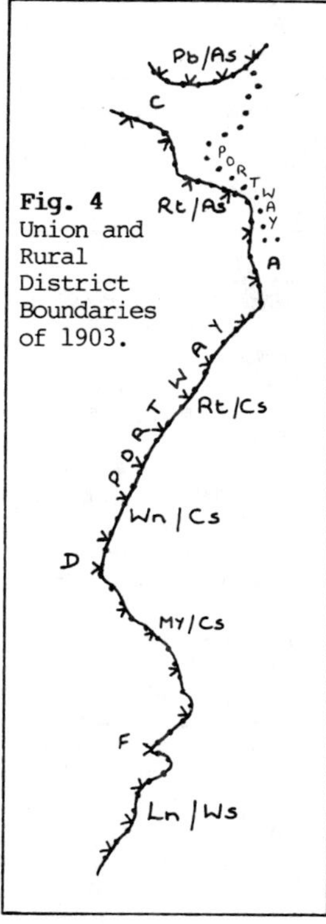

Fig. 4 Union and Rural District Boundaries of 1903.

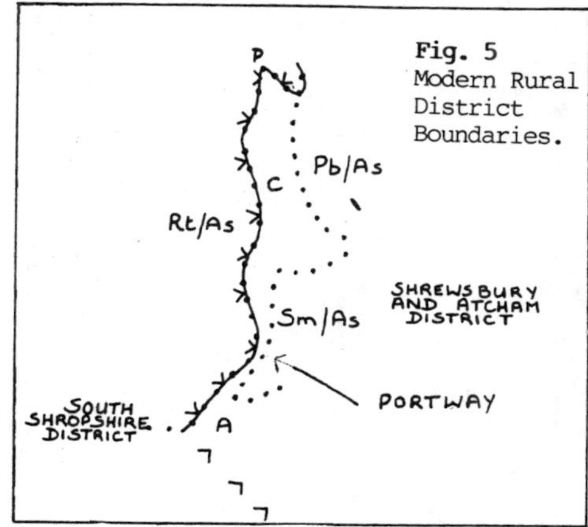

Fig. 5 Modern Rural District Boundaries.

.... parish boundary.
^ ^ district boundary.

A-Duckley Nap.B-Priory Cottage.
C-Thresholds.P-Paulith Bank.
D-top of Minton Batch.
F-Priors Holt.

As-All Stretton.Pb-Pulverbatch.
Cs-Church Stretton.Wn-Wentnor.
Rt-Ratlinghope.Sm-Smethcott.
MY-Myndtown.Ws-Wistanstow.
Ln-Lydbury North.

It was however the parish with its church that perhaps contributed most significantly to the present pattern of the right of way network. Life in the countryside must have revolved around the churches for hundreds of years (and well into the present century), and they can often be seen to be a focal point for footpaths most noticeably when they are isolated from the village.

COMMON FIELDS AND COMMONS

Much of the land on the higher ground of the Long Mynd was common land (see below). Some of the tracks and lanes giving access to this for man and animals were called Outracks. There were also commons and common fields on the lower ground giving rise to ways to them, but these are usually more difficult to figure out.

Common fields have been mentioned in relation to manors. These were open fields ('felled' areas) not bounded by hedges (i.e. not at all like our modern conception of a field) and divided into strips. The strips were allocated to village people for communal farming by the lord of the manor, and part of their payment in return would be to work so many hours or days on the lord's land (demesne land). There were often three common fields and at any one time two would be arable and one would be resting (fallow). There were times when everyone's animals could be turned out together in these fields (just as on the uncultivated common lands) e.g. when a field was fallow or after the corn had been harvested. If one imagines many people each trying to work his strip, it becomes evident how rights of way arose; strips of grass were left between some ploughed strips and were called balks. As the longer main strips (the furlongs) abutted on to short strips (the butts) that had to be created for the awkward corners and were at an angle to each other, balks that became rights of way must have developed some very sharp corners which can be reflected in the angularity of modern lanes that follow their line. A good example of this can be seen between Smethcott and Branmills (see figure 6).

Fig. 6

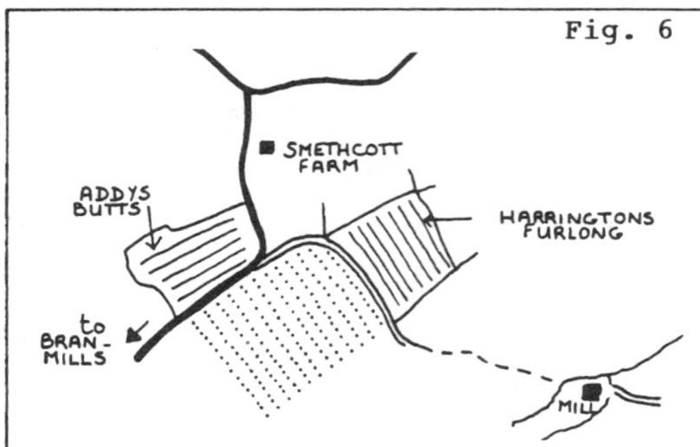

This diagram shows how a lane in Smethcott may have arisen as a balk between butts and furlongs. The plan of ridge and furrow or strips is based on 1844 field names only. The lane is present today as a highway that becomes bridleway (Sm 7). The track to the mill is lost but one hedge remains to show the way it ran.

ENCLOSURE OF LAND, AND SQUATTERS

Woodland, which was abundant in the Middle Ages, was divided up between the lords of the manors but people had common rights in them too. 'Bote' was a term for the right to take material from the common lands for the tenants' use e.g. taking wood for repair work or for firewood. This may be the origin of the name 'Botwood'.

Over the centuries more and more land was being claimed from nature by woodland clearance, an area of cleared land often being called a 'ley'. (Hence, perhaps, the change from 'Botwood' to 'Leebotwood'). Incentives for this were provided by lords of the manors who allowed people (freeholders) to clear woodland and use the cleared land for little rent, with freedom from obligation to work on the lords' lands. With this practice, isolated habitations, now a common sight, first began to appear and more paths and tracks were created by these people going to the village centre or to the mill.

The cleared land was often enclosed and people then tended to lose their common rights; many a fence was torn down in protest. Some of Smethcott Wood however, became an extension of Smethcott Common. Enclosures continued to be made and areas of common land and common fields dwindled; one factor precipitating enclosure was the inability to keep so much arable farmland in use, after The Plague had drastically reduced the population. Many arable fields became grassland for an increasing amount of livestock for which enclosure was necessary.

With these changes, some people became richer, some a great deal poorer (the loss of common land being very much a contributory factor). Increasing poverty led to the appearance of squatters' cottages on the edges of common land. Traditionally it is said that a squatter, who settled on common land without permission, had to erect a rough hut or even just a hearth and have smoke rising from it by morning, before he could have any claim to stay. The small fields that they created around themselves, still often relatively unchanged with grassed-over stone walls, bear names such as 'close', 'croft' or 'allotment' (perhaps where the lord of the manor was tolerant), or 'encroachment' and even 'Snatchfields' where their presence was resented.

A more regulated attempt at enclosing common land was made by Parliament in the 1790s. This is when T.J.Powys put up his boundary stones on the north end of the Long Mynd and when some sections of the parish boundaries were finally determined. Although this led to the creation of fields in this area, Cothercott and Wilderley Hills remained little altered until this century. A legacy too from this period are the long straight roads through the old Smethcott Common which was enclosed at this time; the new roads had to be straight and of a certain width. (Prolleymoor roads are similar but are of a later date). One of the reasons behind increasing enclosure in the 1790s, and thereby (usually) improving land, was the need to produce more corn to raise money towards the Napoleonic Wars. Some of the land on top of the Mynd was used to grow corn then, a practice that persisted for some time but is now only seen near the Thresholds.

MARKETS While the local people continued with their struggles, Church Stretton had grown disproportionately to the other villages and had been granted a weekly market and an annual fair. (The weekly market on a Thursday continues today over 600 years since it was granted). Other places too had been granted markets and fairs e.g. Lydbury North in 1249, Pulverbatch in 1254 and Leebotwood in 1320. Other less ancient fairs and markets would have evolved in the villages, and Church Stretton in this century had several fairs a year. Some tracks, which may have once been just outracks to the hill, became ways to market centred particularly on Church Stretton. These routes may have been only from one side of the hill to the other, used by local people often with laden ponies or in pony and trap, but the same routes were undoubtedly a small part of much longer routes for the same purpose. One long-distance traveller with goods for market was the huckster with his packhorse, the legacy from his era being the Packetstone (Cs 19) and the Huckster Stone (MY 7). The peak of their activity was in the 16th century and likely loads would have been cloth or salt. The use of tracks for getting to markets brought about the name 'portway', a word not just restricted to the Portway along the top of the hill.

ROADS AND THE WELSH DROVERS Parishes were responsible for maintaining roads whether the roads were used mainly by parishioners or were main highways. The Portway was one of the roads that had the status of being part of the King's Highway, which entitled it to enjoy royal protection. As 'traffic' increased considerably in the 17th century and roads deteriorated, there became a need to maintain roads along different lines. In the 18th century, Trusts (often consisting of local landowners) were formed to provide turnpike roads, the toll money from which was to be used to maintain the roads and not for personal profits, other than the accruing benefits from the provision of better routes to markets. Existing roads were normally used, although later new roads were created. A road may have only been intermittently turnpiked but the turnpiked sections had gates, toll houses and milestones. The A49/B4370, the A489 and the minor road on the west (the old Shrewsbury to Bishops Castle road) were turnpiked. The last has many milestones still standing along its verges. Those on the B4370 have fared less well; there is one at Little Stretton and another at Church Stretton, 14 and 13 miles from Shrewsbury respectively. Little Stretton has a Toll House and Pulverbatch a Gate House. The Welsh drovers, who by this time were herding large numbers of cattle to distant markets, were not prepared to pay tolls and once again the old hill routes were used. The Portway, from the southern end of the Mynd to Duckley Nap, was one of their routes; they descended from there to Leebotwood via Woolstaston and thence to the Midlands, after a stop at the Pound Inn, to link up with major routes to London. Other routes on and off the Mynd were also used and two drovers died in bad weather in 1828 near the Thresholds. The blacksmiths along the way, particularly on the east side of the hill e.g. at Lower Wood, shod the cattle before they continued on their journeys on the harder roads.

DEAD MEN

Many other people have lost their lives on this hill. On an old map of Ratlinghope (1698), the spot is marked near the Shooting Box where a dead woman had been found. A dead man was found somewhere near Duckley Nap, perhaps in what was then Woolstaston. The failure of that parish to bury him was amongst evidence used by the people of Church Stretton in 1743, which resulted in Woolstaston losing its common land on the hill. It may have been following this that the batch to the south-east of Duckley Nap became known as Dead Man's Batch. The brook starting on Wilderley Hill was once called Dead Man's Brook, the ford that crossed it lower down was Dead Man's Ford and the lane from Picklescott to the ford was Dead Man's Lane; the last people to succumb in this area were two women in the 1940s. The Reverend Carr just survived a night in the snow in 1865 and on the same night Tom Easterhope died on his way home after tending his animals. The November fair at Church Stretton became known as Dead Man's Fair and Wentnor for a time had bells rung on the night of the fair, to guide people home, after a man lost his way and died; this was known as Dead Man's Peal. Although the name of Dead Man's Fair may not now be remembered, and most of the Dead Man place names have gone out of use, they should serve as a reminder that the Mynd is not to be trifled with.

MORE RIGHTS OF WAY

Rights of way converging on churches have been discussed. If the church is central, as it is in most cases in the area, these rights of way have served a multitude of purposes such as getting to the blacksmith, shop or pub or to a fair in the village. Mills too, not often in the core of the village, have been focal points. So too have the larger houses where many people used to be employed. Some footpaths may have originated more recently with the introduction of schools (19th century), mines, railway stations and bus stops although these have not necessarily created new ways.

THE MOTOR VEHICLE

With the introduction of the bicycle, many people who had walked everywhere chose to get there quicker, particularly adults getting to work. The cyclists forsook the footpaths and joined the ponies and traps using the tracks. A system of relatively more important tracks thus gradually developed which was to become today's network of surfaced roads; it should be realized that this network has evolved from very basic tracks within the space of a lifetime. Fig.7 illustrates some of the events that took

Walkers using the B 4370 in 1913

Fig. 7

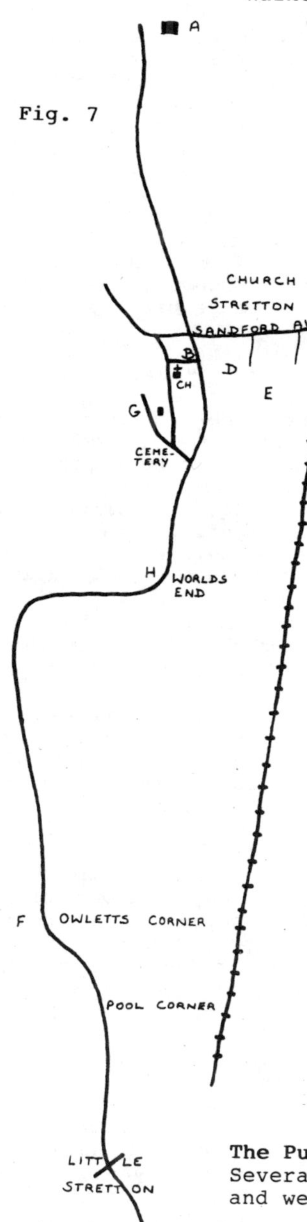

A. **Union Workhouse.**
After doing some work to pay for the night's stay, people from here walked along the B4370 to workhouses at Ludlow or Bishops Castle. (Replaced by the swimming pool).

B. **Market Hall**
This resembled the old market hall in Shrewsbury - open below with a magistrates court above. Many people walked to market here and some attended dances upstairs. (Demolished in 1963).

C. **Railway Station**
This was another focal point. It was later moved to south of the bridge as it is today.

D. **Sheep Sales Field**
This was another busy area. (Now the car park and Kings Court).

E. **Mayfair Field**
The May fair (Bernard Hill's) used to be held here on May 14th (unless this was a Sunday). Crowds of people would have walked to Stretton, and children were given the day off school, to enjoy this exciting occasion. The fair people afterwards went to several places south of Stretton, and processed along the B4370 together with their animals including a bear on a lead. (Now Mayfair House).

F. **Owletts Corner**
(pronounced Ulletts as in full)
Coffins were carried from Little Stretton to the cemetery by Cunnery Road. Bearers had change over points. One funeral procession was caught in a thunderstorm here as the bearers changed over.

G. **The School**
(Now the library).

The Pubs
Several pubs in the centre provided refreshments and were places for parking ponies and traps.

H. **Worlds End**
This was the site of the gas works. People came here for coke and tar.

place along the B4370 between Little and Church Stretton before cars beat along it. The excitement of the arrival of the first motor car in a village is remembered by the elderly. The buses were for many the first form of road transport, and most of the villages around the Mynd were served by them. The earlier buses could not always get up the steep hills when loaded; Cothercott Hill was the walking section for Ratlinghope passengers on Williamsons' Maid of the Mountain. Some footpaths were in use to get to and from the bus stops but many fell into disuse because the lanes had become better to walk along. More and more people acquired cars, while the footpaths and unsurfaced tracks became abandoned by all except school children and postmen. With the advent of postvans and the closure of many village schools, the demise of the footpaths was almost complete in many of the Mynd villages. However, on the open hill it was a different story; walking for leisure had been taking place for some time.

OFFICIAL RIGHTS OF WAY

The creation of a system of public rights of way other than the roads was carried out in the 1950s; these were selected from lists of ways drawn up by each parish council and are now represented on the Ordnance Survey maps. (It is not a rigid system and updating does take place). This new system was important for people to have access to the hill but would have made little difference to walking on the hill itself where a considerable area was (and is) common land. Elsewhere, many of the newly-created public rights of way remained little used and it was to be several years before the village footpaths began to be used again. Even today there are ways with new markers and stiles that still await revival.

THE OPEN HILL

In early mediaeval times, a great area of the Mynd was part of the royal forest extending from just south of Shrewsbury to Craven Arms, and called the Long Forest. Forest originally meant land outside a manor (there were tracts of country, often wooded or untilled, between manors), and was not necessarily woodland as we think of forest today. Hunting in royal forests was reserved for the king and his friends, and strict rules were enforced. John de Cotes was beheaded for a felony in the forest in the 13th century and two men were indicted after their two mastiffs throttled a roe near Asterton. Roger, a prior at Ratlinghope, escaped punishment for taking one of the king's deer by dying first. Many areas withdrew from the jurisdiction of the Long Forest and the village people were able to enjoy common rights in woodland and 'unwooded' forest. A pattern emerged of the common land on the hill being divided up between the manors situated around it. The lords owned it and the people in their manors had common rights on it. The common pasture of the Stretton Hills in Stretton manor was mentioned in 1309 as being 10 leagues in circumference; it was given no value.

One of the main attractions of the Long Mynd is the open hill which tends to equate with the common land that remains today and is where, as one parish council wrote in its survey of paths in the 1950s, 'people walk freely and without hindrance'; this is a habit that is centuries old. The grazing rights however belong to those people who 'occupy land now or previously copyhold of the manor' (quoted from a Court Leet of 1906) i.e. rights are tied up with the old manors, and grazing of animals is not available to all inhabitants of Church Stretton. The number of animals each person can put on the hill is related to the amount of land he 'occupies that gave him common rights of the manor'. The grazing rights, certainly of Church Stretton people, have been jealously guarded through the centuries to the point where the rights of tenants in other manors, particularly in the north, have been questioned. Wilderley and Cothercott manors managed to retain their rights after they were contested in 1527 by Stretton. Disputes over common rights led to riots in Church Stretton in 1612 and Woolstaston lost its rights to Stretton in the 18th century. Batchcott inhabitants were successfully prosecuted for trespass on the Long Mynd in the 18th century, despite rights to common there dating from the 13th century. Picklescott's claims were relatively short-lived. This is all now reflected in the parish boundaries, with Church Stretton parish extending along the top of the hill between Ratlinghope, Smethcott and Pulverbatch, with the Woolstaston boundary (pushed!) well off the hill. The common rights do not include mineral or sporting rights, and the Mynd has always been highly prized by the lords of the manors and their sporting tenants. The combination of many people having common rights, and the good shooting, has resulted in a large area of open common land remaining an open area to this day. Where there were few people in a manor, it was easier to come to some terms regarding division of land on the hill, resulting in enclosures on other parts of the hill.

The Church Stretton Commoners' Association was formed in the 1860s, with the aim of enforcing rules such as not leaving animals on the hill in winter, and to deal with trespassing and encroachments. These had been long-standing rules; one person in 1566 had been fined for unlawfully wintering sheep and another for overburdening the common, both 'to the injury of all the township'. Cattle and goats must have been banned from the hill at some stage as there is no mention of either in 1868; this was a written ban in 1908. Names such as Cow Ridge, Calf Ridge and Bullocksmoor suggest that cows were once on the hill; it is believed that past lords of the manor banned them because they were damaging the shooting butts (the tumps used as shooting butts may have been the old tumuli and are described as being made of earth while boundary tumps contain stones). By 1913, the Committee for the Commoners' Association had members from Ratlinghope, and within a few years had agreed to accept powers over those portions on the Long Mynd that at that time lay within the Ratlinghope and Wentnor estates of the Scott family and were up for sale (1193 acres). At the time of this sale, the occupiers of Coppice Farm, Coates and Medlicott Hall Farm each had rights of turnout for 100 sheep and 10 ponies, twenty other smaller holdings having smaller rights, in all amounting to 1035 sheep and 102 ponies. Little wonder Church Stretton had also been in dispute with Ratlinghope two hundred years before when one Ratlinghope tenant had 900 sheep on the hill! In 1965 under the Commons Registration Act, 106 farmers registered their rights to graze stock on the hill, but not all of these people exercise that right. The common is used almost exclusively for sheep. There are some ponies but far less than there were; this is one factor that has led to the increase of bracken on the hill (see page 97). Animals now stay on the hill in winter; there are better facilities for tending them and the winters have been milder in recent years.

The common land today is only that which lay in the manors of Stretton, Ratlinghope and Wentnor. The National Trust as owner of this area is in the same position as the old lords of the manors.

War and the Long Mynd

The Long Mynd does not appear to have been the site of any battles but soldiers of various eras must have used its routes. A battle is thought to have taken place at Quaking Bridge (near the northern junction of the B4370 with the A49) between the Royalists and the Roundheads. Another battleground in the same war may have been along Stank Lane which runs over Oakley Mynd to the south-west of the Mynd, and which was the last section of ridgeway along an old route, before branching off to get to the Portway; Royalists are certainly recorded as having suffered heavy losses against a smaller number of Roundheads near Bishops Castle, perhaps because the Royalists became trapped in the deep-cut and narrow lane. The people of the Mynd area were largely for the king and a young Walcot was a page of honour at King Charles the First's execution; as a memento of it he was given part of the King's cloak, worn at his execution and stained with his blood.

The hill itself became an important landmark in the Second World War for both sides. American pilots would have recognized it as being near to their base at Condover aerodrome and one of their planes is said to have crashed-landed on Cothercott Hill, as well as a British one on Wildmoor. It may also have been a landmark for the Germans, en route for South Wales. The heather could be set on fire by someone on the ground or by the dropping of bombs, to create a beacon. Some of the pools on the hill may have been created in the war for the sole purpose of providing reservoirs of water that could be pumped (by stirrup hand pumps) onto burning heather, a task that would have been performed by members of the Home Guard who kept a vigil for the enemy on many areas of high ground. A German spy is believed to have lived at Betchcott/Batchcott Hall. He had built a large fishpool a few years before the war, that may have become a landmark in the war. Perhaps this man was lighting heather fires too. He was to disappear before the end of the war and local belief is that he fell, jumped or was pushed from a plane over Belgium or thereabouts. His name survives on the dam of the fishpool - Max Brenner, 1931. Another local personality connected with the Second World War was one of two brothers who had bought Walcot Hall. He went to live in Pole Cottage during the war when the Hall was requisitioned by the army; this must have been an ideal spot to pursue his hobby of falconry but he also became involved in the war, giving advice on the use of predatory birds for clearing airfields of jackdaws and gulls.

Focus on rabbits

Rabbits were introduced to Britain by the Normans who prized them highly, constructed burrows for them and had keepers to look after them (see Portway). Lords of the manors had to apply to the king to get a 'grant of free warren'. This was not always given, particularly when the Long Mynd was part of the Royal Forest (see Background).

Even at the beginning of this century, 'if the lord of the manor like to make a rabbit burrow on the common, the commoners had no right of either to destroy the rabbits or burrows'. Just as the lord could bring action against a commoner for putting too many beasts on the common, so could a commoner bring action against the lord if he thought the rabbits were increasing in numbers and destroying the pasturage.

LONG DISTANCE ROUTES

1. The Portway has been drawn and described in five sections; the total distance is 15 Km/9¼ miles.

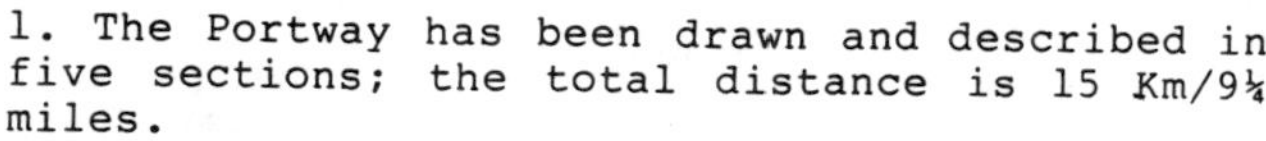

Portway 1 and 2: Plowden to point J (near the entrance to the gliding station) - pages 19, 20 and 22.

Portway 3: J to Q - pages 21 and 22.
Portway 4: Q to V (at the cattle-grid on the Woolstaston to Ratlinghope road) - pages 23 and 24.
Portway 5: V to γ (at the Thresholds) - pages 25 and 26.

Portway 5 and 4 (in reverse): γ to Q - pages 27 and 28.
Portway 3, 2 and 1 (in reverse): Q to Plowden - pages 29 and 30.

2. The return route from Thresholds to Plowden is drawn in two parts, Part I being the north half and Part II the south. The route taken by walkers makes use of footpaths and some lanes, while the route for cyclists and horse riders uses mostly unfrequented highways. The two separate routes are described with each part.
The walkers' route is 13.25 Km/8¼ miles. The cyclists' and horse riders' route is 14 Km/8½+ miles.
Part I is on pages 31 and 32.
Part II is on pages 32 and 33.

The return route from Thresholds to Plowden for walkers equates with the Shropshire Way throughout Part I i.e. as far as Adstone Farm. From Adstone, the Shropshire Way takes a different direction which is briefly outlined on page 32.

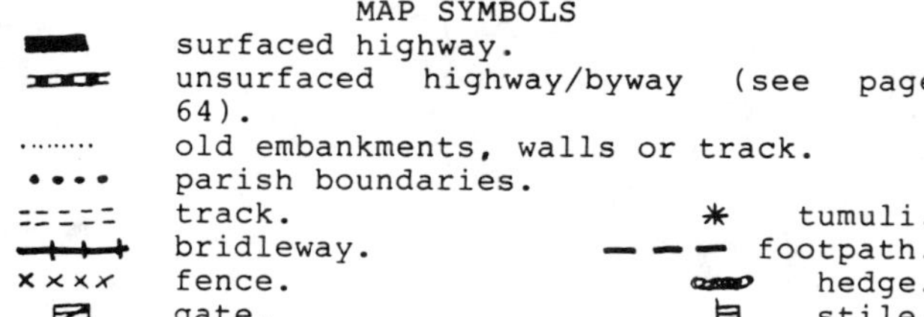

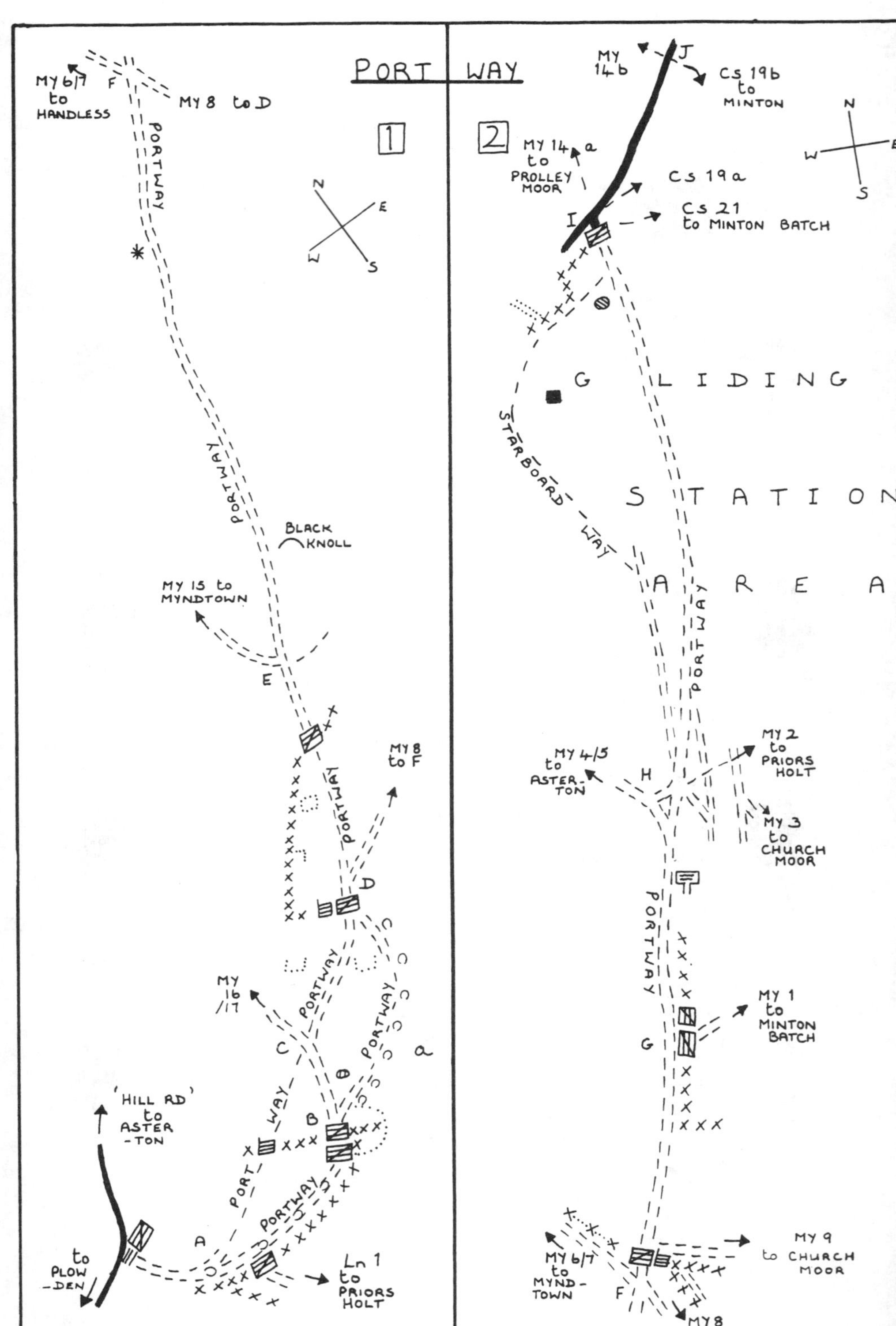

PORT WAY
1
MY 6/7 to HANDLESS
F
MY 8 to D
PORTWAY
N
E
W
S
PORTWAY
BLACK KNOLL
MY 15 to MYNDTOWN
E
MY 8 to F
PORTWAY
D
MY 16/17
PORTWAY
PORTWAY
C
a
'HILL RD' to ASTER-TON
WAY
B
PORT
PORTWAY
A
to PLOW-DEN
Ln 1 to PRIORS HOLT
2
MY 14b
J
Cs 19b to MINTON
MY 14 a to PROLLEY MOOR
Cs 19a
Cs 21 to MINTON BATCH
I
N
W
E
S
G
GLIDING STATION AREA
STARBOARD WAY
PORTWAY
MY 2 to PRIORS HOLT
MY 4/5 to ASTER-TON
H
MY 3 to CHURCH MOOR
PORTWAY
MY 1 to MINTON BATCH
G
MY 9 to CHURCH MOOR
MY 6/7 to MYND-TOWN
F
MY 8

PORTWAY 1 AND 2

The start of the Portway is reached by leaving the A489 at Plowden and taking the lane towards Asterton, passing the old station house but stopping short of Longmynd Cottage. A clear track on the right leaves the lane via a gate and curves around the bottom of the hill before ascending steeply alongside a fence. At point A, before it ascends, a right of way (Ln 1) branches off to the right. This first field shows signs of several faint track marks, a feature that is typical of an old road that reaches a steep hill; generations of people who have used this route have taken the easiest way at the time. The legacy from this 'spread' is that the bridleway and footpath on maps are shown as ascending separately, with a gate at the top of the bridleway and a stile at the top of the footpath, both at point B.

After the stile walkers may notice some faint embankments, thought to be part of an extensive system of Celtic fields possibly dating from circa A.D.75-380. At the gates, riders may notice a faint ring-shaped embankment immediately to the right; this also may be related to the Celtic fields but its role is uncertain.

At point B, the walker bears to the right to join the track from the gate. Rider and walker seemingly ascend together along this track which stands out as a different green to the rest of the field and runs to the left of a small pool. However, the bridleway is shown on maps to veer off obliquely to the right to follow the course of the old Portway, not always in evidence.

From either route the embankments of the Celtic fields are discernible, but from the bridleway at least three tier-like embankments (lynchets) can be seen extending away to the right (a). These lynchets were discovered in 1938 and a plan of them was drawn up in the 1950s using aerial photographs; the plan can be seen at the Local Studies section of the Shrewsbury Library. In this area too there is apparently a pillow mound, a man-made warren for rabbits. Rabbits were once considered to be special, had warrens built for them and a keeper to look after them; this part of the hill is called Rabbit Warren. There are plenty of rabbits and burrows and a deserted Warren House under the hill (for the keeper perhaps) but I have not been able to find a mound.

At the top of this second field the old Portway, alias the bridleway, joins the more modern and clear way, alias the footpath, to pass through the gate at D. (Lying between them, just before they join, is what looks like a green, which is probably what it is; a golf course is shown in this area on the 1937 O/S map).

At D, another old track branches off to the right; this is MY 8 that will eventually rejoin the Portway at F. The Portway itself aims upwards and slightly to the left passing close to another golf green before going through a gate on to the true Long Mynd of bracken, bilberry and heather.

At E, MY 15 branches off to Myndtown. The final steep ascent is made to Black Knoll, the site of the first possible tumulus. The way is now relatively flat with fine views of hills to the south and west. Another rather indistinct tumulus to the left is passed before reaching point F.

At F, MY 6/7 branches off to the left and MY 8 and 9 to the right. The next section passes near to coniferous forest which lies on either side. A considerable area on the right has been cleared.

At G, MY 1 branches off to the right and soon afterwards there is a notice marking the edge of the gliding station.

At H, several routes leave the Portway (MY 4/5, MY 2 and MY 3) and

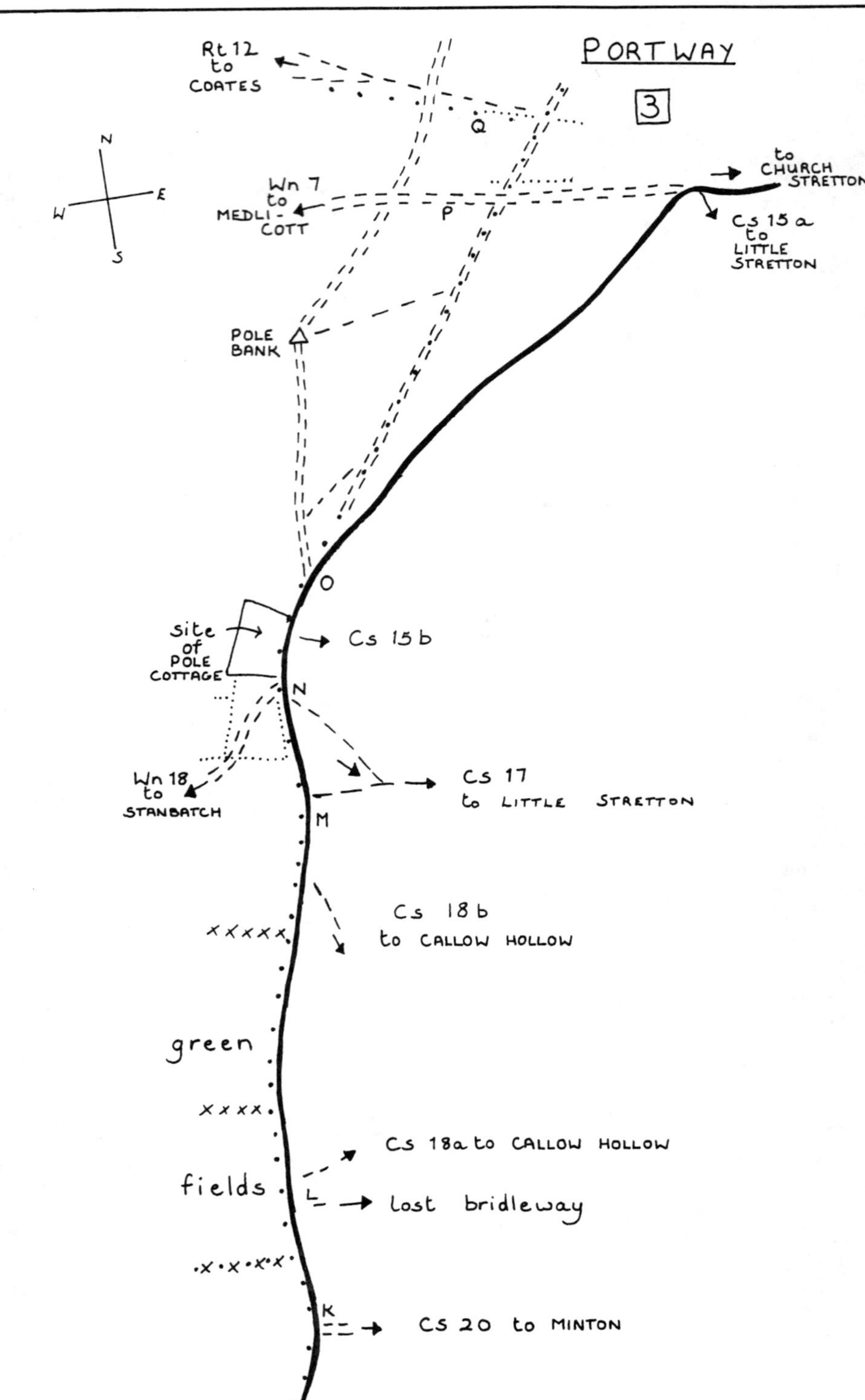
PORTWAY
3
Rt 12 to COATES
Q
N
W
E
S
Wn 7 to MEDLI-COTT
P
to CHURCH STRETTON
Cs 15 a to LITTLE STRETTON
POLE BANK
O
site of POLE COTTAGE
Cs 15 b
N
Wn 18 to STANBATCH
Cs 17 to LITTLE STRETTON
M
Cs 18 b to CALLOW HOLLOW
green
Cs 18a to CALLOW HOLLOW
fields
L
lost bridleway
K
CS 20 to MINTON

the Portway continues across the gliding station. An alternative route is offered to bypass this area and is called the Starboard Way; it is signposted and runs behind the station building and is a much safer way to travel, as well as offering wonderful views to the west. It curves round to rejoin the Portway at the gated entrance to the gliding station (point I), passing to the left of a small pool.

At point I, the Portway becomes surfaced road and MY 14a, Cs 19a and Cs 21 branch off here. Continue along the road as if going to Church Stretton.

PORTWAY 3

At point J, Cs 19b branches to the right and MY 14b, as a vague path, to the left.

At K, Cs 20 turns off as a clear track.

At L, the old bridleway, shown on the maps as branching off to Minton, is lost but a small path (Cs 18a) leads off alongside the boggy hollow and descends into Callow Hollow. On the left is an area of green fields.

Between K and L, a fence running away from the road marks the Wentnor parish boundary as well as the southern boundary of an area of green fields. The Portway, from this point, becomes the Wentnor/Church Stretton boundary.

At M, Cs 17b leads off to the right, soon joining Cs 17a.

At point N, Cs 17a is to the right and Wn 18 to the left.

Between M and N, on the left, are embankments crossing the heather, the first (south) one, running east-west, being an old Medlicott manor boundary. The others are probably related to peat cutting; the poor people of Wentnor were allowed to gather peat for their fires from 6 acres of the moorland here.

Just beyond point N is an old enclosure around what was once Pole Cottage. (More information on Pole Cottage is on page 216 under Wn 19). Cs 15b branches off to the right opposite the enclosure.

Point O is a short way beyond Pole Cottage. A track leaves the road and runs up and over Pole Bank reaching the highest point on the Mynd at 516 metres. This is not a designated public right of way and is not the Portway, but it is the way most people take and is an old route. Once a "Shepherds' Pole" stood at the summit; now there is a toposcope that shows the names of the surrounding hills. This route descends to the Shooting Box at R. For those set on walking the mediaeval way, the Portway leaves the road a little further along from O. It is difficult to find, particularly as there is a short section here that is not used. Either aim for a nick in the horizon and you will soon come to discernible track, or take the Pole Bank track for a short distance before turning off to the right to go along a small path that joins the Portway. The Portway that runs between the two surfaced roads (points O to R) is heather-clad and barely used. Some parts are clearly defined and a small path runs beside it or in it. It continues to be the Wentnor/Church Stretton boundary.

At point P, both the Portway and the Pole Bank routes cross a track from Medlicott to Stretton (Wn 7). Across the Portway at P is a sort of embankment and there is another more extensive one at Q. These act as boundaries, since this tongue of land coming up from Medlicott is not owned by the National Trust; it is privately owned. Q represents an old Medlicott manor boundary as well as the Wentnor/Ratlinghope boundary, but the role of the embankment at P

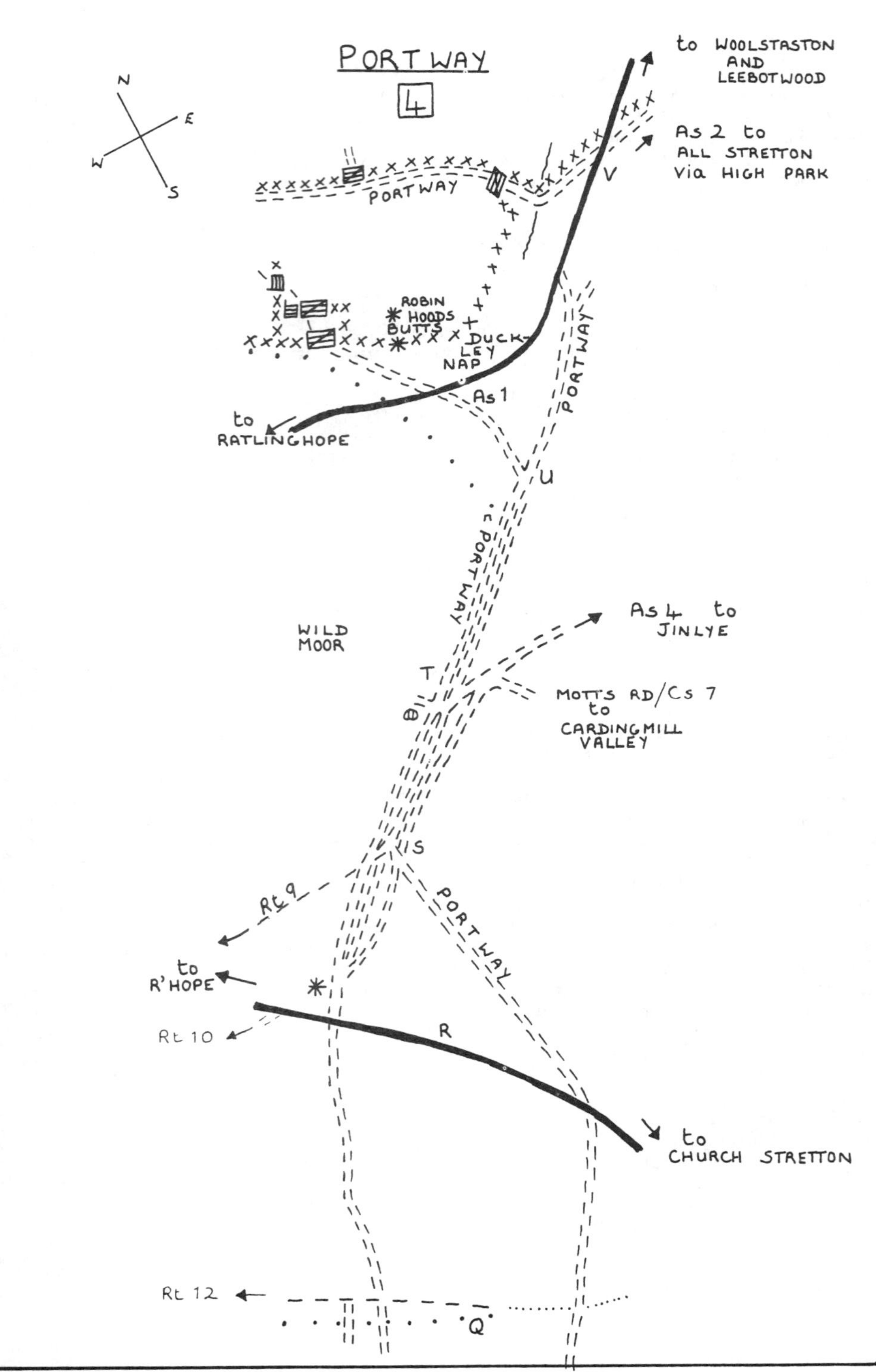
PORTWAY
4
N
E
W
S
to WOOLSTASTON AND LEEBOTWOOD
As 2 to ALL STRETTON Via HIGH PARK
PORTWAY
V
ROBIN HOODS BUTTS
DUCK-LEY NAP
As 1
to RATLINGHOPE
PORTWAY
U
PORTWAY
WILD MOOR
As 4 to JINLYE
T
MOTTS RD/Cs 7 to CARDINGMILL VALLEY
S
Rt 9
PORTWAY
to R'HOPE
Rt 10
R
to CHURCH STRETTON
Rt 12
Q

is less certain. A few people from Medlicott own separate parts of the private 'tongue' of the hill as well as having common rights over a wider area. The Portway from Q becomes the Ratlinghope/Church Stretton boundary.

The Portway and the Pole Bank track continue, and separately cross the Ratlinghope/Stretton road at R.

PORTWAY 4

At point R, the Portway crosses the road and becomes a clear and well-used track once more. The Pole Bank route too continues across the road as a clear track - and this is a good point for horse riders to leave the Portway, taking Rt 10 to Coates and joining the Thresholds to Plowden route there - passing two tumuli before meeting the Portway again at S. The first tumulus is labelled on maps as Shooting Box; a hut, incorporated into the tumulus, once stood here.

From R to U there is a confusing number of parallel paths or tracks; keep to the middle or left-hand ones if going to Duckley Nap.

At Point S, the Pole Bank route (now divided into three) joins the Portway.

At point T, the right-hand track bears off as route As 4 and Motts Road (Cs 7) almost immediately leaves As 4 to descend into Cardingmill Valley.

The reason so many routes cross this area may be that it is boggy and in mediaeval times one was allowed to stray to right or left of the highway if it had become 'floundrous' even if it meant trampling crops. **This is a bleak part of the Mynd running along the top of Wild Moor, but it is a good place for seeing some of the wildlife that frequents moorland, and particularly that which is peculiar to heather.** Red grouse breed on the hill (an estimated 50-75 pairs) and feed on young heather shoots. The hill needs to be managed, in part for grouse, and heather is periodically cut or burned to encourage regrowth and therefore young shoots. **People are encouraged to keep to footpaths, with dogs under strict control, during the breeding season; this also applies for the lambing season at approximately the same time.** Many moths frequent the moorland too, their caterpillars feeding on the moorland plants, some exclusively on heather. The Emperor moth is one such moth which you may see, as it flies by day (in late April/early May) unlike many moths, and has 'eyes' on its brownish wings. Its caterpillar is striking too and although a description of it sounds lurid - bright green with yellow and black markings - it has perfect camouflage on heather.

At point U, the Portway bears off to the right and another route to the left and each meets the Ratlinghope to Woolstaston road separately. Just before U, the Ratlinghope boundary veers off to the left; if you are walking along the 'outside lane' on the left, you will see an old boundary stone, inscribed with the letters T.B.G., standing in a small pool. **The left-hand route (As 1) continues across the road to the tumuli known as Robin Hoods Butts, one predominantly heather-clad and the other in the field (Butts field) grassy; the area is known as Duckley Nap. Route As 1 is dealt with in more detail on page 66. The Portway, having joined the road, continues as the road as far as the cattle-grid at V.**

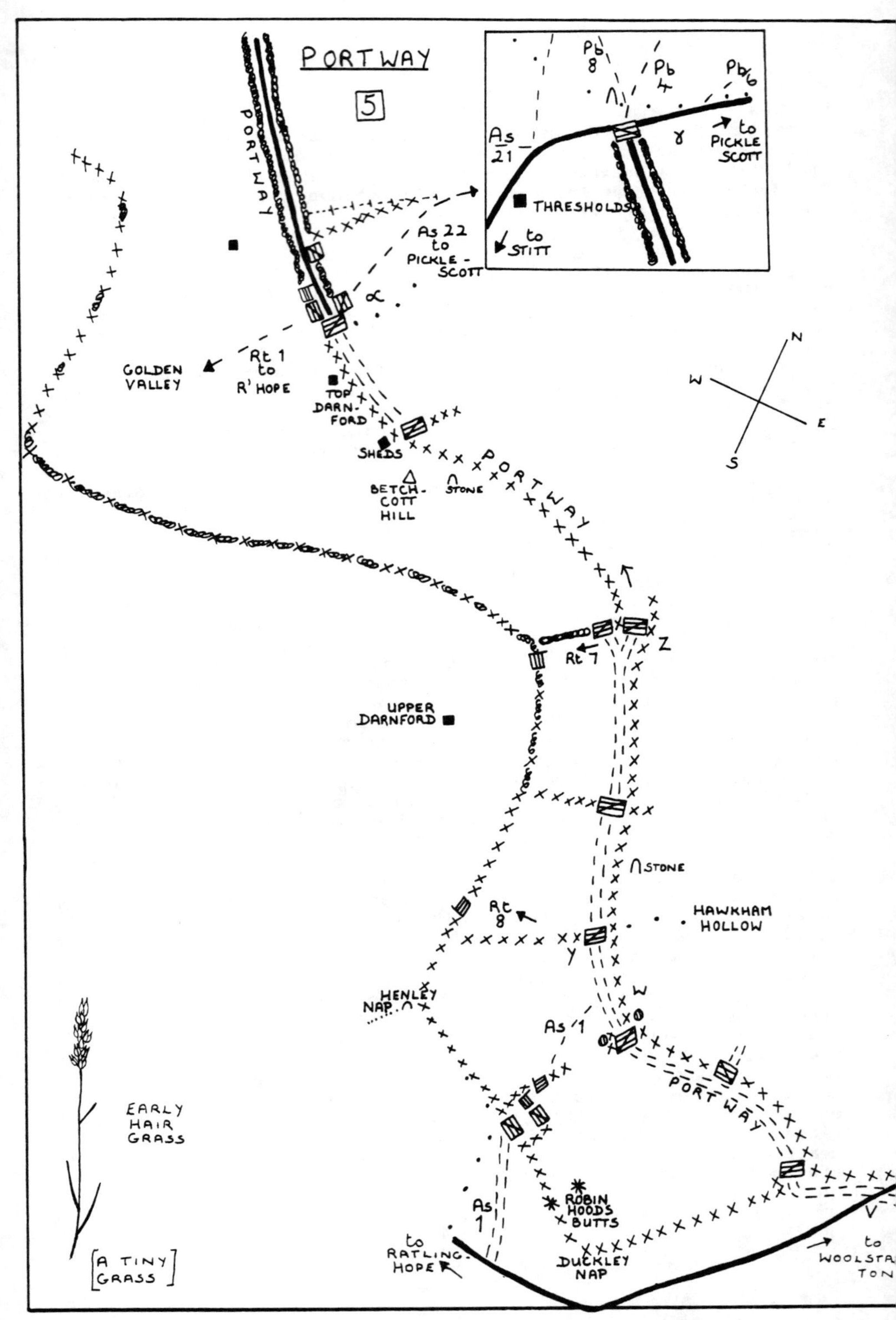
PORTWAY
5
PORTWAY
Pb 8
Pb 4
Pb/6
As 21
γ
to PICKLE SCOTT
THRESHOLDS
to STITT
As 22 to PICKLE-SCOTT
α
GOLDEN VALLEY
Rt 1 to R' HOPE
TOP DARN-FORD
SHEDS
BETCH-COTT HILL
STONE
PORTWAY
N
W
E
S
Z
Rt 7
UPPER DARNFORD
STONE
HAWKHAM HOLLOW
Rt 8
Y
HENLEY NAP
W
As 1
PORTWAY
EARLY HAIR GRASS
ROBIN HOODS BUTTS
As 1
V
to RATLING-HOPE
DUCKLEY NAP
to WOOLSTA-TON
[A TINY GRASS]

PORTWAY 5

At point U, the mediaeval Portway continued down the lane to Woolstaston, where it turned towards Smethcott. The drovers, using the Portway, continued down through Woolstaston to Leebotwood. Perhaps the name of Portway should end here but it tends to refer now to the route that continues to the Thresholds. This section of the Portway runs across an area that has been common land and has seen a few disputes (see Background), but today is an area of green fields. From V, a track follows an old wall into a dip and then up the other side. This wall may once have been the Woolstaston boundary but is now only a field/open hill boundary. **Both wall and track pass a young forest and, immediately after, a track turns off to the right passing High Park Farm** where, in the severe winter of 1963, bales of hay had to be brought by helicopter. On the tithe map, allotments (fields allotted from common land at some time) flank this track as it descends to the High Park to Picklescott lane. **The Portway continues, following fence on old wall on the right, to point W where it is rejoined by As 1.**

At point Y, a little further along, Rt 8 branches off to Upper Darnford. On the right is Hawkham Hollow which forms the south boundary of Smethcott. The Portway now becomes the Smethcott/All Stretton boundary. Hawkham Hollow is a good example of a name that has altered slightly to the ear but markedly in its spelling, to alter its meaning completely. As late as 1840 this was Occwm Beach, occwm perhaps being derived from the Welsh 'oergwm' for 'cold valley', a meaning that would be difficult to arrive at from the word hawkham. **Soon after the Hollow is a 'manor stone', erected in 1791 by T.J.Powys to mark the boundary of Batchcott township (now an area of Smethcott parish and usually referred to as Betchcott).** The part of the hill on the right was Betchcott Common, and the path that ran along the edge of it from Betchcott to the stone, was the way used by one Church Pulverbatch family (and doubtless by many other people) to get to the hilltop to pick wimberries.

At point Z, another path branches off to Upper Darnford along a hedge and the Portway passes through a gate to continue following fence on old wall, but now running along the right-hand side of it. There is no sign of track through this field. Another manor stone is passed near the summit of Betchcott Hill; the metal 'label' has been lost from this stone. After passing through another gate by some sheds, a site where several flints have been found, there is clear track again which soon passes the ruins of Top Darnford.

At α, the Shropshire Way and the walkers' return route to Plowden turn off to the left. To the right is a route to Picklescott (As 22), and the Portway to the Thresholds is a surfaced and enclosed road, resembling other wide, straight roads through old commons.

At the Thresholds, several paths go across Cothercott and Wilderley hills (see Pulverbatch and All Stretton circuits on page 35). A third manor stone stands in the field opposite the end of the Portway. Cyclists and riders (see note below) doing the return route to Plowden, turn left along the lane, descending past the Thresholds farm to reach the start of Rt 4.

N.B. A very short section of this part of the Portway is designated as footpath only - that is, between the dip just north of V and point Y. Cyclists can of course carry their bikes this short distance if necessary, but theoretically horse riders at present must turn off at points R or U and link up with the Thresholds to Plowden return route at Coates or Lower Darnford respectively. Hopefully, this section will be upgraded to bridleway.

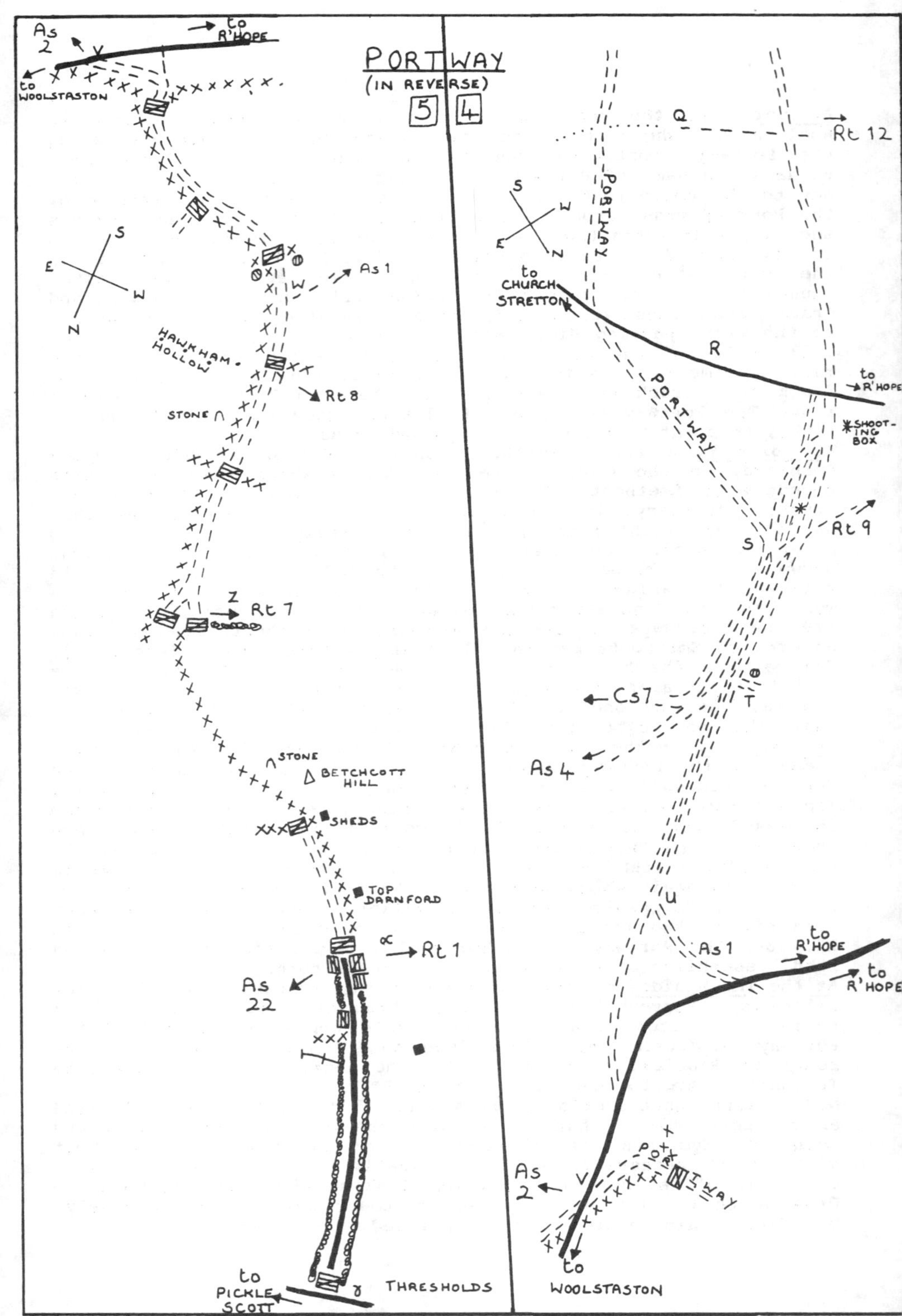

PORTWAY
(IN REVERSE)
5
4
As 2
to R'HOPE
to WOOLSTASTON
V
S
E
W
N
W
As 1
HAWKHAM HOLLOW
Rt 8
STONE
Z
Rt 7
STONE
BETCHCOTT HILL
SHEDS
TOP DARNFORD
α
Rt 1
As 22
to PICKLE SCOTT
γ
THRESHOLDS
Q
Rt 12
PORTWAY
to CHURCH STRETTON
R
to R'HOPE
PORTWAY
SHOOTING BOX
Rt 9
S
Cs 7
T
As 4
U
As 1
to R'HOPE
to R'HOPE
As 2
V
POR TWAY
to WOOLSTASTON

PORTWAY 5 AND 4 (IN REVERSE), THRESHOLDS TO Q

At the Thresholds, turn off the Picklescott to Stitt lane and pass through a gate before proceeding along an enclosed and surfaced road. A second gate is reached after some distance; this is at point α.

At α, Rt 1 branches off to the right and As 22 to the left, both immediately before the gate. The Portway continues through the gate and follows a fence all the way to point V. From α to Z the fence runs along the right-hand side of the Portway; the summit of Betchcott Hill and a 'manor stone' are passed between these two points. This section has no discernible track.

At Z, the Portway passes through a gate and Rt 7 branches off to the right. The way once more becomes clear and runs along the right hand side of the fence. After going through another gate, a manor stone is passed. A short distance beyond the stone, Hawkham Hollow descends as the Smethcott/All Stretton boundary to the left, and another gate is reached at point Y.

At Y, just before the gate, Rt 8 branches off to the right.

At W, route As 1 bears off to the right. The Portway continues along the right-hand side of the fence, passing through two more gates before reaching open hill. After a dip in the terrain, the Portway ascends to the Woolstaston to Ratlinghope road at point V.

At V, the Portway turns right and becomes the road for a short distance. It then leaves the road as clear track obliquely to the left and is soon joined by As 1 at point U.

At U, two clear tracks (the Portway and As 1) join but several tracks and paths have evolved to cross this stretch of the Mynd from U to R.

At T, As 4 and Cs 7 join the Portway creating another track running on the left-hand side to S.

At S, the left-hand track takes on the role of Portway and is the way to take if you are interested in continuing along the mediaeval route; it is also the way to take if going to Church Stretton. Any of the other tracks at S lead to the Shooting Box where they all converge.

At R, both the Portway and the way past the Shooting Box cross the Church Stretton to Ratlinghope road. The latter is the clearer route to follow; it is wide and well used, although it is not a designated public right of way. It ascends to the highest point of the Mynd on Pole Bank. The Portway, crossing the same area , is far less clear; for the most part there is discernible but heather-clad track, and a path runs in it or alongside it.

At Q, the Pole Bank route is crossed by a faint path (Rt 12) and the Portway by an embankment.

N.B. A very short section of Portway 5 is designated as footpath only - that is, between point Y and the dip just short (north) of V. Hopefully this section will be upgraded in the future to a bridleway, to create a through route from the north end of the Mynd to the open hill, thereby providing a long-distance riders' route to Plowden.

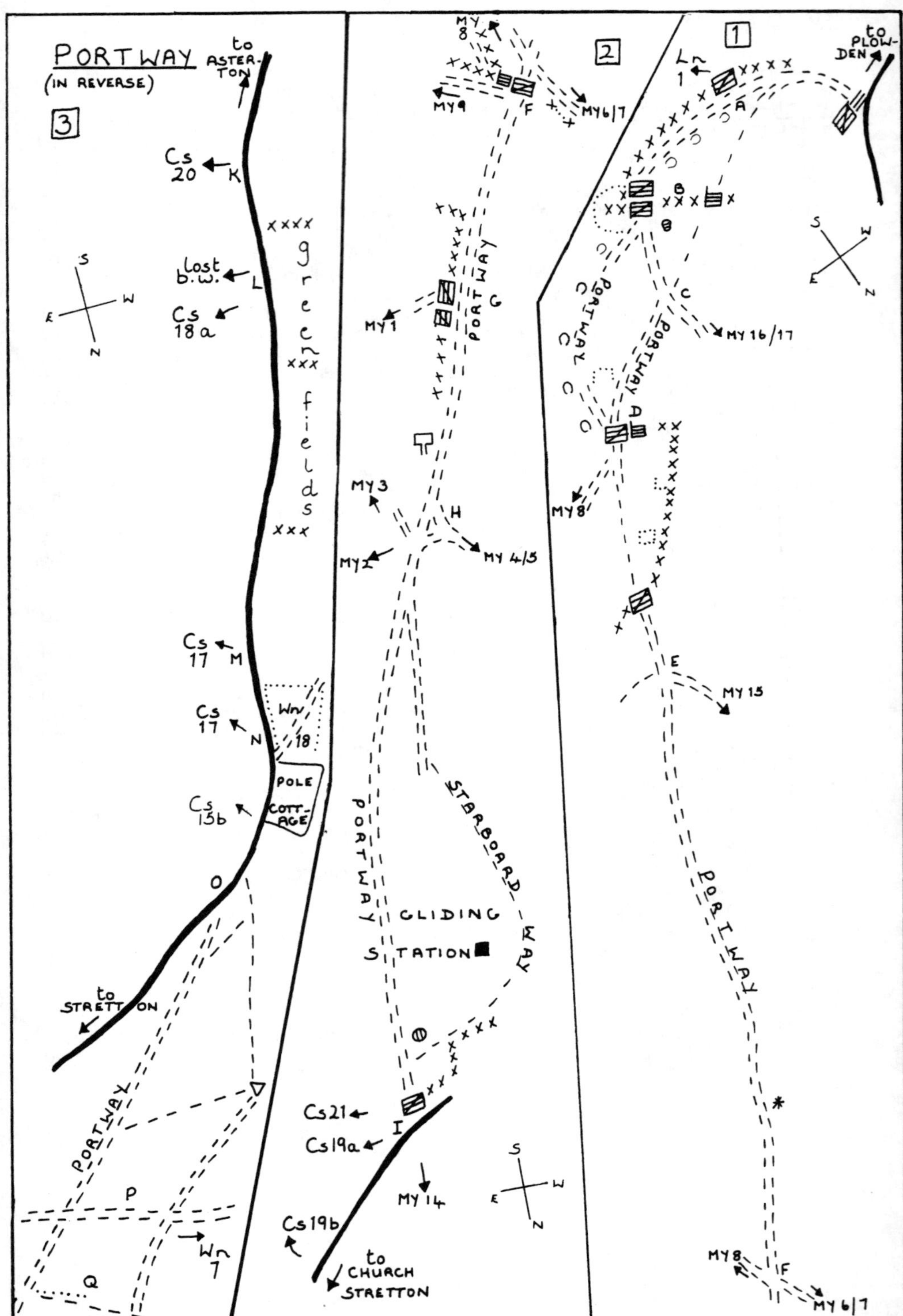
PORTWAY
(IN REVERSE)
3
to ASTERTON
Cs 20
K
lost b.w.
L
Cs 18 a
green fields
Cs 17
M
Cs 17
N
Wn 18
POLE COTTAGE
Cs 15b
O
to STRETTON
PORTWAY
P
Wn 7
Q
2
MY 8
MY 9
F
MY 6/7
MY 1
PORTWAY
G
MY 3
H
MY 2
MY 4/5
PORTWAY
STARBOARD WAY
GLIDING STATION
Cs 21
I
Cs 19a
MY 14
Cs 19b
to CHURCH STRETTON
1
Ln 1
A
to PLOWDEN
B
C
PORTWAY
PORTWAY
MY 16/17
D
MY 8
E
MY 15
PORTWAY
MY 8
F
MY 6/7
S
W
E
N

PORTWAY 3, 2 AND 1 (IN REVERSE), Q TO PLOWDEN

At P, both the Portway and the Pole Bank route separately cross a track (Wn 7). The Portway continues through the heather, a small path running in it or beside it; this path eventually veers away from the Portway and crosses to the Pole Bank route just before point O. The Pole Bank route reaches the highest point of the Mynd after point P and descends to the road at O.

At O, the route is a single one again and follows the road as far as the gliding station at I; it passes the enclosure of Pole Cottage, and several routes branch off from it as shown on the map.

At I, the Portway enters the gliding station area and runs straight across in front of the station building. An alternative route is offered - The Starboard Way - which bears to the right by a small pool and runs behind (west of) the building; small white posts show the way.

At H, the Portway and the Starboard Way unite. MY 2 and 3 branch off to the left and MY 4/5 to the right. The Portway is now a single and simple route to follow, and between H and E is probably the most attractive section, running through heather and with wonderful views to the west. The way passes an area of recently cleared forest with intact forest set back on either side.

At G, MY 1 branches off to Priors Holt.

At F, MY 9 turns off to the left before the gate. MY 8 and MY 6/7 leave the Portway after the gate. The way continues as fairly level walking to Black Knoll, which is the point where the steep descent begins.

At E, beyond and below Black Knoll, MY 15 bears off to the right. A short distance beyond this the Portway leaves the open hill via a gate and enters green fields. Descend through the first field veering slightly away from the fence running down the slope on the right; there is no clear way.

At D, the Portway is joined by MY 8 and passes through another gate (or over a stile). The easiest route to take from D is along a track that stands out as a different green from the rest of the field. This passes the junction with MY 16 at C, at which point the footpath leaves the track and descends to a stile; the track itself descends to a gate at B. The O/S map shows the bridleway descending from the gate at D, looping round to the left and joining the track at the next gate at B; this way is unclear.

At B, riders pass through two gates while walkers may use gates or stile. The bridleway descends as clear track following the fence, which runs downhill on the left. At A, above a wood, the track curves to the right around the end of the hill and exits on to the lane near Plowden. The footpath descends vaguely from the stile rejoining the bridleway at the bottom of the slope.

Focus on the status of the Portway

A to just north of H: Bridleway.
Across the gliding station: Highway, not in general use by traffic.
I to O: Surfaced highway used by traffic.
O to between T and U: Crosses common land but is not designated as a right of way. (The Pole Bank route is bridleway from R to S)
South of U to V: Bridleway to road followed by road to V.
V to dip nearby: Continuation of the bridleway from High Park.
Dip to Y: Footpath.
Y to Z: Bridleway.
Z to α : Unsurfaced highway.
α to γ : Surfaced highway, not in general use.

THRESHOLDS TO PLOWDEN

PART I

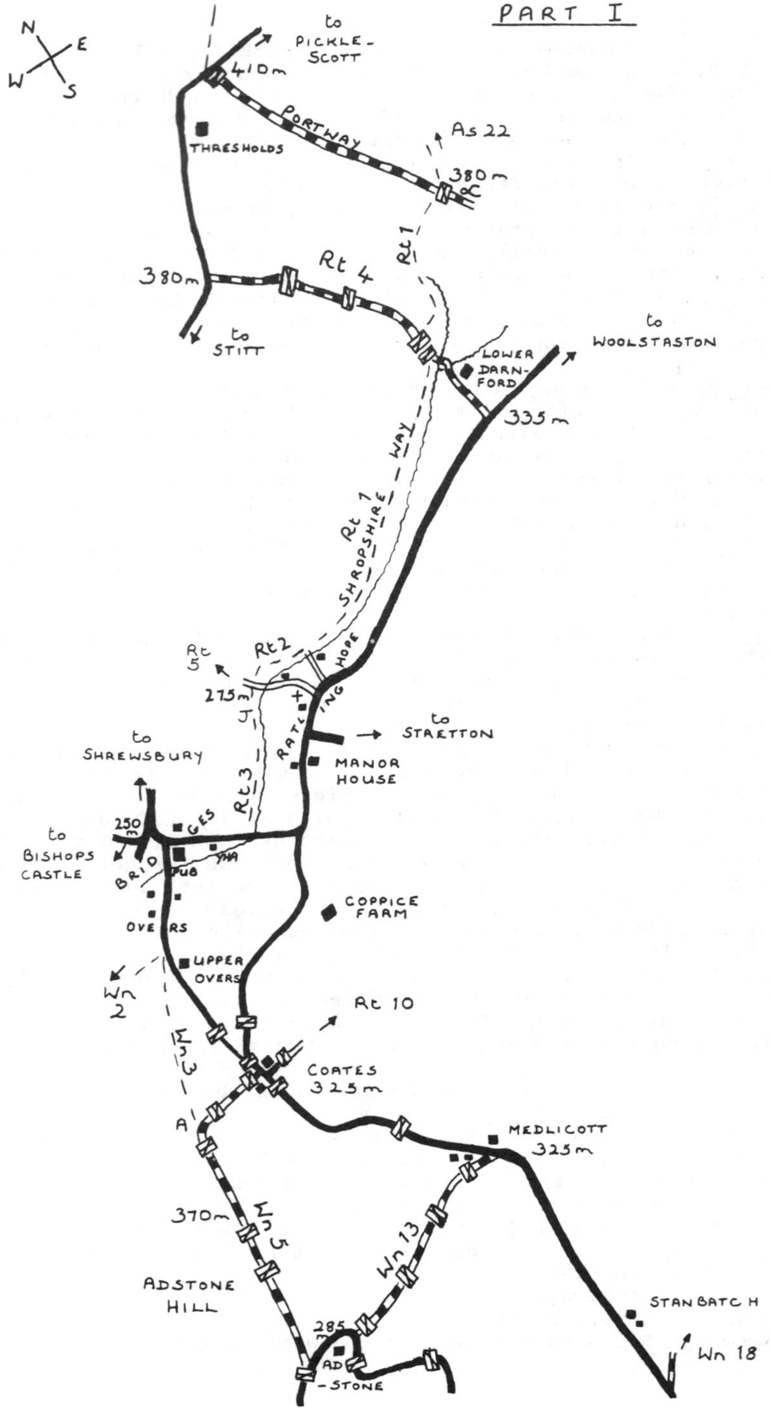

N E S W

to PICKLE-SCOTT

410m

PORTWAY

THRESHOLDS

As 22

380m

Rt 1

Rt 4

380m

to STITT

to WOOLSTASTON

LOWER DARN-FORD

335m

SHROPSHIRE WAY

Rt 1

Rt 2

Rt 5

275m

HOPE

RATL X ING

to STRETTON

MANOR HOUSE

Rt 3

to SHREWSBURY

250 m

to BISHOPS CASTLE

BRID GES

PUB

YHA

OVERS

COPPICE FARM

UPPER OVERS

Wn 2

Rt 10

Wn 3

COATES 325m

A

MEDLICOTT 325m

370m

Wn 5

Wn 13

ADSTONE HILL

STANBATCH

285 m

Wn 18

AD-STONE

RETURN ROUTE from THRESHOLDS to PLOWDEN, PART I

Walkers' route:-

Leave the Portway at ∝, follow Rt 1, 2 and 3 to the Bridges, passing Lower Darnford and Ratlinghope.

Turn left at the Bridges pub (the Horseshoe Inn) and follow the narrow lane up to the start of Wn 3, just before Upper Overs.

Take Wn 3 and link up with Wn 5 to get over Adstone Hill. Up to this point our route has been the same as the Shropshire Way, and to continue along the Way is another possible route to take to return to Plowden (see Shropshire Way below).

Our route leaves the Shropshire Way at Adstone Farm and goes along the lane towards Wentnor. (Move on to Part II).

Cyclists and horse riders:-

At the end of the Portway at the Thresholds, turn left and descend along the lane towards Stitt.

Turn left along Rt 4 (in reverse), which is a gated and unsurfaced highway, and continue over two fords, passing Lower Darnford to exit on to the lane running from Ratlinghope to Woolstaston via Duckley Nap.

N.B. This is the point at which anyone who left the Portway at U, links up with the return route.

Follow the lane downhill passing Ratlinghope Church, a turning to Stretton, and the Manor House.

On a right-angled bend, continue straight on along a gated road, passing near Coppice Farm, to get to Coates. Turn left to pass through Coates itself, following the road as it curves to the right away from the houses.

N.B. This is the point at which anyone who left the Portway at R links up with the return route.

Follow the gated road to Medlicott and continue along the road, running under the hill, to Stanbatch. (Move on to Part II).

N.B. An alternative route from Coates is via Wn 5 to Adstone Farm, thence via lanes across Prolley Moor (not open moorland) to Asterton.

PART II

Walkers' route (continued):-

The lane from Adstone towards Wentnor reaches a road junction (known as Halfway End). There are two ways to continue from here:

1. **Lane to Wentnor/Wn 28 to the Criftins/lane via the Home/lane to Myndtown/MY 10.**
2. **Wn 22/Wn 23/Wn 32(in reverse) to Asterton/lane/MY 10.**

Cyclists and horse riders (continued):-

From Stanbatch, continue straight on along MY 12, an unsurfaced highway. This, as with all the other numbered routes, is dealt with in more detail in the Villages section; for this route refer to MY 12(in reverse).

From Asterton, take the lane towards Plowden. An alternative route to Plowden is to take MY 5 (a steep ascent) up to the Portway at H, and return along the Portway.

THE SHROPSHIRE WAY

This is designed for walkers only. From Adstone Farm, the Way runs as follows:- lane to Prolley Moor/Wn 16 to Stanbatch/MY 14/Portway(in reverse) I to Plowden.

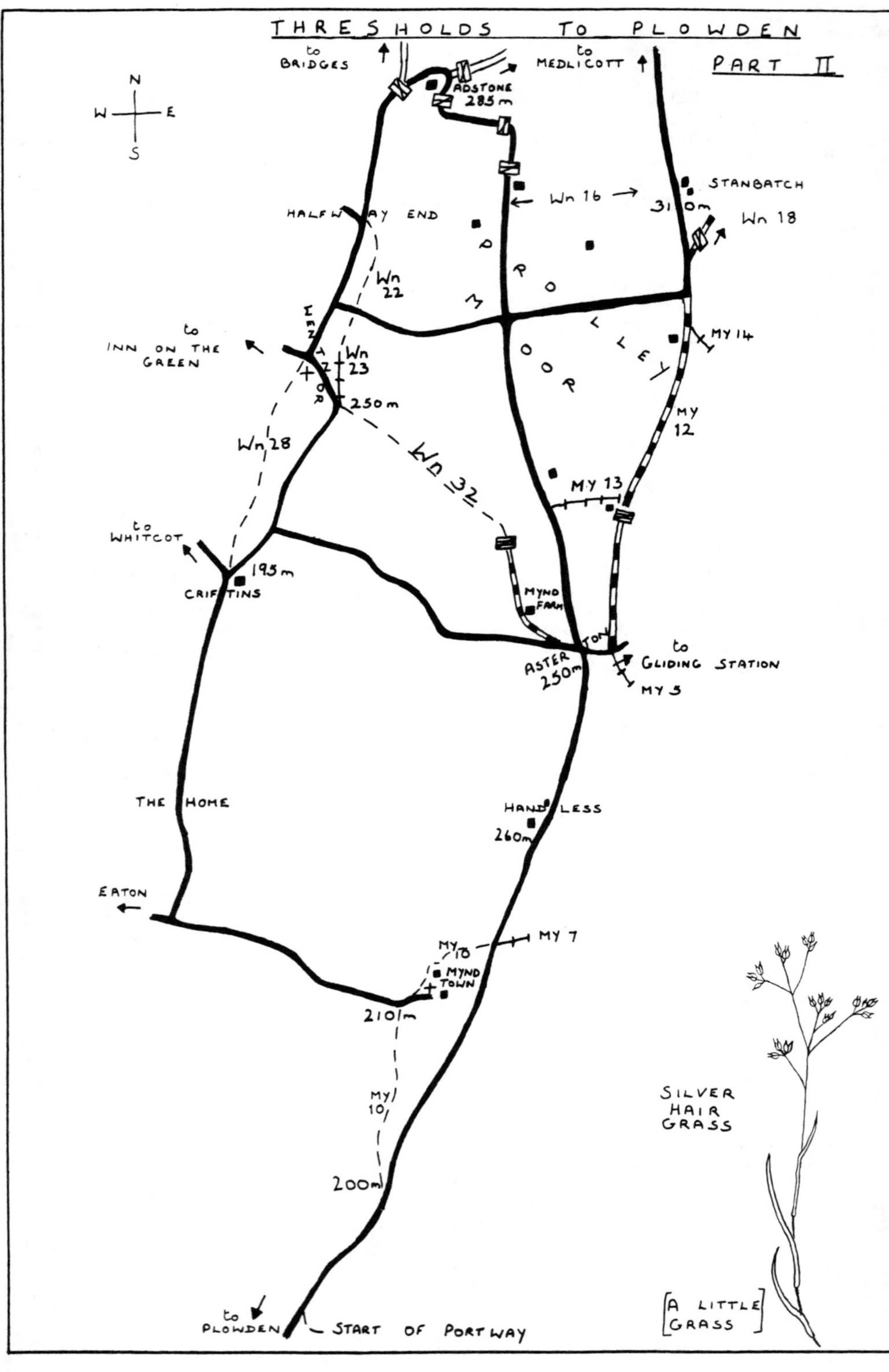
THRESHOLDS TO PLOWDEN
PART II
N
W
E
S
to BRIDGES
to MEDLICOTT
ADSTONE 285m
STANBATCH
310m
Wn 16
Wn 18
HALFWAY END
Wn 22
MOOR
POLLEY
WENTNOR
to INN ON THE GREEN
Wn 23
250m
MY 14
MY 12
Wn 28
Wn 32
MY 13
to WHITCOT
195m
CRIFTINS
MYND FARM
ASTERTON
250m
to GLIDING STATION
MY 5
THE HOME
HANDLESS
260m
EATON
MY 7
MY 10
MYND TOWN
210m
MY 10
200m
to PLOWDEN
START OF PORTWAY
SILVER HAIR GRASS
[A LITTLE GRASS]

CIRCUIT MAPS

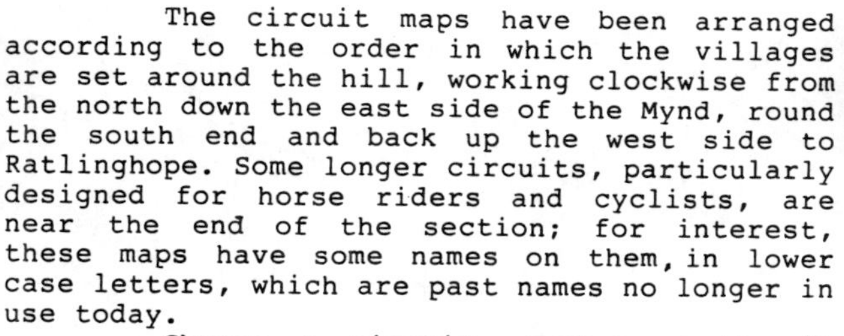

The circuit maps have been arranged according to the order in which the villages are set around the hill, working clockwise from the north down the east side of the Mynd, round the south end and back up the west side to Ratlinghope. Some longer circuits, particularly designed for horse riders and cyclists, are near the end of the section; for interest, these maps have some names on them, in lower case letters, which are past names no longer in use today.

Choose a circuit, perhaps write it down, and then turn to the next section (Villages) and work through the individual rights of way that make up your chosen circuit.

MAP SYMBOLS

surfaced highway.

unsurfaced highway/byway (see page 64).

old embankments, walls or track.

parish boundaries.

track.

bridleway. footpath.

RUPP = road used as a public footpath; these are being gradually reclassified usually into footpath or bridleway.

green lanes in public use (apparently unclassified, but likely to acquire an official status in the near future).

N.B. 'White roads' on O/S maps include public unsurfaced highways or byways, green lanes used by the public, and also private roads.

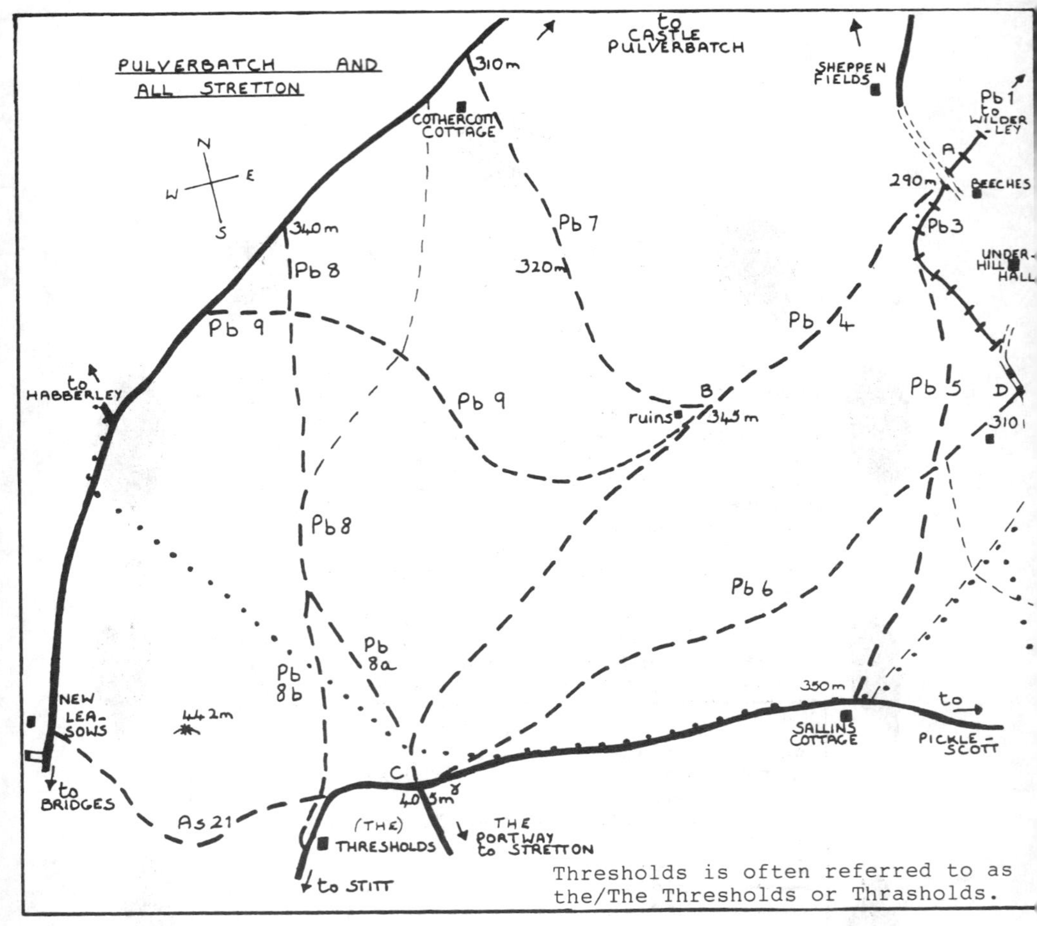

Thresholds is often referred to as the/The Thresholds or Thrasholds.

PULVERBATCH AND ALL STRETTON CIRCUITS

Starting from the Thresholds:-

1. As 21/road/Pb 8(in reverse). 3.75 Km/2¼ miles.
2. As 21/road/Pb 7/Pb 4 B to C. 5.25 Km/3¼ miles.
3. Pb 8/road/Pb 7/Pb 4 B to C. 4.25 Km/2.75 miles.
4. Pb 8/road/Pb 7/Pb 4(in reverse) B to A/Pb 5. 6.25 Km / nearly 4 miles.
5. Pb 8/road/Pb 7/Pb 4(in reverse) B to A/Pb 3(in reverse) A to D/ Pb 6. 6.25 Km/nearly 4 miles.
6. Pb 4(in reverse)/Pb 5. 4.5 Km/2.75 miles.
7. Pb 4(in reverse)/ Pb 3(in reverse) A to D / Pb 6. 4.5 Km / 2.75 miles.
8. Pb 8/Pb 9/Pb 4 B to C. 3.5 Km/2 m.
9. Pb 8/Pb 9/Pb 4(in reverse) B to A / Pb 3(in reverse) A to D / Pb 6. 5.25 Km/3¼ m.

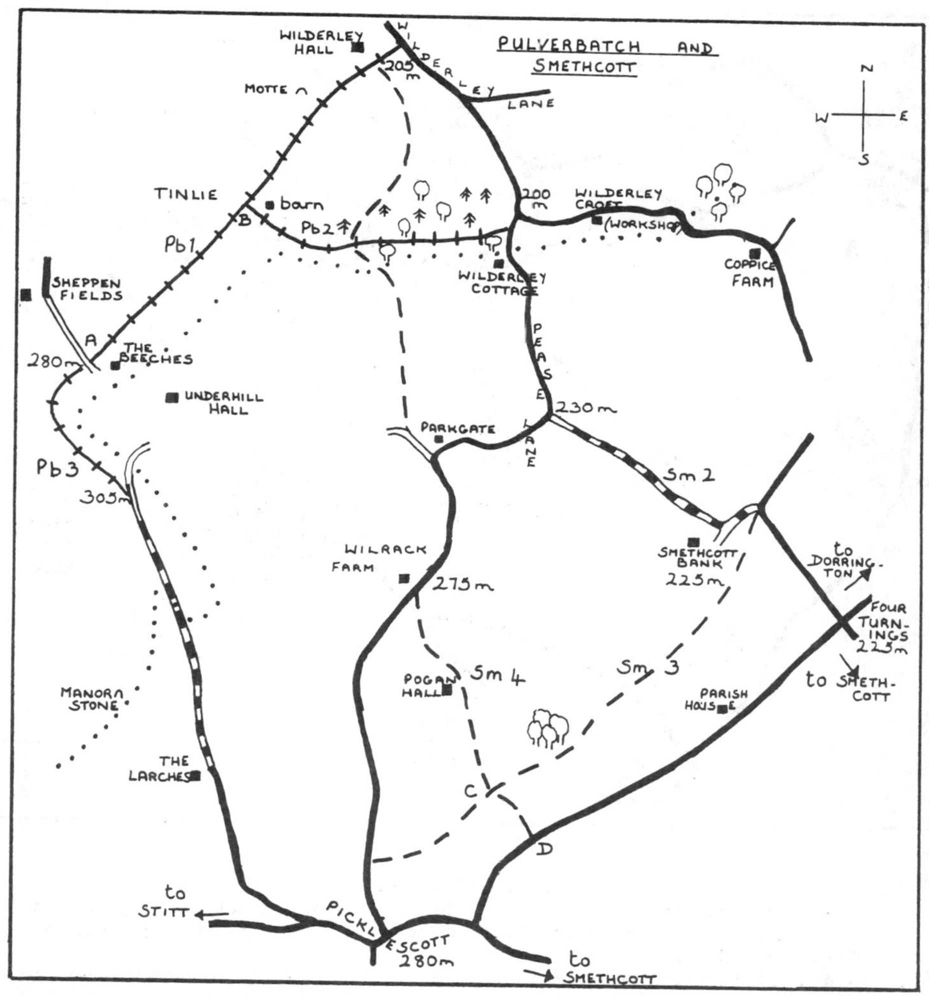

PULVERBATCH AND SMETHCOTT CIRCUITS

*1. Start Smethcott Bank/ Sm 3 to C / Sm 4 C to Wilrack Farm / Pease Lane/Sm 2. 3 Km/1.75 miles.

*2. Start Smethcott Bank/Sm 3/lane/Pb 3/Pb 1 A to B/Pb 2/Pease Lane/ Sm 2. 6.5 Km/4 miles.

*3. Start Smethcott Bank/Sm 3/lane/Pb 3/ Pb 1/ Wilderley Lane/ Pease Lane/Sm 2. 6.75 Km/4¼ miles.

*4. Start Smethcott Bank/Sm 3/lane/Pb 3/Pb 1/Sm 1/ Pease Lane/ Sm 2. 7.5 Km/4½ miles.

5. Start Picklescott/Pb 3/Pb 1/Sm 1/Pease Lane/ Sm 4(in reverse) / lane. 6.25 Km/nearly 4 miles.

* indicates that until Sm 3 is clear, use the lane via Four Turnings and Parish House as the alternative route.

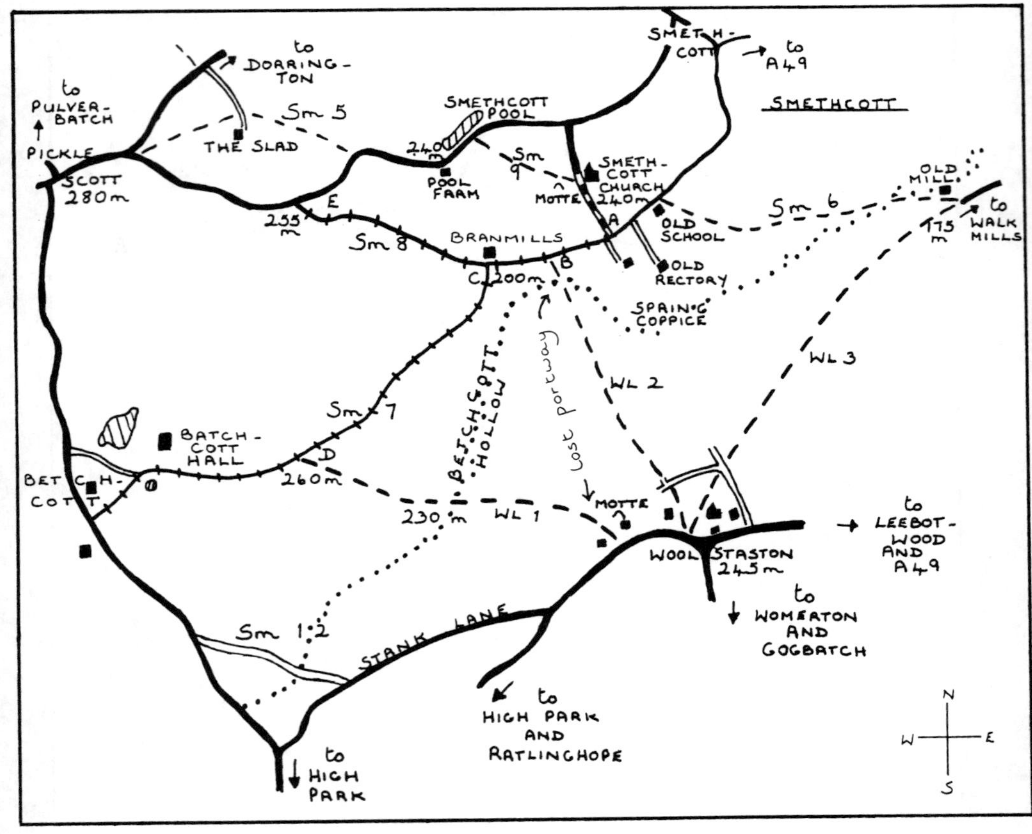

SMETHCOTT CIRCUITS

1. Start Smethcott Church/Sm 9/lane/Sm 5/ lane towards church/ Sm 8 (in reverse) E to C/Sm 7(in reverse) C to A/lane to church. 3 Km/1.75 miles.
2. Start Smethcott Church/ Sm 9/ lane/ Sm 5/ lane to Betchcott via Picklescott/ Sm 7(in reverse) to A/ lane to church. 4.5 Km/ 2.75 miles.
3. Start Betchcott/Sm 7(in reverse) to D/WL 1(in reverse)/WL 2/Sm 7 B to Betchcott. 4 Km/2½ miles.
4. Start Betchcott/Sm 7(in reverse) to D/ WL 1(in reverse)/WL 2/ Sm 7 B to C/Sm 8/lane to Betchcott via Picklescott. 5 Km/3 miles.

*5. Start Smethcott Church/lane to old school/Sm 6/WL 3(in reverse)/ WL 2/Sm 7(in reverse)B to A/lane to church. 3.75Km/2¼+ miles.

*6. Start Smethcott Church/lane to old school/Sm 6/WL 3(in reverse)/ WL 1/Sm 7(in reverse) D to A/lane to church.5 Km/3m.

*indicates that until Sm 6 is clear, these circuits cannot be done.

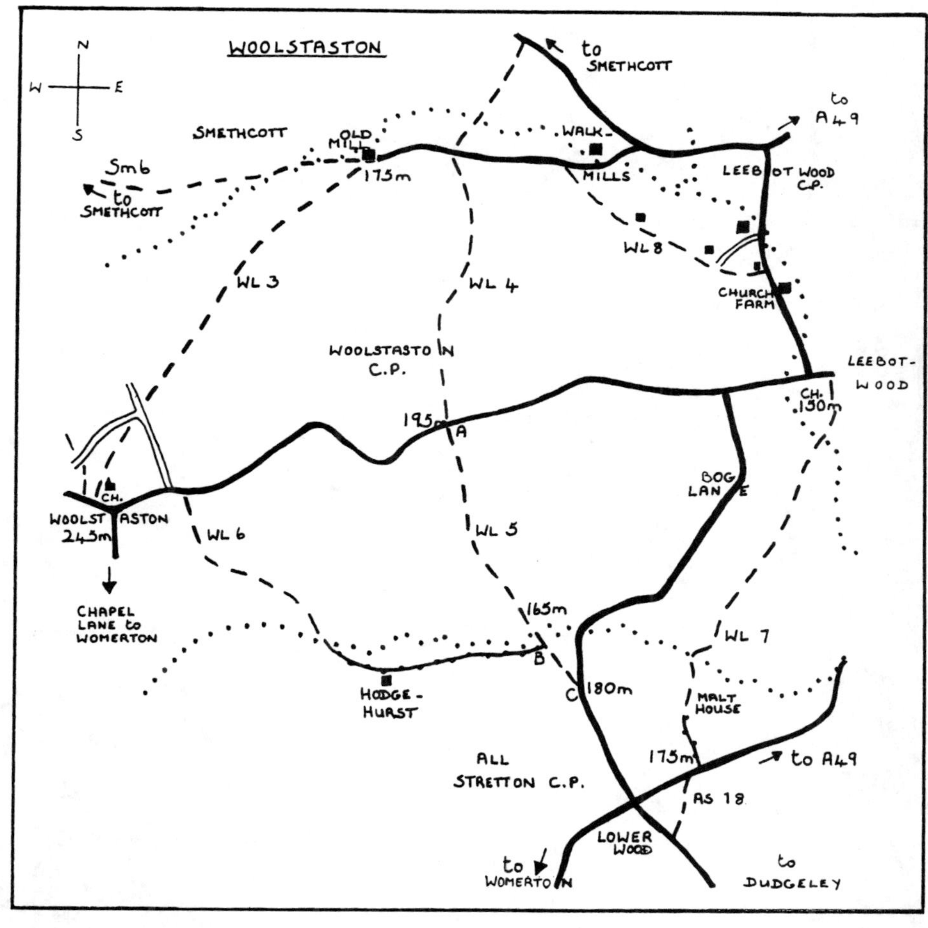

WOOLSTASTON CIRCUITS

1. Start Woolstaston Church/WL 3/WL 4/lane back to church. 3.25 Km/ 2 miles.
2. Start Woolstaston Church/WL 3/WL 4/WL 5 A to B/WL 6/lane back to church. 4.5 Km/2.75 miles.
3. Start Woolstaston Church/WL 3/ lane to Walkmills/ WL 8/ lane to Leebotwood Church/WL 7/Bog Lane/WL 5 (in reverse) C to B / WL 6/ lane back to church. 6.25 Km/nearly 4 miles.
4. Start at junction of WL 4 and 5/WL 4(in reverse)/WL 8/WL 7/ WL 5 (in reverse). 4.75 Km/nearly 3 miles.
5. Start at junction of WL 4 and 5/WL 5 A to B/WL 6/return to starting point via lane. 2.75 Km/1.75 miles.

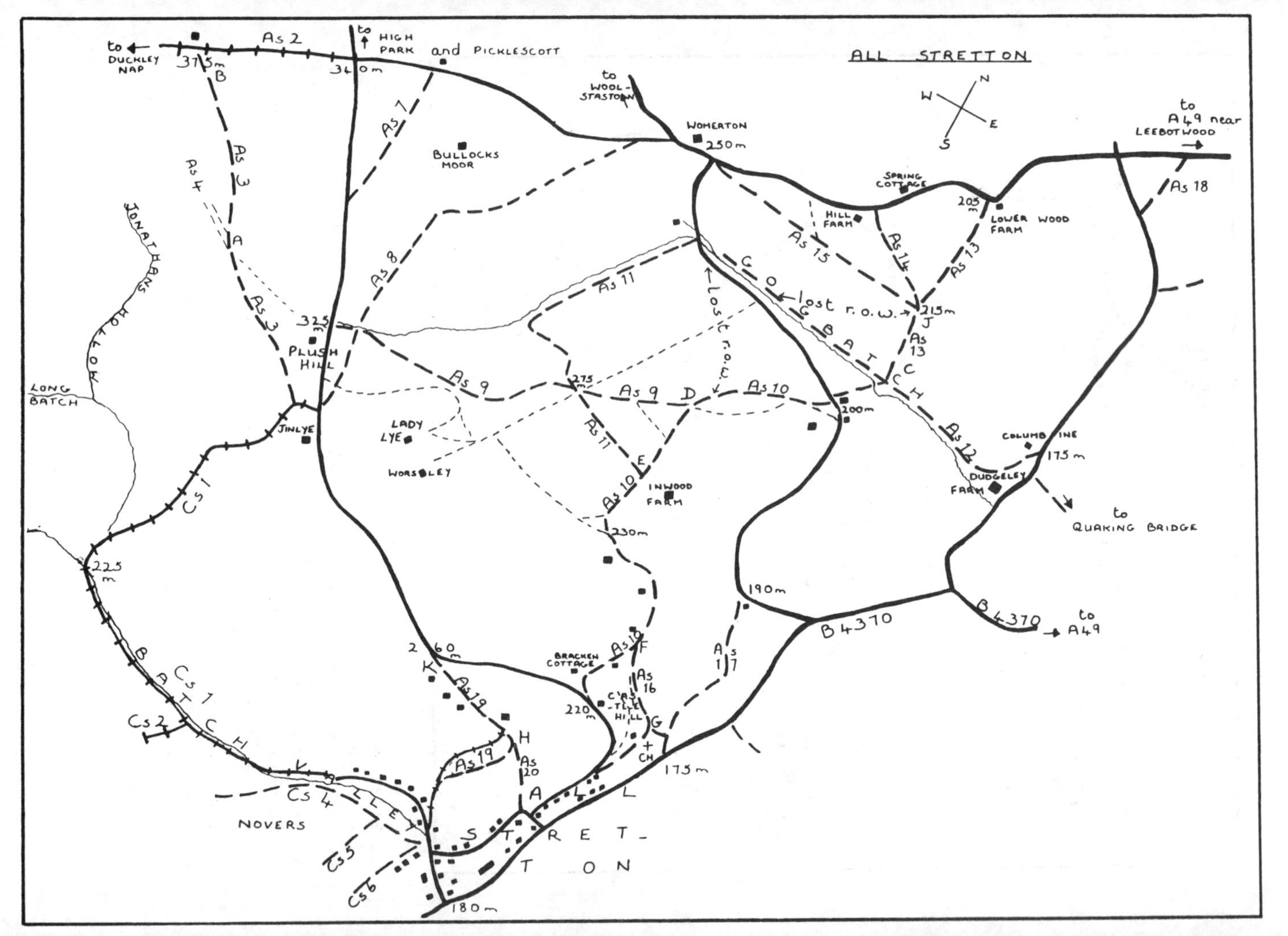
ALL STRETTON
N
E
S
W
to DUCKLEY NAP
As 2
375m
B
to HIGH PARK and PICKLESCOTT
340m
to WOOLSTASTON
WOMERTON
250m
to A49 near LEEBOTWOOD
As 18
As 7
BULLOCKS MOOR
As 3
As 4
A
As 8
SPRING COTTAGE
HILL FARM
205m
LOWER WOOD FARM
As 15
As 14
As 13
As 11
lost r.o.w.
215m
J
COGBATCH
325m
PLUSH HILL
As 9
275m
D
As 10
200m
C
As 12
COLUMBINE
175m
DUDGELEY FARM
to QUAKING BRIDGE
LONG BATCH
JONATHANS HOLLOW
JINLYE
LADY LYE
WORSLEY
E
INWOOD FARM
230m
Cs1
225m
190m
B 4370
to A49
260m
K
As 19
BRACKEN COTTAGE
F
As 16
As 17
CASTLE HILL
220m
G
CH
H
As 20
175m
BATCH
Cs 2
KELLEY
Cs 4
NOVERS
Cs 5
Cs 6
ALL STRET-TON
180m

ALL STRETTON CIRCUITS

Starting from Plush Hill:-

1. As 9/As 10(in reverse) D to Castle Hill/lane to Batch Valley/ Cs 1. 4.25 Km/2½+ miles.
2. As 9/As 10(in reverse) D to F/As 16/lane/As 20(in reverse)/As 19 (in reverse) H to K/lane to Jinlye. 3 Km/nearly 2 miles.
3. As 9/ As 10 D to Inwood/ lanes via Gogbatch and Womerton / As 8. 3 Km/nearly 2 miles.
4. Lane downhill towards All Stretton/As 10/lanes via Gogbatch and Womerton/As 7. 4.25 Km/2½+ miles.
5. Lane towards All Stretton/As 10 to D/ As 9(in reverse) to Plush Hill. 2.75 Km/1.75 miles.
6. Lane towards All Stretton/As 10 to E/As 11/lane via Womerton/ As 8. 4 Km/2½ miles.

Starting from Gogbatch:-

7. As 11(in reverse)/As 10 E to Inwood/lane. 2 Km/1¼ miles.
8. As 11(in reverse)/As 10(in reverse) E to F/As 16 to G/As 17/lane via Inwood to Gogbatch. 3 Km/nearly 2 miles.
9. As 12/lane/As 13(in reverse)/lane. 3.25 Km/2 miles.
10. As 12 to C/As 13 C to Lower Wood/lanes back to Gogbatch. 2 Km/1¼ miles.
11. As 15(in reverse)/As 14/lane. 1Km/½+ mile.

Starting from Batch Valley:-

12. Cs 1/As 9/As 10(in reverse)D to Castle Hill/lane towards Jinlye/ As 19. 4.5 Km/2.75 miles.
13. Cs 1 to Jinlye/lane towards All Stretton/As 19. 3.25 Km/2 miles.

CHURCH STRETTON (NOVERS) CIRCUITS

1. Start Batch Valley/Cs 5/ Cs 4(in reverse). 1½ Km/nearly 1 mile.
2. Start Batch Valley/Cs 4/ Cs 6(in reverse). 1.75 Km/1 mile.

N.B. If you are joining Cs 4 or Cs 5 from the parking area in Batch Valley, use the old grassy track A to B rather than scramble up the steep slope which is becoming badly eroded.

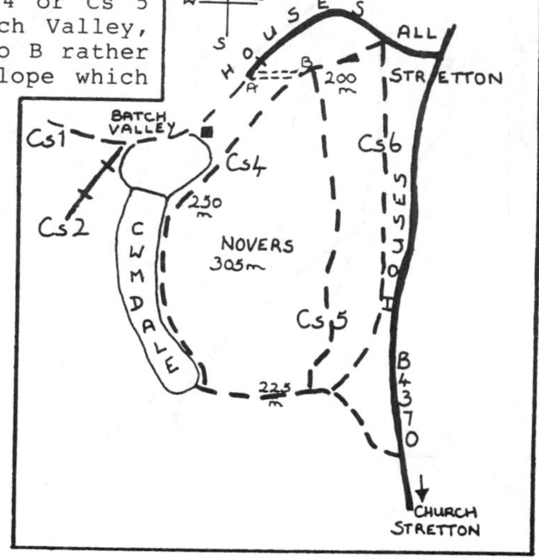

Name meaning. Novers
Novers has arisen from the old English word 'ofer'. Wentnor (Wantenoure in the Domesday Book) and Overs (Ovre in the D.B.) have a similar origin. Ofer refers to steeply sloping land or to the land above a slope but can refer to a hill, as in this case. Wentnor is at the top of a ridge and Overs is halfway up the same ridge at the other (north) end; each place has land falling away on three sides.

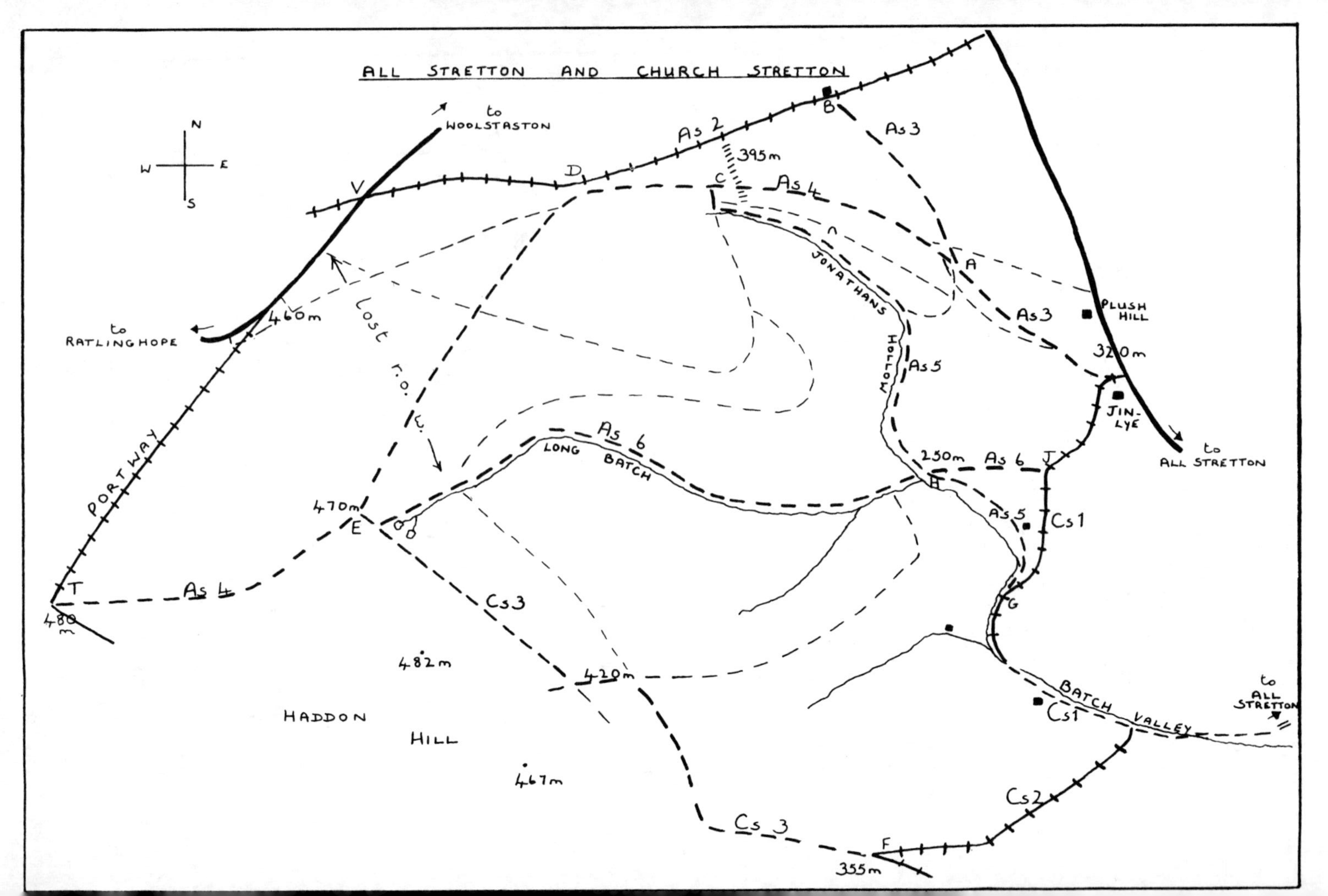
ALL STRETTON AND CHURCH STRETTON
to WOOLSTASTON
N
W
E
S
V
D
As 2
B
As 3
395m
C
As 4
A
JONATHANS
HOLLOW
As 5
As 3
PLUSH HILL
320m
JIN-LYE
to ALL STRETTON
to RATLINGHOPE
460m
Lost r.o.w.
PORTWAY
As 6
LONG
BATCH
250m
As 6
J
H
As 5
Cs 1
470m
E
T
As 4
480m
Cs 3
G
482m
420m
HADDON
HILL
467m
BATCH
VALLEY
Cs 1
to ALL STRETTON
Cs 2
Cs 3
F
355m

ALL STRETTON AND CHURCH STRETTON CIRCUITS

Starting from Batch Valley:-

1.Cs 1 to Jinlye/As 3/As 2 from B to the Portway at V / Portway(in reverse) V to T/As 4(in reverse) T to E/Cs 3 to F/Cs 2(in reverse) to Batch Valley. 7.75 Km/4.75 miles.

2.Cs 2/Cs 3(in reverse) F to E/As 4(in reverse) E to Jinlye / Cs 1 (in reverse). 5.5 Km/3½ miles.

3.Cs 1 to G/As 5/As 4 C to E/Cs 3 to F / Cs 2(in reverse) to Batch Valley. 5.5 Km/3½ miles.

Starting from Jinlye:-

4.As 3/As 2 from B to the Portway at V/Portway(in reverse) V to T/ As 4(in reverse) T to E/Cs 3 to F/Cs 2(in reverse)/Cs 1 to Jinlye. 7.75 Km/4.75 miles.

5.As 4 to E/Cs 3 to F/Cs 2(in reverse)/Cs 1 to Jinlye. 5.5 Km/3½ miles.

6.As 3/As 2 B to the Portway at V/Portway(in reverse) V to T/ As 4 (in reverse) to Jinlye. 6.25 Km/nearly 4 miles.

7.Lane/As 2 to Portway at V / Portway(in reverse) V to T / As 4(in reverse) to Jinlye. 6.5 Km/4 miles.

8.As 3/As 2 B to V/Portway(in reverse) V to T/As 4(in reverse) to E/As 6 to Jinlye.

Starting from Duckley Nap:-

9.Portway(in reverse) V to T/As 4(in reverse) T to E/Cs 3 to F/ Cs 2(in reverse)/Cs 1 to Jinlye/As 3/As 2 B to V.

10.Portway(in reverse) V to T/As 4(in reverse) T to E/ As 6 to Jinlye/As 3/As 2 B to V. 5.5 Km/3½ miles.

Although all the above paths are described in the Villages section in further detail, the circuit map alone may be adequate and simpler to follow. By using the circuit map many other combinations of short sections of paths can be made.

Name meaning

Jinlye

Jinlye has also been spelled Gin Ley. Ley is an old field name and refers to cleared forest land; in this case it could perhaps refer to an area enclosed from woodland or moorland There are several leys in this area including Lady Ley opposite and Worsley. Ley can also mean untilled land and this could apply here too.

Gin, later Jin, suggests that this may have been an area for trapping animals or birds.

Plush Hill

It is unlikely that this hill could have ever been described as plush as we know the word today. Plush is more likely to have derived from a dialect word 'plash' (from an old English word) meaning a 'marshy pool'.

Batch Valley

This is a not infrequent example of a name made up of two words each with the same meaning. This often seems to arise where one of the words is no longer in current use in the English language. Batch is derived from an old English word meaning land in a valley. Cwmdale nearby is another example, cwm meaning valley in Welsh.

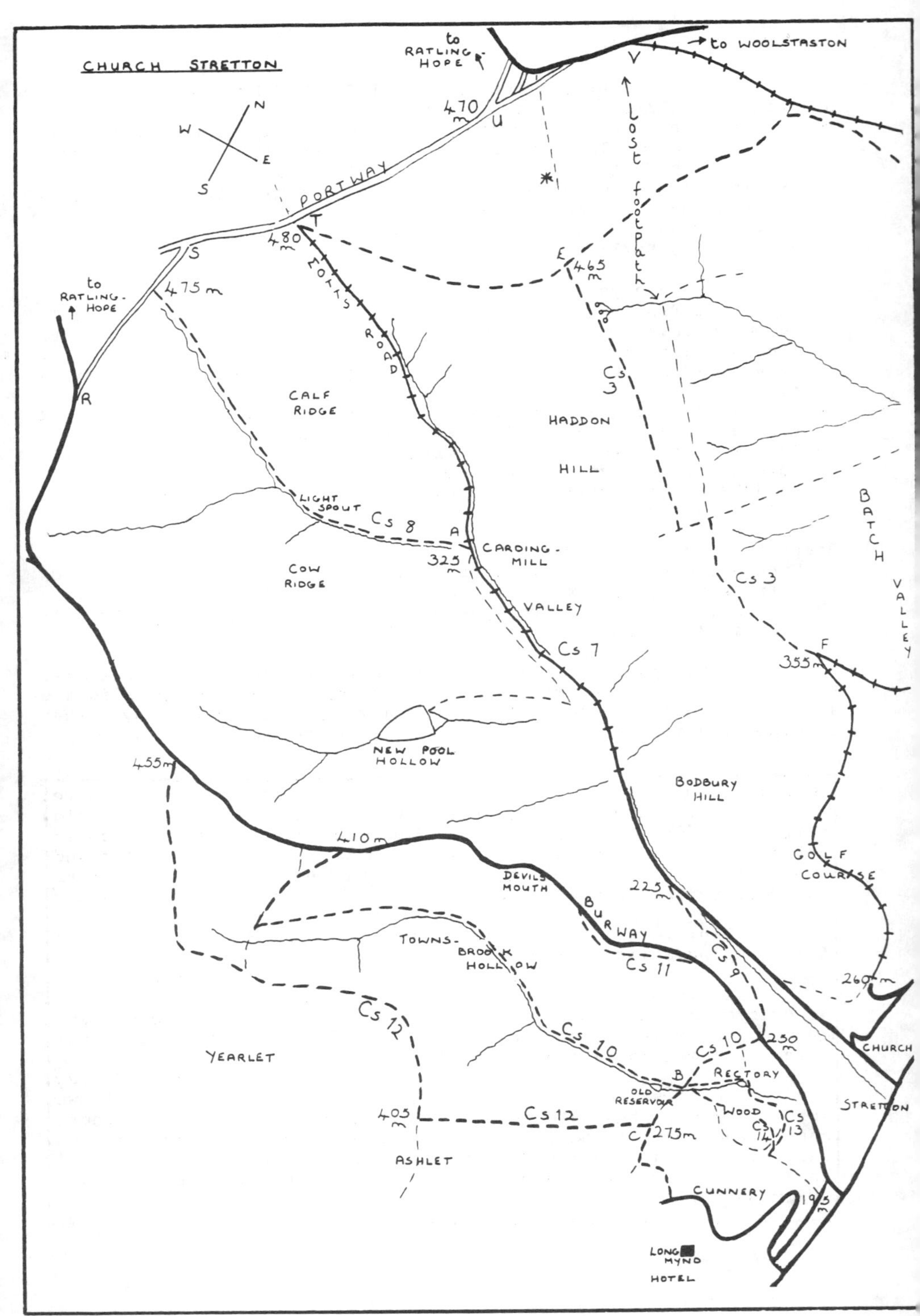
CHURCH STRETTON
N
W
E
S
to RATLING HOPE
to WOOLSTASTON
V
470 m
U
PORTWAY
T
480 m
S
to RATLING-HOPE
475 m
R
MOTTS ROAD
E
465 m
Lost footpath
CALF RIDGE
HADDON
HILL
Cs 3
LIGHT SPOUT
Cs 8
A
325 m
CARDING-MILL
VALLEY
COW RIDGE
Cs 7
BATCH VALLEY
Cs 3
F
355 m
NEW POOL HOLLOW
455 m
BODBURY HILL
410 m
GOLF COURSE
DEVILS MOUTH
225 m
BURWAY
TOWNS-BROOK HOLLOW
Cs 11
Cs 9
260 m
Cs 12
Cs 10
Cs 10
250 m
CHURCH
YEARLET
B
RECTORY
OLD RESERVOIR
WOOD
Cs 13
STRETTON
405 m
Cs 12
C
275 m
Cs 14
ASHLET
CUNNERY
195 m
LONG MYND HOTEL

CHURCH STRETTON CIRCUITS

Starting from Carding Mill Valley:-

1. Cs 7/As 4(in reverse) T to E/Cs 3. 6.75 Km/4 miles.
2. Cs 7 to A/Cs 8/Portway S to T/Cs 7(in reverse). 5 Km/3 miles.
3. Cs 7 to A/Cs 8/Portway S to T/As 4(in reverse) T to E/Cs 3. 7.5 Km/4½+ miles.
4. Cs 9/Cs 10/Burway/Cs 11/Cs 9(in reverse). 4.5 Km/2.75 miles.
5. Cs 9/Cs 10/road/Portway R to T/ Cs 7(in reverse). 7.75 Km / 4.75 miles.
6. Cs 9/Cs 10/road/Portway R to T/As 4(in reverse) T to E/Cs 3. 9.5 Km/nearly 6 miles.

Starting from Church Stretton:-

7. Cs 13/Cs 10 from B/road/Cs 12 to Cunnery/road. 6.25 Km/nearly 4 miles.
8. Cs 13/Cs 10 from B/road/Cs 12 to C/path C to B/Cs 14. 6 Km/ 3.75 miles.

Starting from hilltop:-

9. Portway R to T/Cs 7(in reverse)/Cs 9/Cs 10/road. 8 Km / nearly 5 miles.
10. Portway R to T/As 4(in reverse) T to E/Cs 3/Cs 9/Cs 10/road. 9.5 Km/nearly 6 miles.

Fig.8 **Focus on Stretton reservoirs.**

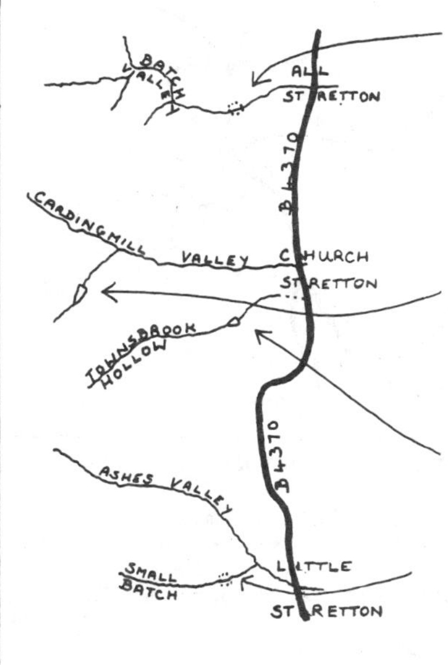

All Stretton reservoir lay at the foot of Novers in Batch Valley. It was in use until the 1960s. The cottage upstream of where it lay is called Old Reservoir Cottage.

The pool in New Pool Hollow was built at the turn of this century and supplied Church Stretton and Little Stretton and much more recently, All Stretton. It went out of use in the late 1970s. There is an old mill pool in the area and the upper car park of Cardingmill Valley was also once a mill pool that was later used as a swimming pool.

The reservoir that served Church Stretton before 1903 is in Townsbrook Hollow.

Little Stretton was served by a reservoir in Small Batch, a branch off Ashes Valley. It is thought to have gone out of use over 100 years ago. Ashes Valley itself had a swimming pool.

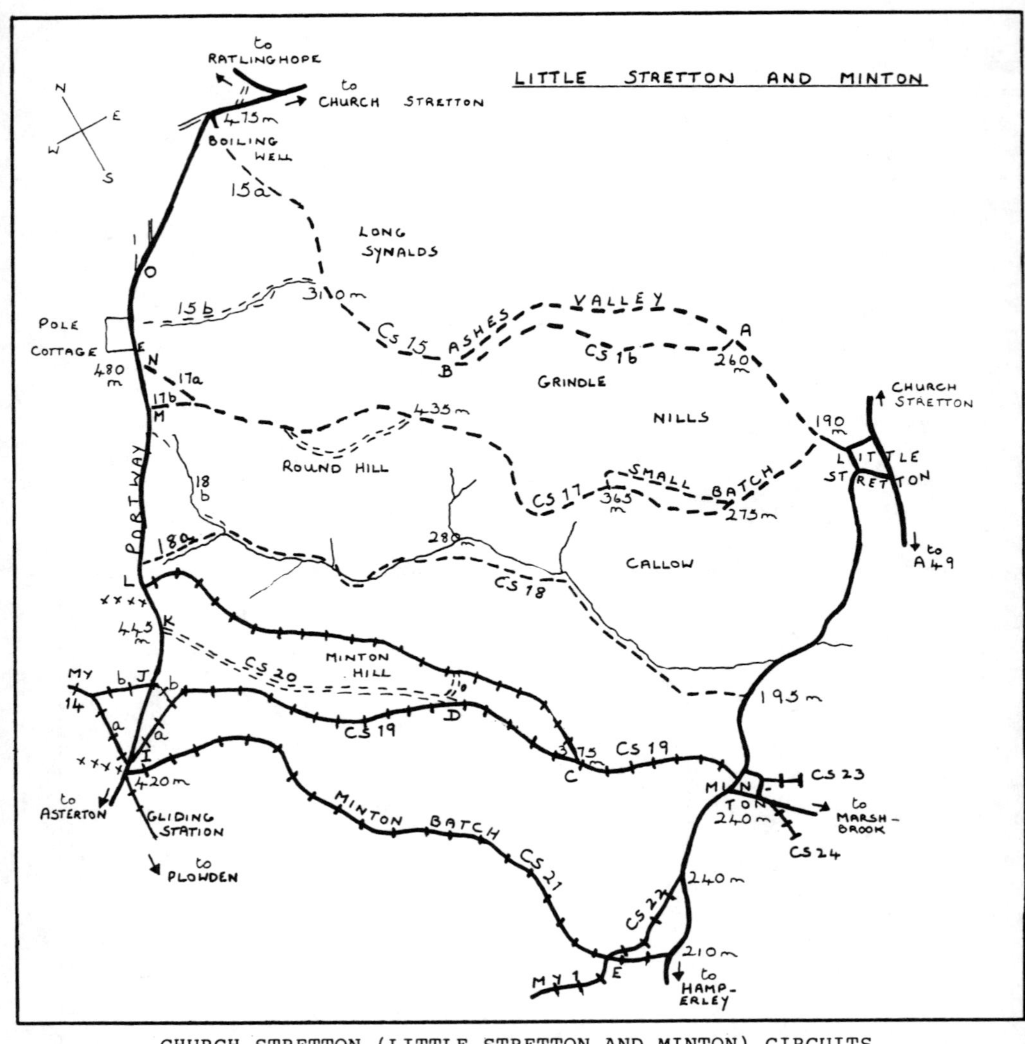

CHURCH STRETTON (LITTLE STRETTON AND MINTON) CIRCUITS

Starting from Little Stretton:-

1. Cs 15/road to N/Cs 17(in reverse). 9.25 Km/5.75 miles.
2. Cs 15 to B / Cs 16(in reverse) / Cs 15(in reverse) A to Little Stretton. 4 Km/2½ miles.
3. Cs 15 to A/Cs 16/Cs 15 from B to Boiling Well/road/Cs 17(in reverse). 9.25 Km/5.75 miles.
4. Cs 17/Cs 18(in reverse)/lane. 9 Km/5½ miles.

Starting from Callow Hollow or Minton:-

5.Cs 18/Cs 20(in reverse)/Cs 19(in reverse) from D to Minton. 6.75 Km/4 miles.

6.Cs 19/Cs 21(in reverse) to E/ Cs 22(in reverse) / lane. 7 Km/4¼ miles.

Starting from Minton Batch:-

7.Cs 21/Cs 19(in reverse)/lane. 7 Km/4¼ miles.

Starting from the hilltop:-

8.Cs 15(in reverse)/Cs 17/road. 9.25 Km/5.75 miles.

9.Cs 17(in reverse)/lane/Cs 18. 9 Km/5½ miles.

10.Cs 20(in reverse)/Cs 19(in reverse) from D to Minton/lane/Cs 18. 7.5 Km/4½miles.

11.Cs 20(in reverse)/Cs 19(in reverse) D to Minton/lane/Cs 22/Cs 21 from E to Portway/road. 6.75 Km/4 miles.

12.Cs 19(in reverse)/lane/Cs 18. 7.5 Km/4½ miles.

13.Cs 19(in reverse)/lane/Cs 21. 7 Km/4¼ miles.

14.Cs 15(in reverse)/Cs 19 to D/Cs 20/road. 10.75 Km/6.75 miles.

15.Cs 15(in reverse)/lane/Cs 18/road. 10 Km/6 miles.

Name meaning.

Callow

Callow comes from an old English word for bald or bare. This name may have at first referred to the hill known as the Callow. Subsequently, the adjacent hollow has become Callow Hollow.

Synalds

This may be derived from a combination of two old English words, 'sid' meaning long, spacious and 'hlaw' meaning hill. If so, Long Synalds is another example of a name, like Cwmdale, combining two words with the same meaning. Locally, Long Synalds is known as Long Signals. An area near the gliding station is recorded on an old map as Synalds, and an area and farm above Batch Valley are also known as Synalds.

Grindle

'Grin' may be derived from the old English word for a snare and '-dle' from hill. Grindle could alternatively have meant green hill. Local people call it Round Hill and have no recollection of the name Grindle ever having been used. It also appears on old maps as Catalls.

Focus on ghost stories

Barristers Plain on Cs 17 is the setting for one ghost story. Locally the old cross dyke here is known as Soldiers Row and some people believe that soldiers were buried here. It was certainly one of the sites, in the last century, for Artillery Volunteer manouvres. More than one person has experienced seeing soldiers in this place, described as approaching at great speed. If the soldiers are coming towards you, this can be a very frightening experience.

Another ghost story is set somewhere approaching Ratlinghope. Here, people have apparently witnessed phantom funeral processions which have appeared real enough for these people to enquire, on arrival at Ratlinghope, who had died.

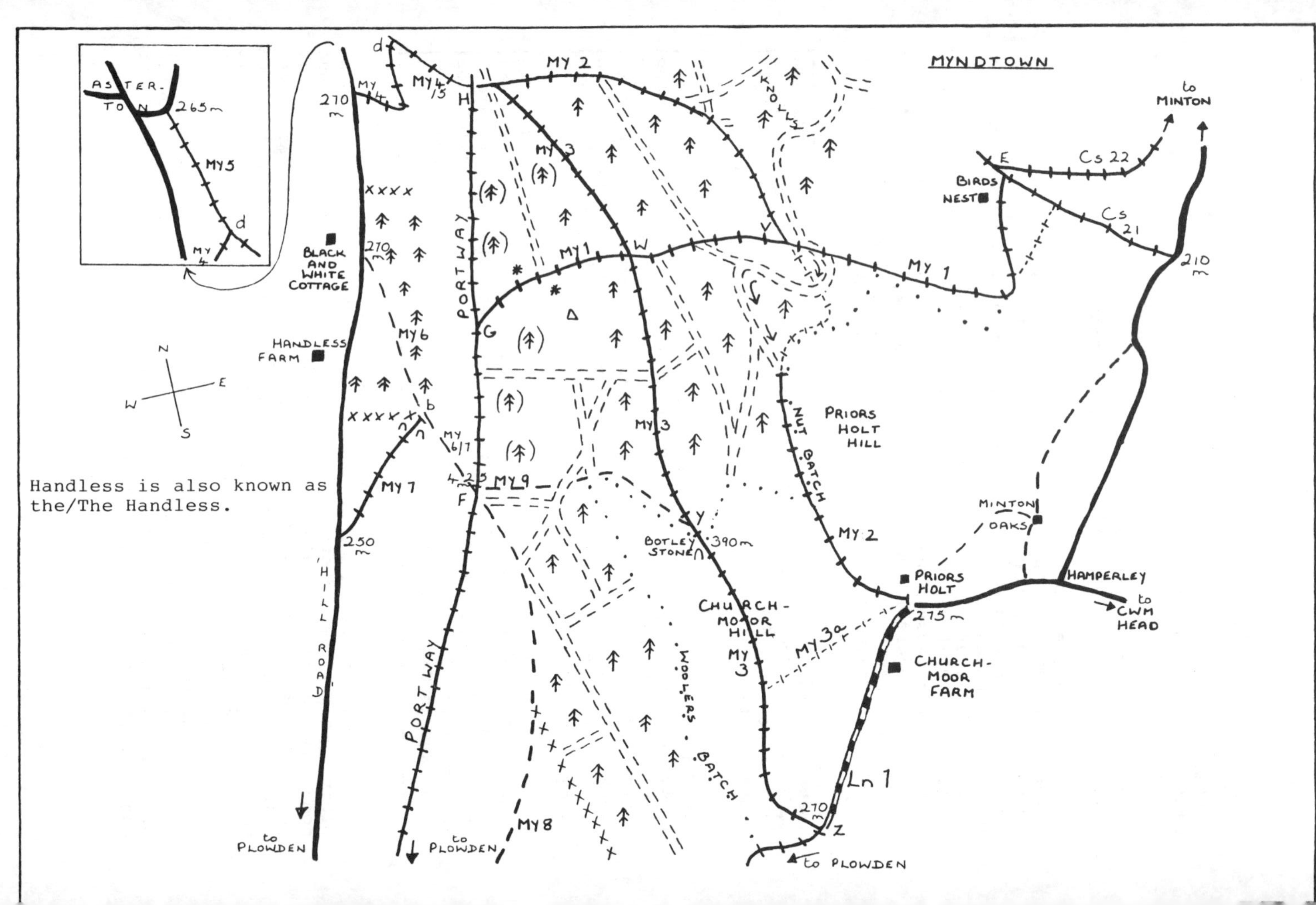

Handless is also known as the/The Handless.

MYNDTOWN CIRCUITS

Starting from Minton Batch:-

1.Cs 21 to Birds Nest/MY 1 to W/MY 3 W to Portway at H/ Portway(in reverse) H to G/MY 1(in reverse) back to Minton Batch. 5.5 Km / 3½ miles.

#2.Cs 21 to Birds Nest/MY 1 to W/MY 3 W to Portway at H/ Portway(in reverse)H to G/MY 1(in reverse) G to W/MY 3(in reverse) W to Z / Ln 1(in reverse) Z to Priors Holt/lane back to Minton Batch. 7.5 Km/4½ miles.

*3.Cs 21 to Birds Nest/MY 1 to V/MY 2 V to Portway at H/ Portway(in reverse) H to G/MY 1(in reverse) back to Minton Batch. 5.75 Km / 3½ miles.

4.Cs 21 to Birds Nest/MY 1 to V/MY 2 V to Portway at H/Portway (in
* reverse) H to G/MY 1(in reverse) G to W/ MY 3(in reverse)W to Z/
\# Ln 1(in reverse) Z to Priors Holt / lane back to Minton Batch. 7.5 Km/4½+ miles.

5.Cs 21 to Birds Nest/MY 1 to W / MY 3 W to Portway at H / MY 4(in reverse)/lane towards Plowden/MY 7/Portway F to G/MY 1(in reverse) back to Minton Batch. 8.25 Km/5 miles.

#6.Cs 21 to Birds Nest/MY 1 to W/ MY 3 W to Portway at H / MY 4(in reverse)/lane towards Plowden/MY 7/Portway F to G/MY 1(in reverse) G to W/MY 3(in reverse) W to Z/Ln 1(in reverse) Z to Priors Holt/lane to Minton Batch. 9.75 Km/6 miles.

*7.Cs 21 to Birds Nest/MY 1 to V/ MY 2 V to Portway at H / MY 4(in reverse)/lane/MY 7/Portway F to G/MY 1(in reverse) back to Minton Batch. 8.5 Km/5¼ miles.

8.Cs 21 to Birds Nest/MY 1 to V/ MY 2 V to Portway at H / MY 4(in
\# reverse)/lane/MY 7/Portway F to G/MY 1(in reverse) G to W / MY 3
* (in reverse) W to Z/Ln 1(in reverse) Z to Priors Holt/lane. 9.5 Km/nearly 6 miles.

9.Cs 21 to Birds Nest/MY 1 to V/MY 2(in reverse) V to Priors Holt/ lane. 4 Km/2½ miles.

10.Cs 21 to Birds Nest/MY 1 to V/MY 2 V to Portway at H/ Portway(in
* reverse) H to G / MY 1(in reverse) to V / MY 2(in reverse) V to Priors Holt/lane. 7.5 Km/4½ miles.

11.Cs 21 to Birds Nest/MY 1 to V / MY 2 V to Portway at H / My 4(in
* reverse)/lane/MY 7/Portway F to G/MY 1(in reverse) to V/ MY 2(in reverse) V to Priors Holt/lane. 9.5 Km/nearly 6 miles.

12.Cs 21 to Birds Nest/MY 1/Portway(in reverse) G to F/ MY 9 / MY 3
\# (in reverse) Y to Z/ Ln 1(in reverse) Z to Priors Holt. 7.5 Km/ 4½+ miles.

13.Circuits 5 - 8 and 11 can be done substituting MY 6 for MY 7.

14.One day in the future, circuits ending with lanes from Priors Holt to Minton Batch may be possible to do substituting the footpaths via Minton Oaks for lanes.

Starting from Handless:-

15.MY 7/Portway F to H/MY 4(in reverse). 3.5 Km/2 miles.

16.MY 6/Portway F to H/MY 4(in reverse). 2.5 Km/1½ miles.

17.MY 6/MY 9/MY 3 Y to the Portway at H/MY 4(in reverse). 4 Km/2½m.

* and #:- circuits 1 to 11 and 15 are made up completely of bridleways and are therefore suitable for riders and cyclists. However,circuits marked by * or # indicate an obstruction but really only to riders. * represents an obstruction on MY 2 near H where the way is crossed by temporary fencing at the edge of the forest. # represents an obstruction on Ln 1 (thereby obstructing the exit of MY 3) where the way is crossed by hurdles near Priors Holt. MY 3a, an old track, is a possible alternative at present but permission to use it should be sought first.

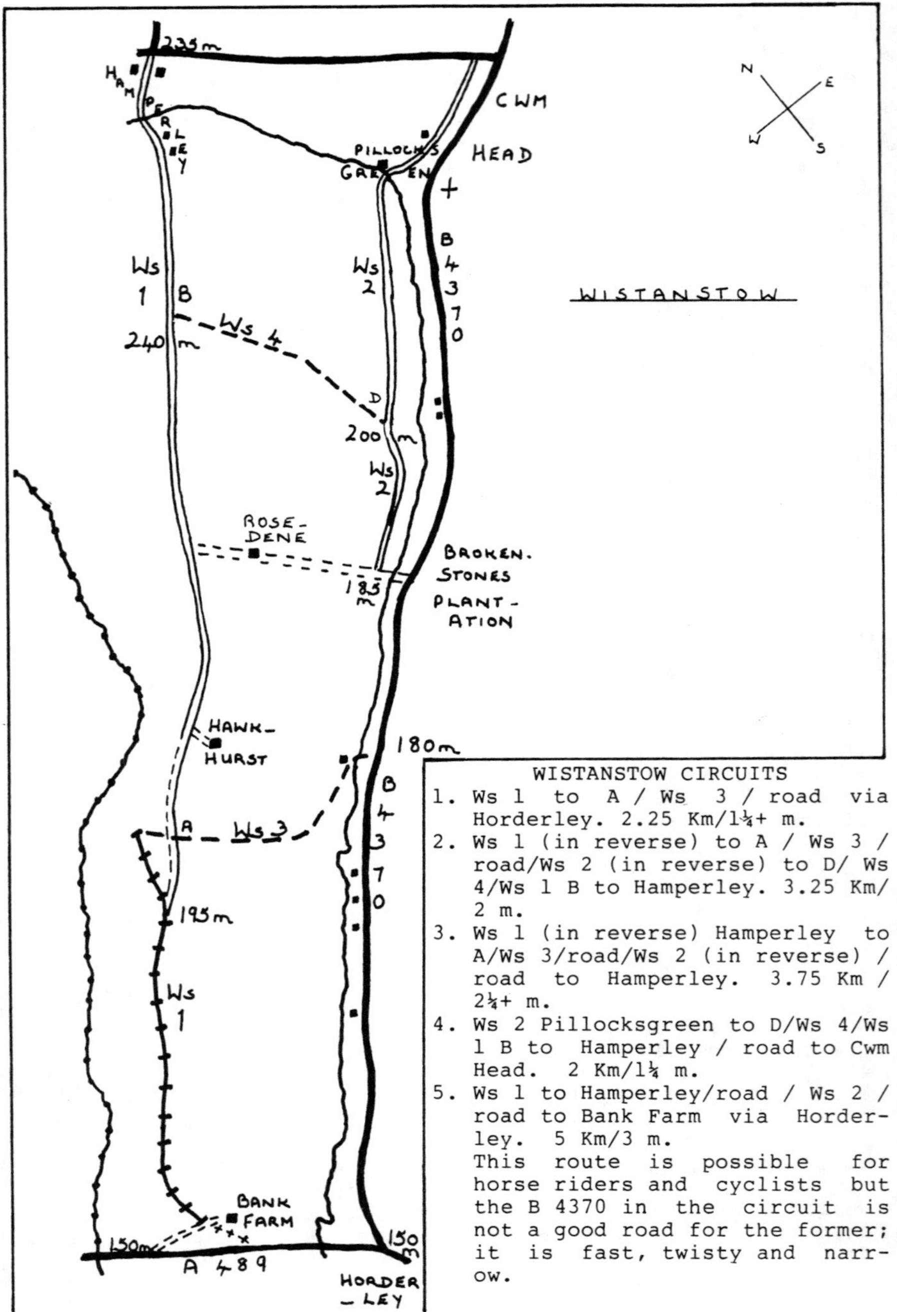

WISTANSTOW CIRCUITS

1. Ws 1 to A / Ws 3 / road via Horderley. 2.25 Km/1¼+ m.
2. Ws 1 (in reverse) to A / Ws 3 / road/Ws 2 (in reverse) to D/ Ws 4/Ws 1 B to Hamperley. 3.25 Km/ 2 m.
3. Ws 1 (in reverse) Hamperley to A/Ws 3/road/Ws 2 (in reverse) / road to Hamperley. 3.75 Km / 2¼+ m.
4. Ws 2 Pillocksgreen to D/Ws 4/Ws 1 B to Hamperley / road to Cwm Head. 2 Km/1¼ m.
5. Ws 1 to Hamperley/road / Ws 2 / road to Bank Farm via Horderley. 5 Km/3 m.
   This route is possible for horse riders and cyclists but the B 4370 in the circuit is not a good road for the former; it is fast, twisty and narrow.

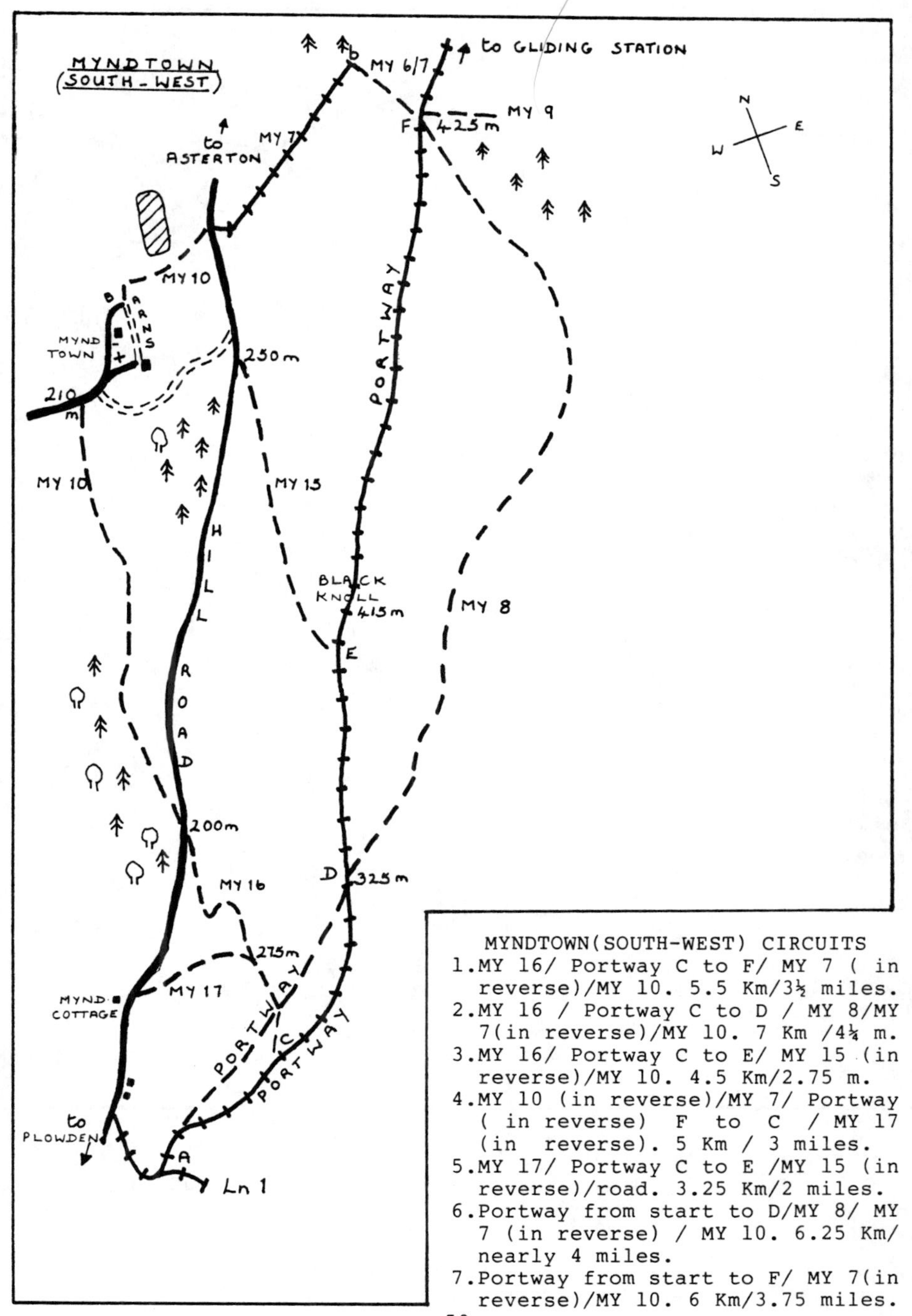

MYNDTOWN(SOUTH-WEST) CIRCUITS

1. MY 16/ Portway C to F/ MY 7 (in reverse)/MY 10. 5.5 Km/3½ miles.
2. MY 16 / Portway C to D / MY 8/MY 7(in reverse)/MY 10. 7 Km /4¼ m.
3. MY 16/ Portway C to E/ MY 15 (in reverse)/MY 10. 4.5 Km/2.75 m.
4. MY 10 (in reverse)/MY 7/ Portway (in reverse) F to C / MY 17 (in reverse). 5 Km / 3 miles.
5. MY 17/ Portway C to E /MY 15 (in reverse)/road. 3.25 Km/2 miles.
6. Portway from start to D/MY 8/ MY 7 (in reverse) / MY 10. 6.25 Km/ nearly 4 miles.
7. Portway from start to F/ MY 7(in reverse)/MY 10. 6 Km/3.75 miles.

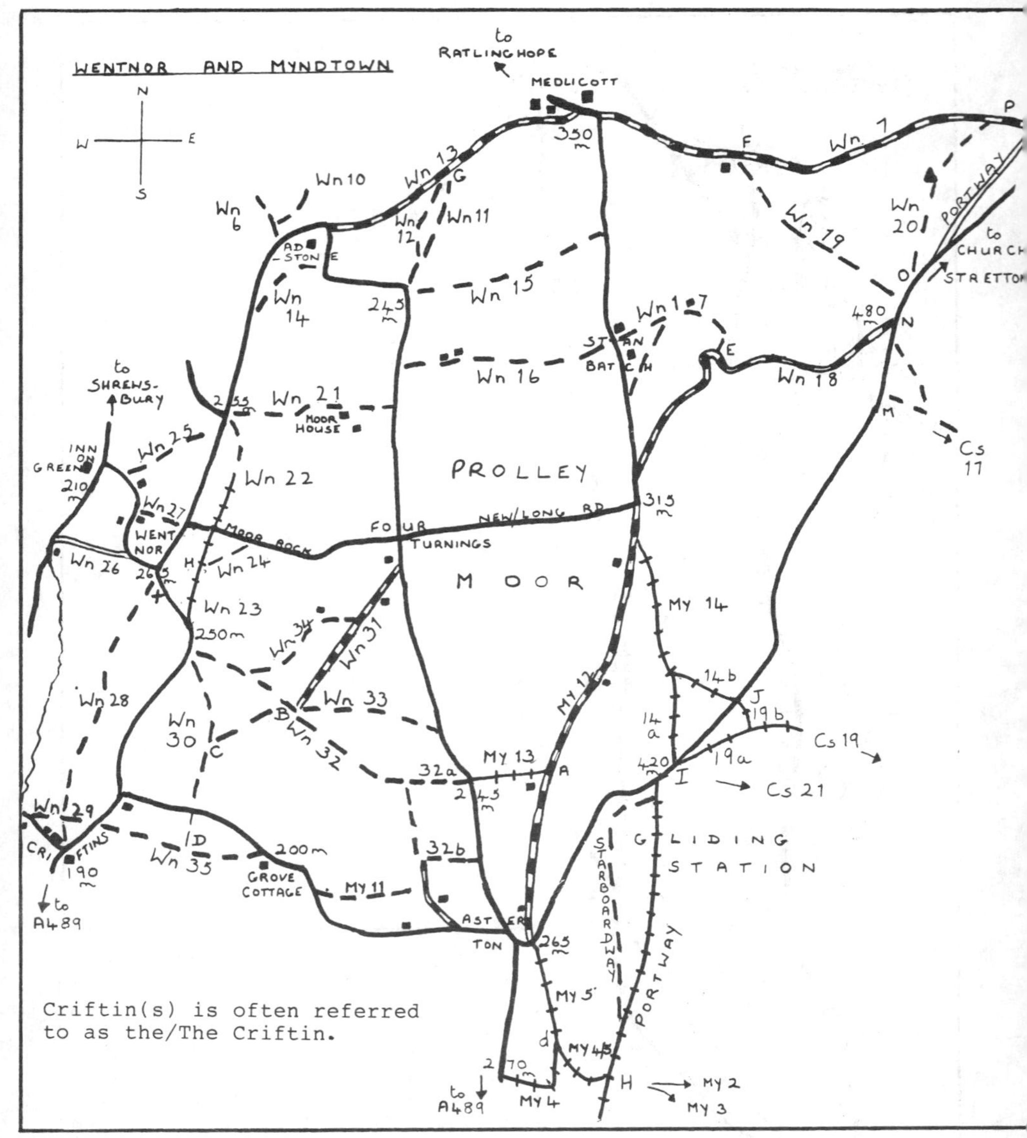

WENTNOR AND MYNDTOWN CIRCUITS

Starting from the Green:-

1. Wn 25/Wn 21/road/Wn 31 to B/Wn 32 B to Wentnor/road/Wn 23(in reverse)/road/Wn 27 or Wn 26/road. 4 Km/2½ miles.
2. Wn 25/Wn 22/road/Wn 27/road. 1.75 Km/1 mile.
3. Road/Wn 32(in reverse),exit via 32a/MY 13(in reverse)/MY 12 A to Prolley Moor/road to Stanbatch/Wn 16(in reverse)/Wn 21(in reverse)/Wn 25(in reverse). 6.75 Km/4 miles.

Starting from Asterton:-

4. MY 5/Starboard Way or Portway H to I/MY 14(in reverse)/ MY 12(in reverse). 5 Km/3 miles.
5. MY 12/road/Wn 31 to B/Wn 32(in reverse) B to Asterton. 5 Km / 3 miles.
6. MY 12 to A/MY 13/Wn 32 to Wentnor/road/Wn 28/Wn 35/ MY 11 / last bit of Wn 32(in reverse).
7. MY 12 to A/MY 13/Wn 33/Wn 32(in reverse) B to Asterton. 5.75 Km/ 3½ miles.
8. Wn 32 to B/Wn 31 B to C/Wn 30 C to D / Wn 35 D to Grove Cottage/MY 11/last bit of Wn 32(in reverse). 3.5 Km/2+ miles.

Starting from Wentnor:-

9. Wn 28/Wn 35 to D/Wn 30(in reverse)/lane. 3 Km/nearly 2 miles.
10. Wn 28/Wn 35/MY 11/Wn 32/lane. 4 Km/2½ miles.
11. Wn 32(in reverse)/lane/MY 5/Starboard Way or Portway H to N / Wn 18(in reverse) to E/Wn 17(in reverse)/Wn 16(in reverse) / Wn 21 (in reverse)/Wn 22/lane. 10.25 Km/nearly 6½ miles.
12. Wn 32(in reverse) to B/Wn 31(in reverse) B to Prolley Moor/lane/ Wn 24/Wn 23. 3 Km/nearly 2 miles.

Starting from Stanbatch:-

13. Wn 17/Wn 18 E to Portway at N/Wn 19(in reverse)/Wn 7(in reverse) F to Medlicott/lane. 3.75 Km/2¼ miles.
14. Wn 18 to Portway at N/Portway N to O/Wn 20 O to P/ Wn 7 (in reverse) P to Medlicott/lane. 4 Km/2½ miles.
15. Wn 18/Portway N to O/Wn 20 O to P/Wn 7(in reverse) from P/Wn 13/ lane/Wn 16. 7.25 Km/4½ miles.
16. Wn 16(in reverse)/lane/Wn 15/lane. 2.25 Km/nearly 1½ miles.
17. Wn 18 to E/Wn 17(in reverse)/Wn 16(in reverse)/lane/Wn 15/ lane. 3.5 Km/2 miles.
18. Wn 18 to Portway at N/ Wn 19(in reverse) / Wn 7(in reverse) F to Medlicott/Wn 13 to G/Wn 12/lane/Wn 16. 6 Km/3.75 miles.
19. MY 12(in reverse)/MY 5/Starboard Way or Portway H to I/ MY 14(in reverse). 4.75 Km/3 miles.
20. MY 12(in reverse)/MY 5/Starboard Way or Portway H to N/ Wn 18(in reverse). 7 Km/4¼ miles.
21. MY 12(in reverse) to A/MY 13/Wn 32 to B/Wn 31(in reverse) B to Prolley Moor/road. 4 Km/2½ miles.
22. MY 12(in reverse) to A/MY 13/Wn 32/ Wn 23(in reverse) / Wn 22(in reverse)/Wn 21/Wn 16. 6.25 Km/nearly 4 miles.
23. Same as 22 but substitute Wn 32 with Wn 33/Wn 32 B to Wentnor.

Starting from near Moorhouse:-

24. Wn 16/lane to Medlicott/Wn 13/lane/Wn 14/lane/Wn 21. 4.75 Km / 3 miles.
25. Wn 16/lane/Wn 13 to G/Wn 12/lane. 3 Km/nearly 2 miles.
26. Wn 16/lane/Wn 13/lane. 3.75 Km/2¼ miles.

Starting from Four Turnings:-

27. Wn 31 to B/Wn 32 B to Wentnor/ Wn 23(in reverse) / Wn 22(in reverse)/Wn 21/road. 3.25 Km/2 miles.

Starting from Pole Cottage:-

28. Wn 20 O to P/Wn 7(in reverse) to F/Wn 19. 3 Km/nearly 2 miles.
29. Wn 20 O to P/Wn 7(in reverse)/lane/Wn 17/ Wn 18 E to N by Pole Cottage.
30. Wn 20 O to P/Wn 7(in reverse)/Wn 13/lane/Wn 15 or 16/Wn 17/Wn 18 E to Pole Cottage. 6.75 Km/4 miles.

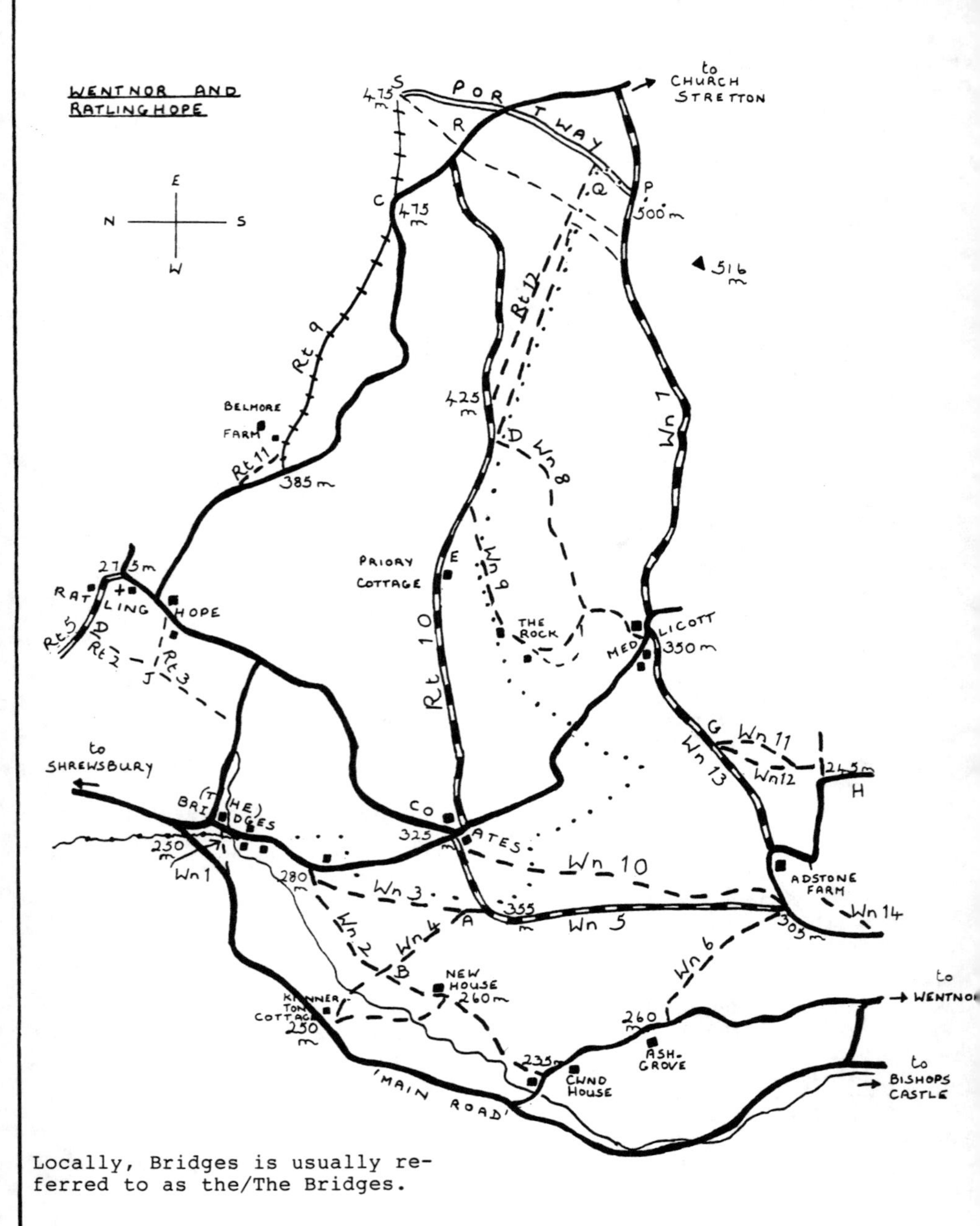

Locally, Bridges is usually referred to as the/The Bridges.

WENTNOR AND RATLINGHOPE CIRCUITS

Starting from the Bridges;-

1. Wn 3/Wn 5 A to Adstone/Wn 6/lane/Wn 2. 5.25 Km/3¼ miles.
2. Wn 3 to A/Wn 4(in reverse) A to B/Wn 2 B to Overs. 2.25 Km/nearly 1½ miles.
3. Rt 3(in reverse)/lane/Rt 11/Rt 9 to C/road / Rt 10(in reverse) / lane. 7.25 Km/4½ miles.
4. Rt 3(in reverse)/lane/Rt 11/Rt 9 to C/road / Wn 20(in reverse) R to P/Wn 7(in reverse)/lane. 7.5 Km/4½+ miles.
5. Rt 3(in reverse)/lane/Rt 11/Rt 9 to C/road / Wn 20(in reverse) R to P/Wn 7(in reverse)/Wn 13/Wn 5(in reverse) to A/Wn 3(in reverse). 9.25 Km/5.75 miles.
6. Rt 3(in reverse)/lane/Rt 11/ Rt 9 to C/road/Rt 10(in reverse) to E/Wn 9/lane. 7.5 Km/4½+ miles.
7. Lane to Coates/Rt 10 to E/Wn 9/Wn 13/Wn 5(in reverse) to A/ Wn 3 (in reverse)/lane. 7.5 Km/4½+ miles.
8. Lane to Coates/Rt 10 to D/Wn 8/Wn 13/Wn 6/lane/Wn 2/ lane. 8.25 Km/5 miles.
9. Lane to Coates/Rt 10 to E/Wn 9/Wn 13 to G/Wn 12/road to Adstone/ Wn 5(in reverse) to A/Wn 3(in reverse)/lane. 8.5 Km/5¼ miles.

N.B. An alternative route from Adstone Farm to Bridges is via Wn 10 (not yet clear) to Coates, returning to the Bridges along the lane.

Starting from the hilltop;-

10. Rt 10(in reverse) to E/Wn 9/Wn 8(in reverse)/Rt 12 / Wn 20 Q to R. 4.75 Km/3 miles.
11. Rt 10(in reverse)/Wn 5 OR 10/Wn 13(in reverse)/Wn 7/ Wn 20 P to R. 8.25 Km/5+ miles.
12. Rt 10(in reverse)/Wn 5 to A/Wn 4(in reverse) to B / Wn 2(in reverse) to Cwnd Cottage/lane/Wn 6(in reverse) / Wn 13(in reverse)/ Wn 8(in reverse)/Rt 10 D to hilltop road. 9.5 Km/6 miles.
13. Rt 10(in reverse)/lane to Medlicott/Wn 7/Wn 20 P to R. 6.5 Km/ 4 miles.

Starting from Ratlinghope Church:-

14. Lane/Rt 11/Rt 9 to C/road/Rt 10(in reverse)/lanes via Bridges/Rt 3(in reverse) to J/Rt 2(in reverse) to D/Rt 5(in reverse) D to church. 8 Km/5 miles.
15. Lane/Rt 11/Rt 9 to C/road/Wn 20(in reverse) R to P/ Wn 7(in reverse)/lanes via Bridges/Rt 3(in reverse) to J/ Rt 2(in reverse) to D/Rt 5(in reverse) D to church. 9 Km/5½ miles.
16. Lane/Rt 11/Rt 9 to C/road/Wn 20(in reverse) R to P/ Wn 7(in reverse)/Wn 13/Wn 5(in reverse) to A/ Wn 3(in reverse) / lanes via Bridges/Rt 3(in reverse) to J/Rt 2(in reverse) to D/ Rt 5(in reverse) D to church. 10.25 Km/6¼+ miles.
17. Lanes via Manor House and Coppice Farm to Coates/Wn 5 OR 10 / Wn 13(in reverse)/Wn 7/Wn 20 P to R/road / Rt 9 from C(in reverse)/ lane. 9.75 Km/6 miles.

Starting from Prolley Moor at point H:-

18. Lane to Adstone Farm/Wn 5 OR Wn 10(in reverse)/Rt 10 to E/ Wn 9/ Wn 13 to G/Wn 12. 6.25 Km/3.75 miles.
19. Lane to Adstone Farm/ Wn 5 OR Wn 10(in reverse)/Rt 10 / Wn 20(in reverse R to P/Wn 7(in reverse)/Wn 13 to G/Wn 12. 9.25 Km/5.75 miles.

Starting from main road at Kinnerton:-

20. Wn 4/Wn 5 A to Adstone Farm/Wn 6/lane/Wn 2 to B/Wn 4(in reverse) B to main road. 4.5 Km/2.75 miles.
21. Wn 4 to B/Wn 2 B to Overs/Wn 3/Wn 5 A to Adstone/Wn 6/lane/ Wn 2 to B/Wn 4(in reverse) B to main road. 5.25 Km/3¼ miles.

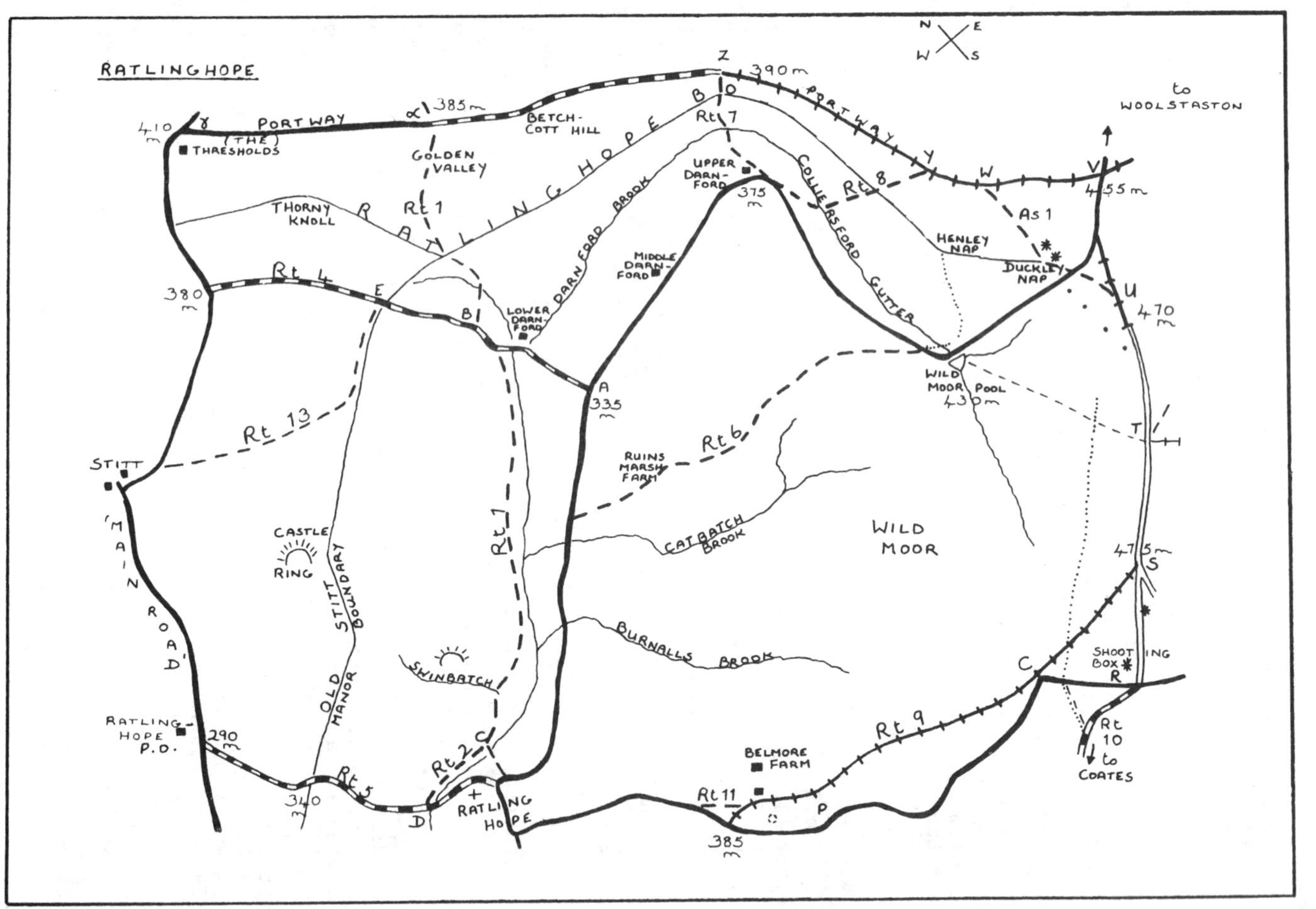
RATLINGHOPE
N E W S
to WOOLSTASTON
PORTWAY
(THE) THRESHOLDS
410 m
385 m
390 m
455 m
470 m
475 m
380 m
335 m
375 m
430 m
290 m
340
385 m
BETCH-COTT HILL
GOLDEN VALLEY
THORNY KNOLL
RATLINGHOPE
DARNFORD BROOK
UPPER DARN-FORD
MIDDLE DARN-FORD
LOWER DARN-FORD
COLLIERSFORD GUTTER
HENLEY NAP
DUCKLEY NAP
WILD MOOR POOL
WILD MOOR
RUINS MARSH FARM
CATBATCH BROOK
BURNALLS BROOK
SWINBATCH
CASTLE RING
OLD MANOR STITT BOUNDARY
STITT
'MAIN ROAD'
RATLING-HOPE P.O.
RATLING HOPE
BELMORE FARM
SHOOTING BOX
to COATES
Rt 1
Rt 2
Rt 4
Rt 5
Rt 6
Rt 7
Rt 8
Rt 9
Rt 10
Rt 11
Rt 13
As 1

RATLINGHOPE CIRCUITS

Starting from the Thresholds:-

1. Portway(in reverse) γ to α /Rt 1/Rt 2 C to D / Rt 5 D to Post Office/main road to Stitt/lane back to Thresholds. 8 Km/5 miles.
2. Portway(in reverse) γ to α /Rt 1 α to B/Rt 4 B to E/ Rt 13 / lane back to Thresholds. 4.5 Km/2.75 miles.
3. Portway(in reverse) γ to α /Rt 1 to Ratlinghope/lane/Rt 6/ lane/ Portway V to W OR As 1 to W/Portway W to γ . 11.5 Km/7+ miles.
4. Portway(in reverse) γ to α / Rt 1 to B / Rt 4(in reverse) B to A/ lane/Rt 7/Portway Z to Thresholds. 6.5 Km/4 miles.
5. Portway(in reverse) γ to α /Rt 1 to B / Rt 4(in reverse) B to A/ lane/Rt 8/Portway Y to Thresholds. 7.5 Km/4½ miles.
6. Portway(in reverse) γ to α /Rt 1/lanes/Rt 11/Rt 9/Portway S to Thresholds. 12½ Km/7.75 miles.

Starting from Ratlinghope Church:-

7. Lanes/Rt 9/Portway S to U/As 1 U to road/road to Wildmoor Pool/ Rt 6(in reverse)/lane back to church. 7.5 Km/4½+ miles.
8. Rt 5/main road to Stitt/Rt 13(in reverse)/Rt 4(in reverse) E to B/ Rt 1(in reverse) B to Portway at α / Portway(in reverse) α to V/road to Wildmoor Pool/Rt 6(in reverse)/lane. 11.5 Km/7+ miles.
9. Rt 5/main road to Stitt/Rt 13(in reverse)/Rt 4(in reverse) E to B/Rt 1 B to church. 5.5 Km /3½ miles.
10. Rt 5/main road to Stitt/Rt 13(in reverse)/Rt 4(in reverse) E to B/Rt 1(in reverse) B to α /Portway(in reverse) α to S/Rt 9(in reverse)/lane. 12 Km/7½ miles.
11. Lane/Rt 6/road/Portway V to W OR As 1 to W/Portway W to α/Rt 1. 9.5 Km/nearly 6 miles.
12. Lanes/Rt 9/Portway S to α /Rt 1. 10 Km/6¼ miles.

Starting from the hilltop (Duckley Nap):-

13. Portway V to α /Rt 1/lane/Rt 6/road. 9.25 Km/5.75 miles.
14. Portway V to α /Rt 1/lanes/Rt 9/Portway S to V. 9.75 Km/6 miles.

Starting from Belmore:-

14. Rt 9/Portway S to U/road/Rt 6(in reverse)/ lanes via Ratlinghope Church. 7.5 Km/4½+ miles.
15. Rt 9/Portway S to α /Rt 1/lanes. 9.75 Km/6 miles.

Starting from Upper Darnford:-

16. Rt 8/Portway Y to Z/Rt 7(in reverse). 1.75 Km/1 mile.

Starting from Wildmoor Pool:-

17. Road/Portway V to W OR As 1 to W / Portway W to Z / Rt 7(in reverse)/road back to pool. 4.25 Km/2½ miles.
18. Rt 6(in reverse)/lanes via Ratlinghope Church/Rt 9/Portway S to U/road down to pool. 7.25 Km/4½ miles.
19. Road/Portway V to W OR As 1 to W/Portway W to α /Rt 1 α to B/ Rt 4(in reverse) B to A/lane/Rt 6 to Wildmoor. 7.5 Km/4½+ miles.
20. Road/Portway V to W OR As 1 to W/Portway W to α /Rt 1 to Ratlinghope/lane/Rt 6 to Wildmoor. 9.25 Km/5.75 miles.

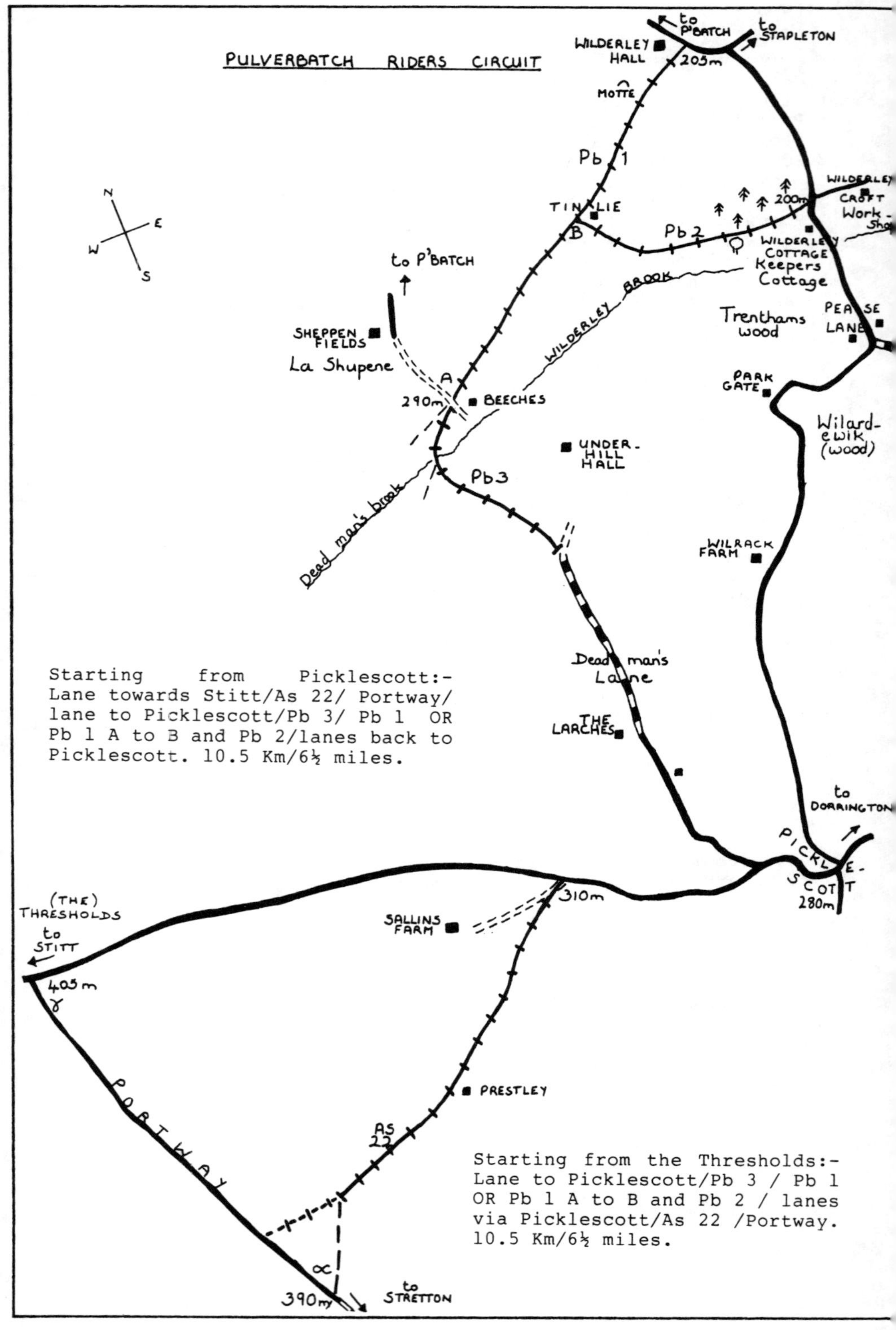
PULVERBATCH RIDERS CIRCUIT
to P'BATCH
to STAPLETON
WILDERLEY HALL
205m
MOTTE
Pb 1
TIN LIE
B
Pb 2
200m
WILDERLEY CROFT
Work-
WILDERLEY COTTAGE
Keepers Cottage
N
E
S
W
to P'BATCH
SHEPPEN FIELDS
La Shupene
A
290m
BEECHES
WILDERLEY BROOK
Trenthams wood
LANE
PARK GATE
Wilardewik (wood)
UNDER-HILL HALL
Pb3
Dead man's brook
WILRACK FARM
Dead man's Lane
THE LARCHES
Starting from Picklescott:- Lane towards Stitt/As 22/ Portway/ lane to Picklescott/Pb 3/ Pb 1 OR Pb 1 A to B and Pb 2/lanes back to Picklescott. 10.5 Km/6½ miles.
to DORRINGTON
PICKLESCOTT
280m
310m
SALLINS FARM
(THE) THRESHOLDS
to STITT
405m
PORTWAY
PRESTLEY
AS 22
Starting from the Thresholds:- Lane to Picklescott/Pb 3 / Pb 1 OR Pb 1 A to B and Pb 2 / lanes via Picklescott/As 22 /Portway. 10.5 Km/6½ miles.
390m
to STRETTON

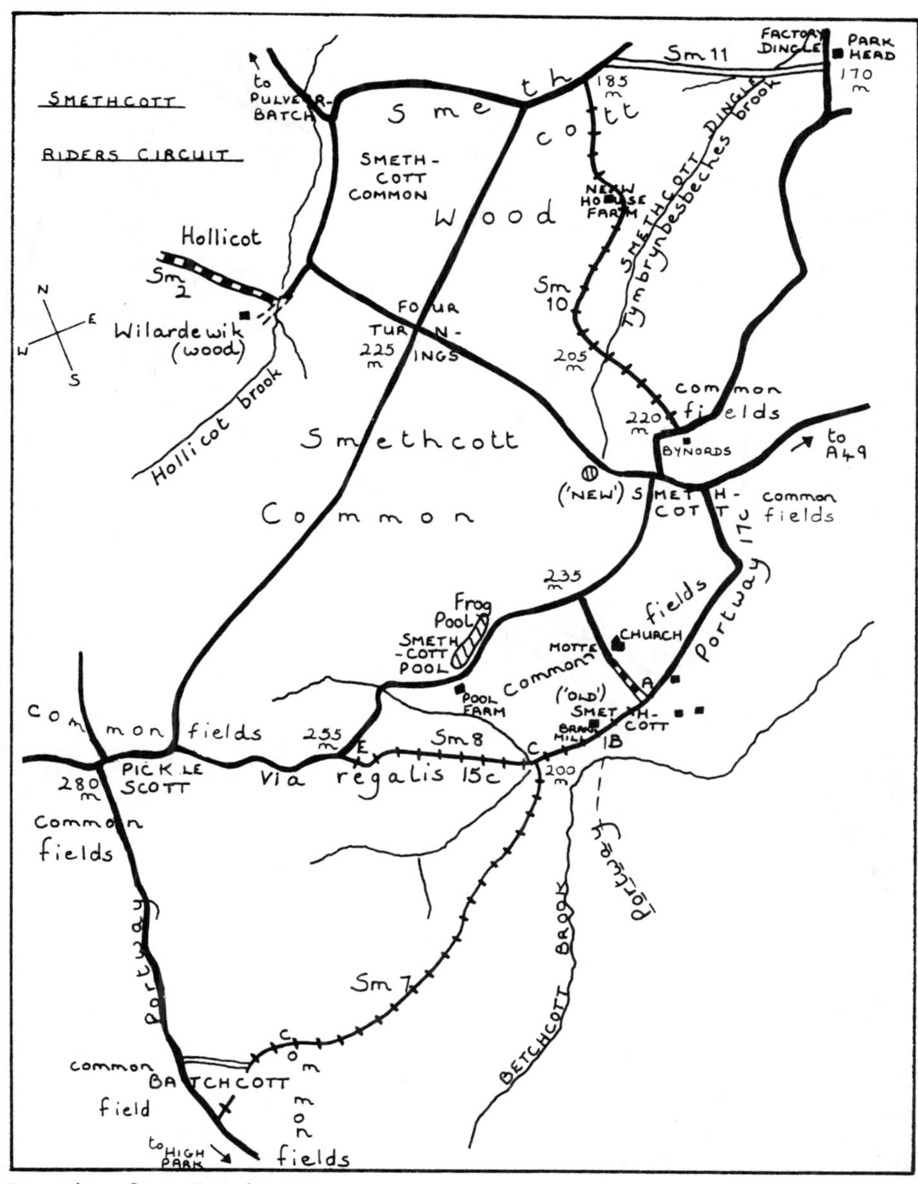

Starting from Batchcott:-

Sm 7 (in reverse) continuing to Smethcott along the mediaeval Portway/lane passing the Bynords (continuation of the mediaeval Portway) to Parkhead/Sm 11/Sm 10. From this point there are two alternatives:

1. lane to Picklescott via church turn and Smethcott Pool.
2. lane as far as church turn/lane passing church/Sm 7 A to C/Sm 8/lanes to Batchcott via Picklescott.

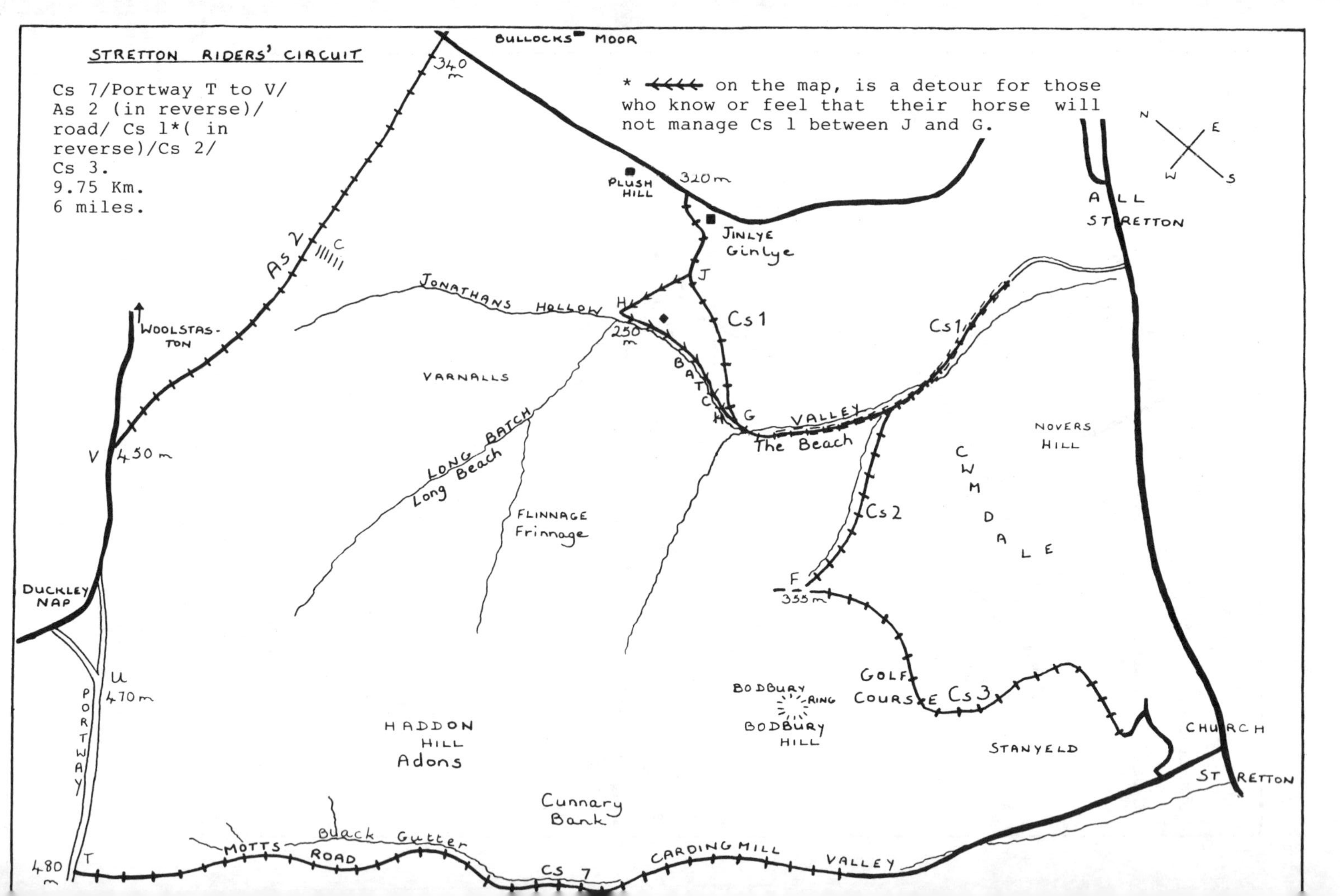
STRETTON RIDERS' CIRCUIT
Cs 7/Portway T to V/
As 2 (in reverse)/
road/ Cs 1*(in
reverse)/Cs 2/
Cs 3.
9.75 Km.
6 miles.
* on the map, is a detour for those who know or feel that their horse will not manage Cs 1 between J and G.
BULLOCKS MOOR
340 m
PLUSH HILL
320m
JINLYE
Ginlye
N
E
W
S
ALL STRETTON
As 2
C
J
H
Cs 1
JONATHANS HOLLOW
WOOLSTASTON
250 m
BATCH
G
VALLEY
The Beach
Cs1
VARNALLS
LONG BATCH
Long Beach
NOVERS HILL
CWMDALE
V
450 m
Cs 2
FLINNAGE
Frinnage
DUCKLEY NAP
F
355 m
U
470 m
PORTWAY
GOLF COURSE
Cs 3
BODBURY RING
BODBURY HILL
HADDON HILL
Adons
CHURCH STRETTON
STANYELD
Cunnary Bank
T
480 m
MOTTS ROAD
Black Gutter
CS 7
CARDING MILL VALLEY

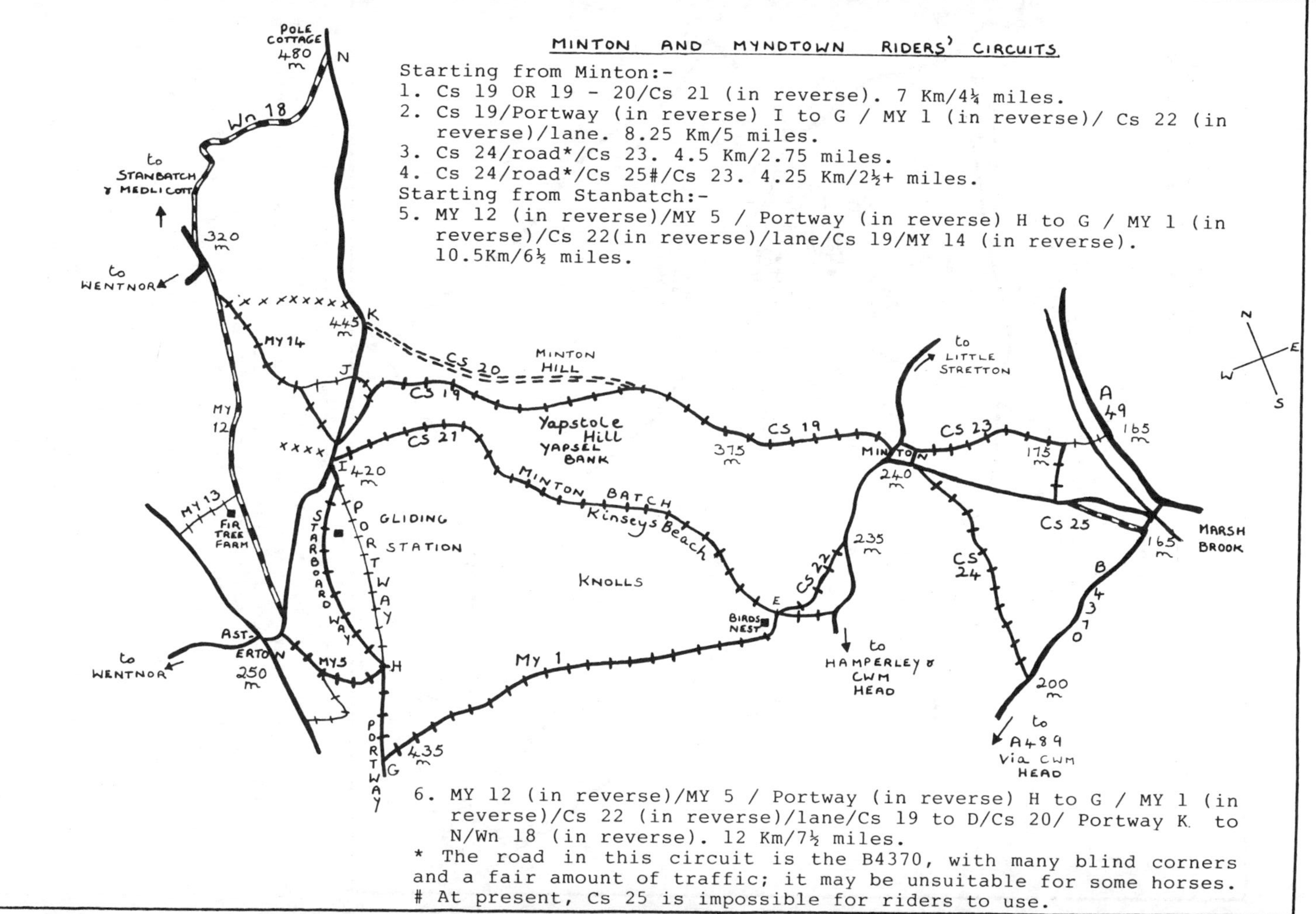

MINTON AND MYNDTOWN RIDERS' CIRCUITS

Starting from Minton:-

1. Cs 19 OR 19 - 20/Cs 21 (in reverse). 7 Km/4¼ miles.
2. Cs 19/Portway (in reverse) I to G / MY 1 (in reverse)/ Cs 22 (in reverse)/lane. 8.25 Km/5 miles.
3. Cs 24/road*/Cs 23. 4.5 Km/2.75 miles.
4. Cs 24/road*/Cs 25#/Cs 23. 4.25 Km/2½+ miles.

Starting from Stanbatch:-

5. MY 12 (in reverse)/MY 5 / Portway (in reverse) H to G / MY 1 (in reverse)/Cs 22(in reverse)/lane/Cs 19/MY 14 (in reverse). 10.5Km/6½ miles.
6. MY 12 (in reverse)/MY 5 / Portway (in reverse) H to G / MY 1 (in reverse)/Cs 22 (in reverse)/lane/Cs 19 to D/Cs 20/ Portway K to N/Wn 18 (in reverse). 12 Km/7½ miles.

* The road in this circuit is the B4370, with many blind corners and a fair amount of traffic; it may be unsuitable for some horses.

At present, Cs 25 is impossible for riders to use.

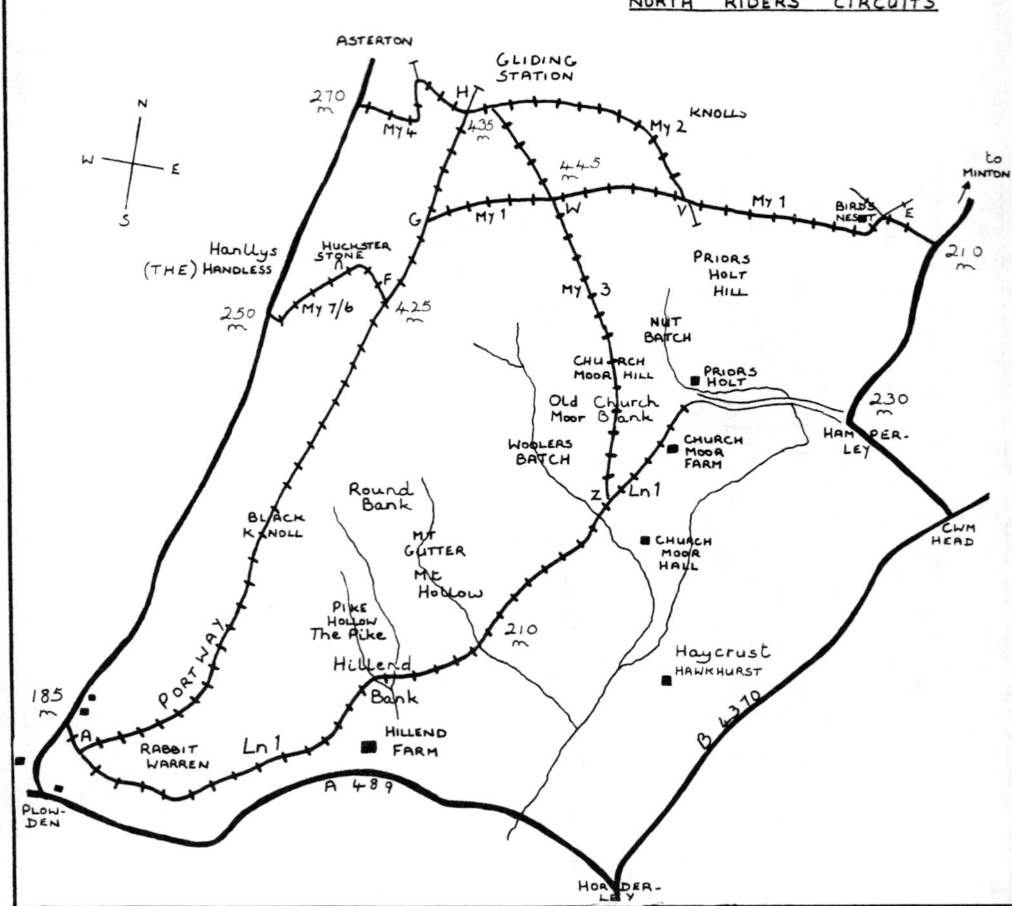

MYNDTOWN AND LYDBURY NORTH RIDERS' CIRCUITS

Most of the rights of way on this end of the Mynd are bridleways. Many of the circuits listed for walkers, therefore, on pages 47 and 48 are suitable for riders.

The additional circuits given on this page, involve a bridleway running around the end of the Mynd from the Portway to Priors Holt; at present it is not possible to use it between Priors Holt and Z.

1. Cs 21 to Birds Nest / MY 1 to the Portway at G / Portway (in reverse) G to A/Ln 1 (in reverse)/lane. 11.25 Km/7 miles.
2. Cs 21 to Birds Nest / MY 1 to the Portway at G / Portway (in reverse) G to F/MY 7 (in reverse)/lane/Ln 1 (in reverse)/lane. 11.25 Km/7 miles.
3. Ln 1/ Portway A to H/MY 2 (in reverse). 10 Km/6¼ miles.
4. Portway A to H/MY 3 (in reverse)/Ln 1. 9.25 Km/5.75 miles.

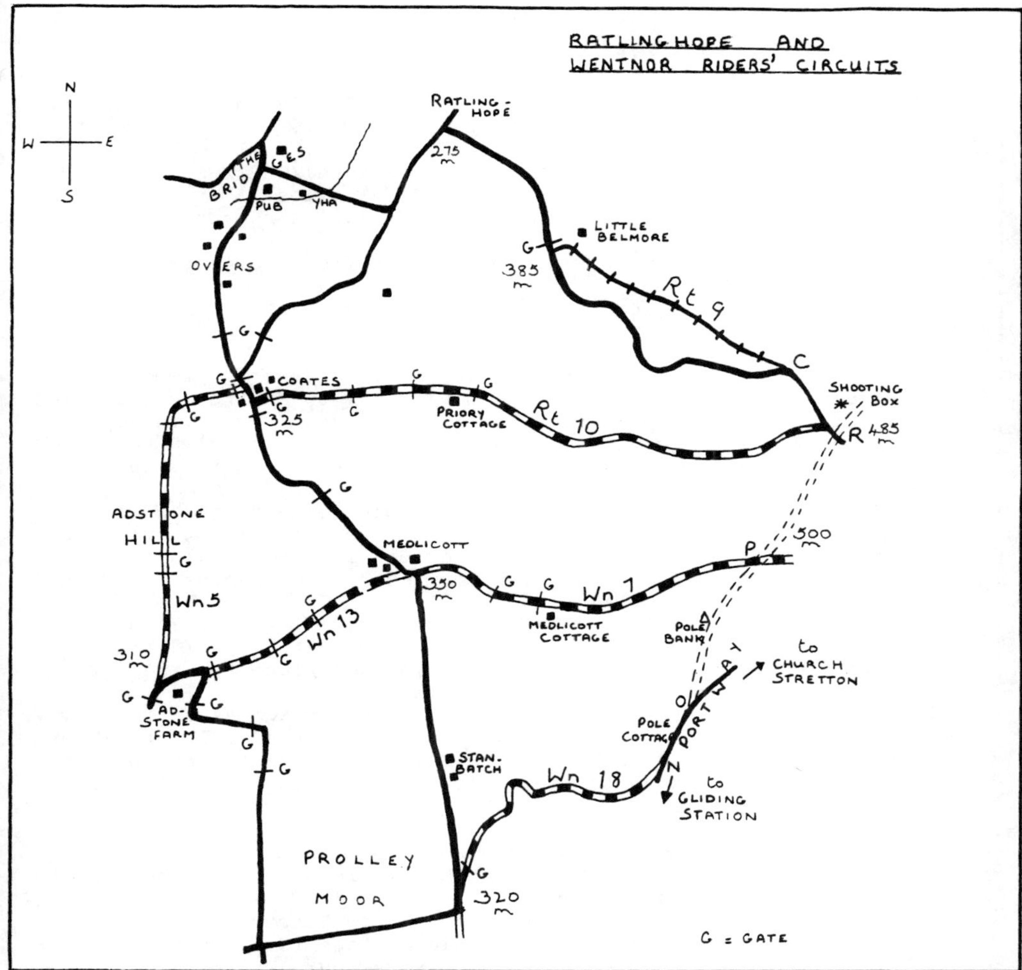

RATLINGHOPE AND WENTNOR RIDERS' CIRCUITS

The Ratlinghope and Wentnor riders' circuits include only one bridleway, but several unsurfaced highways and quiet, often gated surfaced roads. The only section of road likely to have much traffic is between Belmore and the Bridges.

Starting from the Bridges:

1. Gated road via Coates, Medlicott and Stanbatch/ Wn 18 / surfaced Portway N to O, passing Pole Cottage/Wn 20 O to R /road/Rt 9 (in reverse) from C/road to Bridges. 11 Km/nearly 7 miles.
2. As above to point R along Wn 20 / Rt 10 (in reverse) to Coates/ road to Bridges. 11.5 Km/7+ miles.
3. Gated road to Medlicott/Wn 7/Wn 20 P to R/road/Rt 9 (in reverse) from C/road. 9 Km/5½ miles.
4. As circuit 3 to point R along Wn 20/Rt 10 (in reverse)/road. 9.5 Km/5.75 miles.
5. Gated road to Coates/Rt 10/road/Rt 9 (in reverse) from C/road. 7.5 Km/4½ miles.

continued on next page

6. Gated road to Coates/Wn 5/roads through Prolley Moor/Wn 18/surfaced Portway N to O/Wn 20 O to R/road/Rt 9 (in reverse) from C/road. 13Km/8 miles

*7. Gated road to Coates/Wn 5/Wn 13 (in reverse)/Wn 7/Wn 20 P to R / road/ Rt 9 (in reverse)/road. 10.5 Km/6½ miles.

*8. As circuit 7 to point R along Wn 20/Rt 10 (in reverse)/ road. 11 Km/nearly 7 miles.

9. Circuits 1, 2, 7 and 8 could be started from Prolley Moor.

* Wn 13 is difficult for riders to use at present.

SOME LONGER ROUTES

1. Hamperley to Priors Holt/MY 2 to V/MY 1 V to G/Portway G to P/Wn 7 (in reverse) to Medlicott/Wn 13 to Adstone / Wn 5 (in reverse) to Coates/Rt 10 to Shooting Box/Portway (in reverse) R to H/MY 3 (in reverse) to Priors Holt via MY 3a or Ln 1 (in reverse) from Z. 21.25 Km/13¼ miles.
2. MY 1 from Minton Batch/Portway G to Pole Cottage (N)/ Wn 18 (in reverse) to Stanbatch/lane towards Wentnor as far as Four Turnings/lane to Adstone/Wn 5 (in reverse) to Coates/Rt 10 to Shooting Box/Portway (in reverse) R to I/Cs 21 (in reverse) to Minton Batch. 19.5 Km/12 miles.
3. Cs 7 from Cardingmill Valley/Portway T to α /Rt 1, 2 and 3 to Bridges/lane to Upper Overs/Wn 3/Wn 5 to Adstone/Wn 13 (in reverse) to Medlicott/Wn 7 to the Boiling Well/lane towards Stretton/Cs 12 to Stretton. 19.5 Km/12 miles.
4. Cs 1 from All Stretton/As 3 to High Park Cottage/As 2/ Portway V to α /Rt 1, 2 and 3 to Bridges/lane to Coates/Rt 10 to Shooting Box/Portway R to T/As 4 (in reverse) to E/ As 6 to Batch Valley returning along the valley via Cs 1 to All Stretton. 16.75 Km/10½ miles.

SOME ROUTES INVOLVING PUBLIC TRANSPORT

1. Bus from Shrewsbury to Pulverbatch/main road to Cothercott Cottage/Pb 7/Pb 4 B to C/Portway (in reverse) Thresholds (γ) to EITHER T then Cs 7 (in reverse) to Church Stretton/train or bus to Shrewsbury = 6¼ miles OR to Pole Cottage (N) then Cs 17 (in reverse) to Little Stretton/bus to Shrewsbury = 8 miles.
2. Bus from Craven Arms to Plowden (limited days)/lane towards Asterton/Portway A to Pole Cottage (N) continuing along the road to the Boiling Well, just before a road junction/Cs 15 (in reverse) to Little Stretton/bus to Craven Arms. Nearly 7 miles.
3. Bus from Bishops Castle to Bridges (limited days)/Rt 3 (in reverse) to the Manor House/lanes towards Church Stretton/Rt 9 at Belmore to the Shooting Box/Portway (in reverse) R to P/Wn 7 (in reverse) to Medlicott/lane to Stanbatch/Wn 16 (in reverse)/Wn 21 (in reverse)/lane to Wentnor/bus to Bishops Castle. 5 miles.
4. Bus from Shrewsbury to Leebotwood/WL 7 to Malt House / lane to Lower Wood Farm/As 13 (in reverse) to Gogbatch/As 10 (in reverse) to D/As 9 (in reverse) to Plush Hill/As 4 to the Portway/ Portway (in reverse) T to K/Cs 20 (in reverse) linking with Cs 19 (in reverse) at D to Minton/Cs 23 (in reverse)/lane to Marshbrook/bus to Shrewsbury. 8¼ miles.
5. Bus, Shrewsbury to Pulverbatch/lanes to Sheppen Fields/Pb 3 (in reverse) to Picklescott/lane to Thresholds/Portway (in reverse) to V/As 2 (in reverse) to High Park Cottage/As 3 (in reverse)/Cs 1 (in reverse) to All Stretton/bus to Shrewsbury. 7 miles.

THE VILLAGES

The villages have been arranged in alphabetical order. All the villages in this section lend their names to the civil parishes, which appear on the Pathfinder O/S maps. They are as follows: All Stretton (As), Church Stretton (Cs), Lydbury North (Ln), Myndtown (MY), Pulverbatch (Pb), Ratlinghope (Rt), Smethcott (Sm), Wentnor (Wn), Wistanstow (Ws) and Woolstaston (Wl).

Choose a circuit from the previous section and then work your way through the individual rights of way of your chosen circuit, in this section.

Each route map has a symbol to indicate the status of the route. These are as follows:

B.W. bridleway, also for bicyclists. **F.P.** public footpath.

F.P. footpath with no official status, often associated with common land.

B. byway open to all traffic.* **U.C.R.** unsurfaced highway.*

G.L. green lane. **RUPP** road used as a public path

MAP SYMBOLS

- surfaced and public highway/road. RUPP.
- (═ O/S) unsurfaced and public highway/byway *.
- green lane used by the public, with no official status.
- hedge or old field boundary. xxx fence.
- track. .... old embankments, walls or track.
- parish boundaries. tumuli.
- & (— —O/S) bridleway, also for bicyclists. gate.
- (--- O/S) footpath. stile.
- coniferous trees. deciduous trees.

* 'Unsurfaced highway', as a term used in this book, equates with 'unsurfaced county road'. Such roads are open to all traffic although often unsuitable for cars. On O/S maps they appear as white roads as do green lanes and private roads. The only way to be certain that a white road is public is to look at the relevant map in the Highways Department at the Shire Hall in Shrewsbury. Some of these unsurfaced county roads are also becoming registered as 'byways open to all traffic' (this is done through a legal process, although the use of the way is not being altered). Byways are recorded on the definitive maps along with bridleways, RUPPs and footpaths and will therefore ultimately appear on O/S maps with their own symbol.

A note on detours:- in some instances, usually because of an obstruction, a detour has been suggested. Most of the detours included in this book are in use, but that does not make them rights of way. Deviations from rights of way, to overcome an obstruction, are permissible but care has to be taken that it does not involve going onto another person's land. Some of the detours may ultimately replace parts of rights of way but this has to go through an official process.

ALL STRETTON

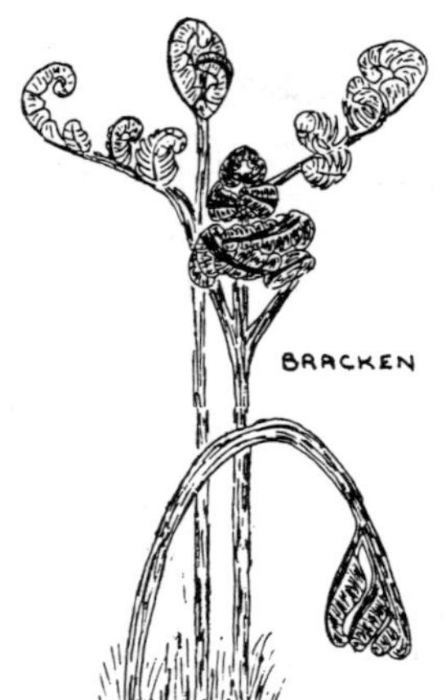

All Stretton is a village centred around the B4370. It is not an ecclesiastical parish but lies in the parish of Church Stretton. It does however lend its name to a civil parish, which is what is shown on present-day maps. All Stretton civil parish does not include the village itself; it extends over the Long Mynd behind, with a tongue of land reaching along the top of the hill as far north as Paulith Bank, just outside the area of this book. The hill area also lies in Church Stretton ecclesiastical parish and its past history, like All Stretton's, is therefore tied up with Church Stretton's.

In the Domesday Book, the manor of Stretton is thought to have included All Stretton; its first recorded names were, in 1261-2, Auredestratton and Aluredestretton. The first part of the name is thought to have derived from a personal name of a holder of land at some time, possibly Alured or Aelfroed. Many people in All Stretton have common rights on the hill because All Stretton was once in Stretton manor.

The All Stretton part of the hill includes Batch Valley, Gogbatch and High Park, and is an area largely covered by bracken and short grass rather than by heather and bilberry. The combination of short grass with gradual slopes and shorter, less dramatic batches lends itself to walkers and riders. There are numerous paths criss-crossing each other, and parts of rights of way shown on the O/S map have disappeared in preference for new routes. There is obviously a great deal of horse riding done in the area, and this has made a large contribution to the path network. This All Stretton network has been the most difficult to sort out and describe, and you may find it easier and sufficient to use the circuit maps alone, without referring to the individual path descriptions.

Amenities:-

Shop - All Stretton Stores.

Refreshments - Yew Tree Inn and Stretton Hall Hotel.

Accommodation - several places, including Paddock Lodge Guest House and Stretton Hall Hotel in the village, with Jinlye Guest House on the hill. At Lower Wood, signposted off the A49 north of All Stretton, there is Bed and Breakfast at Malt House and Willowfields.

Riding - Mynderley Stables at High Park.

Bus service - Midland Red West travels between Shrewsbury and Ludlow via All Stretton, see under Church Stretton. On schooldays, Boultons run an early morning bus northwards to Shrewsbury and an afternoon bus southwards to Bishops Castle via All Stretton.

Name meaning **Duckley Nap**

The name of Duckley Nap may have arisen in the same way as that of the Starboard Way, to match hen and port respectively in their modern sense. Nap, meaning hillock, may refer to the tumuli.

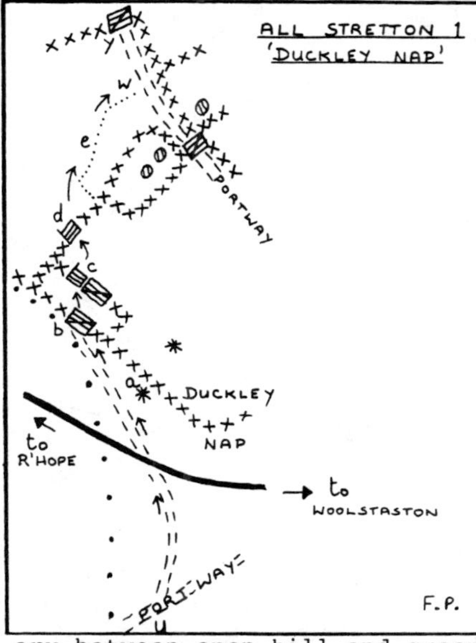

As 1 is an alternative route to the Portway between points U and W. It is not a public right of way but is signposted as a way to the Thresholds. The ancient hilltop route may have continued along the line of this path passing the two tumuli, known as Robin Hoods Butts, which may have acted as route-markers. This route certainly existed much more recently and into this century. The O/S map of 1883 shows As 1 as I have described it but between U and the Butts there was also a track to the left, which equated with the Ratlinghope boundary.

Two large flints were found very close to this route, and a flint knife was found on the actual surface of the Portway just south of U, where As 1 begins. Yet another find was a polished stone axe, discovered in the area to the right of the track near the boundary between open hill and green fields.

The route bears off to the left from the Portway at U, crosses the Woolstaston to Ratlinghope road and continues as a track, passing a large, mostly heather-clad tumulus on the right (a) to reach a gate (b) into green fields. At this point, the fence running to the left has become the Ratlinghope boundary, and some way along it, a boundary tump on Henley Nap is visible against the skyline. **Cross a small enclosure to a stile (c) and turn left over another stile (d). Turn right to travel the same way as the fence but bearing obliquely to the left away from it. It is not easy to find the correct line to take; the embankment (e), which is probably an old enclosure boundary, is a useful line to follow and is approximately the way this old footpath runs to join the Portway at W. W is about halfway between two gates along the course of the Portway.**

Name meaning **Henley Nap**

Nap comes from an old English word for hillock and may in this case refer to the boundary tump here. Henley Nap appears on maps long before Duckley Nap does; it is on a 1698 map of Ratlinghope. 'Hen' may arise from the old English word 'hemme' for 'a border' or from the Welsh word 'hen' meaning 'old'. 'Ley' may indicate a clearing in the moorland at some time in the past. Henley, therefore, could mean an old or a boundary field and there are signs to support either meaning; a striking embankment extends from the tump down the slope in the direction of Wildmoor Pool, and is thought to have been an old field boundary.

Robin Hoods Butts

'Butt' can be a name for a conspicuous hillock (a tumulus in this case). The name 'butts', alternatively, may mean that the tumuli were used as or behind targets for shooting practice.

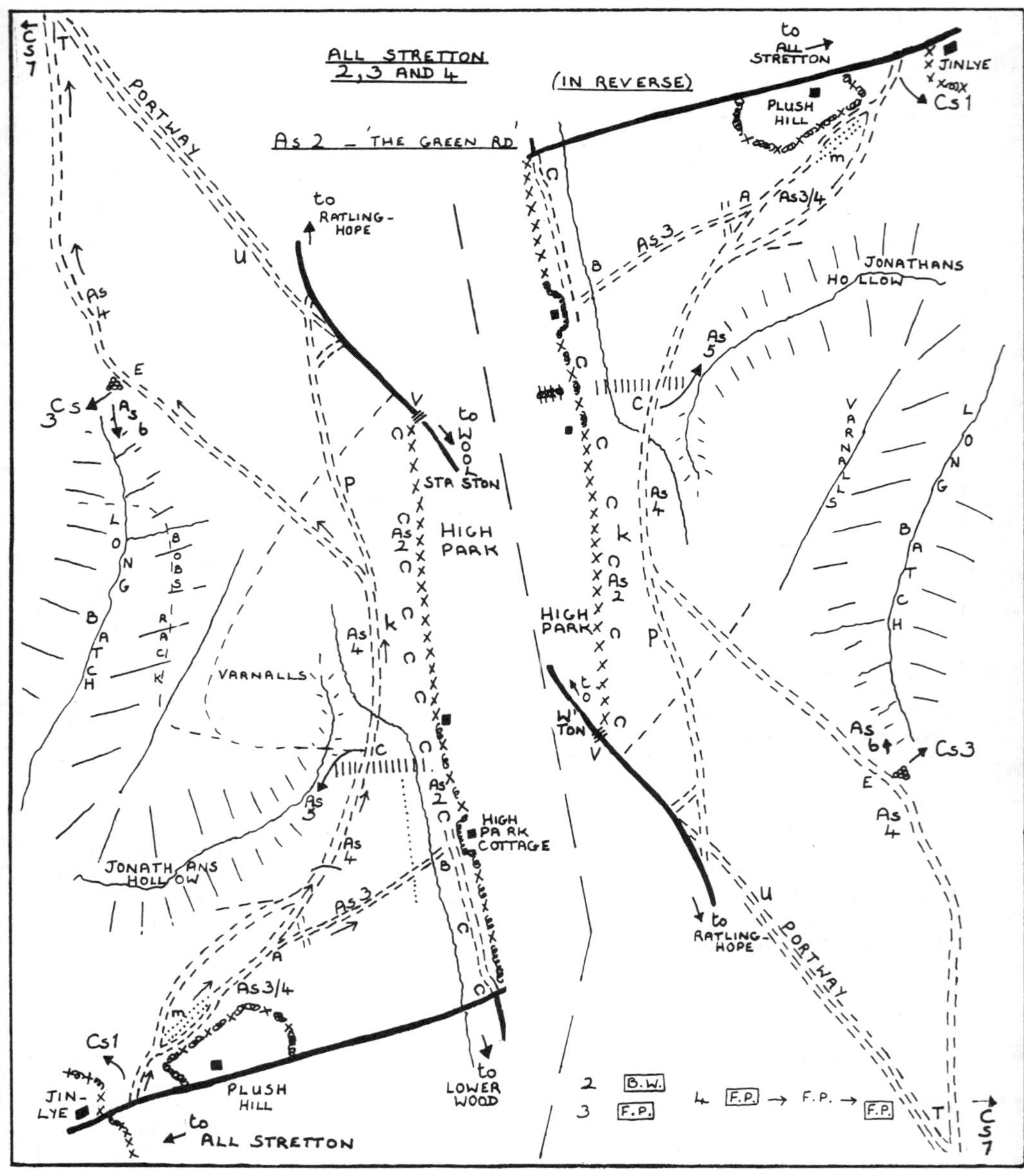

ALL STRETTON 2, PLUSH HILL TO THE PORTWAY AT V 1.5 Km/nearly lm.

As 2 is a bridleway following the old hill boundary. The lower part serves as a driveway to High Park Cottage but a multitude of tracks, made by vehicles that should not be using it, mark the way. This was an important route for Ratlinghope (Darnford) people to get to Stretton with pony and trap.

The track starts at the point where the lane from Lower Wood joins the All Stretton to High Park road, and follows the old hill boundary hedge/fence gradually ascending to the Ratlinghope to Woolstaston road. The route passes a cottage at B and a cross dyke

at C. Laburnum trees in the hedges are a special feature of this walk.

ALL STRETTON 2 (IN REVERSE), PORTWAY AT V TO PLUSH HILL

Turn off the Ratlinghope to Woolstaston road at the cattle grid, which marks the eastern boundary of the open hill. Follow the fence/hedge all the way, descending gradually to the All Stretton to High Park road and passing a cross dyke at C and a cottage at B. As 3 to Jinlye branches off at B.

ALL STRETTON 3 JINLYE TO HIGH PARK COTTAGE 1 Km/½ m+.

As 3 is a public footpath and is an obvious short cut for anyone living in High Park Cottage to get to and from All Stretton. **Take the track that starts clearly between Jinlye and Plush Hill. Keep to the right-hand track and start to ascend. The old enclosures around Plush Hill are passed on the right, but it is when you are above and in line with its north (furthest) hedge at point A, that As 3 veers away from the fields to the left (also away to the right from As 4) as a wide grassy footpath up to High Park Cottage.**

ALL STRETTON 3 (IN REVERSE), HIGH PARK COTTAGE TO JINLYE

Take the grassy track opposite High Park Cottage and follow it until it joins As 4 at A and becomes track, descending behind the enclosures of Plush Hill to reach the road by Jinlye.

ALL STRETTON 4, JINLYE TO PORTWAY AT T 2.5 Km/1½m.

As 4 possibly originated as an outrack sweeping around all the bogs and hollows, and it is still in use today for seeing to the sheep. It passes so close to As 2 at (k), that it comes as no surprise that Ratlinghope people also used this way, turning off from As 2 to go down this track towards All Stretton.

Take the track by Jinlye and ascend the hill via either of the two tracks that are apparent at the present time. Evidence of an old track can be seen at (m). The two tracks join and ascend as a wide grassy area up and over a small brow. The way is now clear up a gradual hill slope and cuts through a cross dyke at C; this old dyke may have been for defensive or enclosure purposes. **Soon after point C is the start of Jonathans Hollow which you can follow down into Batch Valley (As 5). Continue up the hill avoiding other vague tracks. Where the track veers to the left, a well-used track (p) continues straight on to the Portway near point U. As 4 continues as clear track passing the head of the Long Batch Valley. At point E, a heap of stones marks the start of Cs 3 to the golf course.**

From point E continue along the track, passing to the right of Haddon Hill (The Haddons), and join the Portway at T together with Motts road coming up from the left from Cardingmill Valley.

ALL STRETTON 4 (IN REVERSE), PORTWAY AT T TO JINLYE

If approaching from Motts road (Cs 7), turn on to As 4 at the top without quite getting on to the Portway. If approaching along the Portway from the south, keep to the right-hand track at T. At point T, clear track takes you through heather, passing to the left of Haddon Hill.

At E, a heap of stones can be seen to the right; this marks the start of Cs 3 to the golf course. To get on to As 6 at E, turn off along Cs 3 and after a very short distance, before some small pools, turn to the left and follow the outlet from these pools.

ALL STRETTON 4 (IN REVERSE) continued

From E, As 4 continues to descend, curving round the head of Long Batch and on down through the dyke at C.
At C, As 5 branches off to the right.
From C, the way curves down, keeping above the old enclosures of Plush Hill and joining the road to the right of them near Jinlye.

ALL STRETTON 5, BATCH VALLEY TO THE TOP OF JONATHANS HOLLOW

1.25 Km/.75m.

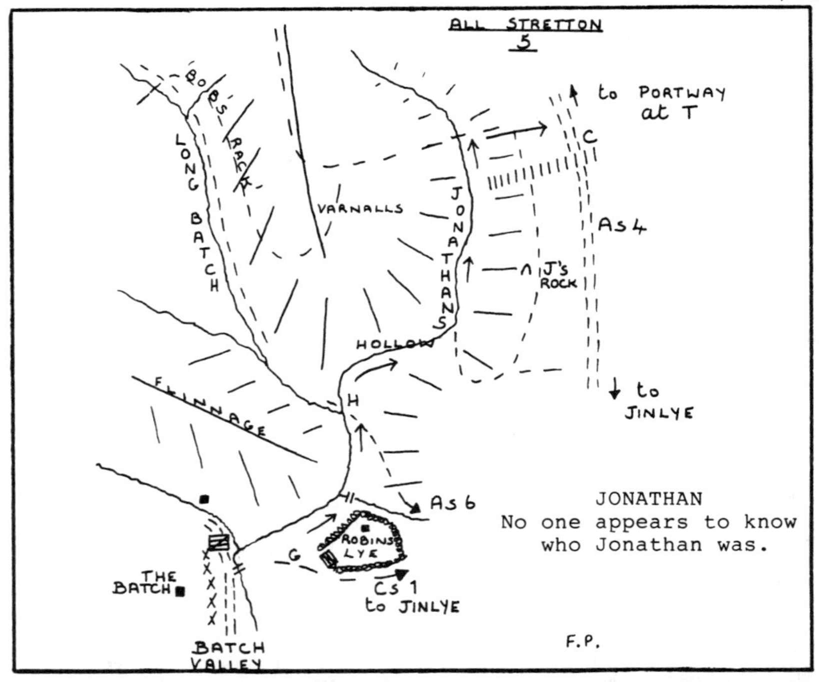

As 5 is a continuation of the track through Batch Valley, and appears to be the main route up the valley. However, the public right of way leaves the valley at G to ascend to Jinlye; I have therefore labelled that as one route (Cs 1) and described As 5 as a branch route off it.

Follow the track up Batch Valley (Cs 1) passing the Batch Cottage. A short distance past the cottage, the path turns to the right and crosses the brook. Continue along the right-hand side of the brook. At G, just before an enclosure, Cs 1 turns off to the right up the hill; As 5 runs alongside the enclosure and bungalow, and remains in the valley. Behind, an old yew dominates the hillside. Cross a small tributary and continue along the right-hand side of the main brook.
At H, the brook divides into several tributaries and the right-hand one is from Jonathans Hollow. As 5 continues along the right-hand side of this tributary and ascends the hollow. On the hillside to the right is Jonathans Rock. The brook dwindles to become a rushy hollow, and by turning right here along vague paths, a point is reached on As 4 near the cross dyke at C.

ALL STRETTON 6, LONG BATCH TO JINLYE 1.75 Km/1m.

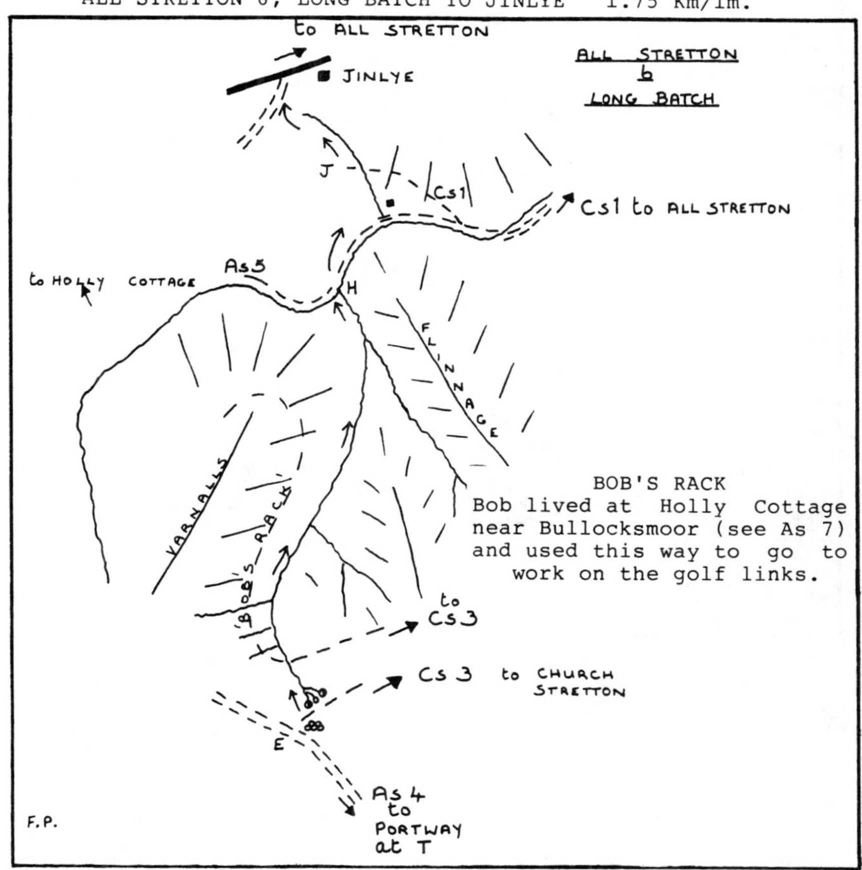

This path starts at the head of Long Batch near point E on As 4. Take the path, branching off from As 4 by a heap of stones, towards some small pools. Just before these pools, turn down to the left and follow the outflow from them all the way down the Long Batch. The brook marks the boundary between the civil parishes of All and Church Stretton and between two districts (South Shropshire and Shrewsbury & Atcham).

Just before H, the brook is joined by another from the right. At H the brook is joined by a tributary from Jonathans Hollow. In this area the valley opens out a little, allowing the sun to warm the shortly-cropped grassy slopes, thereby attracting such butterflies as the Small Heath and the Small Copper; sheep's sorrel, a small plant in the grass, and the grasses themselves, are food plants for the caterpillars of these two species.

Cross the tributary from Jonathans Hollow and take the small path which climbs obliquely across the facing slope. Near the top, the path reaches a small but dramatic little stream. Follow this up to its source and join a track (As 3/4) near the road at Jinlye.

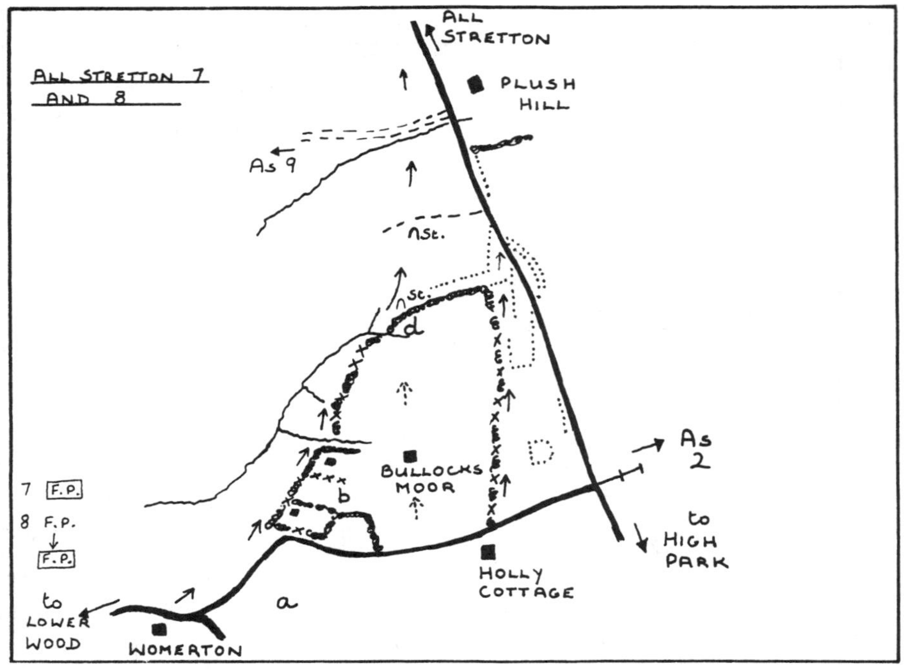

ALL STRETTON 7, HOLLY COTTAGE TO PLUSH HILL 0.25 Km.

As 7 is a short length of public footpath that cuts off a corner of roadway. It runs across open hill, close to the old enclosures of Bullocksmoor, and passes several old embankments that may represent past enclosures. The path was probably created by past inhabitants of Holly Cottage.

ALL STRETTON 8, WOMERTON TO PLUSH HILL 1 Km/½+ m.

As 8 is another example of a public right of way that has altered course. On the O/S map, it runs through Bullocksmoor and on over the open hill to Plush Hill. The first part through Bullocksmoor cannot be done and a different first part has evolved, skirting the enclosed land; this route could not have developed if all the land had been private.

As 8 starts above Womerton Farm. Womerton was a manor in the Domesday Book but later became incorporated into Stretton manor and now consists of only one farm. It had a chapel (possibly St. Peter's) and Chapel Ground (a) is opposite the start of As 8. **Leave the road and follow the hedge that separates the old enclosures of Bullocksmoor** (the name of Bullocksmoor was recorded as long as 400 years ago) **from the open hill. The path soon passes a ruin, a new plantation (b) and a house, before winding on and around some small tributaries that run into the valley below on the left. The path eventually leaves the Bullocksmoor fields at (d), turning left across the open hill and soon passing a large stone,** possibly an old route-marker for past inhabitants of Bullocksmoor; (d) is the point at which the old path left the open hill. **The path passes another large stone, continues across the almost flat area in front of Plush Hill (the house) and ends rather vaguely.**

ALL STRETTON 12, GOGBATCH TO DUDGELEY FARM 1 Km/½+ m.

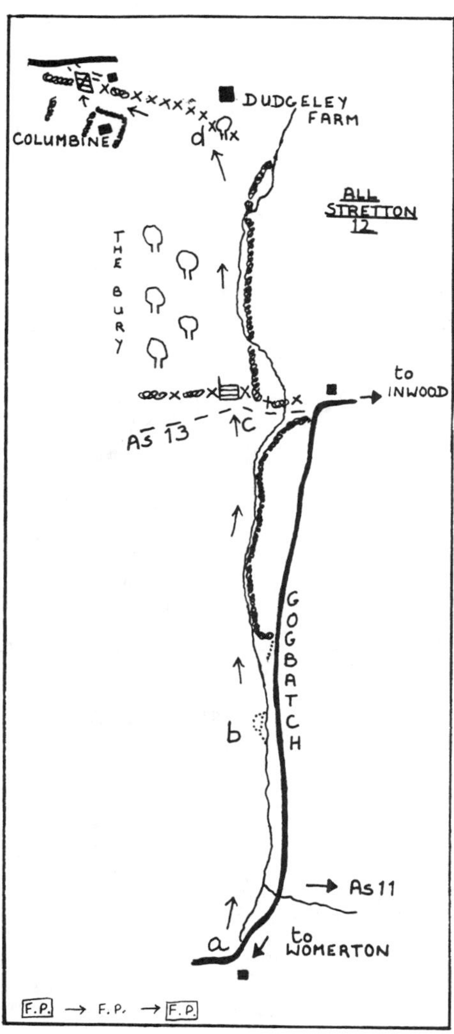

As 12 is made up of parts of two separate public rights of way, joined by a section of simple footpath between (b) and C. A start can be made at any point in the valley although strictly it should start at (a); it must have been created by past inhabitants of the house here. The right of way that forms the first part of this route, from (a) to (b), actually ascends from (b) across the slope away from the valley to reach As 13 at J; there is however no sign of it, although many vertical paths have developed on this slope. **From (a), follow the brook downstream, crossing As 13 at C. The way leaves the open hill via a stile and continues downstream along the side of a slope bearing trees and scrub. The path continues to follow the contour of the hill and gradually leaves the stream. Pass above Dudgeley Farm, bearing to the left to walk along a fence/hedge (d).** The hill on this side is steep and rocky in places, providing a good habitat for certain small plants. **The hedge leads into a corner of the field by a house called Columbine. Exit onto the lane via a gate.** Nearly opposite the end of As 12 is a public footpath, not described in this book, run-ing down to the A49 and crossing the railway. It passes through a field known as Quaking Bridge. This was a place where people congregated to get across the brook to go on to Stretton market. Logs were thrown down to make a bridge across brook and bog.

Focus on plants **Carex dioica and Moenchia erecta**

These two small plants growing in the Mynd area are regarded as uncommon, but they may be more common than is thought. Both are easily overlooked. Moenchia erecta is a species found in dry grassland on steep, sunny slopes where there is little vegetation e.g. the motte at Pulverbatch, the old track and field embankments on Adstone Hill, and some of the batch slopes. Carex dioica is a species of the hill bogs and has separate male and female plants unlike the similar Flea sedge which has male and female 'flowers' on the same spike.

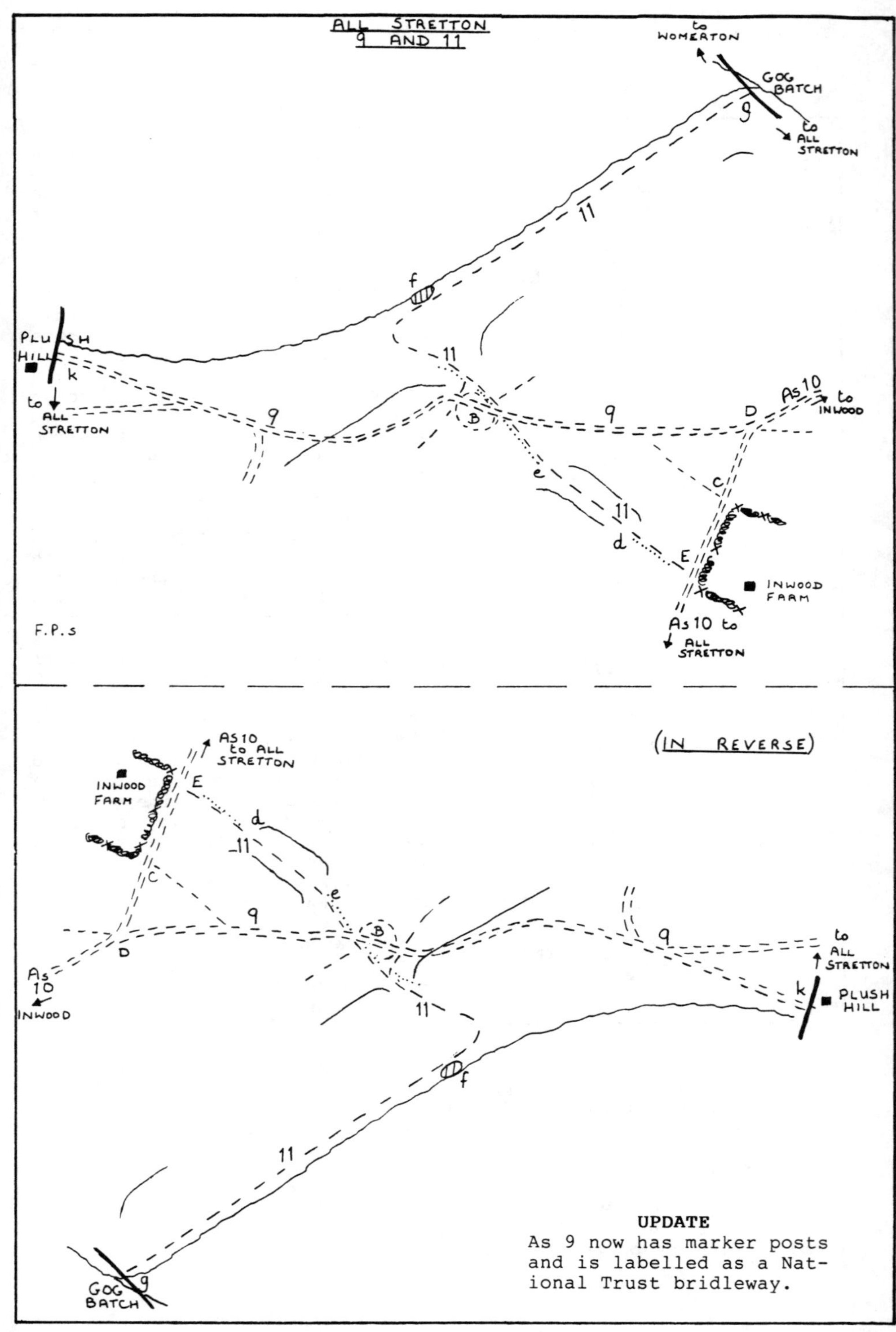

UPDATE

As 9 now has marker posts and is labelled as a National Trust bridleway.

ALL STRETTON 9, 10 and 11

Many paths have arisen on this area of open hill to the south of Gogbatch, and old ones have been modified, a major contributory factor being horse riding. From the maze of tracks, three have been chosen and described in this book. Only one of them (As 10) is a public right of way and even this has been modified (from point D approximately); its original northern end has been lost.

ALL STRETTON 9, PLUSH HILL TO As 10 AT POINT D 0.5 Km/¼ m.

Take a grassy track from almost opposite Plush Hill (the house) at (k), and follow its gradual descent. There is then a short, steeper descent to a circular, grassy hollow at point B, where As 11 and other tracks cross it. Continue straight on along the most clearly-defined track, and descend to point D. At point D, As 9 is joined by another track (As 10) from the right and, as one track, the two routes descend obliquely to the left down to the lane near Inwood House. Another trail continues straight on at D; this rejoins As 9/10 further down the hillside.

ALL STRETTON 9 (IN REVERSE), D ON As 10 TO PLUSH HILL

Leave As 10 at point D, where As 9 branches off as a clear track, on the hillside above and between Inwood House and Inwood Farm, the only two sizeable habitations below. Follow the track up the slope and cross a grassy circular area at B. The track then ascends a short, steep bank before continuing more gradually up to Plush hill (the house) at (k).

ALL STRETTON 11, E ON As 10 TO GOGBATCH 0.75 Km/½ m.

As 11 starts at point E, branching off opposite a right angle in a hedge (N.B. there are two) and above Inwood Farm. The path follows a faint embankment which runs on the left, and then ascends like a wide avenue between two hillocks, from (d) to (e). From (e), the path again follows an embankment on the left until it reaches a natural circular hollow at point B. Keep to the right of this circle and continue straight on, passing between two hills. Descend a short, steep slope. The path then turns to the right, runs past a small pool (f) and follows a small stream down to (g), to join the road running through Gogbatch.

ALL STRETTON 11 (IN REVERSE), GOGBATCH TO As 10 AT POINT E.

As 11 starts from the road at (g) in Gogbatch, just below its steep ascent to Womerton. Follow a small path that runs up the valley near a small stream. Just after a small pool (f), the path curves and ascends out of the valley, passing between two hills before reaching a grassy circular area at point B. Continue straight on, passing to the left of the circle and then following a faint embankment that runs on the right-hand side. At (e), the way becomes like a wide avenue between two hillocks and once more, from (d), runs beside a faint embankment down to join As 10 by a right angle in a hedge.

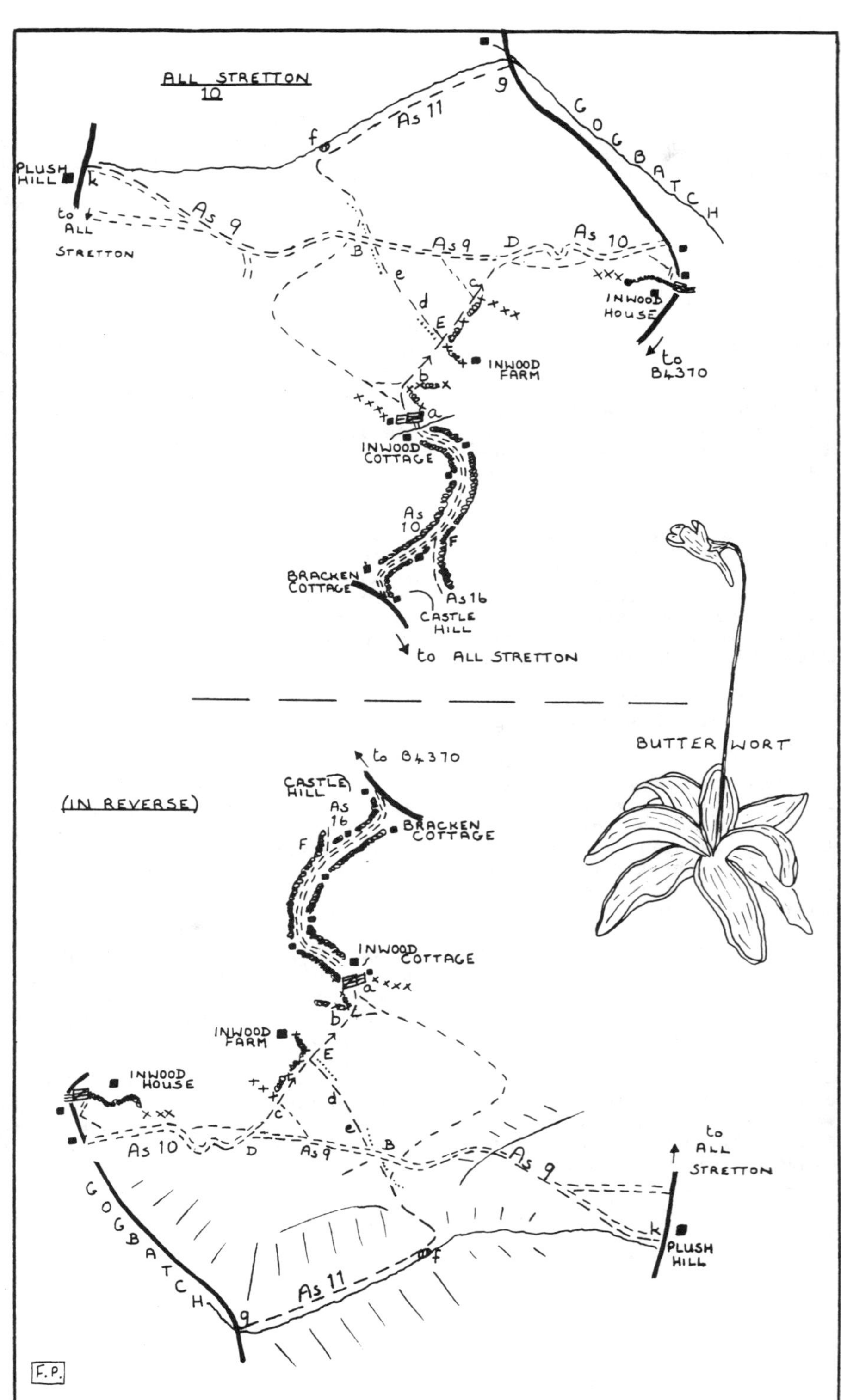

ALL STRETTON
10
GOGBATCH
As 11
f
g
PLUSH HILL
k
to ALL STRETTON
As 9
B
As 9
D
As 10
e
d
c
E
INWOOD HOUSE
to B4370
INWOOD FARM
b
a
INWOOD COTTAGE
As 10
F
BRACKEN COTTAGE
As 16
CASTLE HILL
to ALL STRETTON
BUTTER WORT
(IN REVERSE)
to B4370
CASTLE HILL
As 16
BRACKEN COTTAGE
F
INWOOD COTTAGE
a
b
INWOOD FARM
E
INWOOD HOUSE
d
c
e
As 10
D
As 9
B
As 9
to ALL STRETTON
k
PLUSH HILL
GOGBATCH
f
As 11
g
F.P.

ALL STRETTON 10, ALL STRETTON TO INWOOD HOUSE 1 Km/½+ m.

As 10, a track, branches off from the All Stretton to High Park road by a cottage (no. 5), soon passing Bracken Cottage on the left and continuing past The Paddock to point F. As 16 joins As 10 at point F. As 10 continues as an old track, descending steeply to Inwood Cottage, then crossing a small stream to reach gate (a) which leads onto open hill. The track, as far as here, is likely to have served as an outrack from All Stretton to the open hill; it also linked the open hill common with Castle Hill common (see figure 9). It was also the only way to Worsley before the existence of its present driveway. A few inhabitants of the Gogbatch area may have crossed the hill to join this track to get to and from All Stretton. At least up until the 1950s, a path led from the end of the track at (a) to Gogbatch and became a public footpath. Today, a path goes so far (to D approximately) but has then become modified, turning down to the lane near Inwood House; a continuation to Gogbatch is no longer evident. **From (a), follow the left-hand side of a hedge and avoid taking the small path to the left. After a short distance , the hedge turns away at (b); continue straight on. As 10 is rejoined by hedge, which forms a right angle, at point E. At point E, As 11 branches off to the left. Continue along the left hand side of the hedge and keep straight on at (c) where the hedge once more turns away. At D, As 10 is joined by another track (As 9) and both routes continue as one track, soon curving down to the right. The track descends to join the road near Inwood House.**

ALL STRETTON 10 (IN REVERSE), INWOOD HOUSE TO ALL STRETTON

Leave the Gogbatch road just after it crosses a cattle grid onto open hill. Opposite each of two houses are paths onto the hillside; these soon join to become one track (As 10) which ascends the slope. The track reaches a short, steeper slope where it curves to the left to reach point D. The track divides at this point, As 9 branching off to the right while As 10 bears to the left and soon comes alongside a hedge at (c). Where the hedge turns away at E, As 11 branches off to the right. Continue in the same direction as before, rejoin hedge at (b) and follow this to gate (a). From (a), enclosed track leads past Inwood Cottage and then up a steep bank. It flattens out before reaching point F on a bend; As 16 branches off to the left here. Continue along the track which curves to the right, passing The Paddock, and then to the left, passing Bracken Cottage. Join the High Park to All Stretton road ('Gravel Road') by cottage no. 5.

Focus on bog plants **Insect eaters**

The Long Mynd with its many bogs, is home to two species of 'insect eating' plants, butterwort and round-leaved sundew. It is because these plants live on bogs where nutrients in the soil are low, that they have developed another way of obtaining them, this being to trap and digest insects. Glands on the leaves of these two species produce a sticky substance that attracts and then traps insects, and subsequently the plant digests them. Neither of these species is believed actively to trap insects by movement of its leaves, whereas the Venus fly-trap's leaves close up as soon as an insect touches them. Butterwort is the easier of the two species to find since its rosettes of pale green leaves are striking. Sundew is much more difficult to see, its leaves blending with the colour of the bog.

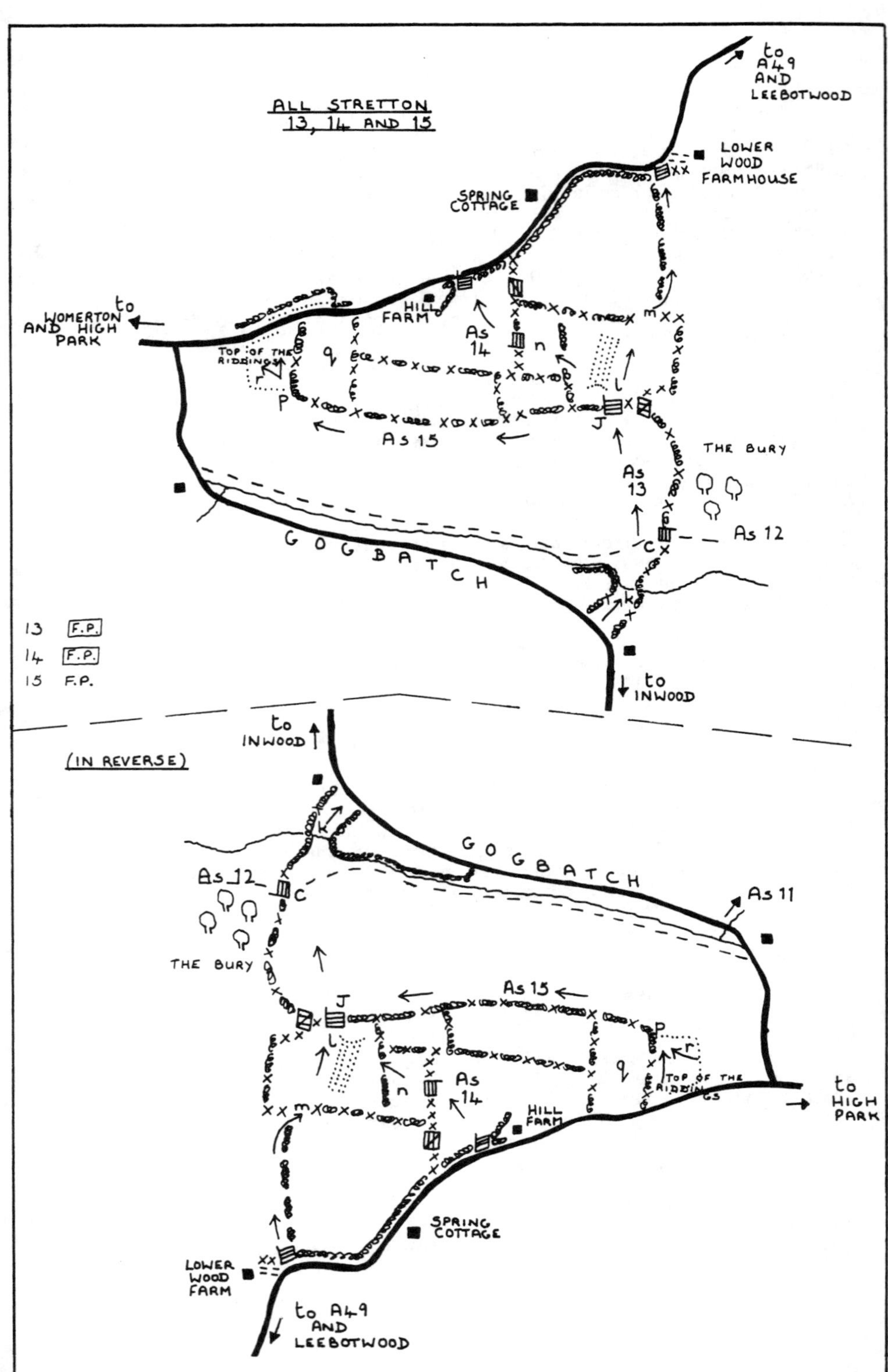

ALL STRETTON
13, 14 AND 15
to A49 AND LEEBOTWOOD
LOWER WOOD FARMHOUSE
SPRING COTTAGE
HILL FARM
to WOMERTON AND HIGH PARK
TOP OF THE RIDDINGS
As 14
As 15
THE BURY
As 13
As 12
GOGBATCH
13 F.P.
14 F.P.
15 F.P.
to INWOOD
to INWOOD
(IN REVERSE)
GOGBATCH
As 12
As 11
THE BURY
As 15
As 14
TOP OF THE RIDDINGS
HILL FARM
to HIGH PARK
SPRING COTTAGE
LOWER WOOD FARM
to A49 AND LEEBOTWOOD

ALL STRETTON 13 AND 14

As 13 and 14 are likely to have been footpaths from Hill Farm and Lower Wood, to All Stretton for church, pub, school etc. and for getting to Church Stretton markets and fairs.

ALL STRETTON 13, GOGBATCH TO LOWER WOOD 0.5 Km/¼ m.

As 13 leaves the road where it enters (or leaves) Gogbatch and descends a steep slope (k), sometimes known as Jacob's Ladder, between fields, to the brook. Follow the hedge on the right up to point C, where As 12 crosses As 13. Continue up the slope, approximately parallel to, but not close to, the hedge on the right. Join another hedge running from left to right at point J at the top of the slope. Cross a stile into field (l). This field has a wide band of ridges across it, resembling the pattern of mediaeval ridge and furrow. There is a grassy mound at one end which may be a 'head' (a heap of soil that gathered at the end of the furrows as the plough was turned). **Cross field (l) in the same direction as the ridges, to reach (m) and enter the next field. Almost immediately turn right into another field and follow the right-hand side of a hedge to reach a stile onto the road by Lower Wood Farmhouse.**

ALL STRETTON 13 (IN REVERSE), LOWER WOOD TO GOGBATCH

Cross the stile by Lower Wood Farmhouse and follow the left-hand side of a hedge to its far end. Turn right into the adjacent field and then immediately turn left at (m) to get into field (l). Cross this field parallel to some ridges, to reach a stile onto open hill at point J. Descend the slope almost parallel to the hedge on the left but not close to it, until a stile in it is reached; this marks point C where As 12 crosses As 13. Follow the right-hand side of the same hedge down to the brook, and then ascend a steep slope between fields, to reach the Gogbatch road.

ALL STRETTON 14, J ON As 13 TO HILL FARM 0.25 Km.

As 14 leaves As 13 at point J, via a stile leading from open hill into fields. Bear obliquely left across field (l) and field (n) to reach a stile into a third field. Aim obliquely right and exit onto the road via a stile, to the right of Hill Farm.

ALL STRETTON 15, J ON As 13 TO WOMERTON 0.5 Km/¼ m.

As 15 is not a public right of way but is well used and on the open hill. As 15 leaves As 13 at point J and follows the open hill boundary along the top of the north side of Gogbatch. It offers a good view towards Caradoc, Ragleth, Helmeth and Hope Bowdler Hill. At (p), the hedge can be followed to the right to get to the road, or you can continue straight on to join the road near Womerton Farm. Field (q) was termed 'encroachment' on the tithe map (see Background). Adjacent to this field, at (r), is another area within embankments; perhaps this was also once an encroachment that was reclaimed by the Commoners, or perhaps it represents a much older enclosure.

ALL STRETTON 15 (IN REVERSE), WOMERTON TO J ON As 13

As 15 begins at the edge of the open hill, between Lower Wood and Womerton. Follow the old hedge that forms the hill boundary, turning left with it at (p) and continuing along the top of the north side of Gogbatch until a stile in the hedge is reached; this is point J where As 15 joins As 13 and As 14.

ALL STRETTON 16, As 10 AT F TO ALL STRETTON (CHURCH) 0.25 Km

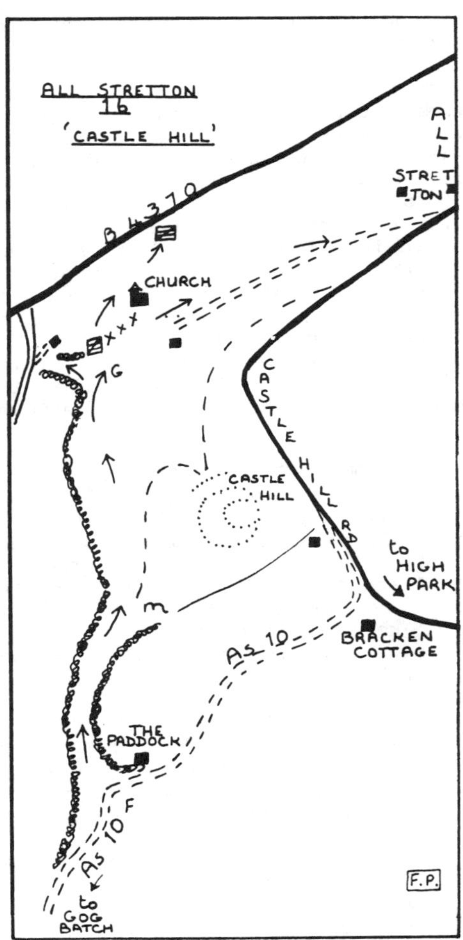

As 16 is the shortest route on foot to take, leaving As 10 at F, to get to All Stretton Church for anyone living at Gogbatch or Womerton. All Stretton has only had a church for just over 90 years and is not an ancient parish; it lies in the ancient parish of Church Stretton and the church is only a 'daughter' church of St. Lawrence's Church.

Leave As 10 on a bend close to The Paddock (a house) at point F, and follow the hedge running down to the left. The first part, from F to (m), appears to have once been a track and is shown as such on the tithe map, linking the common land of Castle Hill with As 10 and thence the open hill (see figure 9). **From (m), continue along the hedge that runs on the left; a diversion can be made to the top of Castle Hill. At G, there are three ways to choose from. One way is to turn down to the left and join As 17 at its junction with the main road. A second way is to go via the churchyard to the main road, and the third way is to walk alongside and above the church to join Castle Hill Road.**

Focus on Castle Hill

Castle Hill is capped by a hill-fort that can be reached by small footpaths. This hill-fort has probably been in use in more than one era, commanding, as it does, an excellent view up and down the Church Stretton valley. It is not thought to be a motte and bailey but there is a resemblance to Pulverbatch's motte in other ways. Both castles are on common land that is no longer in use for grazing animals, a situation that has resulted in the growth of scrub and bracken. (Animals ceased to graze Castle Hill after cattle-grids, placed along the roads off the hill, prevented them from passing freely between the two commons). This is a natural process on land that is left untended and ultimately it reverts to woodland. Woodland these areas undoubtedly once were, and leaving them to revert to woodland would seem a good idea. However, both areas in the interim have become ancient grassland and ought perhaps in parts to be preserved as such. A lesson in land management, relevant to much of the Mynd, can be learned from these two sites and should be remembered before changes, particularly in the ancient grazing traditions, are made.

ALL STRETTON 17, CHURCH TO MAIDENHILL 0.5 Km/¼ m.

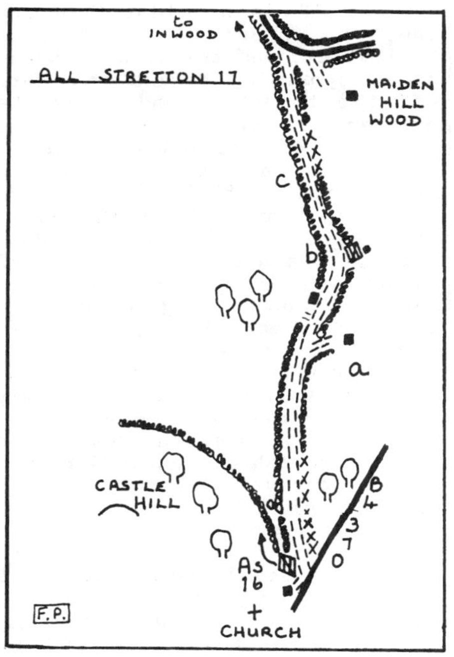

As 17 was once a continuation of the Inwood road down to the main road by the church. This is still apparent today although the surfaced road now curves away from it. As 17 has remained an enclosed track and was usable by vehicles until relatively recently. **Surprisingly, this track has only the status of a footpath; it is highly suitable for riders.**

Leave the main road by the church and take the well-used track signed to Hurst Wood, for which house, and another, the track now serves as a driveway. The track ascends between two small hills. The hill on the right (a), now largely an area of habitation, was once known as Mousehill. Descend to a bend (b) which marks a change from used to disused track. On the left is Bagbatch (c) and on the right another large garden with house called Maidenhill Wood, on the area once known as Little Maiden Hill. The track is narrow, shady and damp here, a good place for ferns and fungi. **Join the Inwood road opposite Maiden Hill itself.**

CASTLE HILL ROAD (GRAVEL ROAD)

Fig. 9

common land and tracks

enclosures

housing

surfaced road

ALL STRETTON 18, WILLOWFIELD TO LOWER WOOD 0.25 Km

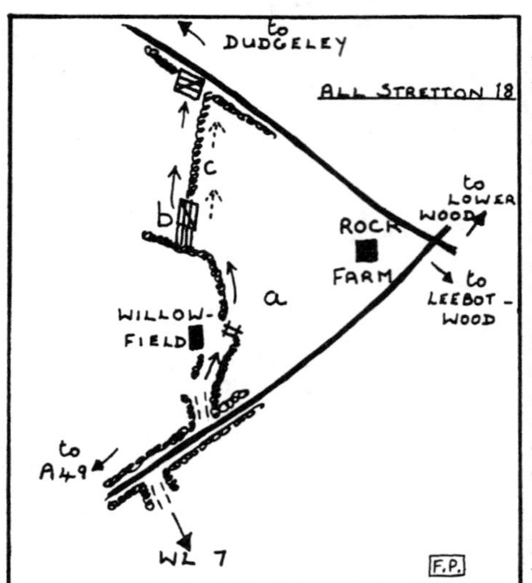

As 18 is a public footpath and a short cut between Willowfield and the area of Lower Wood, bypassing Rock Farm. Turn off the Womerton road along the driveway of Willowfield. At the near end of the house, bear to the right and cross a sort of stile into a field (a). Follow the hedge running to the left, until gate (b) is reached. Pass through the gate, turn right and follow the left-hand side of a hedge (c) up to a gate onto the road. The actual right of way appears to remain in field (a) and to run up the right-hand side of hedge (c), but there is no way out to the road at present.

Lower Wood is an area within the old parish of Church Stretton but for centuries was in Leebotwood manor.

Focus on fungi **Stinkhorn**

The stinkhorn has a very unpleasant smell, resembling that of a dead animal. By simply following your nose, it is not difficult to find them and flies are attracted to them from long distances. Slime covers the heads of these toadstools and by sticking to the flies' legs, gets transported away along with the spores within it. The honeycomb appearance of the heads is only apparent after most of the slime has been eaten or taken away. The stinkhorn is associated with rotten wood. Woodland and shady tracks, such as As 17 and As 19, are possible sites to find them.

Focus on fungi **Inkcaps**

The inkcap bears some resemblance in shape to the stinkhorn. There is no offensive slime but the inkcap does collapse into a black and inky mess as it matures. The shaggy and the common inkcaps are good to eat, although the latter can prove unpleasant if taken with alcohol; it has been used as a remedy to cure alcoholics.

ALL STRETTON 19

As 19 was the old road off the hill down to All Stretton. The road in use today existed on the tithe map as a track at the top and another at the bottom, both ways running to and from the Castle Hill common (see figure 9 on page 80). Its alteration led subsequently to its promotion as the main through route off the hill. It is known as Castle Hill Road or Gravel Road and As 19 as Sunken Road, Coppy Road or Down the Coppy (the term 'coppy' being a commonly used variant of coppice, certainly in this part of Shropshire).

As 19 is classified as public footpath only, although a bridleway exists between (b) and (d), closer to the Synalds enclosures. It runs through a small area of common land that surrounds Buckstone, and is owned by the National Trust.

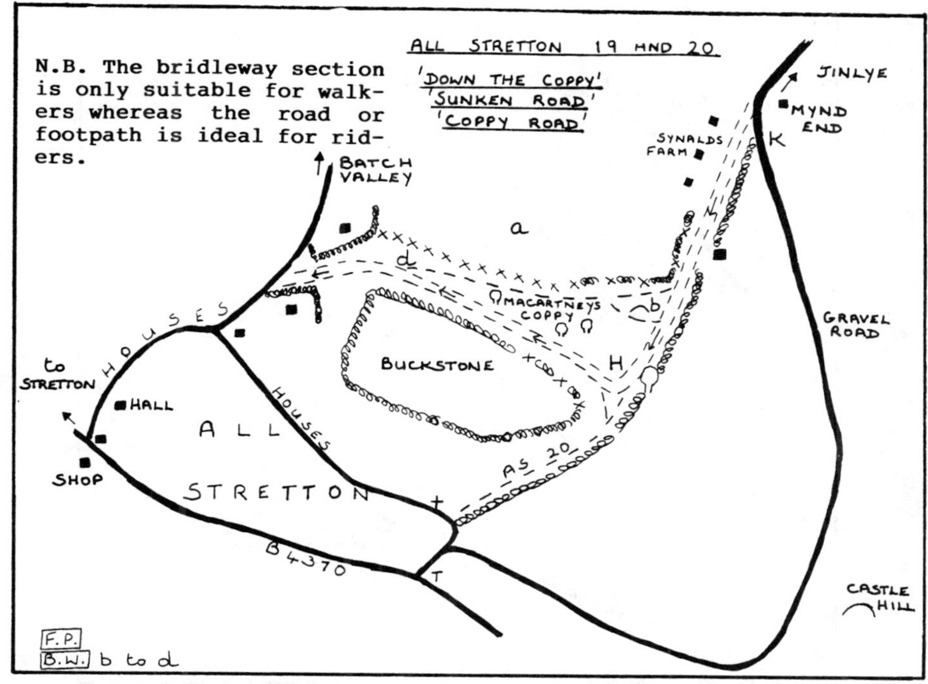

ALL STRETTON 19, SYNALDS TO ALL STRETTON 0.5 Km/¼ m.

Leave the Jinlye to All Stretton road on a bend, in effect continuing straight on, passing Synalds Farm and other houses too. The hillock to the right and its slope (a) down into Batch Valley alongside As 19, was an area of woodland known as Synalds Coppice, hence the name of Coppy Road for As 19. **At (b) is a small open area of old grassland; keep to the left of this alongside the left-hand hedge. At H, As 20 continues straight on as a path down to All Stretton, while As 19 curves to the right and descends as a dark holloway behind an enclosed hillock known as Buckstone.** A holloway (a deep-cut road) represents centuries of erosion by water running down it and has not been created by any feat of engineering. As 19 may, however, have made use of a small valley before it too began to develop into a holloway. The damp, dark banks are home to abundant ferns. **The track emerges from its gloom and joins the road into Batch Valley.**

ALL STRETTON 19 (IN REVERSE), ALL STRETTON TO SYNALDS

Leave the surfaced road into Batch valley, taking a track between two dwellings. The track ascends as a shady holloway, turning sharply to the left at H. Pass several houses and join the All Stretton to High Park road near the Synalds.

ALL STRETTON 20 (IN REVERSE), ALL STRETTON TO As 19

Leave the small road running behind the Manor House, and ascend along the hedge separating field from wood. At H, where As 20 joins As 19, this hedge continues along the right-hand side of the track (As 19).

ALL STRETTON 21
NEW LEASOWES
to SHREWSBURY
to GATTEN
to BISHOPS CASTLE
C
b
a
COTHERCOTT HILL
to PICKLE-SCOTT
THRESH-OLDS
to STITT
F.P.

PAULITH BANK
to HABBERLEY
WEST-COTT HILL
RATLINGHOPE BATCH
P'BATCH
PAULITH BANK
3
2
RATLINGHOPE
PULVERBATCH
MAIN CHURCH ROAD
COTHERCOTT HILL
NEW LEASOWES
to PICKLE-SCOTT
THRESHOLDS
to STITT
STRETTON

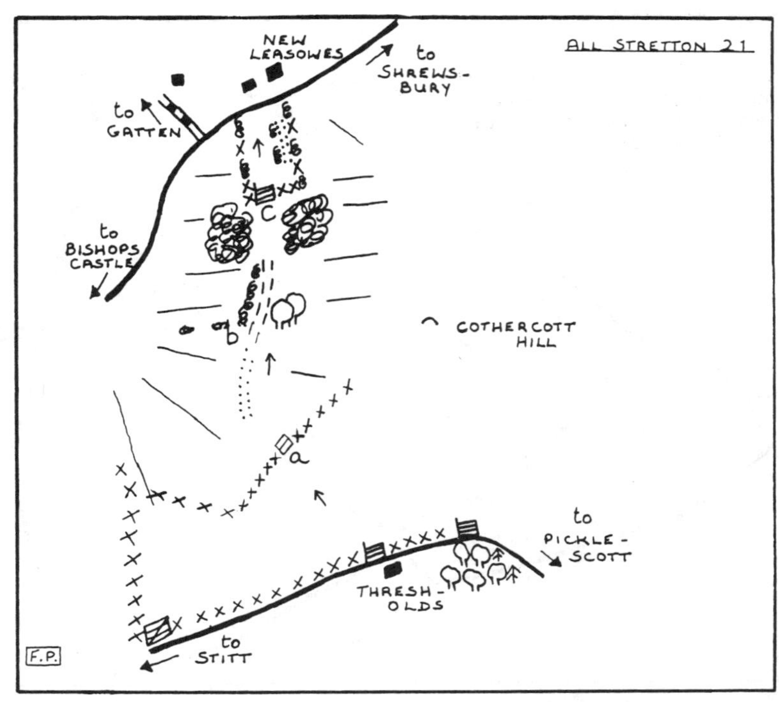

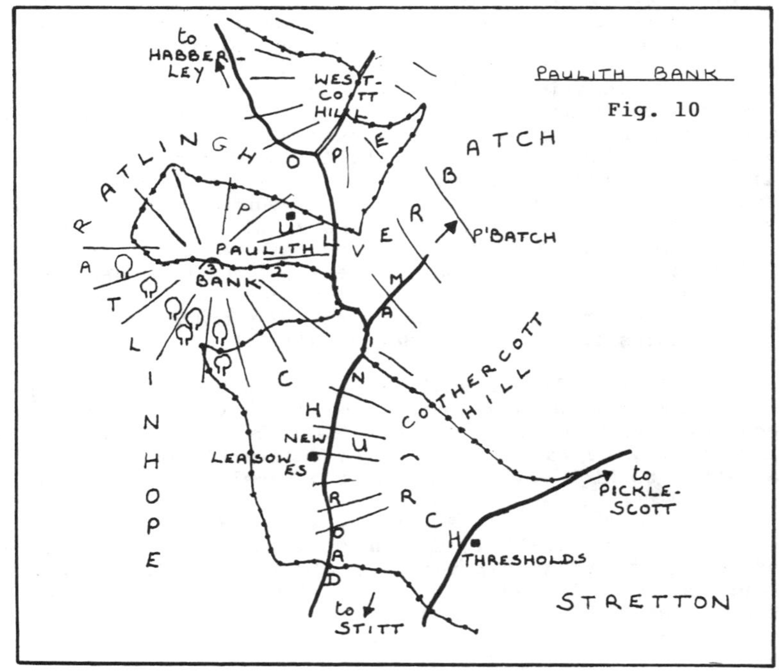

Fig. 10

ALL STRETTON 21, THRESHOLDS TO NEW LEASOWS 0.75 Km/½ m.

Route As 21, although far-flung from All Stretton village, lies in the old parish of Church Stretton and the civil parish of All Stretton. The parish boundary extends onto the edge of the cone-shaped hill (Paulith Bank) visible from this end of the Mynd (see figure 10). Pulverbatch and Ratlinghope also extend onto Paulith Bank. A possible explanation for Pulverbatch is that the manor was granted a portion of Stiperstones Forest in 1314. Perhaps there is a similar explanation for Church Stretton.

As 21 is an old way off the northern end of the hill, and is thought to have been the road in use before the present road from Thresholds to Stitt existed. It is in continuity with a route (unsurfaced highway) over a range of small hills between the Mynd and the Stiperstones. Drovers may have been among the travellers who once used it to get to and from the Portway. Other possible travellers may have been the Romans whose route between the Stiperstones mines and the east remain a mystery (see Background). Roman coins have been discovered very near this route but they were not necessarily dropped here by a Roman traveller.

As 21 is only a public footpath (it would make a very useful link as a bridleway). It begins at a stile opposite a wood of beech and conifers near Thresholds (the house). Bear obliquely left across a sometimes arable field (once, for a short time, a venue for horse races); this direction should take you gradually away from the road which is to your left as you cross the field. The field equates approximately to the old enclosure of Thresholds Bank. To the right is the tumulus on the summit of Cothercott Hill. On the far left is the Wildmoor area of the Mynd while the embankments of an Iron Age fort or enclosure on Stitt Hill are visible against the skyline on the near left. **When the Stiperstones come into view ahead, aim for the largest rock outcrop (Devil's Chair) along its skyline, to get to a small stile (a) in a fence near the top of a slope. From (a), bear obliquely to the right, keeping to the top of the steep part of the slope. A faint track is soon reached; this leads across and down the slope to some ash trees opposite a right angle in a sparse and old hedge (b). The old track becomes more deep-cut as it follows this old hedge and passes through a large area of gorse, a good place to see some interesting small birds such as goldfinches ('seven-coloured linnets') or linnets ('gorse thatcher/gorse bird'). Cross stile (c) into the last section of this track which is fenced off from the hill but open to the road at the bottom end.** There are signs of an older track within the present wide track, a finding that sometimes indicates that a way was a drovers' road; presumably the old road was too narrow for driving large numbers of animals. The wide route itself is bounded by old hedges and contains woodland flowers such as bluebells and moschatel, a finding that suggests there was woodland here in the past (see page 246). On the 1903 O/S map, the track ran alongside the edge of New Leasows Plantation; there was no woodland shown here on the tithe map. Young trees of nut, rowan, ash and hawthorn are growing here, undisturbed by grazing animals or walkers in any numbers, and this area could become a tiny wood again.

ALL STRETTON 22, PICKLESCOTT TO THE PORTWAY AT 1 Km/½+ m.

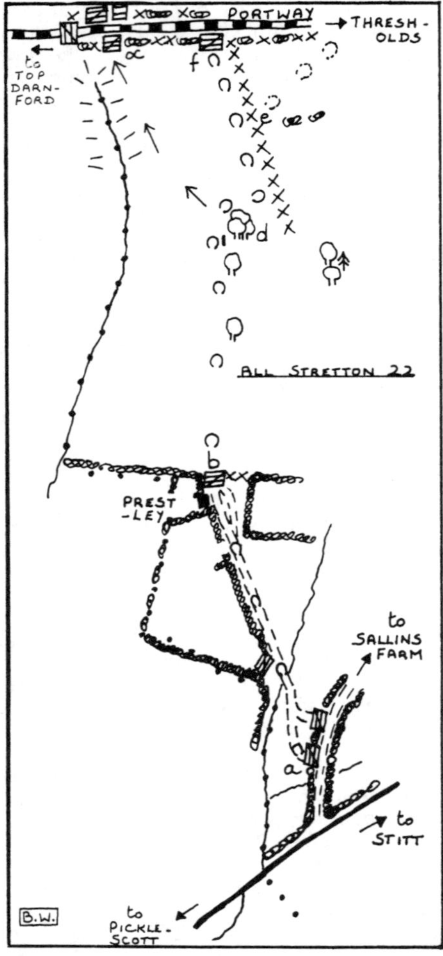

As 22 is likely to have been used as a way on and off the hill linking up with the Portway, and it has sometimes been labelled as Portway on maps. It is also in continuity with Rt 1 to Ratlinghope. As a route on its own, it was a way for the inhabitants of dwellings such as Top Darnford to get to Picklescott and in reverse, it may have once served as an outrack to common land when Picklescott had rights on the hill. The whole route runs in the old parish of Church Stretton, in close proximity to its boundary with Smethcott.

As 22, a bridleway, begins along the enclosed driveway to Sallins Farm. It soon branches off to the left through a gate (a) and runs as an open track across a field to the brook. It ascends from the brook and follows hedge up to a cottage known as Prestley. Presley and Sallins are old names belonging to pastures that lay to the west of Picklescott's common fields, all in the area to the left of As 22. **From Prestley, pass through gate (b) into a large arable field. A narrow strip has been left unploughed and is easy to follow. Two trees also act as route-markers and are remnants of a once enclosed track that ran up to the clump of trees (d) ahead.** The clump of trees represents the site of an old dwelling. **Pass to the left of the clump of trees. Then (walkers only, in theory, riders too, in practice) bear obliquely left to come alongside a small valley, following the top of the valley side to reach the Portway via a gate. Riders should, in theory, use a different route from (d) to the Portway; after passing to the left of (d), turn right and bear obliquely right to a fence at (e). From (e), the bridleway should continue in the same direction as before but it is not possible; it is obvious that some riders are instead following the fence from (e) to gate (f) onto the Portway. It is probably more sensible at the present time for riders to take the walkers' route from (d) to the Portway, since there has been some effort to leave an untilled way here.** Both footpath and bridleway were in continuity with routes on the other side of the Portway. The bridleway continued across to a dwelling known as Golden Valley, now buildings, and on to Rt 4, while the footpath continued, and still does today, as Rt 1 down the Golden Valley.

CHURCH STRETTON

Church Stretton is a parish on the east side of the Long Mynd and is made up of the townships of All Stretton, Church Stretton, Little Stretton and Minton. It was the manor of Stratun in the Domesday Book and is thought to have included All and Little Strettons. Minton was a separate manor. Both manors, before the Domesday Book, had been held by Mercian earls, indicating that they were perhaps already more important than other manors on the Mynd. After the Conquest, the manor passed to Earl Roger de Montgomery. Minton became included in his revenue and was held for the purpose of guarding the Royal Forest. There were Norman castles at Stretton (Brockhurst), All Stretton (Castle Hill) and Minton.

Stretton became a royal manor but was granted to several people in succession, and was even in the hands of the community at one time, until the king gave it to the Earl of Arundel and his heirs for ever in the 14th century (they actually held it until 1802). Stretton became known as Strettonesdale and the other Strettons appeared in records as Aluredestretton and Parva Stretton. Minton (Munetune in the Domesday Book) became known as Muneton in Strettonsdale. Stretton manor extended further south than the parish does now, and the Saxon Church-in-the-Dale may have been near Priors Holt. Stretton had a church by the time of the Domesday Book, at its present site. Little and All Strettons built churches at the beginning of this century while still remaining members of Church Stretton parish. Church Stretton parish is divided into All Stretton and Church Stretton civil parishes and it is these names and boundaries that are shown on modern O/S maps.

Amenities:-

Shop - Church Stretton, numerous. Little Stretton, only one.

Refreshments - there are many cafes, restaurants, hotels, pubs and takeaways in Church Stretton. Little Stretton has two pubs and Mynd House hotel and restaurant.

Accommodation - there are several guest houses and hotels.

Camping - Small Batch, Little Stretton.

Cycle Hire - Longmynd Cycles and Terry's Cycles, Church Stretton.

Train - many trains run daily, including Sundays, between Shrewsbury and the south, stopping at Church Stretton but NOT at Little Stretton.

Bus - Midland Red buses run regularly (not on Sundays) along the A49 between Shrewsbury and Ludlow, passing through the centres of Church Stretton and Little Stretton. On Saturdays, a bus (Horrocks or Shropshire) runs from Shrewsbury to Acton Scott via Church Stretton cross roads; there are two afternoon buses in the opposite direction. On weekdays in term-time, a bus (Boultons or Shropshire) runs between Church Stretton and Shrewsbury, travelling northwards in the early morning and returning at the end of the school day.

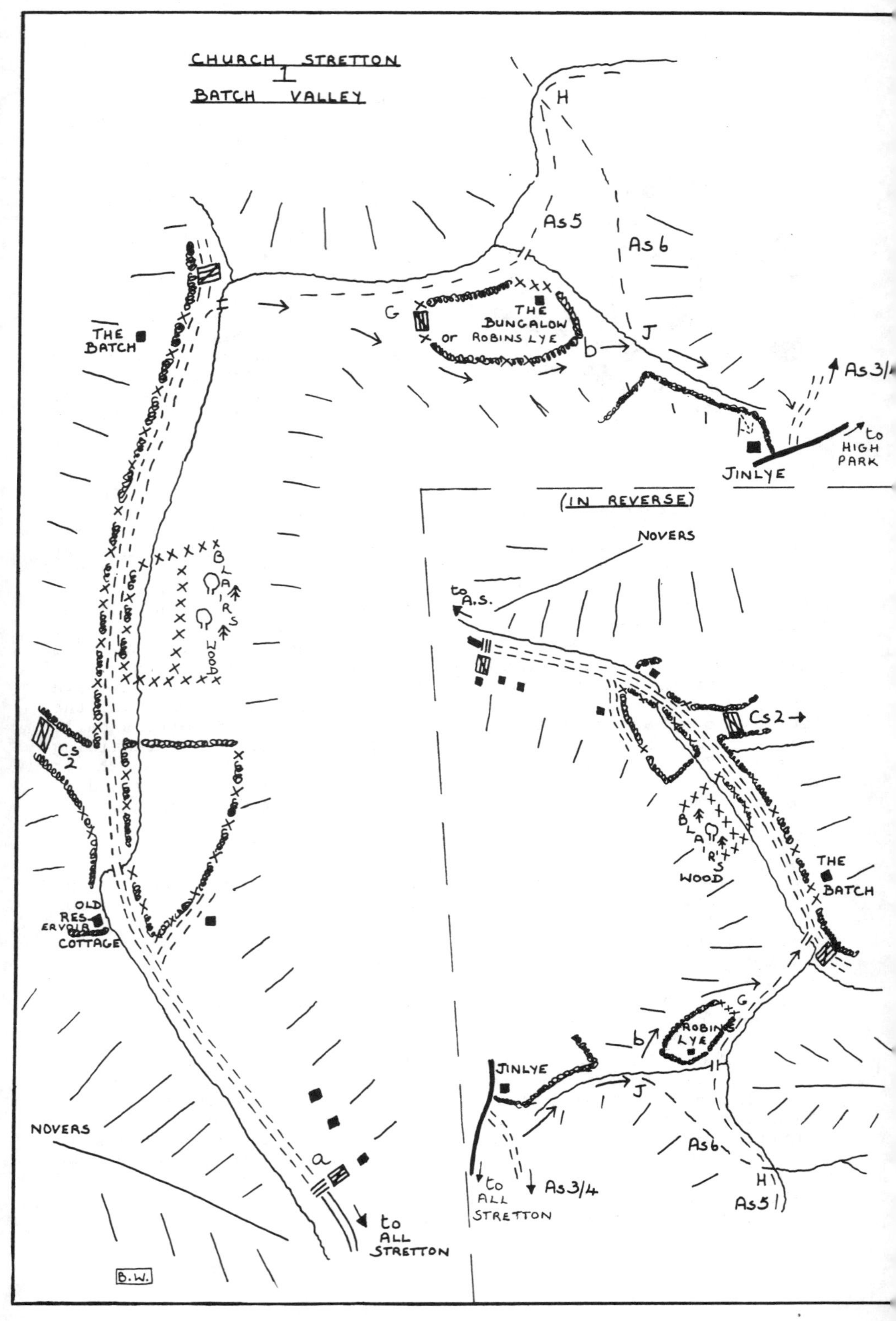
CHURCH STRETTON
1
BATCH VALLEY
H
As5
As6
G
THE BUNGALOW or ROBINS LYE
b
J
THE BATCH
As3/4
to HIGH PARK
JINLYE
BLAIRS WOOD
CS 2
OLD RESERVOIR COTTAGE
NOVERS
a
to ALL STRETTON
B.W.
(IN REVERSE)
NOVERS
to A.S.
Cs2
BLAIRS WOOD
THE BATCH
G
b
ROBINS LYE
JINLYE
J
As6
H
As5
to ALL STRETTON
As3/4

CHURCH STRETTON 1, ALL STRETTON TO JINLYE 1 Km/½+ m.

The track up the Batch Valley is a route well used by walkers and horse riders, and runs through common land. Although I have divided the valley route into two separate ways (Cs 1 and As 5), they form a continuous route with one another. The reason for dividing them is to try and conform to the official status of the ways through the valley, the track along the valley floor being bridleway only as far as Robinslye at G. The end result of this is that the first part of the valley track from (a) to G has been linked with a bridleway running from G to Jinlye to create a riders' route (Cs 1). Unfortunately, the latter section of bridleway, from G to Jinlye, is not very suitable for horses and it is difficult to understand how this became classified as such; a detour has had to be suggested. In the 1930s, this way was certainly only suitable for walkers, when a house move from Robinslye to Jinlye involved the carrying of furniture and sides of ham piece by piece along it.

Cs 1 begins as the road into Batch Valley, opposite All Stretton's shop. Follow the road, passing several houses, and cross a cattle-grid (a) to reach the open hill in the valley. Novers Hill lies to the left. Follow the stony and well-used track and pass a cottage that lies just upstream of the site of the old All Stretton reservoir. The track becomes flanked by old hedges and another track (Cs 2) branches off to the left. Continue up the valley to a cottage called The Batch. Turn right after the cottage and cross the brook; the way is now grassy and follows the brook upstream for a short distance. On looking back, a magnificent old yew tree can be seen on the facing hillside. At G, the more used way continues up the brook as As 5 but Cs 1 bears to the right up the slope as a narrow path only, to follow the boundary hedge of a field and bungalow (Robinslye). At (b), bear away from the hedge and cross a steep bank that overlooks a small ravine (some horses will almost certainly baulk at this). Once safely across this part, cross the stream just above the ravine at point J and follow it upwards to exit onto the road beside Jinlye. An alternative for riders, a detour from the bridleway part of Cs 1 between G and Jinlye, is to continue along the valley from G to H where the valley divides. From H, take another small, but safer path to the right up the slope. This path rejoins Cs 1 at point J just above the small ravine.

CHURCH STRETTON 1 (IN REVERSE), JINLYE TO ALL STRETTON

Leave the All Stretton to High Park road between the houses of Jinlye and Plush Hill but closer to the former. Turn down to the left, following the beginnings of a stream to point J where the slope starts to fall away more steeply. Cs 1 turns left across the stream just above a small ravine and crosses a steep slope to come alongside a hedge at (b); follow this hedge as it runs to the left (not as it descends straight on), and descend to point G. An alternative to this difficult (for horses) section between J and G, is to bear right at J and follow a small, but safer path down and across the slope into the valley, turning left along the valley floor and rejoining Cs 1 at G. From G, follow the brook downstream, cross it and turn left along a well-used and stony track, passing The Batch (a cottage). The track runs down the valley beside the brook. Cs 2 branches off to the right where Cs 1 passes through a shady section. Cs 1 continues and leaves the open hill via a cattle grid at (a).

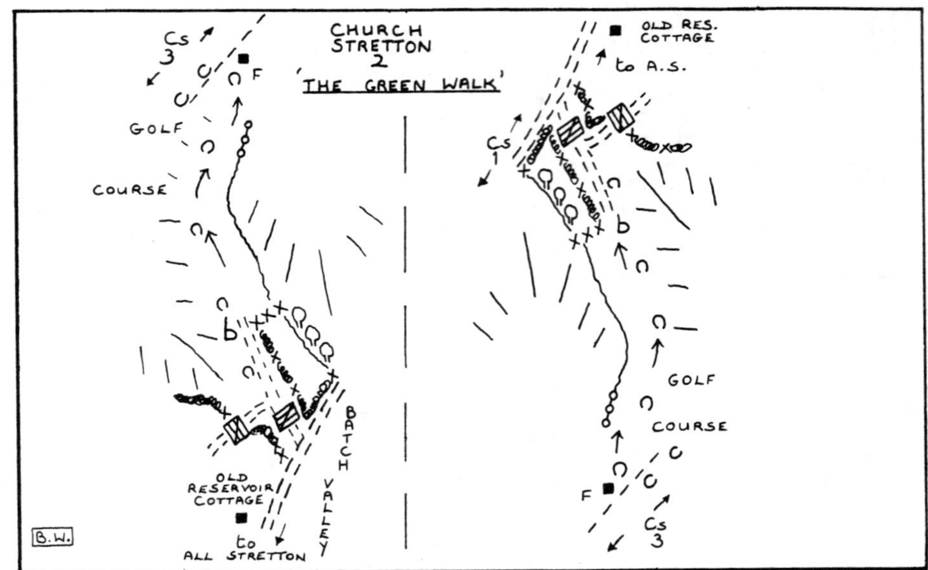

CHURCH STRETTON 2, BATCH VALLEY TO Cs 3 AT F 0.5 Km/¼ m.

Cs 2 is a bridleway and old track up onto the part of the hill which is now the golf course. It is sometimes known as the Green Walk. Cs 2 begins as an enclosed track branching off from Cs 1 in Batch Valley. It passes through a gate onto open hill and follows a hedge which runs on the right. The stream running down the field on the right is flanked by alders and, with the nearby high hedges and woodland, makes a good habitat for some interesting birds such as the tree creeper or the tree pipit. **At (b),** the enclosures end, the stream becomes devoid of trees and **the grassy track continues up the hill, following the stream. The way soon enters the golf course area and a succession of small pools is passed on the right. Aim for a hut which is at point F on Cs 3.**

CHURCH STRETTON 2 (IN REVERSE), F ON Cs 3 TO BATCH VALLEY

Leave Cs 3 on the golf course at a hut and bear obliquely down to the left, passing a succession of small pools. The outflow from the pools forms a stream; follow the right-hand side of this down the valley. Cs 2 becomes a grassy track and at (b) follows a hedge down to a gate that leads off the open hill. Cs 1 is joined after the gate.

Focus on trees **Alders**

Alders grow on wet ground and are often to be found flanking streams. Groups of alder trees on boggy areas are referred to as alder carr. The alder is often called a waller (pronounced 'woller') and commonly features as a field name. The wood was used until well into this century for making the bases for clogs. Clogmen or cloggers bought stretches of alder trees, felled them and made the bases on the spot, out of the 'green' wood. These were sent off to factories to be seasoned and to have soft tops attached. Locally, clogs were sometimes made entirely of wood.

Focus on sheep

Sheep have for centuries been associated with the Long Mynd and have played a large part in shaping its landscape. The Cothercott and Wilderley areas were a sheepwalk in Haughmond Abbey's manor of Boveria, and Le Shupene, which was a house there in the 13th century, has become Sheppen/Shepton Fields. The wool sold provided some degree of prosperity for a while.

Sheep were not allowed to spend the winter on the open hill common and knowing where extra food could be found they would bring themselves down to the farms when food was getting scarce; cattle-grids flanking the hill now prevent their home-coming and many sheep winter on the hill in the milder winters of today.

Movement of sheep in large numbers is a less frequent event than in the past when they used to have to come off the common in winter and, until very recently, for compulsory dipping. The gathering of sheep was a communal and enjoyable event, as was the burning of heather, in the management of the hill. For those who took part in these activities there is a feeling of sadness at another opportunity lost for local people to get together. (Any communal rural event should not be too hastily stopped by those who know little about country life as a whole).

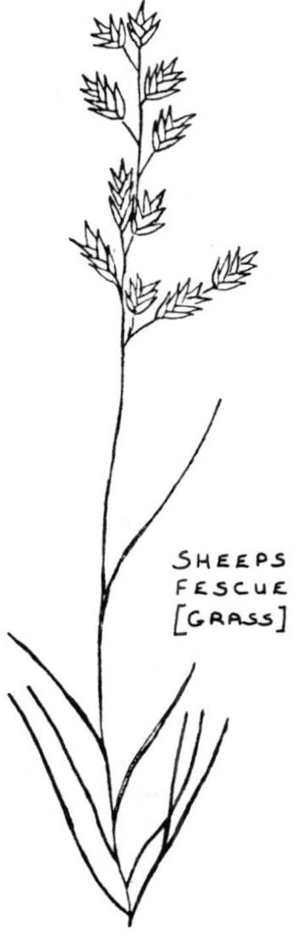

There will always be movement of sheep to markets but, as these are now further afield, the sight of animals being walked to market is no longer a feature of the Mynd tracks. Church Stretton had sheep markets and Sheep Sales Field has now been lost under Kings Court. Sheep sales were held at the Bridges for many years too; Rt 10 was a track used to get there. Sheep sales on a smaller scale take place in Little Stretton today.

The hill sheep are largely the hardy Welsh mountain sheep. They now tend to stay on the hill in winter and lamb there in the spring. Bare hollows often develop on the hill slopes where they take shelter; these were sometimes put into use by the Home Guard in the last war, or new hollows made, to provide shelter for their members to keep watch. One pair of soldiers in a hollow became aware of an increasing weight upon them in the dark and each thought it was the other dropping off to sleep. It was, in fact, a sheep which had decided to rest on their makeshift roof and was gradually sinking onto them. The sheep are surprisingly bold and can be avid picnic-eaters, even butting off a small dog that might be after food too. One sheep which went off with a leather bag was found some time afterwards with its head still through the handles. Its front feet, which were also in the bag, had worn footholes through the leather. The owner's post-office book, also still inside, was subsequently returned!

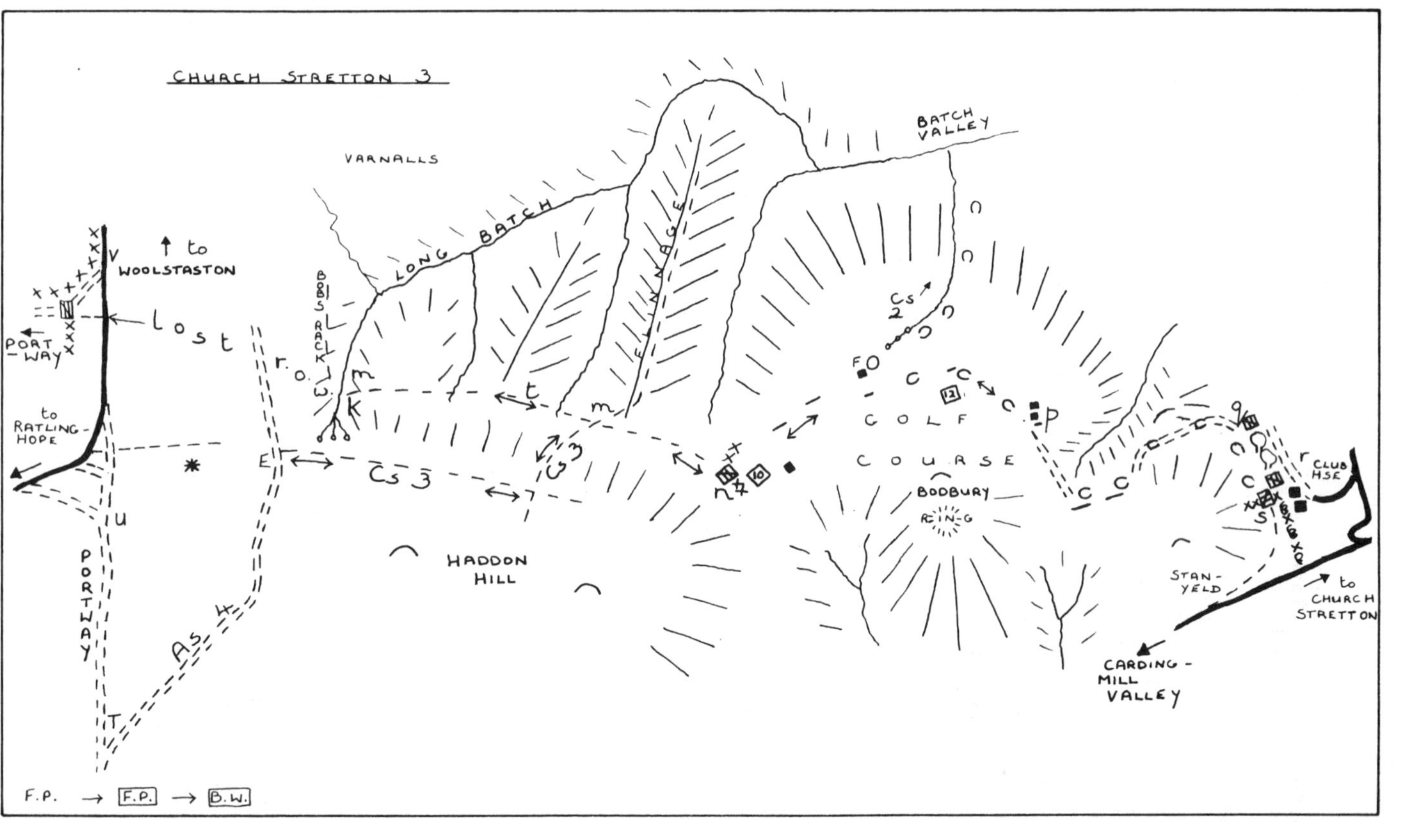
CHURCH STRETTON 3
VARNALLS
LONG BATCH
BATCH VALLEY
BOBS RACK
to WOOLSTASTON
PORT-WAY
to RATLING-HOPE
PORTWAY
HADDON HILL
GOLF COURSE
BODBURY RING
CLUB HSE
STAN-YELD
to CHURCH STRETTON
CARDING-MILL VALLEY
F.P. → F.P. → B.W.

CHURCH STRETTON 3, E ON As 4 TO THE GOLF CLUB 2 Km/1¼ m.

On the O/S map, a public footpath is shown as a continuation from the Portway near V, down and across the golf course, becoming a bridleway at point F. The path must have been created by people living on or near the north end of the Mynd, to get to Stretton. Today the route has altered and it is not possible to find the old right of way between the Portway and the valley (k). The route now begins clearly at E along As 4 and is marked by a heap of stones; it is higher up the hillside than the original route. Almost immediately after branching off along this path, three small pools are passed. Continue along the path, passing to the left of the first of two faint peaks that form Haddon Hill/The Haddons. Just before the second peak, there is a long ridge descending to the left, known as Flinnage; turn left down towards it for a short distance and reach a clear path running from left to right at (m). Turn right along this and continue at much the same height to reach the gate (n) onto the golf course. The gate is at the head of a branch valley of Batch Valley and is also by green number 10 ('Far Hole'). At this point, there is a good view to the right of Bodbury Ring (an Iron Age fort or animal enclosure). Once on the golf course continue straight on, passing some tall posts on the left to get to a hut; there is a way-marker post here, and this is point F where Cs 2 branches off to the left. From F, Cs 3 is a bridleway. Keep to the same direction as before for a little further and then curve round to the right, passing green number 12 ('Excelsior'). Descend to some huts (p) and continue on across the head of a small valley. Turn left after the valley and join a clear track that descends to gate (q). Do not go through (q) but follow the line of trees to the right and exit through gate (r) by the golf clubhouse. Follow the road from the golf clubhouse down to the Cardingmill Valley road. An alternative route for a walker, to get into Cardingmill Valley, is to go through gate (s) by the golf clubhouse and follow a small path down and across Stanyeld.

CHURCH STRETTON 3 (IN REVERSE), GOLF CLUB TO E ON As 4

From the golf clubhouse, take the first gate (r) on the left and follow the line of trees up to gate (q) which you do not use. Turn left at (q), to follow the clear track up a steep slope, and then follow the top of the left slope of a small dingle. Curve round the head of this dingle to some huts (p). From (p), bear slightly to the left up the slope and then curve more sharply to the left round and to the right of green number 12. Continue towards a hut which is at point F, where Cs 2 branches off to the right. Cs 3 goes straight on and up to green number 10 and gate (n), which leads onto the open hill. From (n), bear slightly to the right to follow the contour of the hill, keeping at much the same height, and passing the head of a valley on the right. After passing the valley you will soon find yourself at the head (m) of a long ridge (Flinnage) that descends to the right. Turn left off the path (t) which is going straight on; (t) was the original route but now only leads to the valley at (k) and then takes a completely different course (locally known as Bob's Rack, see As 6) from the right of way on the O/S map. Having turned left at (m), ascend for a short distance, along a vague path, and find a clear path again running to the right. This path leads to As 4 at E near some small pools and by a heap of stones. N.B. This path is not suitable for use in misty weather unless it is familiar to you.

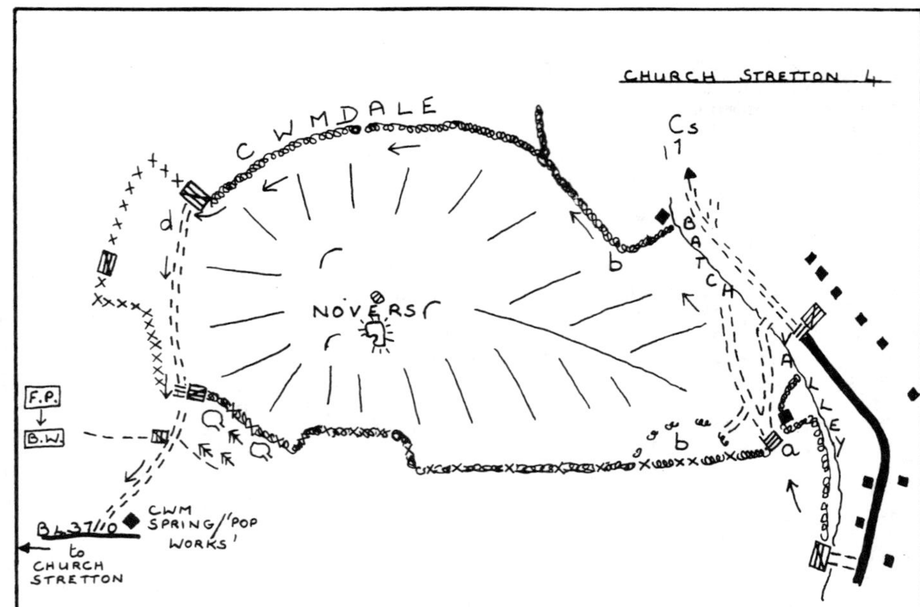

Novers or Novers Hill is best climbed from (a) where ascent is more gradual, up a ridge. Near its summit is a plateau between small hillocks, and this is the site of a pool and a small area surrounded by an embankment, labelled 'enclosure' on the O/S map. The enclosure is not thought to be an ancient one, but to be associated with a cottage that formerly existed in the vicinity.

CHURCH STRETTON 4, BATCH VALLEY TO CWMDALE 1.25 Km/0.75 m.

Cs 4 is a public footpath from its start to (d) and a bridleway from (d) to the Cwm Spring works. It begins off the road into Batch Valley as a track to a gate into a field. Cross the field, aiming obliquely right to a stile (a) close to a house. Take the grassy track that runs almost straight on, but leave it as it starts to descend and aim for the corner of a hedge at (b). The slope between (a) and (b) is steep, and eroded in many places. From (b), follow the hedge around the side of Novers Hill. The hedge is an old boundary between open hill and the enclosures of Cwmdale, and runs in a continuous line to the far end at (d). At (d), join the driveway from the houses of Cwmdale as it runs down the valley. Leave the open hill and pass the Cwm Spring works to join the main road.

CHURCH STRETTON 4 (IN REVERSE), CWMDALE TO BATCH VALLEY

Take the track, by the Cwm Spring works, into Cwmdale and follow it as far as (d) where it leaves the open hill for an area of houses. Turn up to the right and follow the hedge that bounds the enclosures of Cwmdale. This hedge runs around the contour of Novers Hill to (b), where it turns away; Cs 4 continues straight on across a steep, somewhat eroded slope, to get to stile (a) by a house. From (a), cross a field to the far left-hand corner. Exit, via a gate, and cross the brook to reach the road into Batch valley.

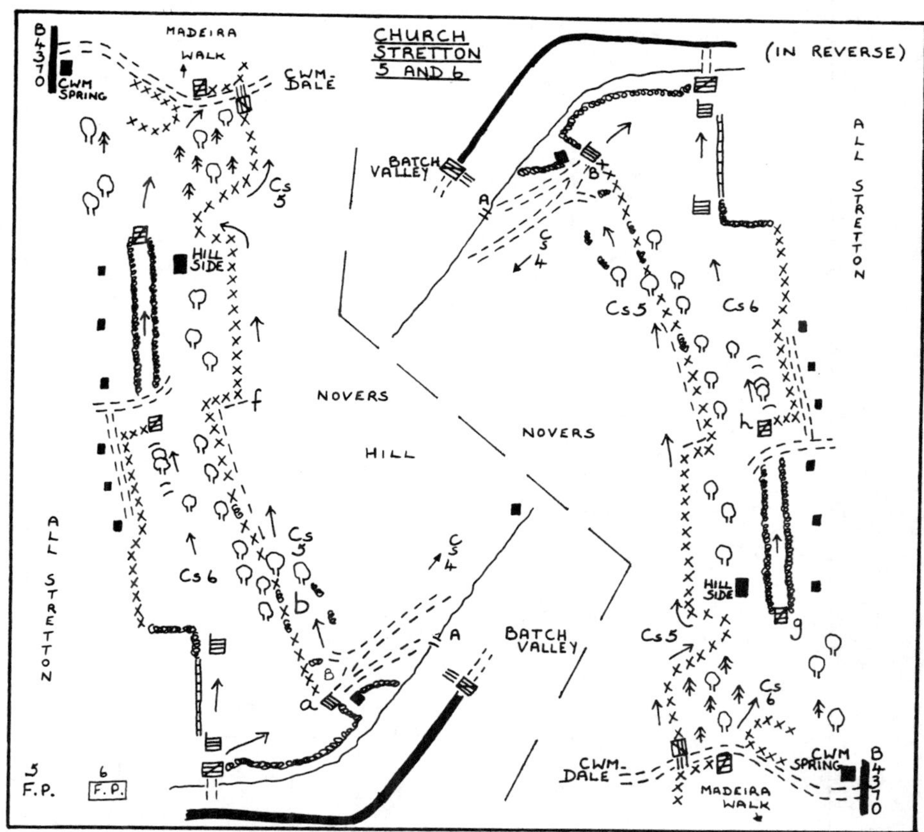

CHURCH STRETTON 5, BATCH VALLEY TO CWMDALE 0.75 Km/½ m.

Cs 5 is a path only, on common land. It runs around the eastern side of Novers Hill, following the old boundary between open hill and enclosures. The path begins from stile (a), near a house, which is reached along Cs 4 or from Batch Valley. Field (b), which is soon crossed, was an 'encroachment'; it is now open to the hill but its hedge remains and contains some old yews. From the yews, a path can be taken along the hill boundary hedge or straight on and across to (f). From (f), follow the boundary hedge to Cwmdale. Novers Hill is best climbed from (a) where ascent is more gradual, and consequently paths are less erosive.

CHURCH STRETTON 6 (IN REVERSE),CWMDALE TO BATCH VALLEY 0.75 Km/½ m.

Cs 6 is a public footpath that runs along the foot of Novers Hill between All Stretton and the north end of Madeira Walk. It begins off the track into Cwmdale, and the first part runs along the lower edge of a wood to gate (g). From (g), the path is enclosed and passes behind some houses. It then crosses the driveway to Hillside, to reach gate (h). From (h), continue in the same direction as before, across a field and on, via stiles, to exit via a gate onto the Batch Valley road.

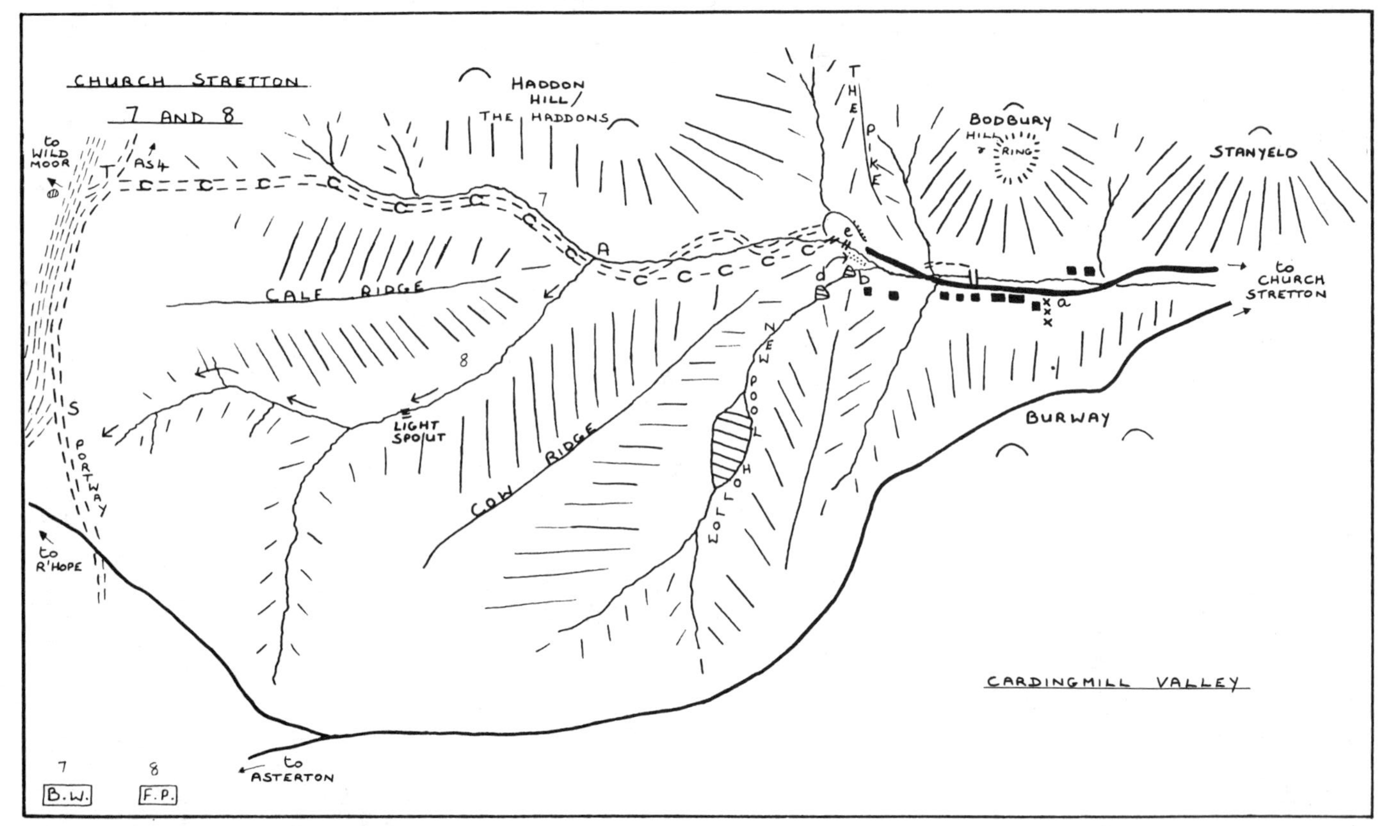
CHURCH STRETTON
7 AND 8
HADDON HILL / THE HADDONS
BODBURY HILL
RING
STANYELD
THE PIKE
to WILD MOOR
AS4
CALF RIDGE
COW RIDGE
LIGHT SPOUT
NEW POOL HOLLOW
PORTWAY
BURWAY
to CHURCH STRETTON
to R'HOPE
to ASTERTON
CARDINGMILL VALLEY
7 B.W.
8 F.P.

CHURCH STRETTON 7, CARDING MILL VALLEY TO THE PORTWAY 2 Km/1¼ m.

The Carding Mill Valley is probably the best known and most used footpath and bridleway on the Long Mynd, with easy access, parking facilities and a National Trust shop, providing information as well as refreshments; the shop is not open in winter. The name of the valley is derived from the presence of the mill, which originally was used for grinding corn but later became a mill for carding wool. The three-storey building was the factory that was added to the mill. **From the lower car park (a), continue along the surfaced road passing the shop and old factory. A footpath then runs along the right-hand side of the brook while the road runs on the left and passes through a ford.** An old mill pool (b) can be seen up to the left on the tributary from New Pool Hollow, and just beyond this point is the line of an old mill race (d); this would have fed the mill pool from the main stream. **The surfaced road ends at the upper car park (e) which was also once a pool;** initially it was a mill pool but later was used as a swimming pool. **From the car park, an old track can be taken which winds back and forth across the brook, or the stream can be crossed by a bridge and followed keeping to the left-hand side. Both routes join just before the turn to Lightspout Hollow and continue as a single wide route that ascends to the top of the valley.** The route is known as Motts Road because a Dr Mott, who lived and worked in Stretton in the last century, apparently helped to fund improvements to it; this was to enable him to get to patients further afield. **The route joins a track just short of the Portway; this is As 4. Continue for a few more yards to reach the Portway at T.** Motts Road, on older maps, is shown as continuing over the hill to Wildmoor, thereby linking with ways to Ratlinghope. Today however, after Motts road has crossed the Portway, it soon dwindles to a small path which can be followed over Wildmoor while aiming for Wildmoor Pool, but because the last part around the pool is vague this route is difficult to pick up in reverse.

CHURCH STRETTON 7 (IN REVERSE), PORTWAY TO CARDINGMILL VALLEY

At point T on the Portway take the track (As 4) that bears off to the right, if coming from the south. Almost immediately, turn off this to the right along a wide path, which is signed as Motts Road. Follow this route down the right-hand side of the stream as far as Lightspout Hollow. From here a path continues along the right-hand side of the stream, crossing it by a bridge at the upper car park. A track also runs from Lightspout Hollow, along the valley floor, to the car park (e).

CHURCH STRETTON 8, Cs 7 TO THE PORTWAY 1.25 Km/0.75 m.

This path starts at point A, which is close to where the track and path from the upper car park in Carding Mill Valley meet, and follows a tributary of the main stream. Paths on either side of this tributary soon unite to run up the hollow on the right-hand side of the stream. It is an attractive little valley with a very well-used path which leads to the Lightspout (a small waterfall). It is possible to continue by climbing rocks on the right of the fall and the path then follows the right-hand side of the stream. The hill to the right is Calf Ridge, that to the left Cow Ridge, names persisting from the days when cattle were allowed on the hill. **The Portway between R and S is reached by keeping to the right-hand side of the main stream but either of two tributaries to the left can be followed to reach the Burway.**

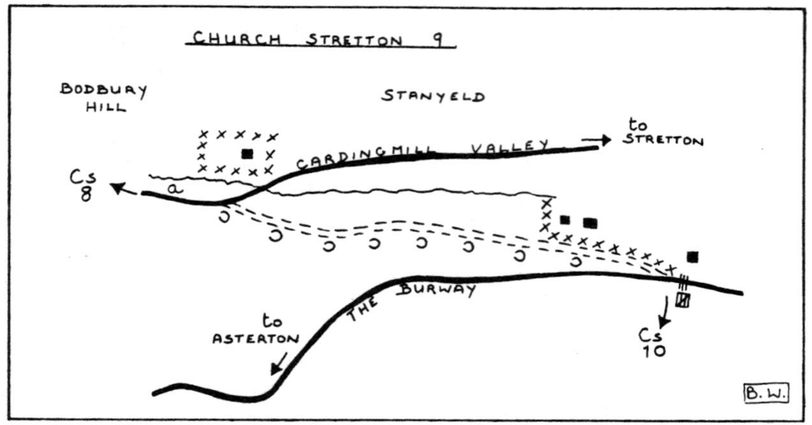

Cs 9 is a bridleway and old track which ascends gently from the car park (a) in Cardingmill Valley to the Burway near the cattle-grid. This may be an older route than the present road in and out of the valley.

Name meaning **The Burway**

The Burway must derive its name from being the way (and it is an old way slightly modified) passing close to, or in view of, the burh or fort on the top of Bodbury Hill opposite.

Stanyeld

This is the name given to the slope opposite Cs 9 and means stony slope. The south-facing slopes in the valleys are rocky and stony with shallow soil. Bracken, which favours deeper soil, is less prevalent on these stony slopes, while gorse is often present.

Haddon Hill

Haddon may derive from two old English words, 'dun' meaning hill and 'haeth' meaning heath or heather.

Friend or Foe **Bracken**

Bracken is regarded as a nuisance and is becoming more widespread on the Long Mynd. It has long been regarded as poisonous to livestock although this is thought to be when the fronds are mature and possibly only when they are bearing spores (not an annual event). Sheep may develop blindness while cattle can get suppression of the bone marrow leading to bleeding into the gut and death. Horses fare a little better but can get a vitamin deficiency if enough is eaten. Animals can live alongside poisonous plants and will normally avoid eating them, but they may do so when food is scarce. Prehistoric man ate both the rhizomes and the croziers (young shoots). There are several caterpillars too that depend on bracken for their diet.

Some areas are densely covered by bracken, which leaves little vegetation for the sheep and ponies but supplies shelter for many creatures. Young tree seedlings also sometimes benefit, as it protects them from grazing animals; this is a feature of some of the enclosed dingle slopes where grazing is not as intense as on the open hill. In the past, the presence of larger numbers of ponies played a part in controlling the bracken by their trampling. Bracken was also cut and gathered, even baled, for use as bedding, a custom that, strangely, was discouraged for some time. Repeated cutting is one way to control it and areas where the gradient is not steep, such as High Park, lend themselves to this method. The steeper slopes pose a much greater problem. Trees are a long-term solution since bracken ultimately disappears beneath their shade. Spraying, ploughing and reseeding is a method of control used on private land but with this practice many other species of plants are lost.

Focus on birds

Ravens

Ravens are sometimes to be seen in the Long Mynd area, particularly from the valley paths, as they fly across the higher slopes or soar in search of food. They are black, considerably larger than rooks or crows, and have a distinctive diamond-shaped tail and a hoarse croak. A stuffed specimen can be seen in Rowley's House Museum in Shrewsbury, which gives an idea of their size.

The raven's history in Shropshire is closely connected with the Long Mynd, Ashes Valley being its last nesting site in Shropshire in the 19th century after relentless persecution. One reason for their persecution may have been that they were regarded as birds of ill-omen, and associated with death. Another may have been that part of their diet includes eggs and birds, and gamekeepers appear as culprits in many accounts. In 1918, when the raven's revival began, its first nesting site was again in Ashes Valley. Revival was sporadic for many years and a small boy in the 1940s remembers the Ashes Hollow nesting site (a cliff face) being pointed out to him as a past event. The same person remembers finding a raven's nest in a pine tree in Callow Hollow in the 1950s and today they are breeding in the Long Mynd area using only tree sites. Breeding in Shropshire is not widespread and is mainly in the south-west. Elsewhere, ravens breed in Wales, the south-west of England and in parts of Scotland, Ireland and Northern England.

Another possible documentary witness to the raven's presence in Ashes Valley is the tithe map of 1840, where several fields above Little Stretton on the lower slopes of Nills are called Raven Doors (see fig.11). Some of these fields abut on to the open hill at the 'doorway' into the valley, and the old nesting site mentioned above is thought to have been near to this point. The field area is called Raven Doors to this day.

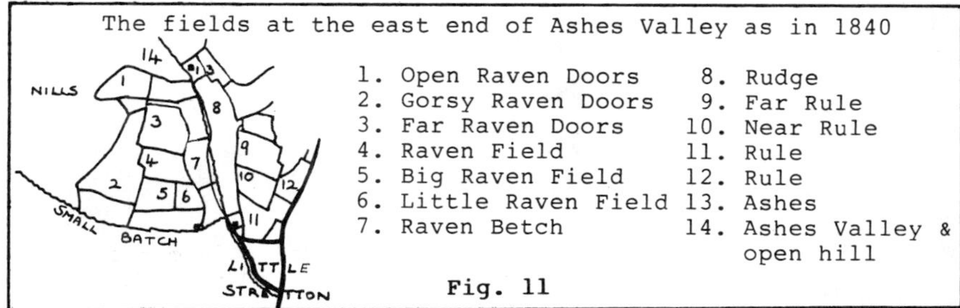

Fig. 11

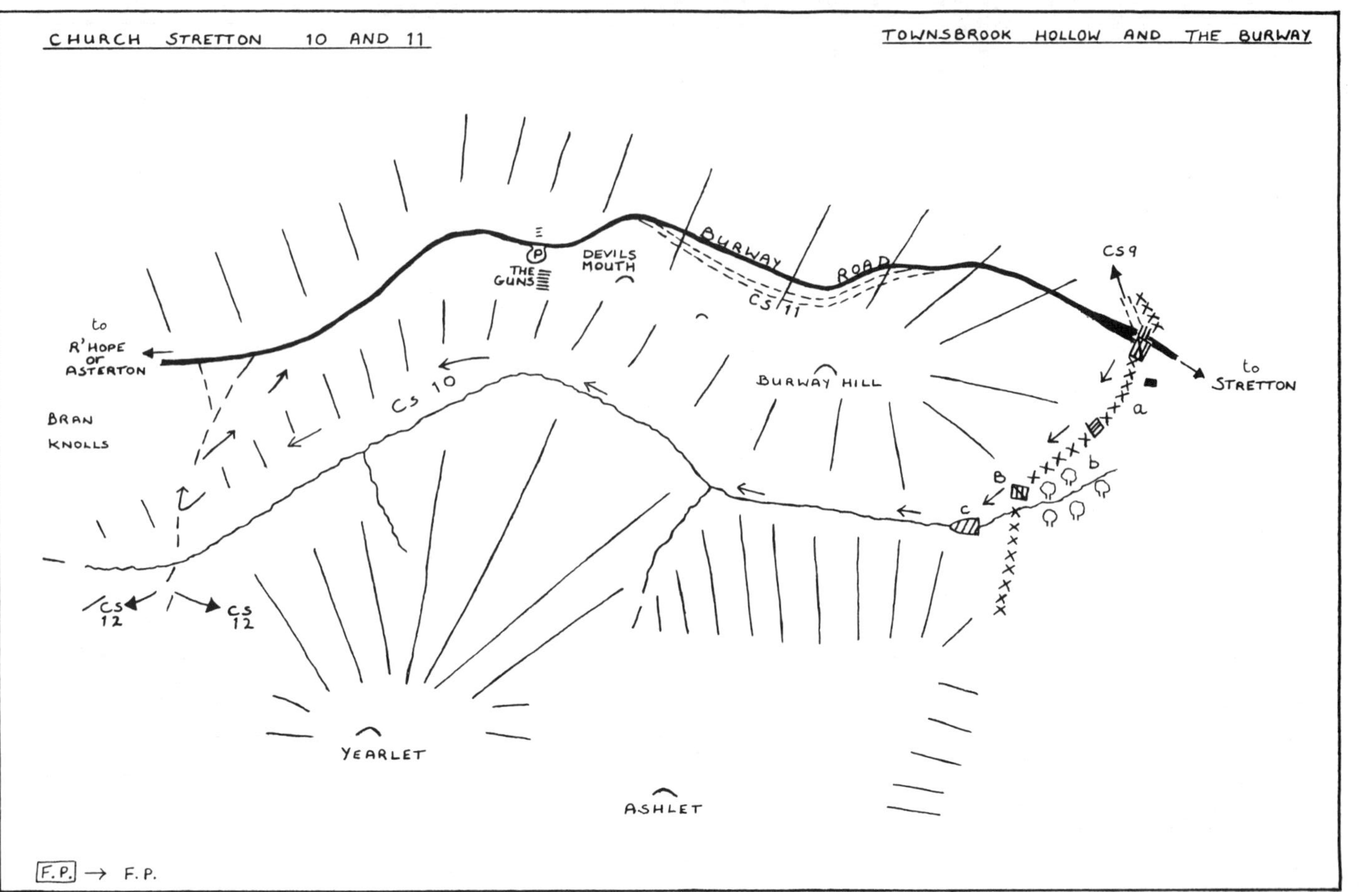
CHURCH STRETTON 10 AND 11
TOWNSBROOK HOLLOW AND THE BURWAY
CS 9
to STRETTON
BURWAY ROAD
CS 11
THE GUNS
P
DEVILS MOUTH
to R'HOPE or ASTERTON
CS 10
BURWAY HILL
a
b
B
c
BRAN KNOLLS
CS 12
CS 12
YEARLET
ASHLET
F.P. → F.P.

CHURCH STRETTON 10, TOWNSBROOK HOLLOW 2 Km/1¼ m.

Cs 10 is another very well-used path that has undergone some work to combat erosion. It passes the old Church Stretton reservoir which lies along the brook. The brook continues from the open hill through Rectory Wood and ran as an open stream through Stretton (along Brook Street, now Burway Road, and Lake Lane, now Sandford Avenue) until some time in the second half of the last century. **This route starts close to the cattle-grid on the Burway Road opposite Cs 9. Turn left after the grid if you are ascending from Stretton and follow the fence around the end of the Burway Hill. Scotchman's Piece (a), on the left, was a field where travelling pedlars, referred to as Scotchmen, gathered; today it is a field and a large house called Scotsman's Field. Rectory Wood (b) lies beyond the field along our route, which soon bears right to go upstream passing the small reservoir (c). On the left are first Ashlet (hill) and then Yearlet. On the right, opposite Yearlet, the hilltop is rocky with many loose stones on the slope below. The path ascends and runs across the slope well above the brook; the brook has a steep beginning, thus creating a valley with a distinct head. Near the head of the valley, a path can be taken to the left which runs around the head to join Cs 12. Alternatively, a path can be taken to the right; this branches and has about three exits onto the Burway road. By taking the right–hand branch the Burway near The Guns is reached.** The Guns is an old embankment, thought to have been used either for defensive purposes or as part of an animal enclosure, and is probably of the same era as Soldiers Row above Little Stretton (on Cs 17) and the embankment at High Park (on As 2 and 4). It was put into use again in the second half of the last century as a place for the Artillery Volunteers to practise; the cannon had to be towed up the Burway by teams of labouring cart horses. A policeman on his bike had to make a very hurried ascent of the Burway one day, having already ridden at full speed from Minton, which was accidentally being shelled.

Today, some of The Guns has been lost to road and car park. Devils Mouth, nearby, may apply to the last cutting the Burway makes before its steep descent begins.

CHURCH STRETTON 11, AN ALTERNATIVE DESCENT TO THE BURWAY

Cs 11 is a grassy track running close to the Burway which represents the older route down this hillside. It has been described as an engineered packhorse trail, and was probably a continuation of the track from Medlicott (Wn 7).

Focus on the Long Mynd ponies

The area around Townsbrook Hollow is one of the places to see ponies. There used to be many more on the Mynd as they were an essential means of transport in the past. Many too were sold to work in mines, and pony fairs were at one time held twice a year. Life for these ponies could be hard; Rev. Carr describes how many had perished in the severe weather of the winter of 1864/5 following the dry season and lack of pasture of 1864. Life was not too good for the ponies that ended up working in the mines; they apparently had to be geldings over four years of age. Winter for them was spent underground where they were warm and well–cared for, but it must have been a pathetic sight to see them blinded by the daylight when they eventually surfaced in the summer. The increased amount of bracken on the hill is attributed to less trampling by far fewer ponies.

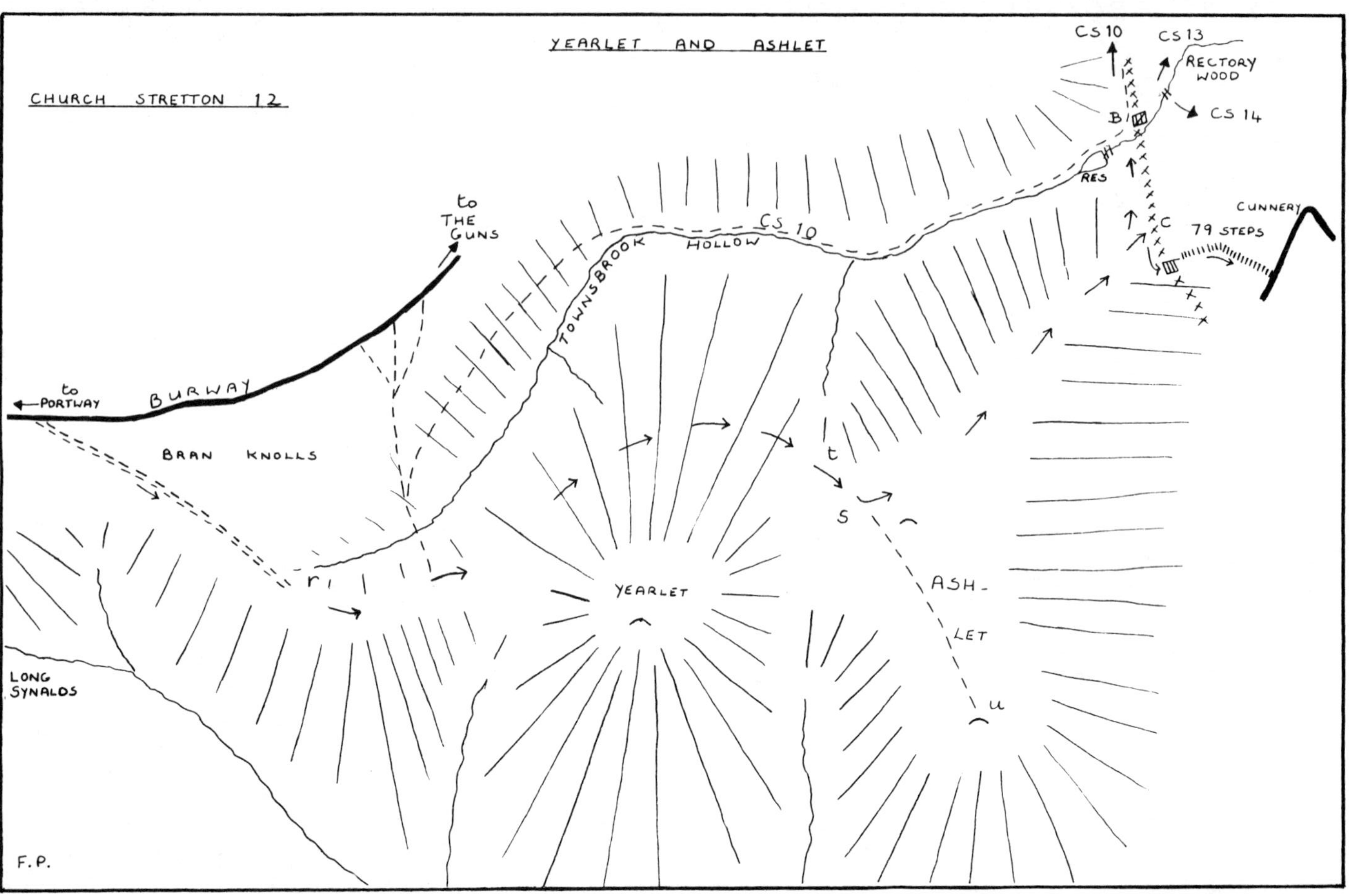
YEARLET AND ASHLET
CHURCH STRETTON 12
CS 10
CS 13
RECTORY WOOD
CS 14
B
RES
C
CUNNERY
79 STEPS
to THE GUNS
CS 10
HOLLOW
TOWNSBROOK
to PORTWAY
BURWAY
BRAN KNOLLS
t
s
ASH-
LET
u
r
YEARLET
LONG SYNALDS
F.P.

CHURCH STRETTON 12, BURWAY TO CUNNERY 2 Km/1¼ m.

Cs 12 starts on the hill plateau between the Guns and the Y junction where the road divides to Ratlinghope or Asterton. Initially the route is a track which descends gradually to the right side of the head of Townsbrook Hollow (r). There are views to the right, of the hills flanking Ashes Valley. The route continues as a path and is joined by a branch from Cs 10. It then runs along the side of Yearlet and looks down into Townsbrook Hollow on the left. The path curves round onto a plateau (s) which is part of Ashlet, on the east side of Yearlet. Hill ponies are often seen here and the name Yearlet may mean that this was once a place used to put yearlings. The area is predominantly bilberry-covered, the small bushes close-cropped and divided by tiny sheep tracks to look like a mosaic. Areas of bilberry mosaics are best seen on the eastern side of these hills. **The path, now quite wide, continues along the plateau to the edge of the hill above Ashes Valley (u) and commands a wonderful view to the south. Our route, however, turns off to the left well before this as a much smaller path, following the contour of a small hollow on the left (t) that descends into Townsbrook Hollow. Cross the higher ground of Ashlet before descending steeply to join an old grassy track. This in turn becomes two paths descending to the fence at C between open hill and enclosures. The fence can be followed to the left to reach Cs 10 by the reservoir, and Rectory Wood. Alternatively, turn right along the fence for a short distance and then turn left down the 79 steps to the area known as Cunnery and on to Stretton by road.**

Focus on plants **Bilberry**

One of the characteristic plants of the Long Mynd is the bilberry, also known as whinberry or wimberry. Picking the fruit has long been a custom for people living around the hill, particularly as a way for poor families to make a little extra money. Wimberry picking sounds an attractive pastime, out in the fresh air on the hill with a picnic and the hum of conversation, but fruit picking all day and several days in a row, with a long walk (e.g. Pulverbatch to Duckley Nap) at each end of the day, was in reality very tedious and tiring. A comb was often used to gather the fruit which was sold to be used in cooking, though much also ended up going by train to be used for dye. Today, wimberry picking is no longer such a feature of the Mynd because there are less bushes through heavier grazing. Sheep also enjoy wimberries and usually get there first. Anyone wishing for wimberry pie will fare better on the Stiperstones.

The history of the bilberry is not just concerned with fruit picking but also involves moths, a number of which feed on it in their larval stage, including the Small Lappet moth. The Long Mynd was one of only a few known localities in Britain for this moth but it has not been recorded from here since 1889 and from Britain since 1965. As it is apparently easily overlooked perhaps experts should keep looking here.

Focus on birds **Chats**

Both stonechat and whinchat can be seen on the Mynd. The whinchat, a summer visitor, is the commoner. Both species, but particularly the whinchat, like the thick bracken that the Long Mynd boasts, for perches and as a cover for their nests which are on or near the ground; gorse too is suitable, hence the lending of its alternative name of whin to the whinchat.

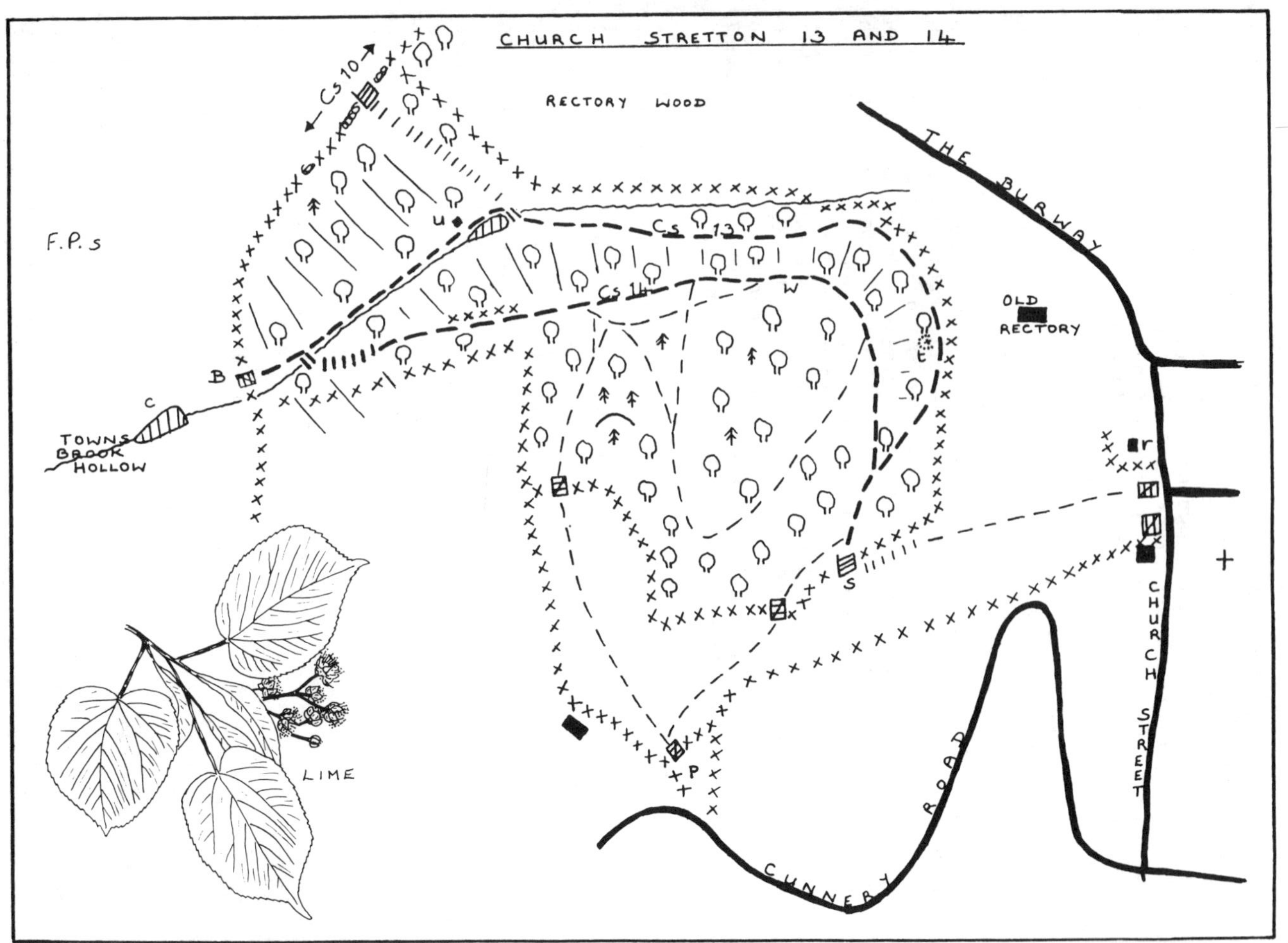
CHURCH STRETTON 13 AND 14
RECTORY WOOD
Cs 10
Cs 13
Cs 14
THE BURWAY
OLD RECTORY
F.P.s
B
C
U
W
S
P
TOWNS BROOK HOLLOW
CHURCH STREET
CUNNERY ROAD
LIME

RECTORY WOOD

This area of mixed woodland was once part of the Rectory's grounds and was acquired by the County Council in 1959. The wood was opened to the public in 1967 when access was from the hill end only. In 1982, the field giving access to the wood from Stretton was also purchased and there are two ways to reach the wood via this field. One way starts at the Scout Hut near the church and crosses the part of the field that was once the Rectory lawn. The other way starts off Cunnery road near the Long Mynd Hotel and there is a small parking area here; this route crosses the part of the field that was known as Near Cunnery. Cunnery is an old term for a rabbit warren, since rabbits were once called conies and only their young were called rabbits.

Rectory Wood was a plantation on the tithe map of 1840 but a painting of 1831 shows that much of it had not then been planted. A wide variety of trees, both evergreen and deciduous, grow here along with a mixture of native woodland plants and 'garden' plants, particularly daffodils. A few true wild daffodils also are present but these are likely to have been introduced. The evergreen trees include almost every native British species - Scots pine, yew, ivy and holly, and the deciduous trees include some fine specimens of beech, sweet chestnut and lime. The biggest tree in the wood is a sweet chestnut at (t), which is at least three hundred years old.

CHURCH STRETTON 13, SCOUT HUT TO TOWNSBROOK HOLLOW 0.75 Km/½ m.

Cross the field from the Scout Hut (r) to reach a stile into the wood at (s). Follow the path to the right which runs near the lower edge of the wood. At (t), signs of an old ice house (a grotto is another suggestion) can be seen in the undergrowth; it is a semi-circular stone wall set into the bank with a sweet chestnut growing at each end (the right-hand one is the very old tree mentioned above). Ice for it may have come from the small pool further along the path. **Continue along the path to the Towns Brook which is then followed upstream to the small pool just mentioned. Cross the outlet of the pool. At this point, there is a branch to the right which ascends via steps to Cs 10 near the Burway. Our route continues along the right-hand side of the stream, passing a small old building (u);** this was used in connection with the water supply from the reservoir upstream, but it had existed before and may have been the home of a hermit (the grotto being suggested as an alternative site). **The path leaves the wood via a gate onto open hill at point B on Cs 10 near the old Stretton reservoir.**

CHURCH STRETTON 14, TOWNSBROOK HOLLOW TO THE SCOUT HUT 0.75 Km/½m.

This route runs between the same points as Cs 13 but does not follow the brook. Enter the Rectory Wood from the hill at point B on Cs 10. A short distance down the stream, cross it via a stone slab which is actually a gravestone with traces of lettering on it. I can find no history attached to this stone; perhaps it was intended as a bridge from the beginning, in memory of someone who had associations with the wood, or alternatively it may have come from a grave in the wood somewhere. Today the lettering is too worn away to read. **Ascend some steps and cross the side of a steep slope through beechwood. Several small paths branch off to the right while our route continues, passing a seat and then curving round to the right. It descends and joins Cs 13 near a large lime tree. After a short distance, a stile (s) leads into a field. Turn left, cross the field to the Scout Hut (r) and exit on to Church Street.**

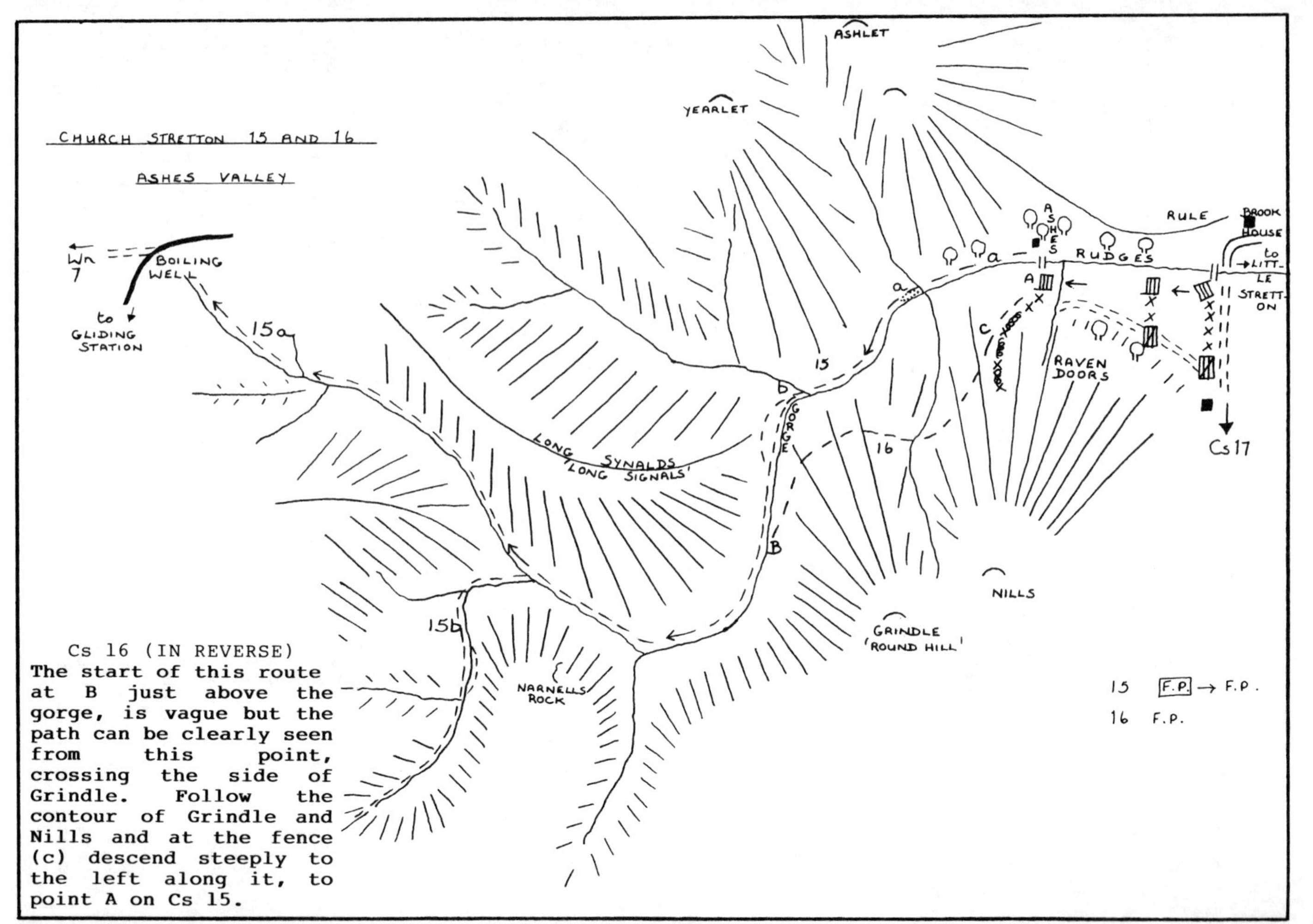

Cs 16 (IN REVERSE)

The start of this route at B just above the gorge, is vague but the path can be clearly seen from this point, crossing the side of Grindle. Follow the contour of Grindle and Nills and at the fence (c) descend steeply to the left along it, to point A on Cs 15.

CHURCH STRETTON 15, LITTLE STRETTON TO THE BOILING WELL 3.5 Km/2+m.

Cs 15 starts just beyond Brook House, where surfaced road ends. Cross the brook via ford or footbridge. The path runs through fields along the flat valley floor and over three stiles, before open hill is reached at A. On the right, running in the same direction as the valley, is a low hill known as the Rule and the Rudges. **At A, cross the brook by footbridge to an empty cottage,** behind which is a wood that was called Ashes; this may have given the valley its name. On an old map of some of the Mynd manors (1828), Ashes Valley was Long Batch Gutter.

A summary:- Follow the right- hand side of the brook from the cottage all the way to the Boiling Well, and although several little paths branch off, particularly alongside tributaries, Cs 15 is the clearest and most well-trodden path. It can prove difficult in parts where short sections cross steep rocks.

A more detailed guide:- The first section, running below Ashlet, has several trees on its slopes. At (a), close to the brook, are some embankments that formed a small swimming pool. **The next section, running below Yearlet, passes through a narrow valley with steep sides** covered with bracken, bilberry and heather and some old trees, mainly hawthorns. Monkey flower grows in the brook, and the bright green rosette leaves of the insectivorous butterwort are conspicuous for much of the year on the steep, wet banks. Rock stonecrop, the cover flower for the Shropshire Flora, has been found here too; it has a very limited distribution in the county. **At (b), the path meets the end of Long Synalds** (locally known as Long Signals). **There is a path up the tributary on the right but the main route crosses the tributary and divides into two for a short distance; a low path follows the brook more closely. The brook runs through a small gorge overhung by willows, holly and birch.** The path, as is the case in most of the valley routes, crosses many patches of bare rock of differing hues. In this area, and elsewhere across the Mynd, the rocks are purple and are termed Synaldian rocks. **Upstream of the gorge, Cs 16 joins Cs 15 and the valley widens out a little. Narnells Rock stands out near the top of a slope as our route becomes steeper and often crosses boggy areas. (15b branches off to follow the next tributary). As the Boiling Well is approached, the path is less steep again and follows a rushy hollow on the left up to the road.** The Boiling Well is so called because it bubbles if you stamp on its margins.

CHURCH STRETTON 15 (IN REVERSE), BOILING WELL TO LITTLE STRETTON

Take the clear path opposite the track from Medlicott, off the Burway to gliding station road, and follow the rushy hollow which becomes a brook, all the way down to Little Stretton. Keep to the left-hand side of the brook. The descent is steepest in the early part of the walk and the path crosses short sections of quite steep rocks, particularly below Yearlet. At a cottage, cross the bridge and follow the right-hand side of the brook through fields and over three stiles to get to surfaced road into Little Stretton.

CHURCH STRETTON 16, ASHES TO LONG SYNALDS 1.25 Km/0.75 m.

Cs 16 starts at A and climbs up along the fence to (c). At (c), an old footpath is joined that ran from Little Stretton up through the fields known as Raven Doors. **Our route continues along this old path following the contours of the hills, and gradually descends to join Cs 15 upstream of the gorge by Long Synalds.**

N.B. On Grindle, this path is narrow and crosses a steep slope.

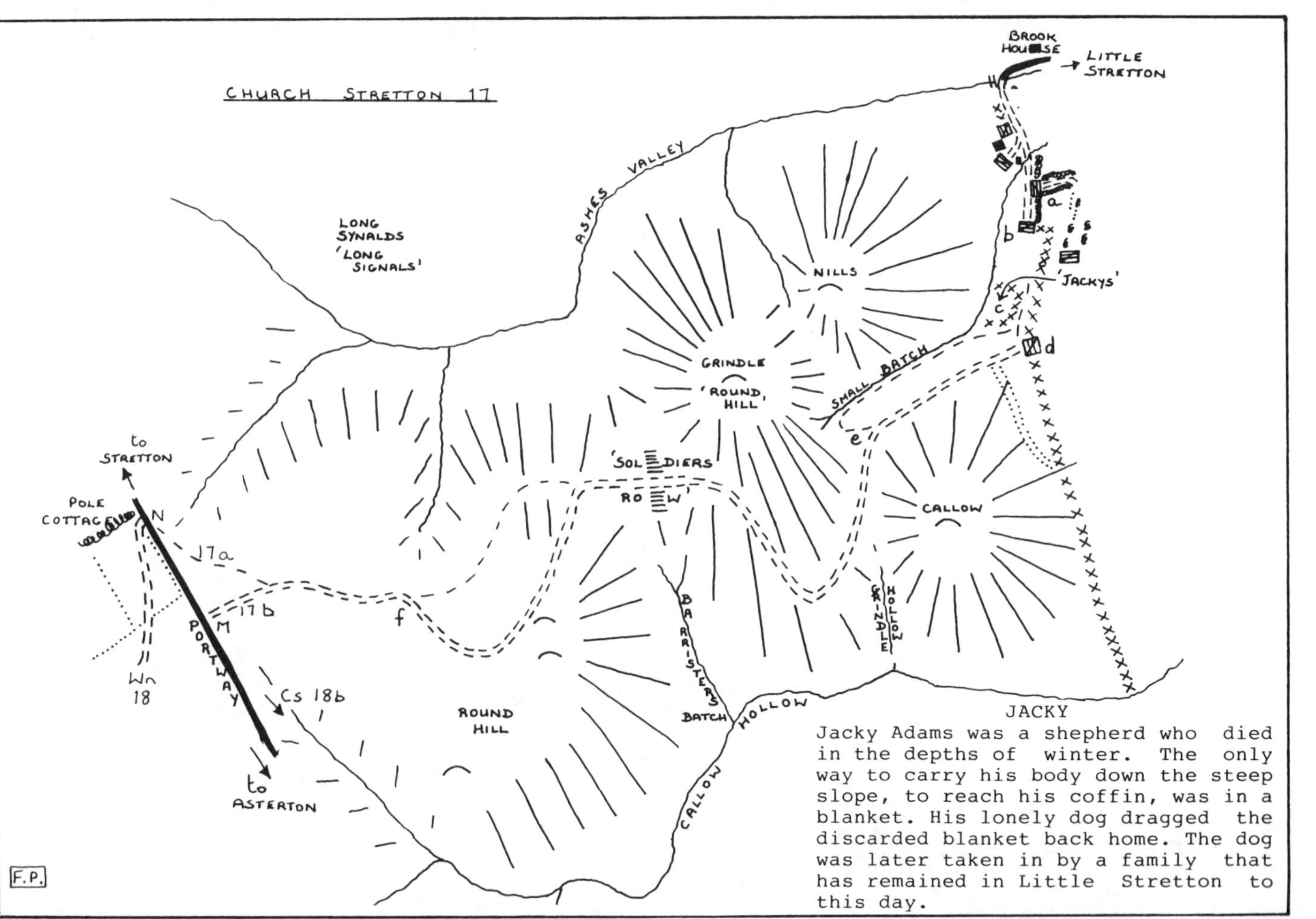

JACKY

Jacky Adams was a shepherd who died in the depths of winter. The only way to carry his body down the steep slope, to reach his coffin, was in a blanket. His lonely dog dragged the discarded blanket back home. The dog was later taken in by a family that has remained in Little Stretton to this day.

CHURCH STRETTON 17, LITTLE STRETTON TO POLE COTTAGE 3.25 Km/2 m.

Cs 17 is a public footpath and begins at the ford near Brook House. After crossing the brook, follow the track past a house on the right. Immediately after this house, keep to the left hand track which runs in the stream bed for a short distance. At (a), an old track is visible, turning off to the left, and higher up the slope it curves round and runs up the ridge; this is the old way that Cs 17 began and ended. **Today, Cs 17 continues through a gate (b) onto open hill and ascends a steep slope. In the valley on the right, known as Small Batch, was the site of Little Stretton's reservoir, marked only by Scots pines today. Upstream of the pine trees is an enclosed area (c)** that was an encroachment and a dwelling on the tithe map. A past inhabitant, but not the last, was Jacky who died at the turn of this century. This area has since been known as Jacky's or Jacky's Hollow. **By this enclosure, a path branches off and follows the brook up the batch; it rejoins our route at (e). Cs 17 ascends a little further to join a grassy track at (d), which runs to the Portway.** This track was continuous with the track at (a), and was an old route for travelling over the hill. By the time that cannon were being hauled up to Barristers Plain along this route (see below), the way past Jacky's was in use. **Continue from (d) and ascend gradually along the north side of the Callow above Small Batch. Cs 17 is joined at (e) by the path that ran up the side of the brook from Jacky's. The track then curves around the south side of Grindle (known locally as Round Hill) and looks down into Callow Hollow.** Grindle had a tumulus on its summit and has two more above Cs 17; these may have acted as signposts along an ancient route (see Background). After skirting Grindle, the track comes to a narrow flat area called Barristers Plain. The cross dyke here is thought to have been for defensive purposes but may have been part of an animal enclosure. Locally it is known as Soldiers Row; in the last century soldiers practised artillery fire here across the valleys, the dyke serving as a brake for the cannon. Shells were often found and kept as trophies until many were taken away from people in World War II for recycling. **The track (this part is in use today for tending livestock) runs over the summit of the true Round Hill (the Round Hill shown on the map) while a path runs along the north side of the hill with views down into Ashes Valley. Track and path reunite at (f) and pass another tumulus before reaching the Portway near Pole Cottage, either by continuing straight on or by branching to the right.**

CHURCH STRETTON 17 (IN REVERSE), POLE COTTAGE TO LITTLE STRETTON

A track leaves the Asterton road, just south of the Pole Cottage enclosure, and descends gently to point (f). At (f), the track continues over the top of Round Hill while a path branches to the left and skirts the northern slope of Round Hill; track and path rejoin at Barristers Plain, a small plateau crossed by an embankment known locally as Soldiers Row. The route continues as an old track which bears to the right round the south slope of Grindle (N.B. this is also known as Round Hill) overlooking Callow Hollow on the right. The track then curves to the left to follow the north slope of Callow Hill and looks down into Small Batch. At (e), continue along the track or turn down sharply and follow the brook in the batch. Both routes meet again at (c) by Jacky's and descend steeply in a tongue of open hill to a gate (b). Track leads from this gate down to Brook House and Little Stretton.

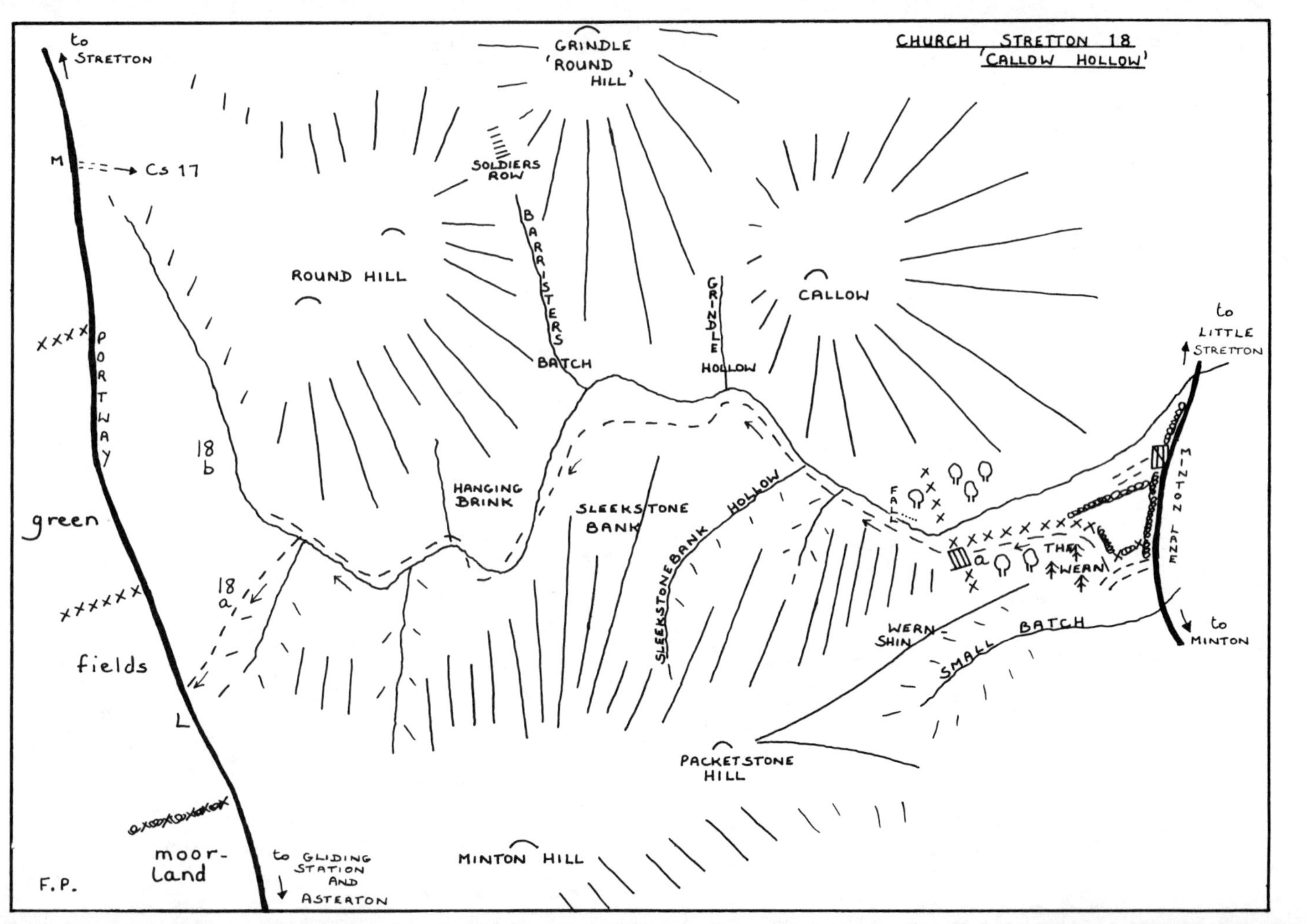
CHURCH STRETTON 18
'CALLOW HOLLOW'
to STRETTON
GRINDLE 'ROUND HILL'
M
Cs 17
SOLDIERS ROW
ROUND HILL
BARRISTERS BATCH
GRINDLE HOLLOW
CALLOW
to LITTLE STRETTON
PORTWAY
18 b
HANGING BRINK
SLEEKSTONE BANK
SLEEKSTONE BANK HOLLOW
FALL
THE WERN
a
MINTON LANE
green
18 a
WERN-SHIN
SMALL BATCH
to MINTON
fields
L
PACKETSTONE HILL
moor-land
to GLIDING STATION AND ASTERTON
MINTON HILL
F.P.

CHURCH STRETTON 18, MINTON LANE TO THE PORTWAY 3 Km/1.75+ m.

Cs 18 is not a designated public right of way but is recognized as a footpath by the National Trust; the first section, Minton lane to (a), runs through an area of woodland (The Wern) which has only recently been acquired by the National Trust. The path on the open hill can be difficult in places, and along Sleekstone Bank runs as a narrow path across a steep slope quite high above the brook. Callow Hollow is probably the most attractive valley on the Mynd, with its steep sides well-endowed with old hawthorn trees that attract birds for their shelter and fruit. The fruit may persist on the trees well into the winter and attracts many redwings and fieldfares, birds that only visit us in winter.

Minton Lane is the lane between Little Stretton and Minton; Cs 18 starts where the road begins to ascend to Minton, by turning through an open gateway into forest. Almost immediately, a signpost guides you to the right and the path follows the fence along the edge of the wood to a stile (a) onto open hill. The path now follows the brook along the left—hand side and very soon reaches a waterfall called Oakleymill waterfall. Downstream on the other (north) side is the line of the old mill race which disappears where the slope becomes steep and eroded. Downstream of the fence the fields were called Hockleymill Ground but the exact site of the mill is unknown. **The path continues along the left side of the brook under the Callow; it can be difficult in places where rocks are crossed. Across Sleekstone Bank the path runs well above the brook. It then descends again to the brook and follows it upstream, passing under Hanging Brink; the path is vague in this area. Near the top of the valley, follow either tributary; the left hand one is a shorter and easier way that joins the Portway at L nearly opposite the Wentnor boundary which equates with the green field/moorland boundary. The right-hand tributary and path join the Portway at M near the end of Cs 17. The upper reaches of any of these streams become boggy hollows and walking beside them can be wet.**

CHURCH STRETTON 18 (IN REVERSE), PORTWAY TO MINTON LANE

Follow the boggy hollow nearly opposite the fence between green fields and moorland at the gliding station end. The bog becomes a stream and soon joins another stream which Cs 18 follows down the valley, passing below Hanging Brink. Lower down the valley the path runs across Sleekstone Bank on the right of the brook and well above it. The path descends again to follow the brook more closely under the Callow and soon reaches Oakleymill waterfall. A little way downstream from the fall, a fence marks the end of the open hill; bear to the right to find the stile at (a). Follow the lower edge of the wood along the fence and emerge from a small coniferous plantation onto Minton Lane.

Focus on birds **Ring ouzel**

This summer visitor to the Long Mynd is of very limited distribution in Shropshire and the upper parts of some of the Stretton valleys are almost the only areas in the county where you may see one, singing on a far-off perch. They resemble blackbirds, to which they are closely related, but have a prominent white half-collar on the upper breast. One important reason for staying on footpaths rather than wandering at will is to preserve this special and very shy bird in its habitat.

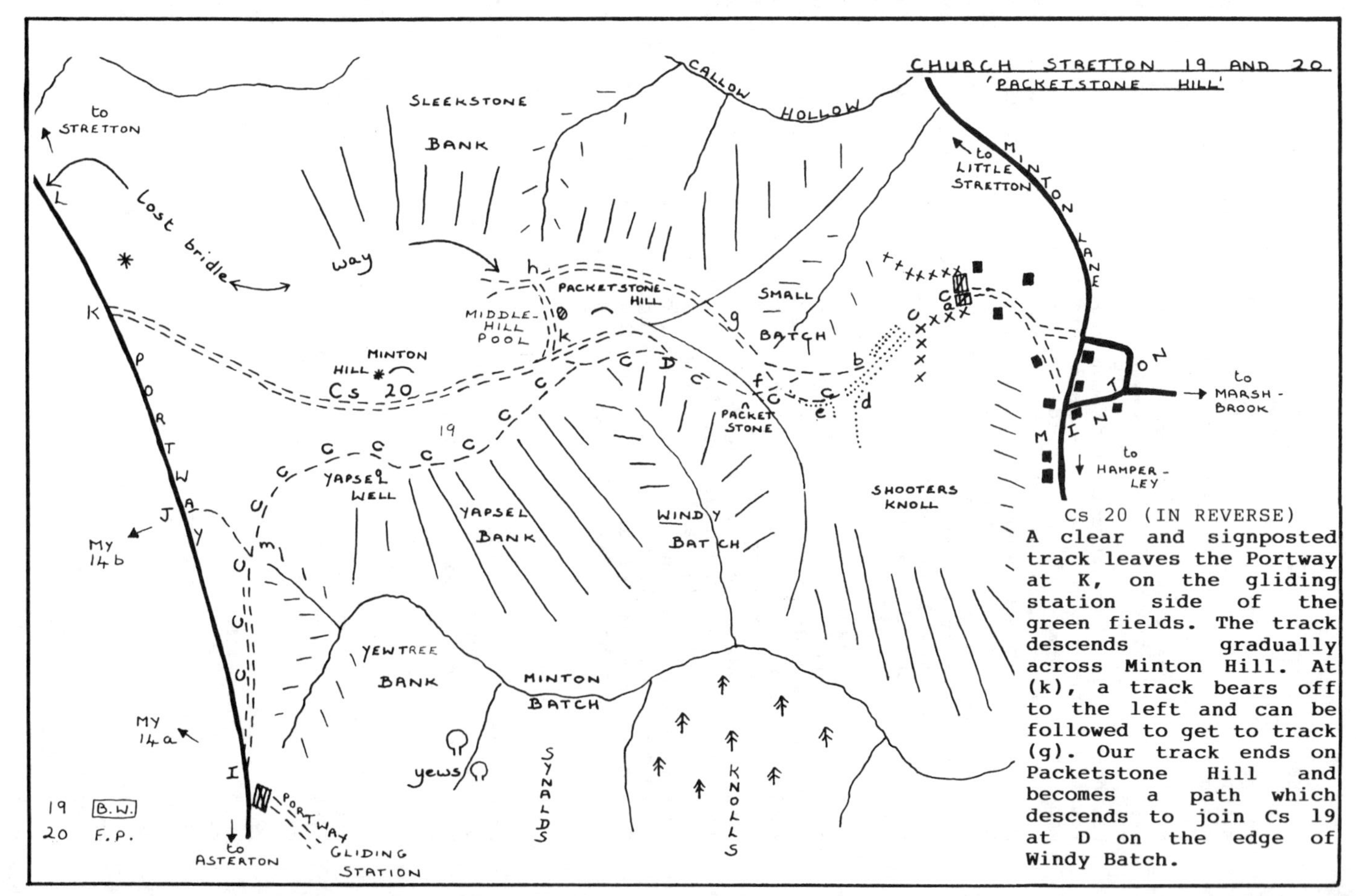

Cs 20 (IN REVERSE)

A clear and signposted track leaves the Portway at K, on the gliding station side of the green fields. The track descends gradually across Minton Hill. At (k), a track bears off to the left and can be followed to get to track (g). Our track ends on Packetstone Hill and becomes a path which descends to join Cs 19 at D on the edge of Windy Batch.

CHURCH STRETTON 19, MINTON TO THE PORTWAY at I OR J 2.5 Km/1½ m

Cs 19 is a bridleway and is thought to be an old packhorse trail. The route starts as a track from Minton village green to the open hill, passing between Long Mynd (Cruck) House and Yew Tree Cottage. Pass through the gate at (a) into a downward projection of the open hill, known as the Outrack. At the top of the Outrack, there are signs of two old tracks ascending steeply, the left-hand one being the more pronounced and continuing further. A clear path bears off to the right at (b); either this or the old track can be followed to get to point (f). The left-hand side of the old track develops into a small embankment which turns off at (d) and runs across to Shooters Knoll to the left; this probably marks an old enclosure. The track is joined by another small embankment at (e) with which it runs before crossing it; the embankment then peters out. Soon after this point, take a path to the left, passing to the left of an area of springs (f).

N.B. If you use the path from (b), turn left just before the head of Small Batch to join the paths passing to the left of (f). An alternative route is to follow the clear track (g) which is marked on the map as a bridleway passing through point (h) to reach the Portway, but the bridleway from (h) is lost. Instead, take an old track from (h) that runs across to Cs 20 passing Middlehill Pool.

From (f), ascend to the Packet Stone on the edge of an appropriately named Windy Batch. There are two stories attached to this stone. One is that it was the place where the loads on packhorses were adjusted before or after the steep descent or ascent. The other is that this was the spot where packets were left for Asterton people when they were afflicted by the plague in the Middle Ages. Continue round the head of Windy Batch. At D, a path bears off to the right to become the track that is Cs 20 from the brow of the hill (see below). Cs 19 continues a little further round the head of the Batch before it too bears off to the right; this joins Cs 20 near point (k) but just before doing so Cs 19 turns off to the left as a small path through the heather. The path does become a little clearer as it runs along the top of the north side of Minton Batch. On Yapsel Bank, the path passes above a spring known as Yapsel Well. Yapsel may originally have been Yop's Well, Yop being the name of an Asterton family of many generations. The path becomes wider and exits near the gliding station to join the Portway at I. Alternatively a path can be taken from (m) to join the Portway at J.

CHURCH STRETTON 20, PACKETSTONE HILL TO THE PORTWAY at K 1.5 Km/1m

Cs 20 is a clear track from Packetstone Hill and runs over Minton Hill to the Portway at K. This, in combination with the first part of Cs 19, is the best route to take if you are not familiar with the hill.

CHURCH STRETTON 19 (IN REVERSE), PORTWAY at I TO MINTON

A clear and wide path leaves the Portway at I near the gliding station and runs along the top of the north side of Minton Batch. The path becomes narrow as it runs through the heather. Follow the head of Windy Batch round, passing the Packet Stone and descend towards the head of Small Batch. Take one of the paths to the right that descend along the ridge between Small Batch and Minton Batch; a tongue of open hill leads to gate (a) off the hill onto track to Minton village green.

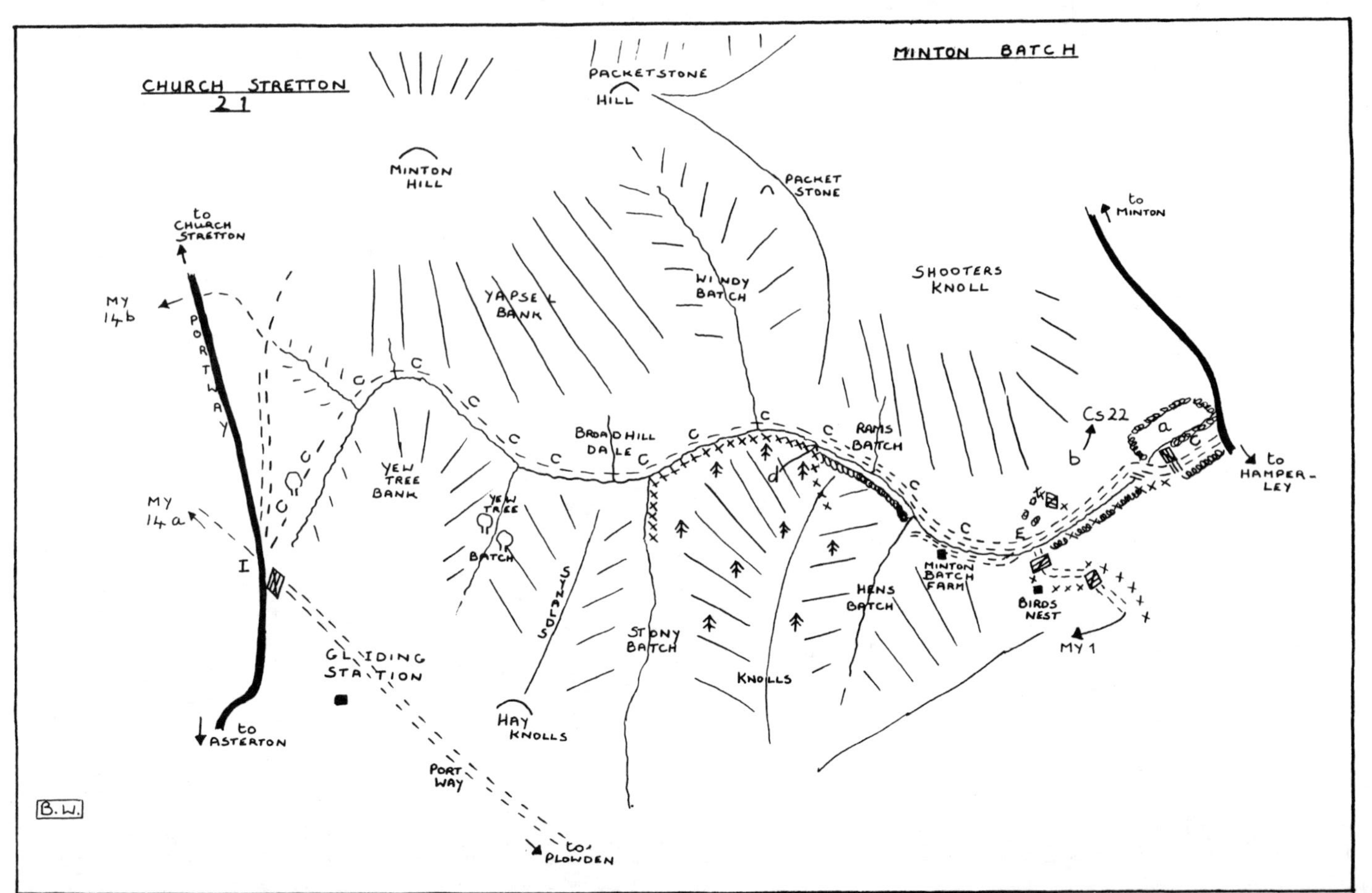
CHURCH STRETTON
21
MINTON BATCH
PACKETSTONE HILL
MINTON HILL
PACKET STONE
to MINTON
to CHURCH STRETTON
MY 14b
PORTWAY
YAPSEL BANK
WINDY BATCH
SHOOTERS KNOLL
Cs22
a
b
c
d
E
I
RAMS BATCH
BROADHILL DALE
YEW TREE BANK
YEW TREE BATCH
SYNALDS
STONY BATCH
HENS BATCH
MINTON BATCH FARM
BIRDS NEST
to HAMPERLEY
MY 1
MY 14a
KNOLLS
GLIDING STATION
HAY KNOLLS
to ASTERTON
PORT WAY
to PLOWDEN
B.W.

CHURCH STRETTON 21, MINTON BATCH TO THE PORTWAY 2.75 Km/1.75 m.

Cs 21 is a bridleway that follows the course of the brook which runs down the Minton Batch. It is track for much of its length but in parts is only a path. An old map (1831) marks this route as an occupation road, an old term for a private road and Minton Batch was called Kinseys Beach. The brook forms the boundary between the civil parishes of Church Stretton and Myndtown but in the past was the boundary between the township of Asterton in Norbury Parish and the ancient parish of Church Stretton; it has also been a district boundary.

Turn off the Minton to Hamperley road, in the hollow, and take the track to Minton Batch and Birds Nest. There used to be a holy well in this area, either by the road (local information) or in the first field (a) on the right (a hand-written insertion on an old O/S map in the library). The well was in use within living memory and was good for sore eyes. The hillside on the right is called Yells after the names of the fields at the Minton end (Yeld, Far Yeld, Little Yeld, Hole in the Yeld and Near Yeld); yeld derives from the old English word 'helde' meaning 'slope'. The fields at the Minton Batch end, on the right of the start of Cs 21, were Water Holes (b) and Oseley(a); the latter may simply mean 'a field that oozes'. **Follow the track on the left of the brook, then cross the brook by ford or footbridge and continue along the right hand side.** The brook is flanked by alders, or wollers as they are often called. **Just before the turn to Birds Nest (a house) is a small old field on the right with yew trees in its hedges; this was the site of a dwelling and is the point at which Cs 22 branches off. The track to Birds Nest is MY 1. Continue along the right-hand side of the brook, passing a spring beside the route and Minton Batch Farm on the other side of the brook. The alders along the brook and the fields on the left end at the forest which covers the slopes on the far side of the brook.** A stone (d) with the letters I.J. stands by the brook in line with the edge of the forest. **Several subsidiary batches are passed. Windy Batch sweeps up to Packetstone Hill and the Packetstone on the right. On the left, Stony Batch marks the far edge of the forest and the next batch on that side is Yew Tree Batch, flanked by two yew trees. Continue along the right-hand side of the brook under Yapsel Bank and opposite Yew Tree Bank. Soon the path starts to ascend and reaches an old rowan tree with a gliding station warning sign; the station is in close proximity to the last part of this route. The path follows the rushy hollow to exit on to the road (the Portway) at I.**

CHURCH STRETTON 21 (IN REVERSE), PORTWAY TO MINTON BATCH

Follow the left-hand side of the rushy hollow that lies near the entrance to the gliding station, on the east side of the road. Descend alongside the hollow which soon becomes brook and continue along the left-hand side of the brook. A forest is passed on the right and, downstream from this, Minton Batch Farm. The turn to Birds Nest is MY 1 and just after this point Cs 22 branches off to the left onto enclosed hillside. Cs 21 continues as a clear track, crossing the brook via ford or footbridge and soon joining the Minton to Hamperley lane.

Focus on bog plants **Bog Pimpernel**

This is one of the most attractive plants to be found in many of the Mynd bogs and is found in few other places in Shropshire.It creeps along the ground and has conspicuous pale pink flowers.

CHURCH STRETTON 22, MINTON TO MINTON BATCH 0.5 Km/¼+ m.

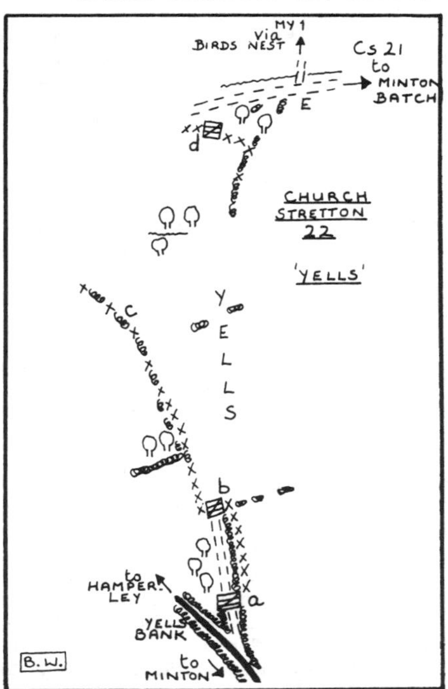

Cs 22 is a bridleway and a short cut between Minton and Minton Batch e.g.for schoolchildren who used to go to Acton Scott school. **The way starts off the Minton to Hamperley lane. Take the track to the right as the road starts to descend Yells Bank, passing through a gate (a). Continue alongside the hedge above alder carr. Enter a large sloping field, known as 'Yells', via gate (b). Follow a hedge until it turns sharply away at (c) to the left. Bear obliquely right following the contour of the hill across boggy land. Exit through gate (d) on to Cs 21 by a small old enclosure.**

CHURCH STRETTON 22 (IN REVERSE)

Leave Cs 21 by yew trees , passing through a gate into a sloping field. Follow the contour of the slope round to join a hedge at (c). Continue along this hedge, leaving the field through gate (b). The last part is trackway, alongside alder carr, which exits on to the lane via gate (a).

CHURCH STRETTON 25, MARSHBROOK TOWARDS MINTON 0.5 Km/¼+ m.

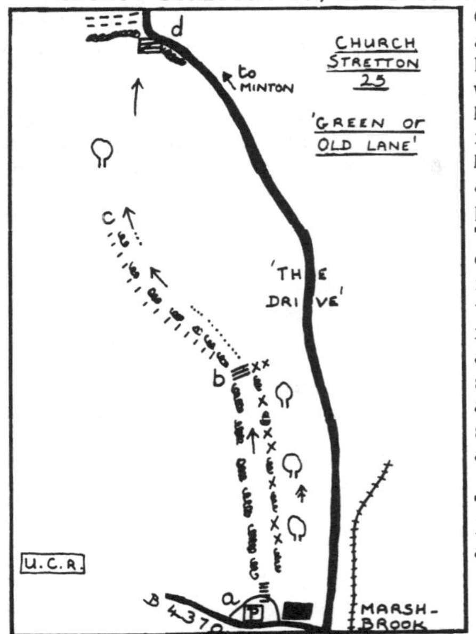

Cs 25 is an unsurfaced highway but at present is impossible for a horse rider to use. This was the way the lane from Minton to Marshbrook used to run. The 'new road' (The Drive), from (d) to Marshbrook, was built by a squire at Minton and was initially private (see page 116).

The way starts from the car park of the Wayside Inn (a) via a flight of rotten wooden steps. At the top of these, a clear trackway runs along the edge of the wood to a wooden fence at (b). After (b), signs that this was an old track are still evident; the left-hand side is marked by a line of trees along a short steep bank. From (c), the track has been lost. Telegraph poles initially and a lone tree mark the way across to a gate on to the lane at (d).

CHURCH STRETTON 23, NEW HOUSE TO MINTON 1 Km/½+ m.

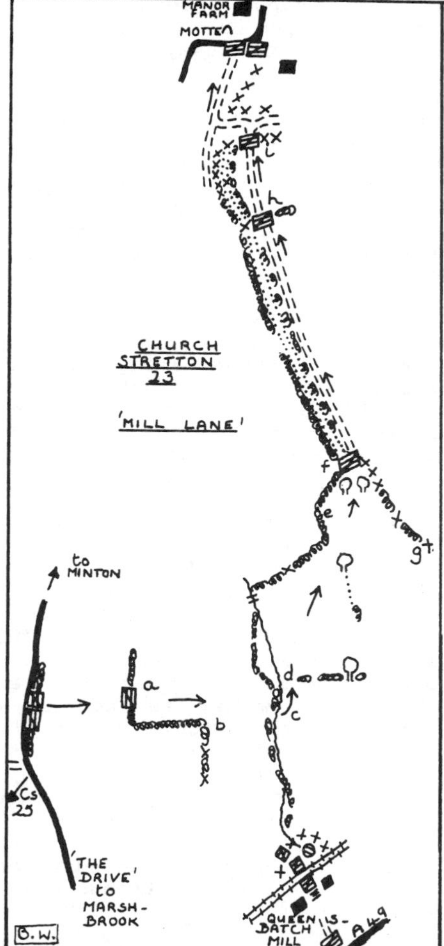

Cs 23 starts nearly opposite the end of Cs 25 and the drive to New House Farm. Pass through a gate and bear obliquely left to gate (a). After gate (a), descend a slope aiming slightly to the right, reaching the brook in line with a right-angled corner (b) at the top of the slope behind. A hedge with gaps runs beside the brook. Pass through a gap but beware of the irregular fence on the other side of the brook. At this point (c) another bridleway is joined, running between Minton and Queensbatch Mill, which must have been used often when the mill was working. I have not included the section of bridleway from (c) to the mill (see below). Turn left after crossing the brook and pass through the gap at the lower end of a hedge at (d). Ascend obliquely right up the slope, aiming to the left of a lone ash tree at the top, to reach a hedge (e) running up the slope from the left. Follow this hedge to gate (f) where hedges (e) and (g) converge. The route from this point to Minton is old trackway. On the tithe map, this track ran from Minton and continued along hedge (g) reaching a dead end on the top of the slope; it was not a track to the mill. **The way from (f) is a well-used track running beside the old one and passes through gates (h) and (i). From (i), keep to the track as it bends to the left to skirt the farm yard and buildings and exit on to the lane.** On the other side of the lane is a motte and Manor Farm. In this area there was also once a chapel, possibly an appendage to an old manor house, which is thought to have been dedicated to St Thecla; St Thecla's day was celebrated long after the chapel ceased to exist (see page 257).

N.B. The section of bridleway from (c) to Queensbatch Mill I do not feel can be recommended to riders because it crosses two railway tracks on a long bend.

Focus on the dead and rights of way

By common tradition, a right of way could be created if a coffin (full) was taken that way, and funeral processions were not allowed to go from Minton via The Drive (see Cs 25) for this reason. The Drive was also closed for one day each year, on Good Fridays, to prevent it from becoming a right of way.

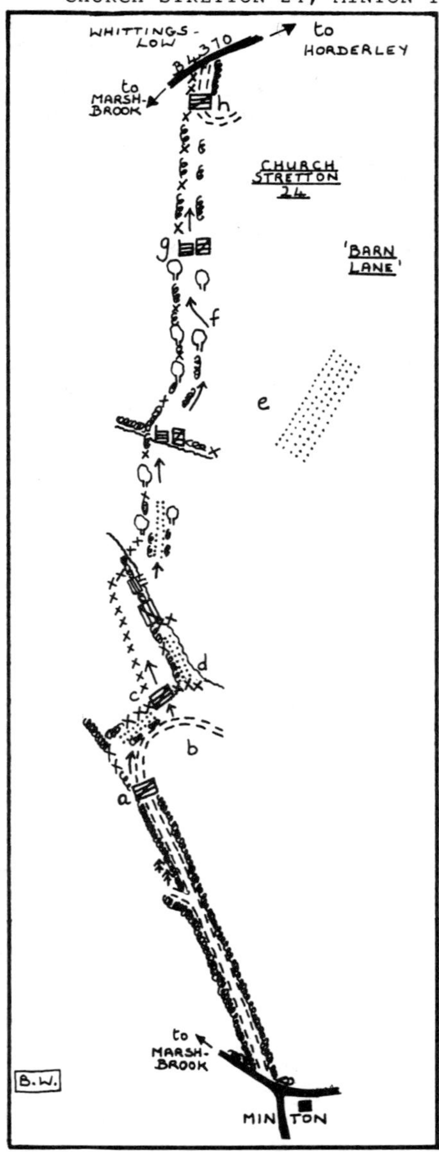

On old maps, Minton radiates tracks. Three have become roads and three bridleways, while one has not become a right of way. Cs 24, one of these tracks, is a bridleway and must have once been a link between Minton and Whittingslow, perhaps when these two old manors were included in the manor of Stretton. For most of its length it is apparent that this was an old, enclosed road. **The first part of this route is well-used and enclosed track as far as gate (a). In field (b), the old track is evident but not usable. Continue along the new track down the slope but turn away from it to pass through gate (c). Follow fence on one side, hedge and brook on the other to get to the crossing over the brook.** The old track can be seen running beside the brook at (d). **Riders use gate and ford, walkers stile and footbridge. Ascend a slope through trees, following the cutting of the old track. Stile and gate lead into field (e). This is a large field with a faint pattern of ridge and furrow. Again the track with its hedges is evident through this field, but initially is too overgrown to use. From (f), the track becomes a usable, grassy way and passes through stile and gate at (g). At (h), it joins a well-used track, passes through a gate and descends to the B4370 near Whittingslow.**

Focus on the Cedars of Minton

Cedars of Lebanon are to be seen on the old Minton estate, and are apparently four in number. An elderly resident's father, as a small boy, helped to plant one of these (he had a hand on it as it was planted); this dates them as being about 110 years old.

LYDBURY NORTH

Lydbury North is a parish which lies on and to the south of the Long Mynd. The parish is made up of Choulton, Eyton, Plowden, Totterton and Lydbury townships, each with a small hamlet as its centre; Lydbury's centre is the more sizeable village of Lydbury North that contains the church. Lydbury was the large manor of Lideberie in the Domesday Book and had a church then. The manor had been and continued to be held by the Bishop of Hereford until the 16th century. Lideberie had been given to Hereford Cathedral in Saxon times when its owner was cured of the palsy after a visit to the shrine of St. Ethelbert at the cathedral. 'North' was added later to distinguish this Lideberie from Ledbury in Herefordshire which was also held by the bishop. A castle was built for Lydbury manor and became known as the bishop's castle; this area soon (in about 1200) became part of the separate parish of Bishops Castle. The old manor included Asterton and Norbury, while Choulton, including Eaton, was originally a separate manor. Eaton is shown to have a motte on the O/S map but this may be the barrow where a number of urns containing burnt bones were once found which are thought to be Roman.

Tenants-in-chief under the bishop included the Plowdens and the Walcots. Plowden (Hall) has been the seat of the Plowden family from the 11th century until the present day while the Walcots remained at Walcot (Hall) until the 18th century. Walcot was bought by Lord Clive of India, whose son married the sister of the Earl of Powis. At the Earl's death, she inherited his estates but not the title and her husband was (re)created the 1st Earl of Powis on his own merits. In this way the Long Mynd became linked with the Earls of Powis. The Plowdens, Walcots and Earls of Powis have played a role in the story of the Mynd as owners of land and as lords of the manors of Lydbury North, Myndtown and Wentnor.

Only a small part of Lydbury North falls into the area of this book and includes Hillend, Old Churchmoor Hill, Priors Holt and the southern end of the Mynd known as Rabbit Warren. The area around and including Churchmoor Hall now lies in Lydbury North but it was extra-parochial until the late 19th century.

A railway ran along the Onny from Craven Arms to Bishops Castle, although the original intention had been to link the Shrewsbury to Hereford main line with another main line near Montgomery, and provide a short cut between the two. The railway functioned, often struggling financially, only from the 1860s until the 1930s and both Plowden and Eaton boasted stations. Traces of the railway are visible as is the old station house at Plowden.

Lydbury North lies on the B4385. Plowden, which is at the foot of the Mynd, lies on the A489.

Amenities: -

- Shop - at Lydbury North, 2 miles from Plowden and the Mynd.
- Refreshments - Powis Arms at Lydbury North.
- Accommodation - Powis Arms.
- Camping - Powis Arms.
- Bus Service to Plowden - Midland Red West runs one return journey between Craven Arms and Bishops Castle along the A489, on Fridays and Saturdays.

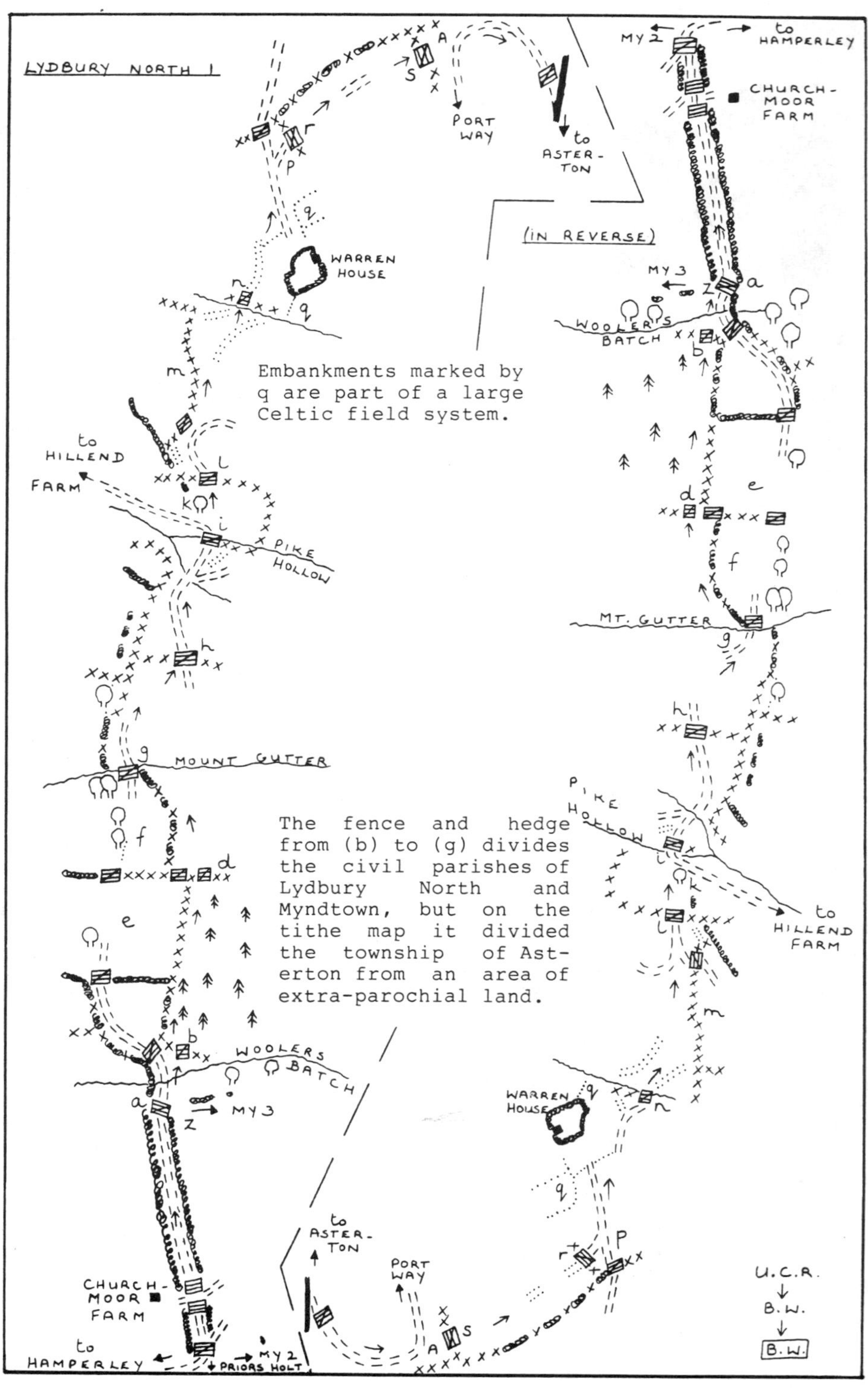

LYDBURY NORTH 1
(IN REVERSE)
Embankments marked by q are part of a large Celtic field system.
The fence and hedge from (b) to (g) divides the civil parishes of Lydbury North and Myndtown, but on the tithe map it divided the township of Asterton from an area of extra-parochial land.
MY 2
to HAMPERLEY
CHURCH-MOOR FARM
PORT WAY
to ASTER-TON
WARREN HOUSE
MY 3
WOOLERS BATCH
to HILLEND FARM
PIKE HOLLOW
MOUNT GUTTER
MT. GUTTER
PRIORS HOLT
U.C.R.
B.W.
B.W.

LYDBURY NORTH 1, CHURCHMOOR TO PLOWDEN 3.75 Km/2¼ m.

There are signs to indicate that a track, enclosed or accompanied by a hedge, ran from Priors Holt as far as (l) via fields (e) and (f). Ln 1 leaves the track at (b) and rejoins it at (g). At (l), the track appears to have continued alongside hedge down to the road, while another track branched off to cross open hillside towards Warren House; it is the latter that has become the continuation of Ln 1.

Ln 1 is a bridleway (see below) and the first section is unsurfaced highway; at present it is not possible to use on horseback. The way begins as an enclosed track opposite the turning into Priors Holt. Follow the track, passing close to Churchmoor Farm and crossing two sets of hurdles, to gate (a). MY 3 branches off to the right at this point. Descend, cross the brook in Woolers Batch, leave the track and enter the forest via gate (b). Follow the boundary fence of the forest, which initially runs with a marked embankment. (N.B. The first part through the forest is not yet an official bridleway). Exit from the forest via gate (d) and descend along the left-hand hedge to join a well-used track at (g). Cross a brook in Mount Gutter and follow the right-hand side of a fence, passing through gate (h). On the left side of the fence is a line of trees and shrubs that must have bounded the old track. Leave the fence at the start of Pike Hollow, keeping to the well-used track that crosses two small streams in the hollow and passes through gate (i). From (i), leave the well-used track (which descends to Hillend Farm) and climb up a slope to the right to reach a lone tree (k). From (k), cross to gate (l) in the far corner of the field. From (l), set out along a well-used track but keep straight on along fence when the track starts to bend up to the right onto the hill. Continue at much the same height across the slope, leaving the fence when it turns away at (m), and find a faint track. This leads to a rocky hollow where it bends to run upstream; leave it at the bend and drop down a short slope to a wicket gate (n). From (n), an old grassy track runs up out of the hollow and continues, well to the left of the field of Warren House. There are abundant rabbits here. Join a grassy track from Warren House and follow it to (p), branching off at this point to pass through gate (r). Follow the right-hand side of an old hedge (there is a good view of the old Plowden Mill) to gate (s) and the Portway at A. Follow the Portway to the left to reach the road.

LYDBURY NORTH 1 (IN REVERSE), PLOWDEN TO CHURCHMOOR

Leave the Portway at A and pass through gate (s). Follow a hedge, pass through gate (r) and turn left up towards Warren House along grassy track. Branch off to the right (vague) to pass well to the right of Warren House and its field. An old grassy track soon becomes evident; follow this down into a rocky hollow and pass through a wicket gate (n). Climb straight up out of the hollow and join a faint track. Turn right along this and follow the contour of the hill round to come alongside a fence at (m). Follow fence to join a track off the hill. Continue along this track to gate (l) and go straight on across a field towards a lone tree (k) on a bank. From (k) descend to a well-used track, turning left along it and following it through Pike Hollow and along a fence to gate (h). Continue along fence and descend to the brook in Mount Gutter. Just before a gate, turn left and follow the hedge up to the forest. Enter the forest and follow its boundary. Exit via gate (b) and join clear track which runs through Woolers Batch, through gate (a) and on, as enclosed track, to Priors Holt.

Focus on bellringing

HAREBELLS

The ringing of bells in the churches around the Mynd has been carried out for centuries. When and how they were rung will have varied from village to village and with the passage of time, but their prime function was always meant to be a way of summoning people to church.

Generations of bellringers must have trodden the footpaths to and from the churches, and between church and pub. The sexton is (or was) another character to beat a regular trail to the church, one of his duties being the simple chiming and tolling of the bells for some services, particularly funerals.

Pulverbatch, Church Stretton, Lydbury North and Wistanstow, at different times, each had their number of bells increased, as well as rehung in such a way (attached to a wheel to which the rope is fixed) as to be able to perform the more controlled ringing that became the art of bellringing. As bellringing advanced, so it tended to develop an identity unconnected with religious observance, and there was a long period when unruly behaviour occurred in towers, with bells being rung on any occasion for the ringers to make money and have a good time. This was eventually brought under control and most towers have lists of rules regarding behaviour as well as ringing.

In the four churches mentioned above, the bells can be rung up. This means that they can be made to swing in an ever increasing arc until they are upside down. A simple mechanism, involving a projecting piece of wood called a stay, prevents each bell from swinging right over. It is with the bells up (swinging from an upside down position on one side to the same position on the other with each pull on the rope) that changes can be rung. 'Rounds' are bells ringing in the order of their numbers. 'Changes' are when the order is changed. All the four towers mentioned above ring 'call changes' whereby one person calls out the changes to be made by all the bells. The next stage from this, both historically and as part of the learning process, is 'method ringing' whereby each person has to manage his own changes, following a particular pattern e.g. in 'plain hunting' a bell has to work its way from first position to the last position and back to first. There are many methods with names like Grandsire Doubles, Kentish Delight, Cambridge Surprise, Stedmans and many others. (Stedman introduced the idea of method ringing in the 17th century). At present, the only church attempting any of these methods is Church Stretton.

Amongst the remaining churches, Wentnor has the most bells and occasionally a 'peal' is rung on them. A 'peal' used to be rung on the night of Dead Mans Fair in November, to guide people home from Stretton; this was termed Dead Mans Peal.

A true peal is the ringing of over 5000 changes in one go, a not too frequent event. Many towers have a few records of peals performed, often in the form of framed lists of ringers who took part in the peal, the method and the time taken.

MYNDTOWN

Myndtown is a parish at the south end of the Long Mynd. As a civil parish, it also includes Asterton township but the ancient ecclesiastical parish does not. Asterton is in Norbury parish. However, since Norbury became a chapelry of Myndtown in 1894 (it was previously a chapelry of Lydbury North), Asterton is now ecclesiastically linked with Myndtown. In the Domesday book Myndtown was the manor of Munete meaning 'mountain', the 'town' being added later. At the same time Asterton and Norbury lay in the Bishop of Hereford's great manor of Lydbury. The 'civil' Myndtown has three centres of habitation. Myndtown itself is situated on a knoll below the steep south-west escarpment of the Mynd and includes the church of St.John the Baptist. Asterton is a larger hamlet lying even closer to the base of the hill; a steep road, locally known as the Portway, ascends from here to the gliding station and on to Church Stretton. The Handless is a very small centre lying between Myndtown and Asterton.

Asterton had a mediaeval chapel and a modern Methodist chapel which can be found in ruins above the hamlet along MY 12. The township of Asterton extends over the top of the Mynd, the extension down the eastern slope including all the coniferous forest, the gliding station and the settlement of Minton Batch. On the west, the township includes some of Prolley Moor.

For nearly seventy years both Myndtown and Asterton could boast proximity to a railway station; Myndtown was only 1¼ miles from the station at Plowden.

Myndtown and Norbury (with Asterton) parishes were joined with Wentnor and Ratlinghope parishes about thirty years ago. The primary school children from all these parishes attend Norbury school.

Asterton is reached from Church Stretton via the Burway road and gliding station, or from the A489 at Plowden. It can also be reached by lanes from Wentnor. Myndtown lies at the end of a lane which branches off from another lane running between Eaton on the A489 and Wentnor (via the Home and the Criftin).

Amenities:

Shop, pub, refreshments and riding are all available at Wentnor, 1.75 miles from Asterton, 2.75 miles from Myndtown.

Camping - The Poplars, Asterton. Also, see Wentnor.

Bus - Horrocks' bus runs on Fridays to and from Bishops Castle. It leaves Bishops Castle at 9.50, reaches Eaton (nearest stop for Myndtown) at 10.00, Asterton at 10.08 and returns to Bishops Castle via Wentnor by 10.30. The circuit is reversed in the afternoon; the bus leaves Bishops Castle at 13.10, arrives at Asterton at 13.32, Eaton at 13.40 and returns to Bishops Castle for 13.50. Horrocks also run a bus via Wentnor to and from Shrewsbury on a Tuesday (see under Wentnor).

N.B. These 1993 times are included more as a guide to the length of the journey; departure times may alter. The days are likely to remain the same since they are both market days.

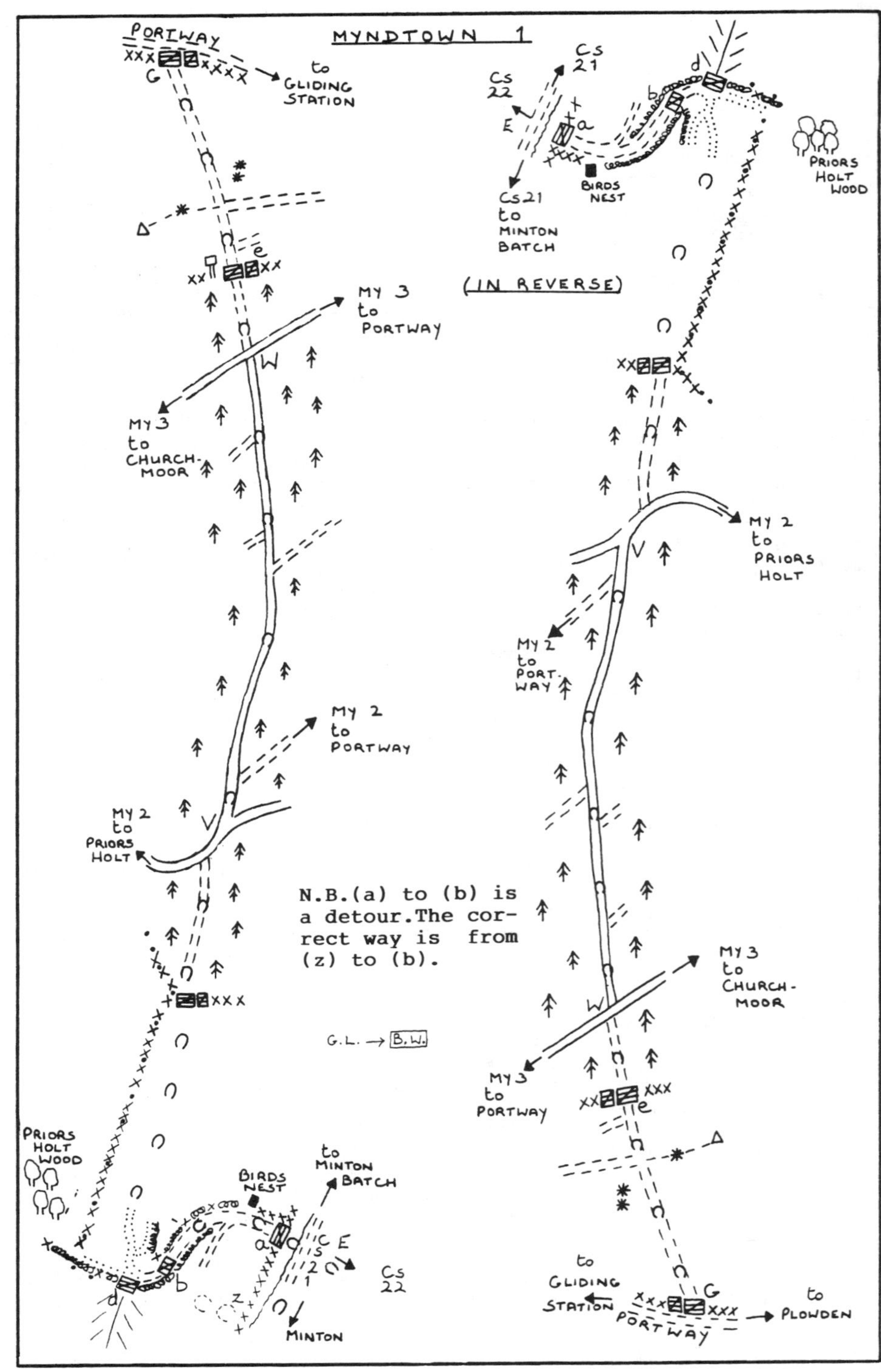

MYNDTOWN 1
PORTWAY
G
to GLIDING STATION
e
My 3 to PORTWAY
W
My3 to CHURCH-MOOR
My 2 to PORTWAY
My 2 to PRIORS HOLT
V
N.B.(a) to (b) is a detour.The correct way is from (z) to (b).
G.L. → B.W.
PRIORS HOLT WOOD
BIRDS NEST
to MINTON BATCH
a
b
d
z
E
Cs 22
MINTON
(IN REVERSE)
Cs 21
Cs 22
Cs21 to MINTON BATCH
BIRDS NEST
PRIORS HOLT WOOD
My 2 to PRIORS HOLT
My 2 to PORT-WAY
My 3 to CHURCH-MOOR
My3 to PORTWAY
to GLIDING STATION
to PLOWDEN
PORTWAY

MYNDTOWN 1, MINTON BATCH TO THE PORTWAY AT G 2.25 Km/1¼+ m.

MY 1 was an old route across the hill in conjunction with MY 7, and is now a bridleway. Except at the Minton Batch end of MY 1 there are no signs of its antiquity, probably because there has been disturbance of land over most of its extent.

Take the track off Minton Lane (Cs 21) towards Minton Batch and follow it as far as the open hill at point E. Turn left along another track, ford the brook and go through gate (a). The track ascends past a house (Birds Nest) and passes through gate (b). Follow an old hedge on the left to gate (d). This gate is used as a landmark only; it is on a ridgeway running from left to right and is the approximate point at which to turn right up the hill. The old hedge just mentioned runs across to Priors Holt and forms the boundary between Church Stretton and Lydbury North for most of its length. In the past it has also been a union and rural district boundary. **Having turned right at gate (d), ascend the steep ridgeway which merges into a grassy hillside stretching up towards the forest. On the left a gully and fence also run up the hill** (Myndtown and Lydbury North boundary). **Aim towards the top end of this fence by the forest and enter the forest via a gate.** This large area of forest belongs to the Forestry Commission and lies within the old township of Asterton in Norbury ecclesiastical parish; much of the forest boundary too corresponds with the old township boundary which today has become the civil parish boundary of Myndtown. All the Mynd in the Asterton township was open common land on the tithe map of 1846 and the boundary was marked by stones and tumps only, probably well into this century. The forest is post World War 2. **Continue along a grassy track to join a good forest road at point V. Follow the forest road, in effect straight on. (Turn left along this road if following MY 2 to Priors Holt. Another good road branches off to the right but it is the grassy track to the right just after this that is MY 2). At a crossroads W, where MY 3 crosses MY 1, continue straight on along grassy track and leave the forest via gate (e). Cross an area of heathland and cleared forest that lies at the south end of the gliding station territory.** A tumulus is passed on the left and two on the right; a flint was once found nearby. **Join the Portway via a gate at point G; a flint was found here too. The O/S map shows a bridleway continuing diagonally to the left to join MY 7 near the Huckster Stone, but it is not possible to use this way. Reach MY 7 by turning left along the Portway and passing through a gate at F.**

MYNDTOWN 1 IN REVERSE, PORTWAY AT G TO MINTON BATCH

Leave the Portway at point G via a gate and cross an area of heathland and cleared forest, passing tumuli on either side, to reach a gate (e) into the forest. Continue along grassy track to a crossroads at W, where MY 3 crosses MY 1, and go straight on along a good forest road. This descends gradually through the conifers and eventually bends to the right at point V. From this bend take the grassy track, that is in effect straight on and descend to a gate at the edge of the forest. Descend the grassy hillside bearing obliquely away to the left from the fence that also runs down the hill. A short steep slope is part of a ridge that descends to gate (d) in an old hill boundary hedge. Turn left at the gate and follow the hedge through gate (b). Descend enclosed track, passing a house (Birds Nest), to reach another track (Cs 21) via gate (a). Turn right along this to get to Minton Lane. If using Cs 22, turn right and then left by some yew trees into a field.

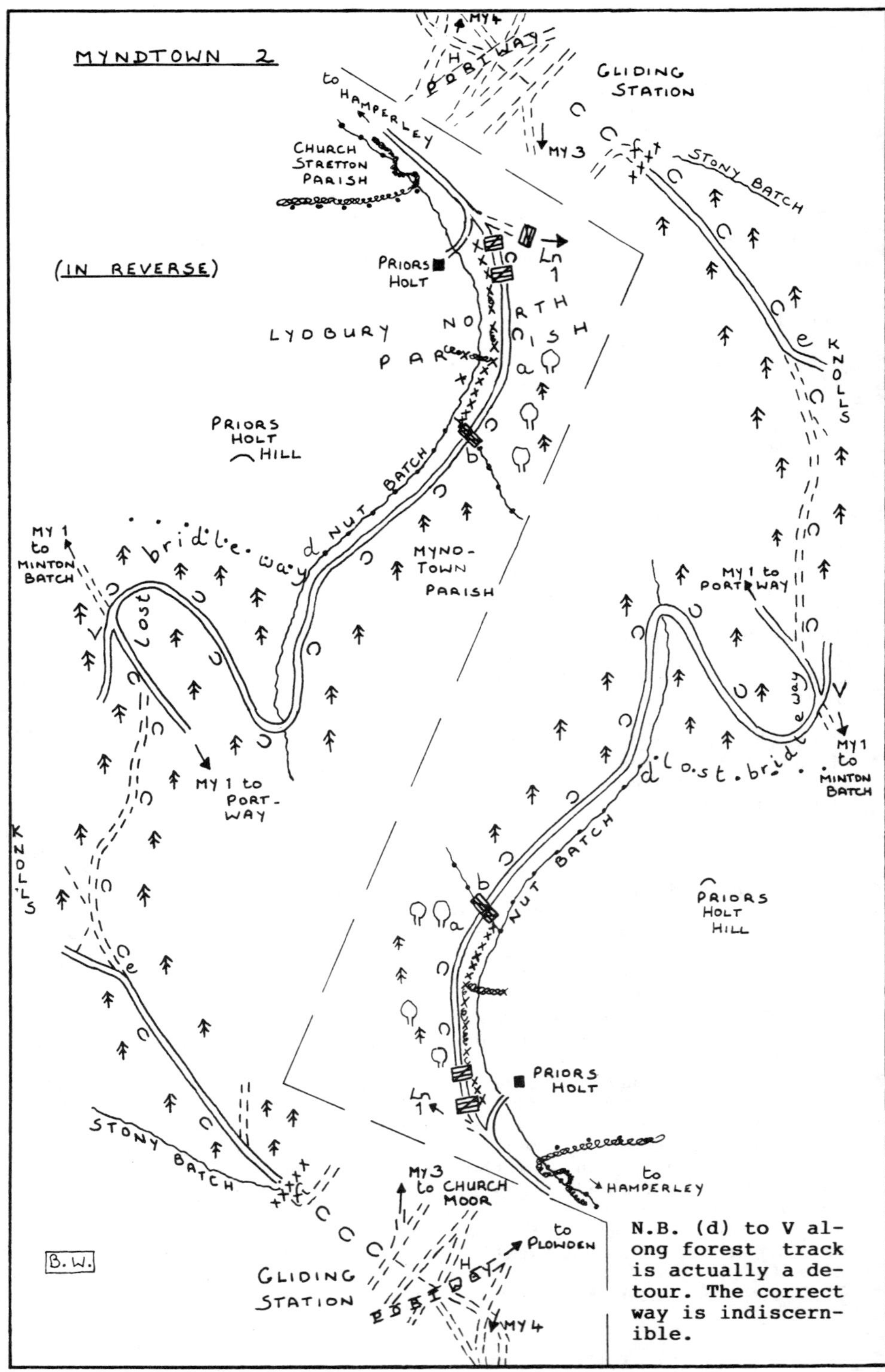
MYNDTOWN 2
(IN REVERSE)
MY 4
PORTWAY
H
GLIDING STATION
to HAMPERLEY
MY 3
STONY BATCH
CHURCH STRETTON PARISH
PRIORS HOLT
Ln 1
LYDBURY NORTH PARISH
PRIORS HOLT HILL
NUT BATCH
KNOLLS
MY 1 to MINTON BATCH
bridle-way
lost
MYND-TOWN PARISH
MY 1 to PORTWAY
MY 1 to PORT-WAY
lost bridleway
MY 1 to MINTON BATCH
NUT BATCH
PRIORS HOLT HILL
KNOLLS
PRIORS HOLT
Ln 1
STONY BATCH
to HAMPERLEY
MY 3 to CHURCH MOOR
to PLOWDEN
GLIDING STATION
PORTWAY
H
MY 4
B. W.
N.B. (d) to V along forest track is actually a detour. The correct way is indiscernible.

MYNDTOWN 2, PRIORS HOLT TO THE PORTWAY AT H 2.75 Km/1.75m.

MY 2 was another old route across the hill in conjunction with MY 4/5. The second part, from V to the Portway at H, may have originated as a branch track of MY 1 with the first part being only a footpath; this is how it appears on a map of 1831. Another map (1828) shows only the second part, as a continuation of MY 1, but a short section of the first part, along the hill boundary, is 'green rack'. There are no signs of antiquity along its route as there has been disturbance of land, and for the same reason the way has become altered. Priors Holt does not seem to have had connections with a priory but a church is thought to have once stood in a field there. An old map apparently records Priors Holt as Briars Hold.

The road from Cwm Head to Hamperley continues to Priors Holt where it ends. A track to the right descends to Priors Holt itself, Ln 1 turns to the left and MY 2 goes straight on as a good forest road. Pass through two gates. On the left is an old plantation (a). At gate (b), the Myndtown C.P./Lydbury North C.P. boundary (once the Lydbury North/Asterton township boundary) is crossed and **the forest begins.** The boundary follows the brook upstream and turns away from it to the right, as did the original bridleway, at (d) which is level with the forest edge on Priors Holt Hill. **Today, follow the forest road up the left-hand side of the brook and around the head of the valley known as Nut Batch; the old route through this area is completely lost in the trees.**
At V, on a second long bend, our route is joined by a grassy track from the right which is MY 1 and just beyond this point a good forest road turns off to the right. Keep to the road bending round to the left and as the corner ends take the grassy track to the right. This eventually joins another good forest road at (e); turn left along it to the edge of the forest (f). Recent forest clearance has altered the forest boundary as shown on O/S maps; it is now approximately at the head of a small batch, Stony Batch, running down to the right. At the time of walking this route the exit point here was crossed by temporary fencing. From the edge of the forest, aim straight across the heathland (following track for a short distance after which there is no clear way) but beware of gliders and winching apparatus; this area is part of the gliding station. Join the Portway at H where it runs along the western edge of the Mynd; MY 4 is straight on and down the slope.

MYNDTOWN 2 (IN REVERSE), PORTWAY AT H TO PRIORS HOLT.

Leave the Portway at H where the Starboard Way and MY 4 join it. With the steep slope behind you, go slightly to the left of straight on to cross heathland where there is no clear way; aim for forest road running straight into the forest and join this road just before you reach the forest boundary. This area is part of the gliding station so watch out for gliders and winching apparatus. At the forest boundary, at the head of Stony Batch (further east than on the O/S map, due to recent forest clearance) is a temporary fence (f) across the road to be followed. Continue along this stony track until it veers off to the left at (e). Here take the grassy track that carries straight on for a short distance and then curves round to the right to descend through the conifers.
At V, a good forest road is joined; turn left along it and follow the long bend round and down. Another long bend curves around the head of Nut Batch and the road continues down this valley, leaving the forest at gate (b) and passing through two more gates to get to Priors Holt.

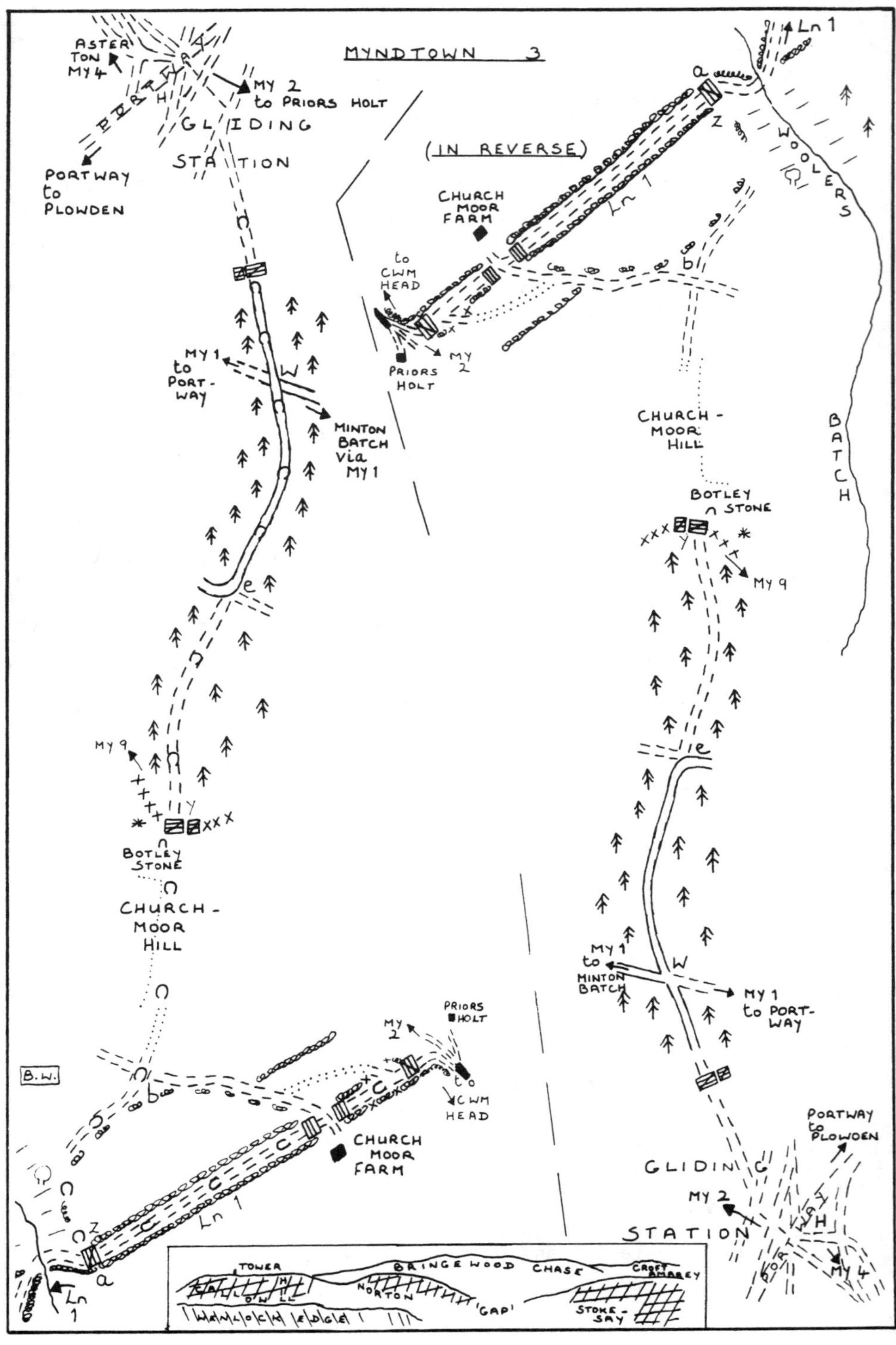
MYNDTOWN 3
(IN REVERSE)
ASTERTON MY 4
MY 2 to PRIORS HOLT
PORTWAY
GLIDING STATION
PORTWAY to PLOWDEN
MY 1 to PORTWAY
MINTON BATCH via MY 1
MY 9
BOTLEY STONE
CHURCH-MOOR HILL
B.W.
PRIORS HOLT
MY 2
to CWM HEAD
CHURCH MOOR FARM
Ln 1
WOOLERS
BATCH
MY 1 to MINTON BATCH
MY 1 to PORT-WAY
PORTWAY to PLOWDEN
MY 4
TOWER
TITTERSTONE CLEE HILL
BRINGEWOOD CHASE
CROFT AMBREY
NORTON 'GAP'
STOKESAY
WENLOCK EDGE

MYNDTOWN 3, CHURCHMOOR TO THE PORTWAY 2 Km/1¼ m.

MY 3 is an old route across the hill in conjunction with MY 4. There were a few ways on and off Churchmoor Hill; one descended directly to Priors Holt but it was the one that descended to Ln 1 near Woolers Batch that became the bridleway of today.

The start of this bridleway is some distance along the track (Ln 1) at point Z, after it has started to descend and where it bends to the right to pass through a gateway (a). Turn right at this point into a large area of grassland that extends over the hillside known as Churchmoor Hill (in the past, Old Churchmoor Hill or Bank). Keep to the top of the dingle slope where an old hedge soon becomes apparent. Follow this sparse line of old trees to a sharp corner and turn right to continue along it; it has now become a marked old hill boundary wall with a track running alongside it. Keep to this track; it reaches the apex of the boundary wall at (b) and then bears to the left up the hill, crossing another track. It continues but as it becomes very faint keep straight on with a small brow to the right. There is a very faint embankment running along on the left-hand side, to guide you almost to the forest edge. At the top is a stone near the corner of the forest and in front of a gate into it. This must be the Botley Stone which was at one time a boundary stone between Asterton township and Lydbury North; today it marks the boundary between the civil parishes of Myndtown and Lydbury North. A grassy tumulus lies nearby. **Pass through the gate into the forest; this is point Y where MY 9 branches off to the left. Ascend a muddy track to reach a forest road.** The sight of mature fir trees (Sitka spruces) with branches sweeping down on either side of this moss-bordered track is striking. Here, two species of bird to look out for in particular are the goldcrest and the coal tit, which have adapted to coniferous woods. **At W, our track continues over a crossroads (MY 1 crosses our route). Keep straight on, leaving the forest area via a gate and crossing heathland (still on a track) to get to point H on the Portway near the western edge of the Mynd.**

MY 3 (IN REVERSE), PORTWAY AT H TO CHURCHMOOR

With your back to the western slope of the Mynd and the end of MY 4/5, the Portway is running from left to right and another track branches off obliquely to the right. Move forwards and cross another track. Move forwards again to another track running from left to right which has a branch off it which is MY 3. This crosses heathland to the forest, entering it via a gate. The track continues as forest road passing through the crossroads W where MY 1 intersects it. Continue straight on until the road bends to the right; turn left down a muddy track and reach grassy hillside via a gate. A stone, probably the Botley Stone, lies just inside the field. Descend the hillside aiming obliquely to the right. In your sights should be Bringewood Chase (a long and wooded hill on the horizon), and a gap between two wooded hills in the middle distance (see inset). A faint embankment on the right is another guideline. A faint track is reached which descends to an old hill boundary wall at (b) and follows it down to the right to join Ln 1 near Woolers Batch at Z. Since Ln 1 is blocked, an alternative way off the hill (with permission) is to follow a track running to the left from near (b); this divides into an old track running through gorse to Priors Holt (difficult to use) and a well-used track running down to Churchmoor Farm. Leave this second track and exit along the field side of Ln 1.

MYNDTOWN 4 AND 5

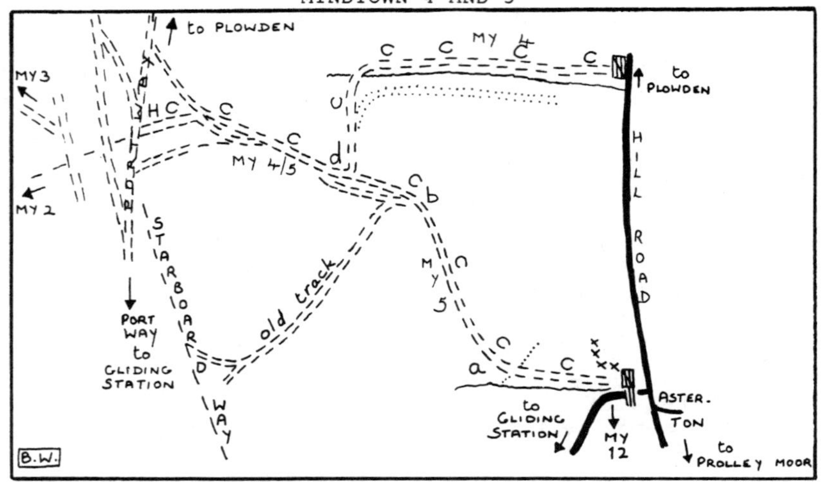

MYNDTOWN 4, THE HILL ROAD TO THE PORTWAY AT H   0.75 Km/½ m

MY 4 and 5 are both bridleways and are old tracks running up the slope behind Asterton, joining at (d) and continuing as one track up to the Portway. They may have originated as outracks but by their continuity with MY 2 and 3 became old routes across the hill. Within living memory they appear to have been little more than wimberry picking routes, MY 5 being known as the North Road, but now they are well used by walkers and riders.

MY 4 starts off The Hill Road between Asterton and Handless. It passes through a gate and follows a stream, crossing it higher up. An older track runs on the other side of the stream; **It then ascends to join MY 5 (another track) and continues as MY 4/5 up to the Portway. Just before the Portway it divides into three, with the central track in continuity with MY 2.**

MYNDTOWN 4 (IN REVERSE), PORTWAY AT H TO THE HILL ROAD

MY 4 leaves the Portway near the start of the Starboard Way and descends as a clearly-defined track (initially there are three tracks but they soon converge). At (d), it turns left off MY 5 and descends to The Hill Road between Asterton and Handless.

MYNDTOWN 5, ASTERTON TO THE PORTWAY AT H   0.75 Km/½ m

As the road starts to climb from Asterton towards the gliding station, a cattle-grid leads to open hill (not common land here). MY 5 bears off to the right and follows a small stream for a short distance as a faint track, before turning away and rising steeply as a much more clearly-defined track (a). At (b), several deep-cut tracks have formed (a feature of steep slopes, see Portway on page 20); keep to the right-hand one. A little further up at (d), our route is joined by MY 4 (another track) and as one track ascends to the Portway, dividing into three just before joining it.

MYNDTOWN 5 (IN REVERSE), PORTWAY AT H TO ASTERTON

MY 4/5 leaves the Portway near the start of the Starboard Way and descends as a clearly-defined track (initially there are three tracks but they soon converge). At (d), MY 4 turns off to the left. MY 5 descends the hill, bending steeply and sharply at (a) to the stream which it follows down to the cattle-grid near Asterton.

MYNDTOWN 9

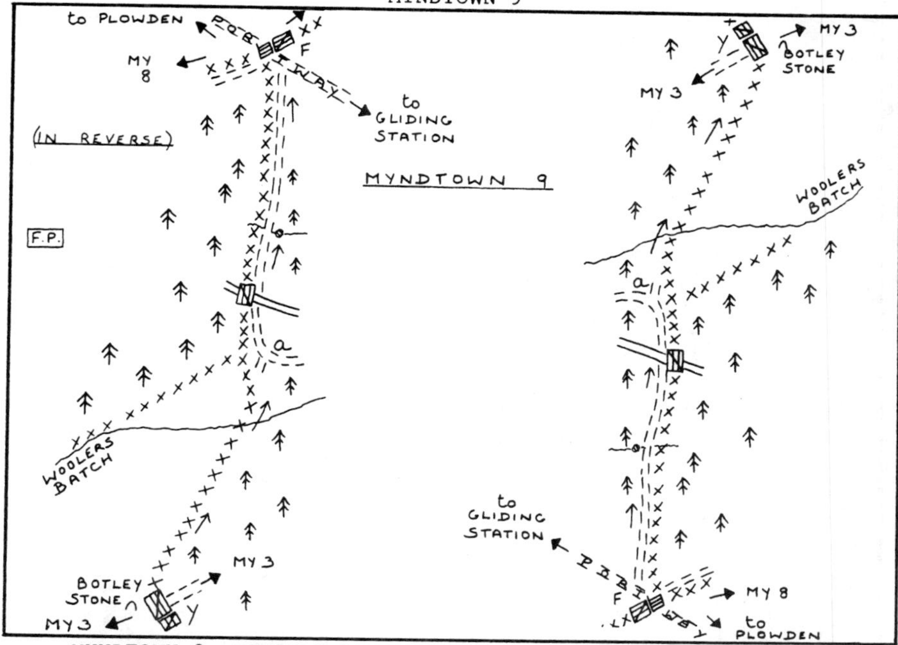

MYNDTOWN 9, PORTWAY AT F TO THE BOTLEY STONE 1 Km/½+ m.

This route starts on the north (forest) side of the gate at F on the Portway and, as a track, follows a fence down through the forest. It crosses another track before reaching (a). At (a), MY 9 leaves the track and continues along the fence all the way to gate Y, passing the head of Woolers Batch which descends to the right as a deep-cut valley. MY 3 is joined at Y. The Botley Stone lies near Y in the field and serves as a boundary stone (see MY 3). A tumulus is also discernible near the stone; the name of Botley Stone has also been applied to this.

Most plant species avoid coniferous plantations, as do many birds, but several species of fungi abound and the wood is by no means devoid of bird-song. Some bird species to look out for here are the goldcrest, the coal tit and the sparrowhawk.

Focus on forests

The first new forests were planted in the eighteenth century and were both deciduous and coniferous, the conifers including larch, Scots pine and Norway spruce. Two world wars used up a huge amount of timber from these and from the older woodlands too. The Forestry Commission was established in 1919 to embark on a large afforestation scheme. Conifers were chosen because they develop quickly into saleable timber on quite poor soils and initially native continental trees (European larch, Norway spruce and Scots pine) were planted. Later, species from the west coast of North America (where the climate actually resembles our own more than the Continent's does) were found to be successful here and were widely planted. The Sitka spruce found growing in the Longmynd forest is one such species.

MYNDTOWN 6 AND 7

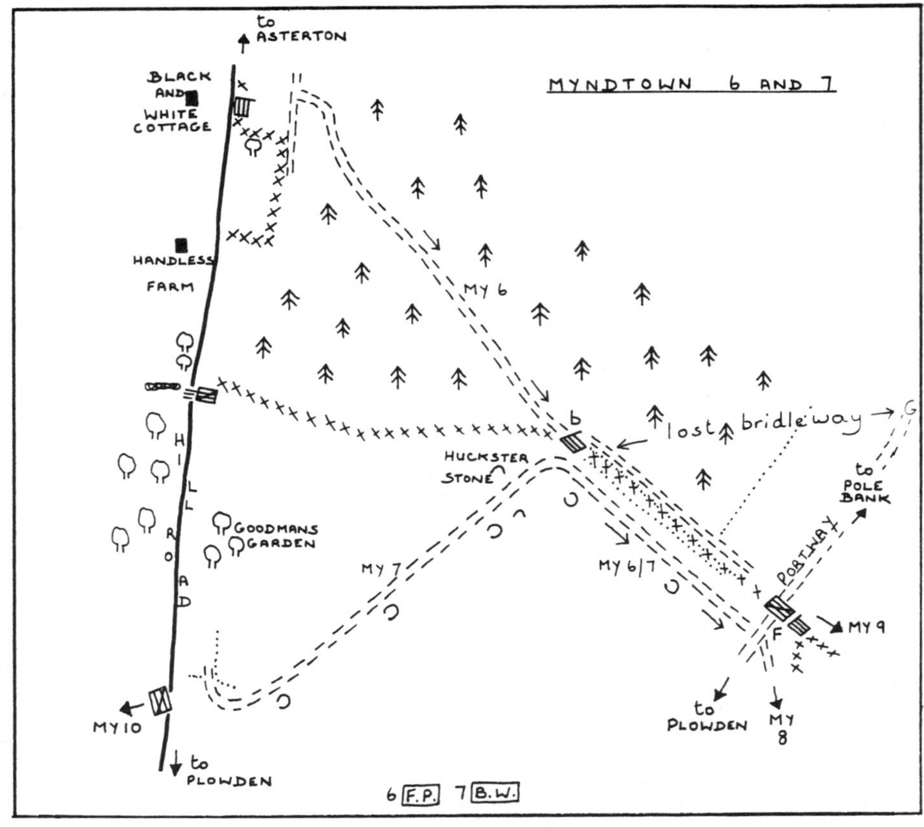

MY 6 (a footpath) and MY 7 (a bridleway) are shown as crossing over at (b) on the O/S map and on older maps too. However, the section of MY 7 from (b) to G is not always shown on old maps, suggesting perhaps that this was a less important section. MY 7 joined MY 6 at the Huckster Stone and thence was in continuity with MY 9 and 3 to Churchmoor, and MY 8 along the parish boundary. Via the section from (b) to G, MY 7 was in continuity with MY 1 to Priors Holt. MY 7 from (b) to G on the Portway cannot now be followed and I have therefore put MY 6 and 7 as joining at (b) and continuing as one route to the Portway at F, as they did on the 1846 tithe map and a map of 1828. MY 7 is obviously an old track as far as (b) but MY 6 has been disturbed by forestry. From (b) to the Portway, signs of an old track and/or embankment run with the fence; this is also the ancient parish boundary of Myndtown. There are no signs of the continuation of MY 7 to G although it crosses an area of seemingly undisturbed heathland. Another interesting feature of MY 7 is the presence of the Huckster Stone which could be one of two natural rocks that flank the track. The name suggests that this was an old route used by hucksters.

MYNDTOWN 6, HANDLESS TO THE PORTWAY AT F 0.5 Km/¼+ m

Leave The Hill Road at Handless opposite Black and White Cottage, via a stile into forest. Follow the edge of a field to a grassy track running from left to right. Turn left along this for a very short distance and find a vague track off it that ascends into the forest. This soon curves to the right and ascends obliquely through dense fir trees. It may be off this slope that an avalanche fell onto a Handless cottage in 1814; although all the family were sleeping in one bed, some children survived but the parents and one child died (see leaflet at Norbury Church). **Emerge at a stile that leads onto an old track (MY 7).** At the edge of the forest, you may see the toadstools of fairy-tale pictures (red with white spots); these are fly agarics and are poisonous. **Follow a wide path that runs alongside fence, up to the Portway at F.**

DOUGLAS FIR CONE

MYNDTOWN 6 (IN REVERSE), PORTWAY AT F TO HANDLESS

Leave the Portway at F, taking a grassy track that follows the Plowden (south) side of a fence down the hillside. At (b), a marked track bends off to the left but MY 6 turns right, over a stile into dense forest. Follow a track down through the trees and as Handless is approached it curves to the left and joins a grassy track. Cross this track and follow the edge of a field to exit onto the road via a stile. This is Handless or the Handless but in the past it has appeared as Henllyss i.e. probably Welsh, meaning 'old hall'; if so, there is no evidence of an old hall.

MYNDTOWN 7, THE HILL ROAD TO THE PORTWAY AT F 0.5 Km/¼+ m

This route starts opposite the end of MY 10 and soon becomes an old track ascending the steep slope; it may once have been linked with Myndtown via MY 10 and from there with Bishops Castle. All the early 19th century maps show MY 7, suggesting that it was an important route, but it features as a continuation of The Hill Road from Plowden. **The track reaches the Huckster Stone, which is probably the large conglomerate rock on the left rather than the one on the right. Just beyond this, at the forest edge (point (b) where MY 6 joins our route), the track bends to the right. It continues as MY 6/7, running upwards beside a fence to join the Portway at F.**

MYNDTOWN 7 (IN REVERSE), PORTWAY AT F TO THE HILL ROAD

Leave the Portway at F and follow the fence on the Plowden side down to point (b). MY 7, as a clear and old track, bends away from the forest and descends the steep slope, passing the Huckster Stone on the right and continuing down to The Hill Road.

Focus on birds

Wheatear

Another bird associated with the uplands (but not exclusively) is the wheatear, which is one of the earliest summer migrants to arrive here. The short grass of the Mynd, particularly where it is steep and rocky, is an ideal breeding habitat for them, nests being made in rock crevices, stone walls and rabbit burrows. One of the wheatear's distinctive features is its white rump, which is the meaning of its name.

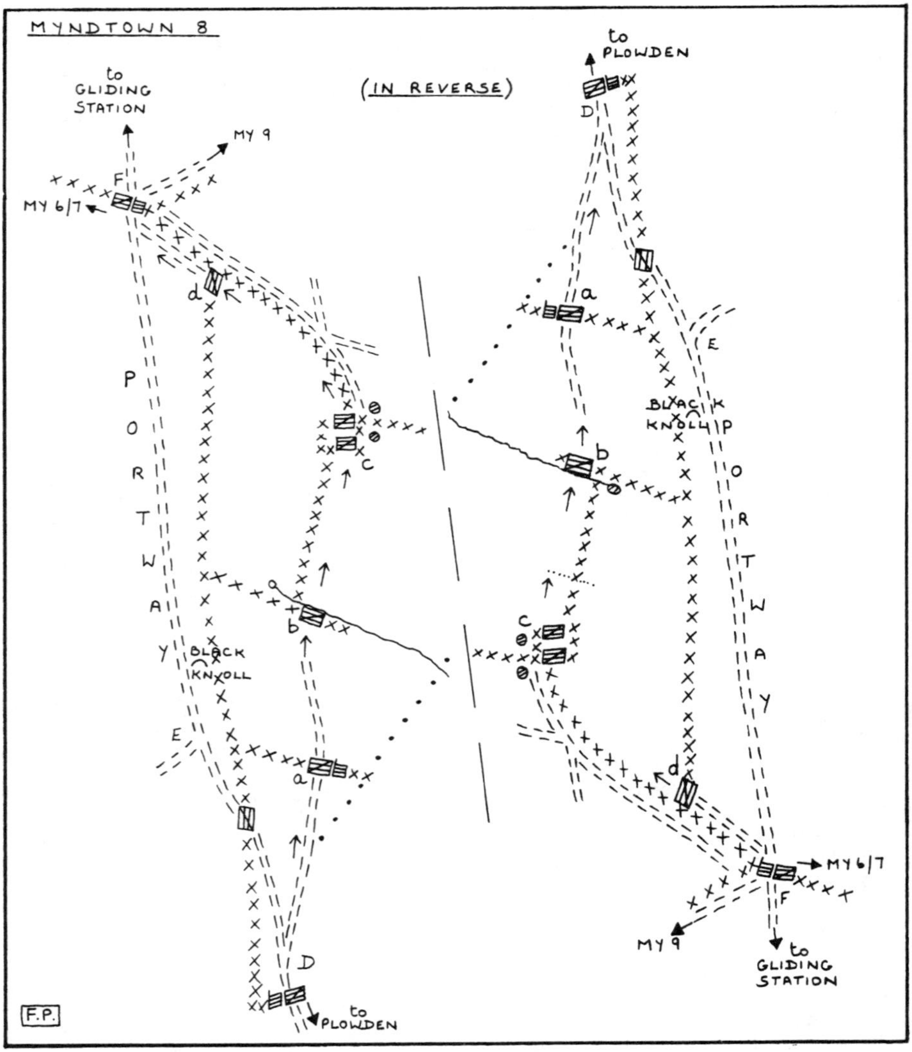

MYNDTOWN 8

(IN REVERSE)

to GLIDING STATION

MY 9

MY 6/7

F

d

c

b

a

D

to PLOWDEN

PORTWAY

BLACK KNOLL

E

F.P.

THE HUCKSTER STONE

MYNDTOWN 8, PORTWAY AT D TO PORTWAY AT F 2.25 Km/1¼+ m

MY 8 is another old route that is described on one old map (1828) as a 'green rack'. It was, together with a few tumps and stones, the old manor boundary and the ancient parish boundary of Myndtown. Today, only a short section of old track is visible, near point D.

After passing through the gate across the Portway at D, bear obliquely to the right along an old track which leads to a gate and stile at (a). This whole area of fields is one of improved grassland and at the right time of year may well be covered with mushrooms and other fungi. It lies in the civil parish of Myndtown but to the left is the ancient parish of Myndtown and to the right is a tongue of Norbury parish. **From (a), cross another field to a gate (b) and pass through this to continue along a fence.** There are some faint embankments along this section. **At (c), a fold is reached by some old pools and the start of forest.** These pools form a welcome splash of colour against the green forest and grassland, with the yellow of lesser spearwort and irises, the blue of marsh forget-me-nots, the white of marsh bedstraw and the red of the large red damselflies. Near the pools fragments of Roman pottery (probably 4th century A.D.) have been found and a large whetstone too.

Pass through the fold at (c) and follow the fence that forms the forest boundary to a gate (d). The forest here consists of Scots pines and the track that runs on the other side of the fence (the old 'green rack' perhaps) has abundant toadstools, particularly in the autumn. Species include the fly agaric or Amanita muscaria (red with white patches) and the blusher or Amanita rubescens (rosy brown with white patches). N.B.Many Amanitas (a group that includes the death cap and the destroying angel) are poisonous. **Pass through gate (d) onto what appears to be open hill (but which is not common land) and join the Portway at F.**

MYNDTOWN 8 (IN REVERSE), PORTWAY AT F TO PORTWAY AT D

Leave the Portway at F and follow the forest boundary fence, passing through gate (d), to reach a fold by some pools at (c). Pass through the fold via two gates and continue along the fence to gate (b). From (b), a track is soon picked up and this leads to the Portway at D, passing through another gate at (a).

Focus on trees **Scots pine**

The Scots pine is our only native pine and a few thousand years ago it may have grown all over the Long Mynd until other trees took its place (see Background). Today, most of the Scots pines on the Mynd are likely to have been planted but some self-set young trees can be seen in the heather near the south end of the Mynd (heathland being an ideal habitat for them to pioneer). Part of the forestry near the south end of the Mynd consists of areas of Scots pine. Elsewhere, trees tend to be scattered and old, often in woods or along old hedges. In some places a line of them marks the edge of an old plantation long since gone e.g. near the New Leasows (As 22) where there was a New Leasowes plantation. These old and attractive trees with their dense crowns offer good nesting sites for such birds as the buzzard or raven.

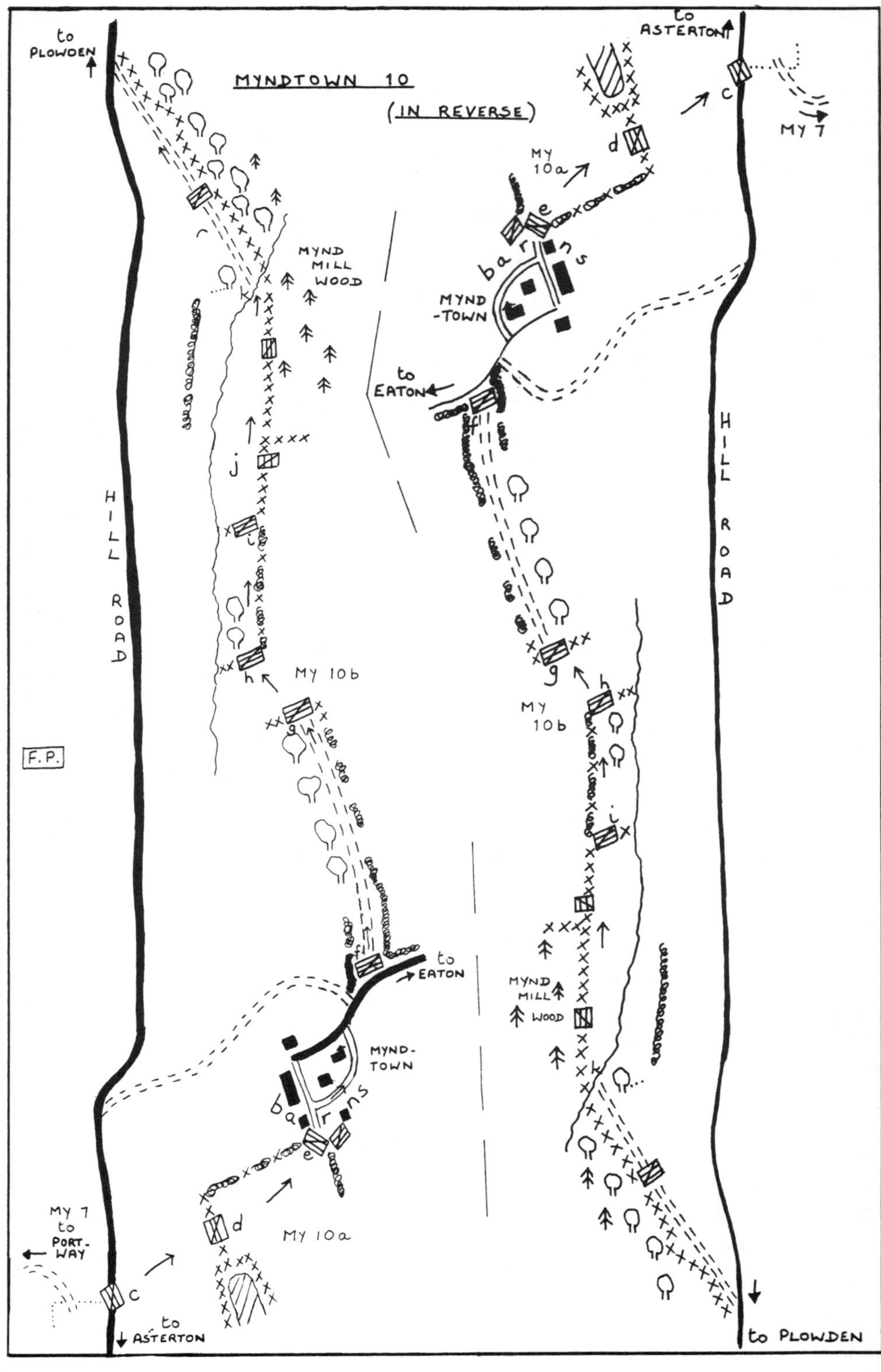

MYNDTOWN 10
(IN REVERSE)
to PLOWDEN
to ASTERTON
MYND MILL WOOD
MYND-TOWN
to EATON
barns
HILL ROAD
MY 10a
MY 10b
MY 7
MY 7 to PORT-WAY
F.P.
to ASTERTON
to PLOWDEN
c
d
e
f
g
h
i
j
k

MYNDTOWN 10, HANDLESS TO PLOWDEN VIA MYNDTOWN 1.5 Km/1 m.

MY 10 is made up of two paths to and from Myndtown. 10a links up with MY 7 to the hilltop and would have been a way for Myndtown inhabitants to see to their animals on the hill, or part of a longer route over the hill. 10a also linked Myndtown with Asterton. Asterton had a shop and Myndtown the church; Asterton people only used this church after 1894. Today 10a shows no signs of antiquity. 10b, by contrast, retains features along its route to suggest that it is an old track. Much of it was probably enclosed, as it is today flanked by hedge or lines of trees. 10b would have been a route to open hill, but it was also a link with Plowden for the mill, main road, railway station and a Catholic school. A past inhabitant of Asterton remembers going to this school with children from Handless but there were then no children living at Myndtown; if there were at any time, it is likely that they went to the same school. As well as people going to the mill, the miller with his cart delivered flour certainly to Asterton and possibly along MY 10 to Myndtown. (This mill was working until about 1939).

Leave the Asterton to Plowden road (The Hill Road) through a gate (c) and descend into a shallow valley. Pass through gate (d) near an enclosed area of trees and pool. Ascend to the top left hand corner of the field and exit between barns onto a lane that forms a loop behind the church. 10b starts at gate (f) off the lane to and from Myndtown. Just before (f), another track (well-used) branches off to the Asterton to Plowden road. After passing through gate (f), continue straight on along old track. At gate (g), there was almost certainly a branch track to Myndmill Farm which may have been a link between Myndtown hamlet and the mill or main road. (It is uncertain when or even if a mill existed here). **The way crosses the corner of a field between gates (g) and (h) and then runs close to the brook to reach gate (i). The field after (i) was called Flood Acre and is full of yellow irises, witnesses to its dampness. A coniferous forest on the right (Scots pine and larch) extends up onto a ridge as Myndmill Wood** (less extensive and known as Ridgeback Wood on the tithe map), **and the way follows its lower border to the brook at (k). 10b then ascends as a clear track, still following the wood boundary, up to the road.**

MYNDTOWN 10 (IN REVERSE), PLOWDEN TO ASTERTON VIA MYNDTOWN

Leave the Plowden to Asterton road taking the track that follows a wood boundary down to the brook at (k). Continue along the lower border of Myndmill Wood to gate (i). Follow hedge to gate (h) and then cross the corner of a field to gate (g). An old track leads to the road via gate (f). Turn left just before the church and follow a road round to some barns at a T junction. Turn left again and enter a field through gate (e). Descend to gate (d) in a shallow valley near a pool, and then ascend to The Hill Road at (c) opposite MY 7.

Focus on trees

Oaks

There are two species of oak native to Britain, the pedunculate and the sessile oaks. Their names derive from the way in which their acorns grow, those on the sessile oak having no stalks. Although sessile oakwoods tend to grow on steep hillsides in the west and pedunculate oakwoods, with larger trees, on the lowlands (a pattern that may have evolved from rivalry a long time ago), either tree will grow well in both habitats. The fine trees growing on low ground along MY 10 are sessile oaks.

MYNDTOWN 11, GROVE COTTAGE TO MYND FARM 0.5 Km/¼ m.

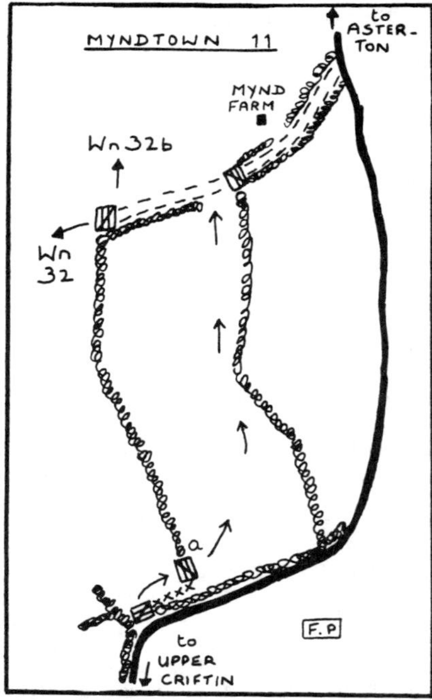

Leave the Criftin to Asterton lane on a sharp corner beyond (east of) Grove Cottage and pass through a gate. Turn right and go along the inside of the lane hedge to gate (a). From gate (a), aim obliquely across the field to the top far corner of the opposite hedge. At this point a track is reached (Wn 32). Turn right to get to Asterton passing Mynd Farm, or turn left to follow Wn 32 to Wentnor.

MY 11, in conjunction with Wn 35 and Wn 29 must have been a route used at some time to get to Whitcot, although it does not appear to be much shorter than going by road and it has been used little within living memory. Whitcot itself had both mill (only in use from the late 19th century until 1916) and blacksmith, and was also on the way to Norbury where the blacksmith's was in use more recently than at Whitcot. Asterton people used the church at Norbury until the end of the last century, and most children have attended Norbury school since it was built in 1874 (a few went to Plowden). The Criftin, near Whitcot, became the bus stop for Asterton people although some buses went to Asterton itself as does the infrequent bus of today.

Focus on 'beating the bounds'

Perambulation of the bounds of a parish was an old custom that appears to have become associated with Rogationtide (in May), although it originated as a separate event. Perambulation of the bounds took place as an annual survey of the boundaries of a parish, manor or estate to see that they were unchanged or still in existence. The officials making the survey were usually accompanied by parish boys, who struck the boundaries with peeled willow wands, hence the popular name of 'beating the bounds'. Rogationtide is a time of intercession for God's blessing on the fruits of the earth and has long been associated with processions through fields of crops (the practice in fact predates Christianity, as a pagan ritual). The combination of the two customs resulted in the beating of the bounds becoming a religious ceremony in some places, and certain boundary trees became known as 'gospel trees' (there appear to be none in the Mynd area). Rogationtide is still observed by some churches today, although usually without the procession.

There is a record of a formal perambulation of the boundaries between the manors of Lydbury North and Wentnor as far back as 1278, and Asterton and Norbury were at that time in the manor of Lydbury North. This perambulation was to fix the boundaries, and was objected to on the first occasion because it was performed by four freemen and only eight belted knights. Thirteen knights performed the second perambulation and this seems to have been acceptable. Familiar names mentioned as boundaries are the 'Bassebrok rivulet' and the 'King's Highway on La Longamunede'. The former, the Buzz or Criftin Brook, remains a boundary between the old township of Asterton (in Norbury parish) and Wentnor parish. The latter, the Portway, is crossed twice by the old Asterton boundary, and a short section of it is a boundary between Asterton and Myndtown.

There appears to be no recollection of beating the bounds in the area, but the small parish of Edgton just south of the Mynd performed this ceremony in May 1993.

Focus on birds **Skylarks and pipits (titlarks)**

Two similar-looking, brownish birds commonly found on the Mynd are the skylark and the meadow pipit. The skylark is easily recognized by its song flight; it sings and rises vertically from the ground, hovers high in the sky and then drops like a stone to the ground again. Its song for many people means sunny, summer days. The meadow pipit also has a distinctive song flight; it rises steeply from the ground, singing, but does not reach such great heights or hover as long as the skylark. Its descent has far more style, as it glides down on outspread wings and tail.

Skylarks remain with us all year round, while many meadow pipits leave us for the winter. Meadow pipits, although not exclusively birds of the open hill, are less likely to be seen on farmland than skylarks. The skylark's association with farmland, however, is proving its downfall and a dramatic decline in their numbers has taken place, greater than with any other once common species. One reason is the switch from spring to autumn ploughing and sowing, with a loss to the skylark of winter stubble that served as a food store.

The meadow pipit's close relative, the tree pipit, is hard to distinguish from the meadow pipit. Its habitat is slightly different in that it frequents the edges of the open moorland, where some trees or scrub are present. Its similar song flight is likely to be to and from a tree.

The lives of skylark and pipit are linked with two other birds in particular - cuckoo and merlin. The cuckoo's song, like the skylark's, is associated with a season, while the meadow pipit is one of the birds that may have to contend with a cuckoo's egg to hatch and rear; its Welsh name (gwas-y-gog) means 'cuckoo's servant'. If undisturbed by the cuckoo, the pipits should rear their own young successfully but they then may fall victim to the merlin; they are said to be its favourite prey. The merlin, a small bird of prey, can sometimes be seen on the Mynd but it is a rare and shy bird.

Friend or foe **Ragwort**

Ragwort is an attractive plant often associated with wild and rough land. Insects visit the flowers and the cinnabar moth caterpillars feed on its leaves. It is, however, not a friend to man with livestock. Ragwort is thought to be dangerous when it is dying but this coincides with the time of year the normal vegetation in the animals' diet is becoming scarce and whatever is available may be eaten. As with all poisonous plants, animals can coexist with it and not come to any harm but if it is eaten by cattle or horses the liver is affected and they develop the 'staggers'.

MYNDTOWN 12 AND 13

MY 12 (sometimes known as Chapel Road) is an unsurfaced highway and MY 13 is a bridleway.

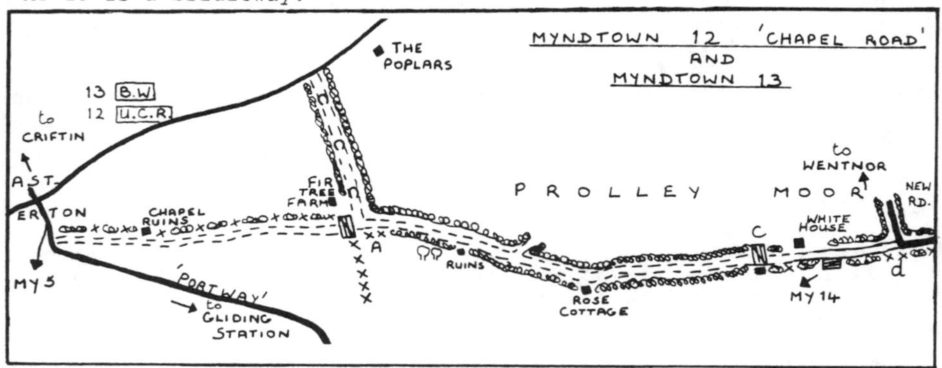

The section of MY 12 from A to (d) is a narrow and very evidently old track and probably predates other routes crossing Prolley Moor. On the tithe map this section is shown running along the upper (eastern) edge of an open Prolley Moor with a strip of small fields and a few habitations flanking it. Near this old road, on the moor, two bronze implements (a flat axe and an unlooped palstave, 1500-1400 B.C.) were once found and can be seen in Rowley's House Museum. The continuation of the road south to Asterton was shown as a track on the tithe map, following the hill boundary, as it runs today. MY 13 appears to be a branch of MY 12. It was open track on the tithe map, running along the southern edge of Asterton Prolley Moor; today it is enclosed and partly surfaced and serves as a driveway for Fir Tree Farm. The other roads of today that cross Prolley Moor ran a similar course across open moor on the tithe map, but as open tracks. They are not identical to today's because they were changed into straighter roads with well-spaced hedgerows when the moor was enclosed, possibly in the mid 19th century; the road from Wentnor to Medlicott is still called the New Road.

The Hurricane Tombstone

A cottage in Asterton, possibly along the old road, was the site of a tragedy in 1772. Many people were there for a 'caking', which was a sort of gaming party; the cottager made cakes and sold them to the others who used them as stakes in card games. It appears that many people must have stayed and gone to sleep there because the following is the verse on the tombstone of Samuel and Mary Perkins and their son, in Wentnor church:

One Sunday morn Bout Nine a Clock as we Lay in our Bed,
By Hurricane of Wind and Snow all three were killed Dead.
The house and we were Blown away as many well Did know,
And for that day Could not be found all for the depth of Snow.
Fourteen Poor Souls were under it, but with us were killed Seven,
I hope the Lord hath Pardoned us and Received our Souls in Heaven.

The tombstone is referred to as 'the hurricane tombstone'. The hurricane was a separate event from the avalanche which occurred at Handless in 1814 and which appears in the church records of Norbury.

MYNDTOWN 12, ASTERTON TO PROLLEY MOOR 1.75 Km/1 m.

Turn left off the Asterton to gliding station road (known locally as the Portway) **just after the cattle-grid and follow the track along the hill boundary hedge. The ruins of a Methodist chapel are passed;** this was built in 18?39 (the date is over the doorway but is unclear) and is thought to have been in use until about 40 years ago. Asterton also had a mediaeval chapel. **Pass through a gate by a house (Fir Tree Farm) at A. MY 13 joins our route from the left. My 12 continues as a narrow and enclosed track. Remains of past dwellings are represented by heaps of stones and many old bushes of box. Gate (c) is reached by some sheds and the track continues past White House. MY 14 branches to the right and a little further on New Road is joined** (both the road to the left and straight on are referred to as New Road).

MYNDTOWN 12 (IN REVERSE), PROLLEY MOOR TO ASTERTON

MY 12 is a continuation of the road from Medlicott to Stanbatch running under the steep slope of the Long Mynd. MY 14 branches off just after point (d). MY 12 passes White House and becomes unsurfaced road. Gate (c) by some sheds leads to a narrow and enclosed old road which passes Rose Cottage and some ruins before reaching Fir Tree Farm at A. MY 13 branches off to the right. MY 12 passes through a gate and runs as a grassy track along old hill boundary hedge, to exit onto the Asterton to gliding station road close to Asterton.

MYNDTOWN 13, FIR TREE FARM TO THE POPLARS ¼ Km

This is an open-ended track that bears off from MY 12 to pass in front of Fir Tree Farm. It descends between hedges to join another road running from Prolley Moor to Asterton.

MYNDTOWN 13 (IN REVERSE), THE POPLARS TO FIR TREE FARM

Take the clear track which starts near The Poplars. It ascends gradually to join MY 12 by Fir Tree Farm at A.

Focus on hedges

This is an appropriate place to consider hedges since some of those around Prolley Moor are very distinctive.

A recognised method of dating a hedge is to imagine that the original hedge was likely to have been hawthorn (quickthorn) or blackthorn (sloe), and for every other species found in a 30 metre stretch to add 100 years. This is a method of dating which is controversial for Shropshire where mixed-species hedges may have been planted as such or may be remnants of woodland. Prolley Moor is a good example of mixed-species planting, with large tree species included; many of these hedges are little more than 150 years old and quite a large proportion are now rows of trees. The straightness of the hedges, as also the roads, is perhaps the feature that is most suggestive of a short history, whereas a mixed -species hedge that winds with a track is likely to be old.

The hedges of Prolley Moor seem to have been deliberately planted and managed with trees in mind, and tall hedges are very attractive. However they tend to become thin and their original function of keeping animals enclosed is lost unless they are supplemented by fencing. To preserve a hedge and its function, it needs to be pleached (cut and laid), and there are several sites around the Mynd where there is evidence of recent pleaching.

MYNDTOWN 14

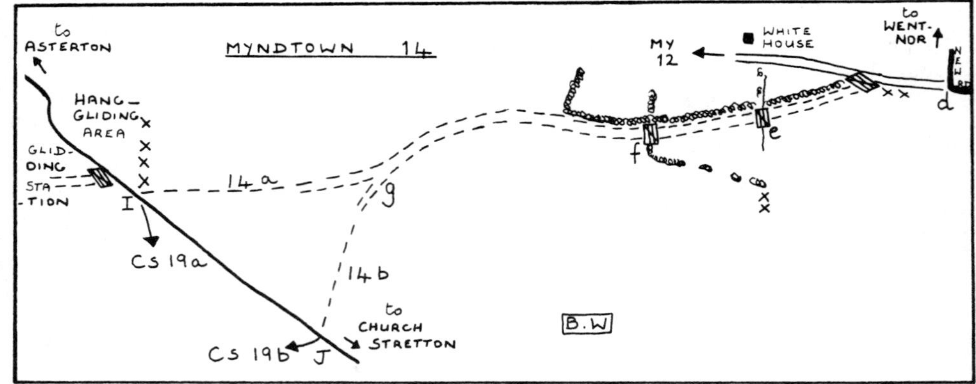

MYNDTOWN 14, PROLLEY MOOR TO THE PORTWAY AT I 0.75 Km/½ m.

MY 14 is a bridleway and another old route up onto the hill, where it divides into two, both routes dwindling to small paths before joining the Portway at I and J. On the west, it joins MY 12 and after a 'dog-leg' continues to Wentnor. On the tithe map, the route to Wentnor was directly opposite. On the east, MY 14 is in continuity with the bridleway and supposedly old route (Cs 19) to Minton via the Packetstone. On the tithe map, there appears to be a crossroads at I, the Asterton to Church Stretton road crossing the Portway (from the south) in continuity with MY 14a (14b is not shown).

The track leaves MY 12 near (d) on New Road via a gate and ascends along an old hedge of mixed trees including larch, cherry and laburnum. At the second gate (e), a small stream is crossed and this marks the Asterton township/Wentnor parish boundary; the boundary extending up the hillside to the left was marked by tumps, while to the right the stream takes over (dividing Prolley Moor into Asterton Prolley Moor and Wentnor Prolley Moor) until it joins the Criftin or Buzz Brook. **Pass through another gate (f) and continue up the hillside to the heather zone. At (g) the track divides into two which very soon become small paths through the heather. The right-hand one (14a) is the clearer of the two and ascends to join the Portway beside the enclosed hang-gliding area. The left-hand route (14b) is vague but follows a slight hollow in the contour to join the Portway at J. MY 14a links with Cs 19a and MY 14b links with Cs 19b.**

MYNDTOWN 14 (IN REVERSE), PORTWAY TO PROLLEY MOOR

MY 14a starts at point I on the Portway (surfaced road here). Leave the road nearly opposite the gate to the gliding station, beside the fence bounding the hang-gliding area. Do not follow the fence but bear away from it along a narrow path. As this descends through the heather, it becomes an old track which continues down the hillside. MY 14b is vague and starts opposite Cs 19b which is a little clearer; follow a slight hollow to get to point (g) where a grassy track (MY 14a) is joined. MY 14 descends from (g) to a hill boundary hedge, soon passing through gate (f). Continue along this hedge passing through two more gates to reach MY 12 near (d) on New Road.

MYNDTOWN 15, THE HILL ROAD TO BLACK KNOLL 0.5 Km/¼ m.

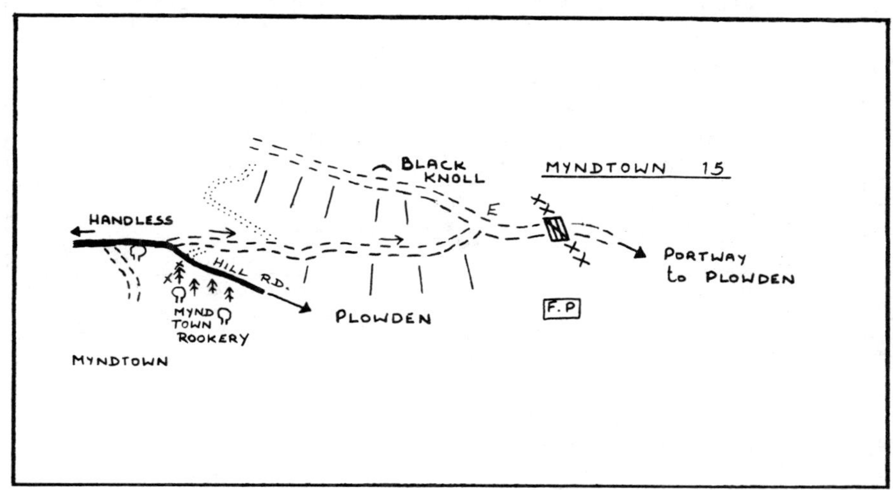

MY 15 is classified as a public footpath. It is a clear and modernized track, in use as a way up onto the hill to tend animals. It links up with a private track to and from Myndtown. In the past too it was a route between Myndtown and the hilltop, where it joins the Portway at E. It followed a more zigzag route in 1831, reaching the Portway at a point further north than today's route (this old route was obviously well used and is still carved into the hillside); the 1903 O/S map shows a similar course to today's and it is remembered as once being a grassy track. **The track leaves The Hill Road almost opposite the south end of Myndtown and ascends the hillside as an ungated track. The wood below is Myndtown Rookery.** Exactly opposite this wood, a short section of the original track can be seen ascending to join today's track. Some distance up the new track, when approximately in line with the middle of Myndtown Rookery, the old track bears away sharply to the left from MY 15. **The Portway is joined at E, a point just below a short steep ascent to Black Knoll.**

MYNDTOWN 15 (IN REVERSE), BLACK KNOLL TO THE HILL ROAD

MY 15 leaves the Portway just after (if coming from Plowden) leaving the fields on the south end of the Mynd. A clear and modernized track curves away from the Portway just below Black Knoll and descends the steep western slope of the Mynd. The Hill Road is reached nearly opposite the tiny hamlet of Myndtown.

Between the starting points of MY 15 and MY 16, a copper mine was cited on a map of 1831 and one of the hollows running down the hill was called Mine Hollow. Apart from a few old quarries, signs of past activity below the road can be seen about halfway along and this is believed to have been a mine.

MYNDTOWN 16 AND 17

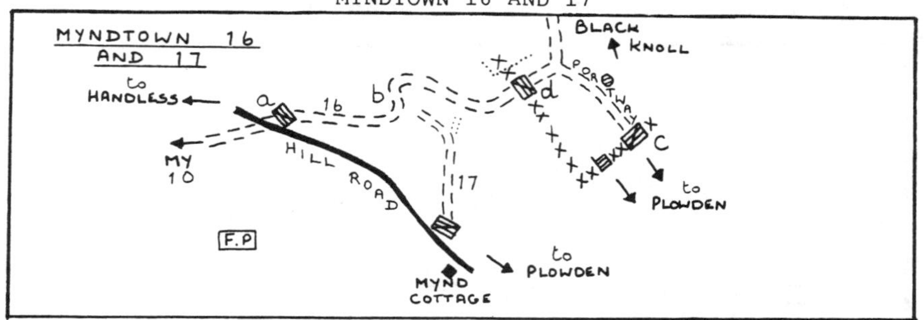

These are two more routes up onto the hill that join at (b) and continue as one track to the Portway; they scarcely feature on old maps and are footpaths on the 1903 O/S map but they are remembered as once being grassy tracks. MY 16 has been modernized and MY 17 has been diverted to join it lower down the slope than the original route. MY 16 is in continuity with MY 10 to Myndtown and may have been a route used by Myndtown people, whereas MY 17 was probably used by people living at the south-west end of the Mynd. Today, with animals on the hill being reached by car or van, MY 16 is the way used for this purpose.

The Myndtown boundary runs from The Hill Road up the ridgeway just to the south of MY 17 and curves round to cross the Portway at the beginning of MY 8. Mynd Cottage, nearly opposite the start of MY 17, is just in the parish of Myndtown and a boundary stone (Myndtown/Lydbury North parishes) stands near the south-west corner of its small field; the stone is quite small and bears the letter P, which probably represents the Plowden family name.

MYNDTOWN 16, THE HILL ROAD TO THE PORTWAY AT C 0.5 Km/¼ m.

Leave The Hill Road via a gate (a) and follow a well-used track. Ascend the slope to a gate into improved pasture at (d). This area falls within the extensive system of Celtic fields (see Portway 1) and faint embankments can be discerned. Join the Portway near C, where it appears as a grassy track with a different green to that of the surrounding grassland.

MYNDTOWN 17, MYND COTTAGE TO THE PORTWAY NEAR C 0.5 Km/¼ m.

A grassy and little-used track leaves The Hill Road via a gate almost opposite a small white cottage (Mynd Cottage) and ascends a hollow. It appears to have originally continued straight on to join MY 16 but today it turns left and crosses to MY 16 at a lower point (b). Turn right onto the well-used MY 16 track and follow this through gate (d). Cross improved grassland to reach the Portway track.

MYNDTOWN 16 AND 17 (IN REVERSE), PORTWAY NEAR C TO THE HILL ROAD

MY 16 and 17 leave the Portway just north or uphill from point C and a small pool. As one route they cross to a gate (d) and, leaving grassland for rough pasture, the way descends the hillside via a well-used track. The continuation of the track down to The Hill Road at (a) is MY 16. MY 17 branches off from MY 16 at (b) on a long bend; turn left to get onto a relatively newly-made track and follow this across to and then down a hollow to join The Hill Road via a gate.

PULVERBATCH

Pulverbatch is a village on the north-east of the Long Mynd and is made up of the old townships of Castle Pulverbatch, Wilderley, Cothercott, Church Pulverbatch and Wrentnall. The north end of the Long Mynd lies in the townships of Wilderley and Cothercott and the rights of way described in this book are only some of those crossing or descending from Wilderley and Cothercott Hills. (All other rights of way in Pulverbatch have been described in a separate booklet).

Pulverbatch was the manor of Polrebec in the Domesday book; 'bec' means 'valley' but the meaning of 'polre' is uncertain. Wilderley, Cothercott and Wrentnall were also manors although Wrentnall soon became part of Pulverbatch. Mottes and baileys were built at (Castle) Pulverbatch and Wilderley. Both mottes are well preserved, as is the bailey too at Pulverbatch. The motte at Pulverbatch (known as The Knapp) is in an impressive site and is common land; it has been a focal point for centuries for fairs, church services and picnics. The church is unusually situated in another township, that of Church Pulverbatch; it is on a hilltop and is thought to be on the site of something much older, since it has a circular churchyard. There has been a church here since at least the 13th century.

Cothercott and Wilderley manors for a few centuries formed part of Haughmond Abbey's manor of Boveria (see Background) and the hill slopes were used largely for sheep, hence the name of Sheppen Fields for one old farm on the hill. Tenants of these two manors had common rights on the north end of the Mynd until this century. Tenants of the manor of Pulverbatch had common rights on the hill too, from the 13th to the 17th century; the outrack that was used to get to and from the hill runs along the valley at the foot of the Mynd below Cothercott Hill and is still evident today in parts. It is a public footpath for most of its length.

Cothercott and Wilderley consist of a few scattered farms and houses. There are larger groups of dwellings at Castle Pulverbatch, Church Pulverbatch and Wrentnall. Pulverbatch is reached via the minor road from Shrewsbury to Bishops Castle, or via lanes from Dorrington. Castle Pulverbatch is approximately three quarters to one mile from Wilderley Farm, The Beeches and Cothercott Cottage.

Amenities (only at Castle Pulverbatch):-

Refreshments - The Woodcock and The White Horse pubs.

Bus Service - Williamson's Motors or Midland Red, approximately five return journeys a day (not Sundays) between Shrewsbury and Castle Pulverbatch.

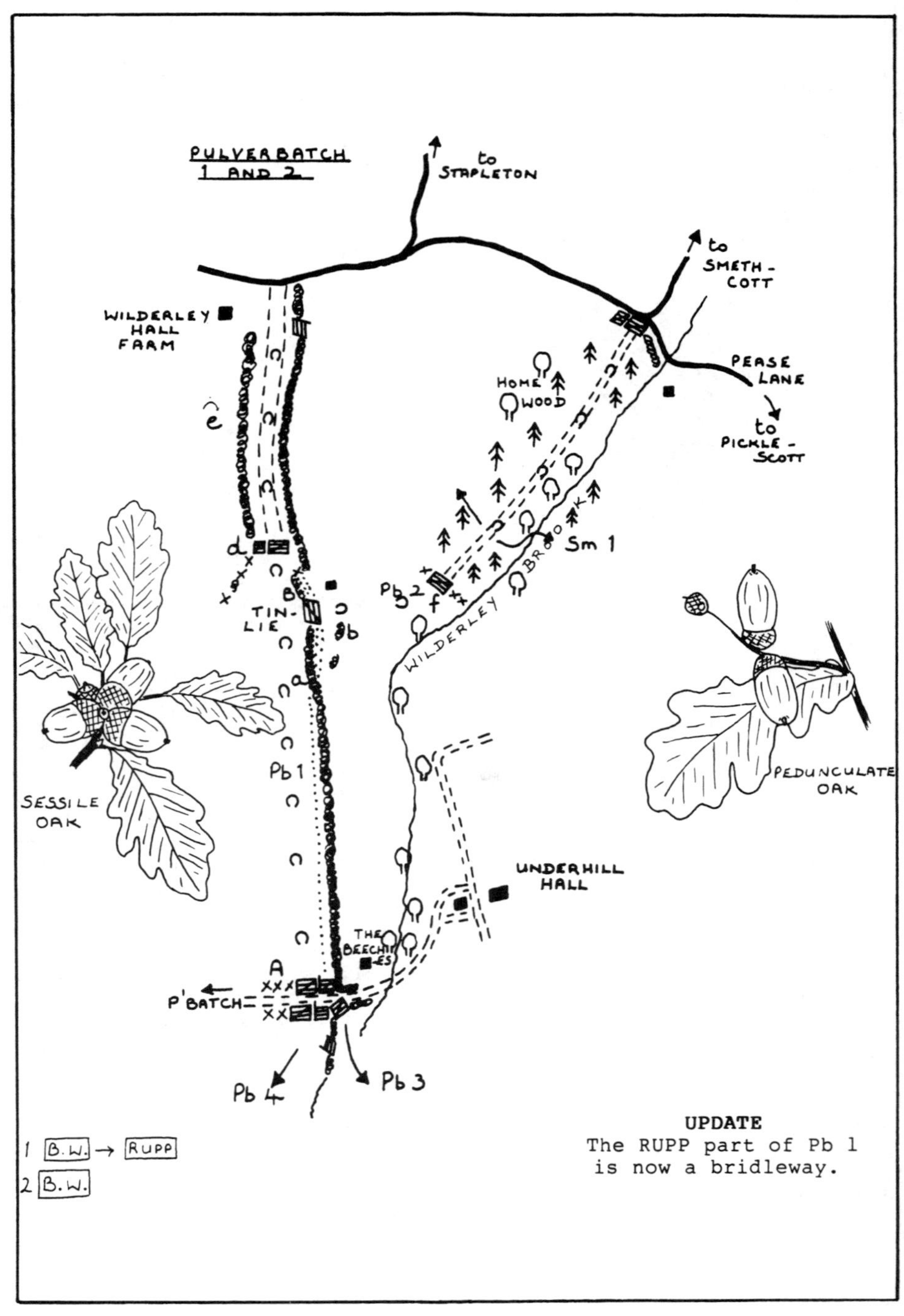

UPDATE
The RUPP part of Pb 1 is now a bridleway.

PULVERBATCH 1, THE BEECHES TO WILDERLEY HALL FARM 1 Km/½+ m.

Pb 1, in continuity with Pb 4, was an old route that ran from Wilderley up to (the) Thresholds, there linking up with the Portway. **Pb 1 is a bridleway,* although the lower part from (d) to Wilderley is, strictly speaking, a RUPP (see WL 6 on page 250). The way begins by The Beeches, entering a large field via gate or stile. Follow the left-hand side of a hedge.** To the right, a field's breadth away, the dingle of Wilderley Brook runs in the same direction. There are many beech trees in the area between The Beeches and Underhill Hall, also to the right on the far side of the brook. Underhill Hall belonged to the Powys family of Berwick, (not to be confused with the Earls of Powis, also connected with the Mynd) who owned the manor of Wilderley and subsequently also the manor of Cothercott, from the early 18th century until the beginning of this century. The large and ancient oak (also to the right on the far side of the brook), which can be seen in winter from Pb 1, is called the Powys Oak after the family. **Continue to descend gradually along old hedge.** The gully along the hedge may be the original old track, which at (a) can be seen to pass through to the other side of the hedge and run beside an area of past habitation (b). **At B, an area known as Tinlie, Pb 2 branches off to the right through a new gate, close to an old barn. Continue downwards into a funnel-shaped corner of the field. Pass through gate (d) onto enclosed track, which runs down to Wilderley Hall Farm.** At (e), Wilderley's old motte can be seen; it is a prominent mound covered by trees and woodland plants, but is easily passed unnoticed. This motte is described in the Victoria County History as having been 'designed to command one of the roads formerly running northwards from the Long Mynd towards the Severn valley'.

PULVERBATCH 2, TINLIE TO PEASE LANE 0.75 Km/½ m.

Pb 2, another bridleway,* leaves Pb 1 at Tinlie, passing through a gate into an area of former habitation. Pass an old barn and aim across the often arable field to a gate (f) into woodland, by an old and half-dead sweet chestnut tree. There is usually a thin trail blazed through this field but no signs of the original track. At gate (f), enter woodland and follow clear track through it. This wood is a mixture of conifers and a wide variety of deciduous trees including beech and elm and some non-native poplars. There are patches of bluebells, seen at their best in an area of larch trees on the right after passing through gate (f). Snowdrops abound on the flat ground alongside the Wilderley brook and foxgloves among the conifers. This is an unfrequented wood and the damp track, used and crossed by wild animals, provides good examples of animal footprints. **Exit from the wood (sometimes known as Home Wood) via a wicket gate onto the junction of Pease Lane with the Wilderley to Smethcott lane.**

***Both Pb 2 and Pb 1 (not the RUPP section, which is recorded correctly) are marked as footpaths on the O/S Pathfinder map. They are however both bridleways on the definitive map and are correctly marked on the O/S Landranger map.**

Name meaning	Tinlie
A ley or lye means land enclosed from the forest. Tin is another field name for land that has been enclosed.	

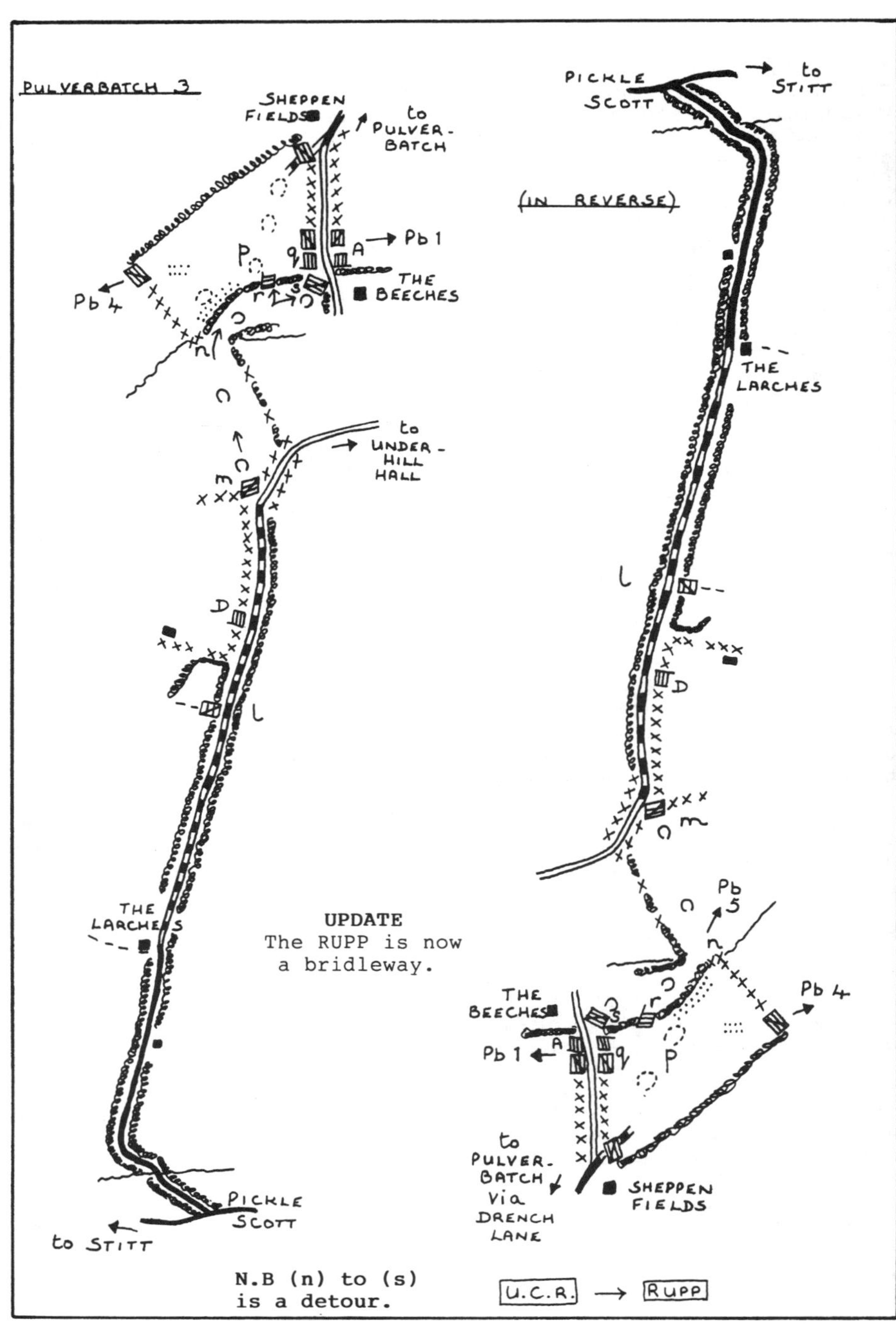

UPDATE
The RUPP is now a bridleway.

N.B (n) to (s) is a detour.

PULVERBATCH 3, PICKLESCOTT TO THE BEECHES 1.75 Km/1 m.

Pb 3 is a highway, starting just above the centre of Picklescott. It is surfaced as far as The Larches but unsurfaced from this point onwards. At a slight curve in the course of this track, Pb 3 enters a field via gate (m), while the track continues as a private road to Underhill Hall. The way that Pb 3 has taken is the old road from Picklescott to Pulverbatch and is, from point (l), a RUPP (road used as a public path, a term whose ambiguity has led to the gradual reclassification of these routes), which should be usable at least by riders and walkers. Continue straight on from (m), parallel to an old hedge that forms the Pulverbatch/Smethcott parish boundary; there is little sign of the old road to follow. Descend towards a brook at (n), from which point difficulties arise at present.

The correct way: The RUPP crosses the brook at (n) (once called Dead Mans Ford), ascends along the hedge (the old track is still discernible here) and crosses the field to exit close to Sheppen Fields; at (p), a short section of bridleway (part of Pb 4, also the Shropshire Way) can be taken to exit via gate (q). The end of Pb 5 should ideally use the (n)/(p)/(q) route too, not (n)/(r)/(q).

The detour: Turn right at (n) and follow the right-hand side of the hedge to gate (s) opposite the start of Pb 1. In effect, this detour is following the direction of the RUPP to (p) and the bridleway from (p) to (q), but on the wrong side of the hedge.

PULVERBATCH 3 (IN REVERSE), THE BEECHES TO PICKLESCOTT

Leave the track to Underhill Hall via gate (s) to the left of the gate and stile (q) that mark the continuation of the Shropshire Way (also Pb 4). Follow the left-hand side of the hedge down into the hollow at (n). N.B. This is a detour; the correct routes are EITHER Sheppen fields via (p) to (n) OR (q) to (p) to (n) but there is an obstruction at (n). **Turn left at (n) and ascend a slope parallel to an old hedge running on your left. Gate (m), somewhat tricky to use at present, leads onto a grassy track which is a pleasant and easy route to follow to Picklescott; it becomes a surfaced road from The Larches onwards and joins the Thresholds road just above the centre of Picklescott.** Pb 3 was once called Dead Mans Lane and more than one person has succumbed in the snow along its way (see Background).

Focus on tracks **Badgers**

The Mynd area offers good habitats for many animals and, although you may never see some of them, as most people are walking by day, there are plenty of animal signs to look for. You have, however, a good chance of seeing badgers and foxes in the area, particularly at dusk. One sign of badgers is a well-worn path, which could even lead you astray if it is in use more than the right of way. If the path is damp, look for characteristic footprints, each with the imprint of four or five round pad-marks in a neat row. Badger hair can be found where paths run under low strands of barbed wire. The conclusive evidence of a path's being a badger trail is the discovery of a latrine area; badgers dig holes to soil in, like a cat, but they leave the holes open and use an area repeatedly. It is never by the sett, which again is unmistakable because of the large size of the holes, often in a group and with huge mounds of soil outside the entrances. The sett area is clean, unlike a rabbit warren, and trees or bushes nearby, often elder, have scratch-marks, or are even barked, near the ground.

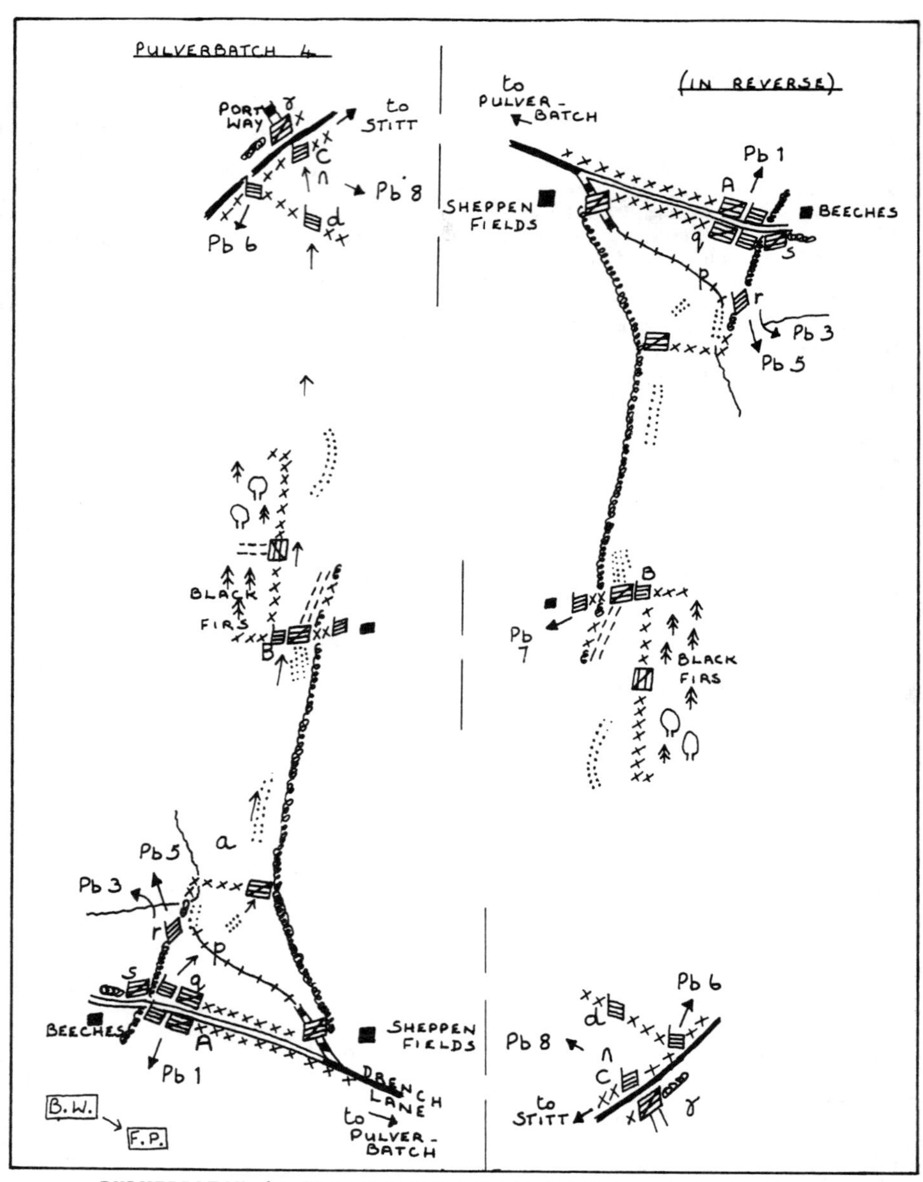

PULVERBATCH 4, THE BEECHES TO THRESHOLDS 1.75 Km/1 m.

Pb 4, in continuity with Pb 1, is an old route up onto the Long Mynd, linking up with the Portway. It must also have been used by Cothercott and Wilderley tenants to get to and from common land on the hill. **Pb 4 is bridleway from (q) to (p) and then becomes public footpath.** This strange pattern is explained by looking at an old map; Pb 1 ascends from Wilderley, becoming today's Pb 4, with no interruption until it joins and crosses the old Picklescott to Pulverbatch road at (p), there being no track to Underhill Hall.

Enter field via gate or stile at (q) and ascend to the top right-hand corner. Pass through another gate into field (a). This field is an oasis, in a large area of improved grassland, of relatively undisturbed land with rushy areas providing habitat for snipe and a few interesting plants such as red rattle, now difficult to find elsewhere in Pulverbatch. **The old track is still discernible running up the field but is too shrouded in gorse or too boggy to use today; keep to the left of it and ascend parallel to the hedge on the right, to reach gate and stile at B. Follow the edge of the forest (Black Firs), or the faint track near it, to the top and then continue in the same direction to stile (d) in a fence. From (d), cross the corner of the field, passing a 'manor stone' (see Pb 8), and exit onto lane opposite the Portway.**

PULVERBATCH 4 (IN REVERSE), THRESHOLDS TO THE BEECHES.

Cross the stile opposite the Portway and walk to the 'manor stone'. Bear right to stile (d) in a fence. From (d), aim obliquely to the left to get to the top left-hand corner of the forest. Descend alongside the forest to gate and stile at point B. From B, follow the right-hand side of the hedge (not closely) through rushes and bog down to gate (a). From (a), bear right down to the bottom right-hand corner of the field and exit opposite the start of Pb 1 near The Beeches.

PULVERBATCH 5, THE BEECHES TO SALLINS COTTAGE 1.25 Km/0.75 m.

Pb 5 is one of a few footpaths across Wilderley Hill, not all of which have been described in this book but which have been indicated on the route maps. **Pb 5 is a public footpath that begins at gate and stile (q), with Pb 4. A short distance from (q), cross stile (r) and follow the left-hand side of the hedge into the hollow at (n). Aim obliquely left up the slope to reach a double stile (t) amidst a row of conifers. From (t), continue straight on until a lumpy circular area (u) is reached, above and to the right of a right angle in a fence (v). From (u), keep to the same course, bearing away gradually to the right from fence (w). As you approach hedge (y), turn more to the right to keep away from it, not joining it until you get to the top of the field at a small farmyard opposite Sallins Cottage. Alternatively, from (u), follow fence (w) to the corner of the field and then turn right and follow hedge (y) to Sallins Cottage (this alternative route is also following rights of way).**

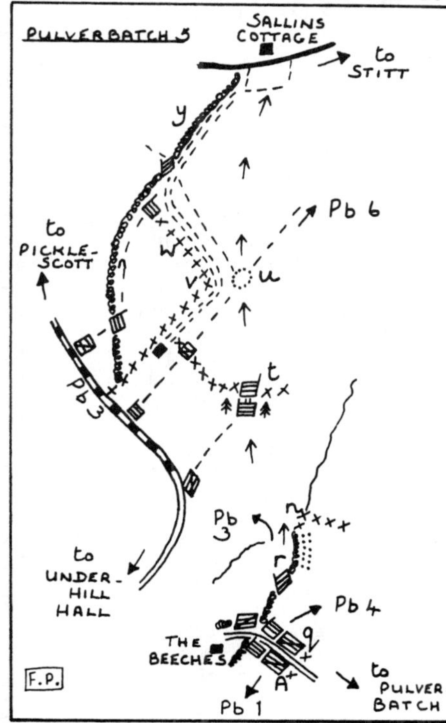

PULVERBATCH 6, Pb 3 AT D TO THRESHOLDS 1.25 Km/0.75 m.

Pb 6 begins off Pb 3 at D, just after the hedge on the left-hand side of the track changes to fence. Cross a stile. A faint track turning off to the left may have been an old route to Sallins Cottage that followed the Pulverbatch/Smethcott parish boundary, an old hedge (a) that must have also once served as the open hill boundary; a 'manor stone' is situated along this hedge marking the boundary of the manor of Wilderley in 1791. **Continue straight on to gate (b), passing a new, barn-like house. From (b), the way follows a fence up to a right angle (v) and soon reaches a lumpy circular area (u). Ascend the slope ahead, aiming straight on and to the left of the forest, to reach stile (d) in a fence.** To the right is a gully that forms the upper reaches of Wilderley Brook which on the tithe map was called Dead Mans Brook; it once formed the boundary between the manors of Cothercott and Wilderley and still strictly divides Cothercott Hill from Wilderley Hill, although as pasture, both now form one uniform expanse of grassland. The forest nearby has existed for about 80 years and is a mixture of conifers of varying ages and deciduous trees typical of this hill before it was improved (hawthorn, rowan and birch). Some further planting has recently taken place. In the forest, and visible from (d), is an almost circular embankment (e) which may be another Iron Age animal enclosure or an 'entrenchment' (1903 map). **From (d), continue straight on across grassland, keeping just to the left of some higher ground, to reach the top left-hand corner of this vast 'field'. Exit onto the road nearly opposite the Portway.** Cothercott and Wilderley Hills, forming as they do the north end of the Long Mynd, offer magnificent views but are disappointing in that much of the land has been tamed. Apart from the small gullies, the area is improved grassland or arable, a change that began during the last war when much of the area was ploughed up and potatoes planted. Before the war, the hill was a large expanse of bracken, rushes, gorse and small trees criss-crossed by cart tracks. Not surprisingly, the potatoes tasted of 'fern' (as bracken is commonly termed) and were only suitable for animal food.

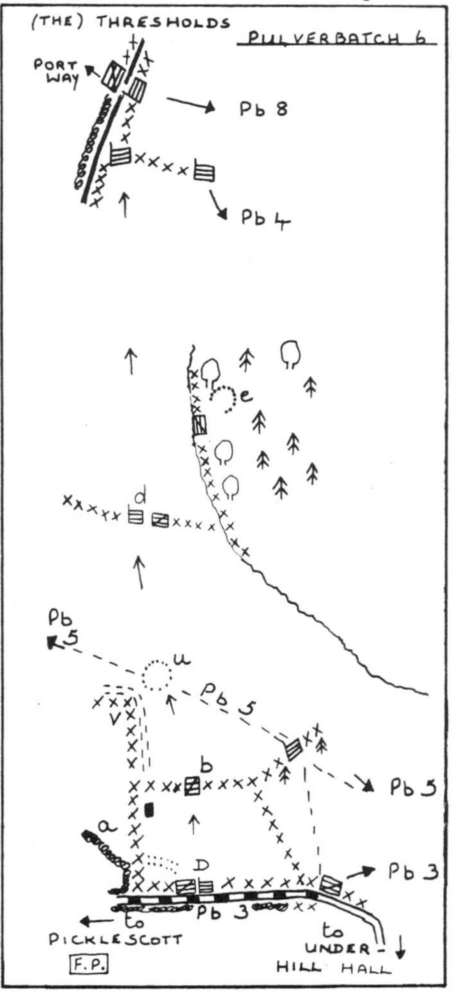

THE SUNKEN ROAD
(As 19)

THE LIGHTSPOUT
(Cs 8)

WINTER'S DAY AT POLE COTTAGE
(Tumulus in the background)

OAKLEYMILL WATERFALL IN CALLOW HOLLOW
(Cs 17)

THE KNAPP, PULVERBATCH
(A motte and bailey castle)

DRENCH LANE TO SHEPPEN FIELDS, PULVERBATCH
(continues as Pb 3 to Picklescott)

ALDERS IN THE LONG ROUGH
(Pb 7)

THE HUCKSTER STONE
(MY 7)

LOWER DARNFORD
(Rt 4)

RATLINGHOPE BEECHES
(Castle Ring on Stitt Hill in the background)

BRANMILLS AND SMETHCOTT CHURCH
(from Sm 7)

AN OLD WAY TO SMETHCOTT SCHOOL
(near Sm 6)

WALKMILLS BROOK, SMETHCOTT

HIGH ARKOLL
(Wn 7)

THE SOUTH-EAST SIDE OF THE MYND
(from Ws 1)

RIDGE AND FURROW, NEAR THE RUINS OF NETNESS/NETTLES
(near Hamperley)

PULVERBATCH 7, COTHERCOTT COTTAGE TO BLACK FIRS 1 Km/½+ m.

Pb 7 is a public footpath and an attractive route, passing through long-established fields adjacent to the open hill. Leave the main road just below Cothercott Cottage, so called on maps but now called Cothercott Hill Farm. Both Cothercott Cottage and the old Cothercott Hill Farm, now a ruin in the area known as the 'desert' (see Pb 8), were originally squatters' cottages (see Background) and the small fields passed on the right represent the efforts of early inhabitants to shape the land from the open common. The fields appear to have undergone little change and as old pastures have many wild flowers in them, creating a colourful contrast to the neighbouring fields. **Bear left across the field, away from the boundary hedge of Cothercott Cottage, aiming for the top far corner when it comes into view. Cross stile (a) into an area known as the Long Rough (an apt description).** The upper part of the Long Rough is old grassland and extends up to the area of the old Cothercott barytes mines (in operation in the early part of this century). The lower part of the Long Rough is a very attractive area of woodland, grazed enough to keep it clear of brambles but not enough to disturb the abundant bluebells and other woodland plants. It is, however, at risk of gradually dying out (see wood leasow on page 180). **Descend obliquely to the right to the small stream and climb up the steep far side to reach stile (b) in a fence. Turn half-right and cut across the corner of the field to stile (c). From (c), bear obliquely left, aiming for the bottom of the forest and the far left corner of the field. Join Pb 4 via stile (d), close to the ruins of Upper Sheppen Fields.** It may have been past inhabitants of this house who created this footpath.

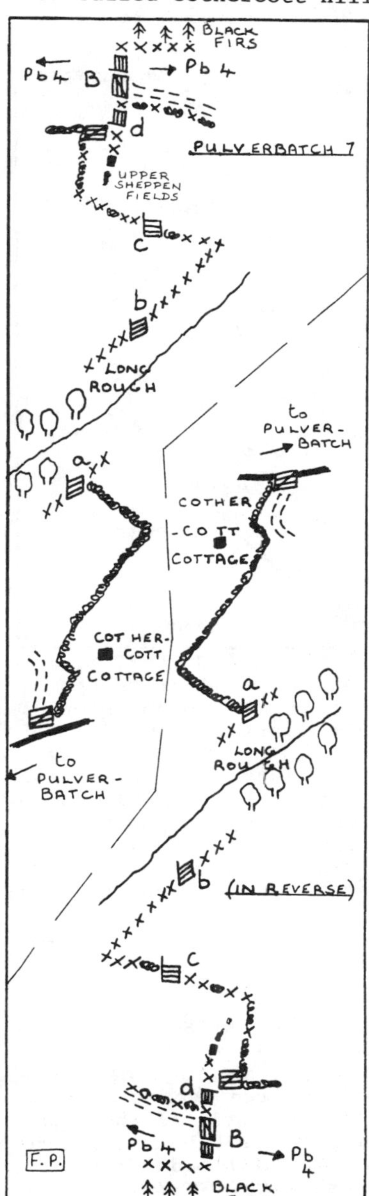

PULVERBATCH 7 (IN REVERSE)

Leave Pb 4 via stile (d) near Black Firs. Cross the first field obliquely to the right to reach stile (c). Bear slightly left across the corner of a field to get to stile (b). Pass obliquely to the right, through the steep-sided Long Rough, to get to stile (a). From (a), again bear obliquely right to get to the far right corner of the field. Go along a short track to reach the main road.

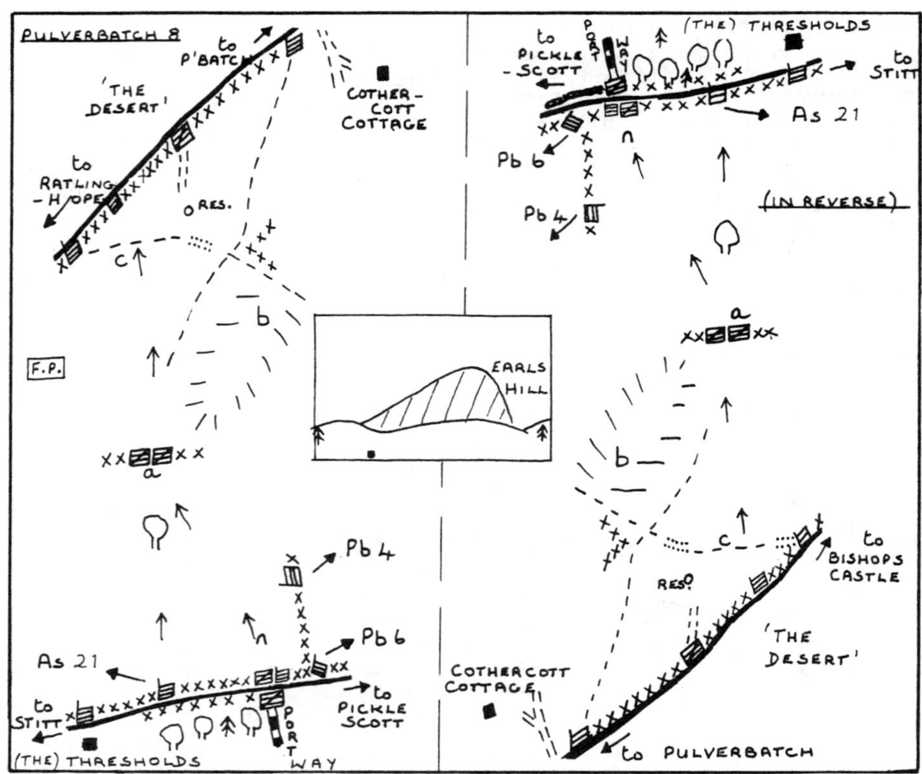

PULVERBATCH 8, THRESHOLDS TO THE MAIN ROAD 1.25 Km/0.75 m.

Pb 8 begins opposite the Portway and is a public footpath. Enter a sometimes arable field and cross to the 'manor stone', erected by T.J. Powys (see Pb 1) in 1791 to mark the boundary of Cothercott manor; today it functions as a parish boundary-marker. **Continue across this field, aiming to the right of a lone tree (another boundary-marker and once in a line of trees), to get to twin gates (a). From (a), descend the gradual slope of Cothercott** (locally known as Cuthercott) **Hill, passing well to the left of a small valley (b),** the site of old barytes mines, **and aiming to the left of Earls Hill in the distance (see inset). At (c), as the road is approached, Pb 8 crosses Pb 9,** which in parts represents the course of the old mine railway that ran from left to right to the mines. **Exit onto the road via a stile.** Opposite is an area known locally as 'the desert'.

PULVERBATCH 8 (IN REVERSE), MAIN ROAD TO THRESHOLDS

Leave the main road via the middle one of three stiles along this section of the road. Aim straight on to ascend the slope. Soon, the twin gates (a) and the lone tree near them come into view ahead; these are now the targets. Pass well to the right of a small valley (b) to get to the twin gates (a) that lead into a sometimes arable field. To reach the road by Thresholds from (a), EITHER continue straight on past a lone ash tree, OR veer to the left away from it, passing a 'manor stone'.

PULVERBATCH 9, COTHERCOTT ROAD TO BLACK FIRS 1.25 Km/0.75 m.

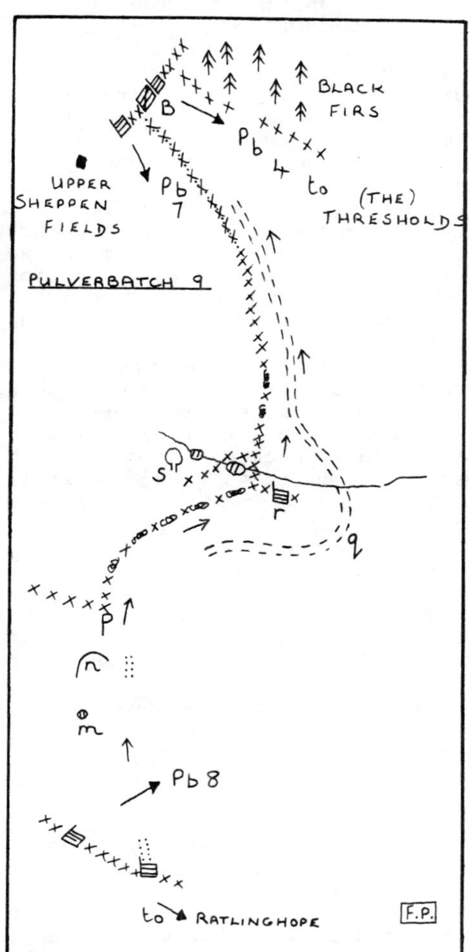

Pb 9 begins at a stile along the main road, on the Ratlinghope side of and near to the end of Pb 8. Ascend from the stile, bearing obliquely right up and away from the road. Pass to the right of the concrete remains of an old reservoir (m). On looking back, Paulith Bank, a cone-shaped hill, can be seen. A line running up the middle of it is an embankment (2 to 3 on figure 10) marking the Pulverbatch/Ratlinghope parish boundary; it has also always served as a district boundary, and appears to have been an old hundred boundary too. **Beyond the reservoir is a small hillock (n); pass between this and the main slope of Cothercott but keep to the right, out of the hollow. The way runs along a short length of built-up grassy track;** this is a remnant of the old railway line that ran from the main buildings opposite the Westcott turn on the main road, to the barytes mines ahead. **Join a right angle in a fence (p) and follow the fence as it runs to the right and descends into a valley.** The railway line veers away from (p) and can be seen as a track (q) curving round the contour of the valley. **Cross stile (r)** (to the left at (s) is an ancient oak tree) **and then a stream.** Two small pools on the left are a favourite haunt for mallard ducks. **Climb out of the valley and join a track which is a continuation of the old railway line.** Past mining activity is evident on either side. **Follow the track, along the old hill boundary wall, to point B at the bottom end of Black Firs, a fir plantation;** some areas of the forest have now been planted with young deciduous trees. **Pb 9 joins Pb 4 at B.**

Focus on birds

Snipe

Cothercott Hill, despite its taming, still provides enough areas of rushy marsh to attract snipe and it is not unusual to flush one when walking on the hill. The Mynd as a whole, with its wet hollows, offers a good habitat; there are few other places in Shropshire that do so. When disturbed, the snipe flies off, keeping near to the ground in a zig-zag flight. At the right time, the male's spectacular courtship display may be seen or heard.

Focus on trees **Yews**

Many old yew trees can be found in the Mynd area. The yew is the only tree still to have a Celtic name, fitting for a tree that in some cases has lived for centuries, longer than any of our other trees. The yew may have been regarded as special in early times since it was one of only four evergreen trees in Britain, the others being holly, Scots pine and juniper. Yews are commonly found in churchyards, where they are often very old e.g. at Ratlinghope, and may even predate the existing church in some instances. They are popular in gardens too and there are several Yew Tree Farms and Cottages still with their yew trees, e.g. at Minton. Elsewhere there are trees scattered across the countryside; some of these are undoubtedly serving or have served as boundary-markers, e.g. as an old manor boundary-marker between Myndtown manor and Asterton township near Handless, as a field boundary-marker in Home Wood which lies along Pb 2 and as a parish boundary-marker between Pulverbatch and Pontesbury. Smethcott has a Yew Tree Leasow next to the old boundary between fields and open hill, as does the area of Bullocksmoor in Stretton. Some trees are also thought to have been route-markers, and of all the fields named after yew trees, now mostly absent, many are adjacent to routes e.g. Yew Tree Leasow is by Sm 8 and another is by the Woolstaston to Duckley Nap road. Both the Yew Tree Leasows in Pulverbatch are by roads, the one still having a yew tree which grows in the roadside hedge. Old yews on Yew Tree Bank (Minton Batch) and on a slope facing Batch Valley may have been territory markers on the open hill.

It was believed that to fell a yew tree brought misfortune, but to judge from the disappearance of yews from most fields named after them this superstition no longer holds. Anyone with livestock is extremely wary of them; the leaves, bark and seeds, but not the fleshy red part of the fruit, are poisonous to man and his livestock. The male trees, which lack berries, are no less poisonous than the female but, as with other poisonous plants, animals can coexist alongside yews without harm for years.

The yew tree has the added mystique of having been used in the past to make bows. The wood is described as being hard, elastic and durable.

Focus on tracks **Foxes, hares and rabbits**

Many animal holes, trails and tracks can be found along the rights of way. Rabbit burrows are usually in a group or warren and are smaller than those of the fox or badger. Pellet-like droppings lie all around the warren and in the burrow entrances. The fox's larger hole or earth is often solitary and may, like the badger's, have a mound of soil by the entrance. Hen feathers or rabbit fur in the hole entrance, are signs of the fox's presence, as is a strong smell of fox. The hare makes no hole, only a snug 'form' in long grass.

A fox's footprints resemble a dog's of the same size but the pad-marks are less compact. A line of such prints, more obvious in snow, without accompanying human prints, almost certainly indicates a fox. Rabbit and hare footprints form a very distinctive pattern in the snow (see drawing), only differing from each other in size; unless the animal is moving slowly, the small prints of the front feet appear behind the larger prints of the back feet.

hopping rabbit bounding rabbit resting hare

RATLINGHOPE

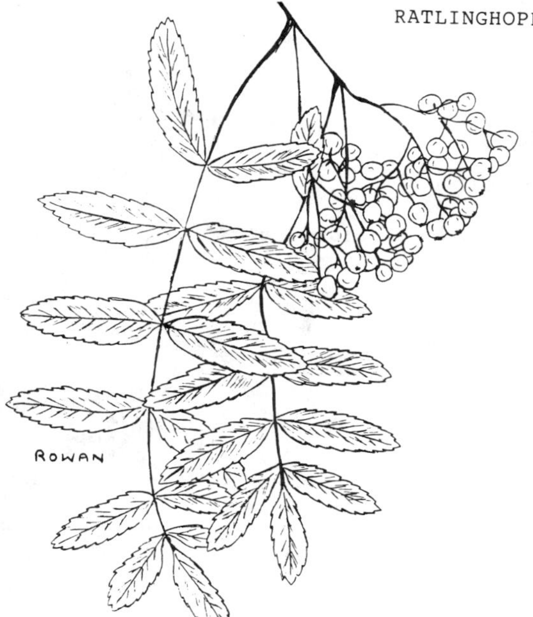

Ratlinghope is a parish situated on the north-west of the Long Mynd. It is made up of the old townships of Ratlinghope, Stitt and Gatten, the latter township lying outside the area covered in this book. Ratlinghope was the manor of Rotelingehope in the Domesday Book and Stitt lay within it. The name means 'secluded valley associated with Rotel', Rotel being a personal name. The manor was given to Wigmore Abbey, but Stitt and Gatten became part of Haughmond Abbey's manor of Boveria. The prior and his brethren who came from Wigmore may have been the first people to cultivate the valley and their successors remained probably until the time of the Dissolution of the Monasteries. The parish had come into being by the 16th century and a church that had been founded earlier still stands; the monastic buildings may have been nearby but no trace of them has been found. Stitt and Gatten were annexed to the parish after the Dissolution.

Ratlinghope is a parish with several small groups of habitations and scattered farms. Around the church is one such small group. Others are at Stitt, Coates and (the) Bridges. Integrated with Bridges is Overs, the site of a Domesday manor now lying just in the parish of Wentnor. Yet another small area of habitation has developed from the old school and vicarage, along the main road. Stitt also lies on the main road; it was a larger hamlet in mediaeval times with its own chapel.

Ratlinghope can be reached via the minor road from Shrewsbury to Bishops Castle. It can also be reached from the A49 via lanes across the Mynd EITHER from Leebotwood via Woolstaston OR from Church Stretton via the Burway road.

Amenities:-

Shop - none. Post Office only, on the main road.

Refreshments - Horseshoe Inn at Bridges. N.B. Not open every lunchtime. Brow Farm, near the church, is open as a cafe at weekends and bank holidays and also, by arrangement, for groups.

Accommodation:- YHA at Bridges. Bed and Breakfast at Lower Stitt Farm on the main road.

Campsites:- Brow Farm, near the church (all year). Middle Darnford, along the road from the church towards Woolstaston.

Bus service - Horrocks Coaches, Tuesday only. Leave Bishops Castle at 09.10, Ratlinghope Post Office at 09.39 and arrive at Shrewsbury at 10.30. Leave Shrewsbury at 13.00, Ratlinghope Post Office at 13.54 and arrive at Bishops Castle at 14.23. (1993).

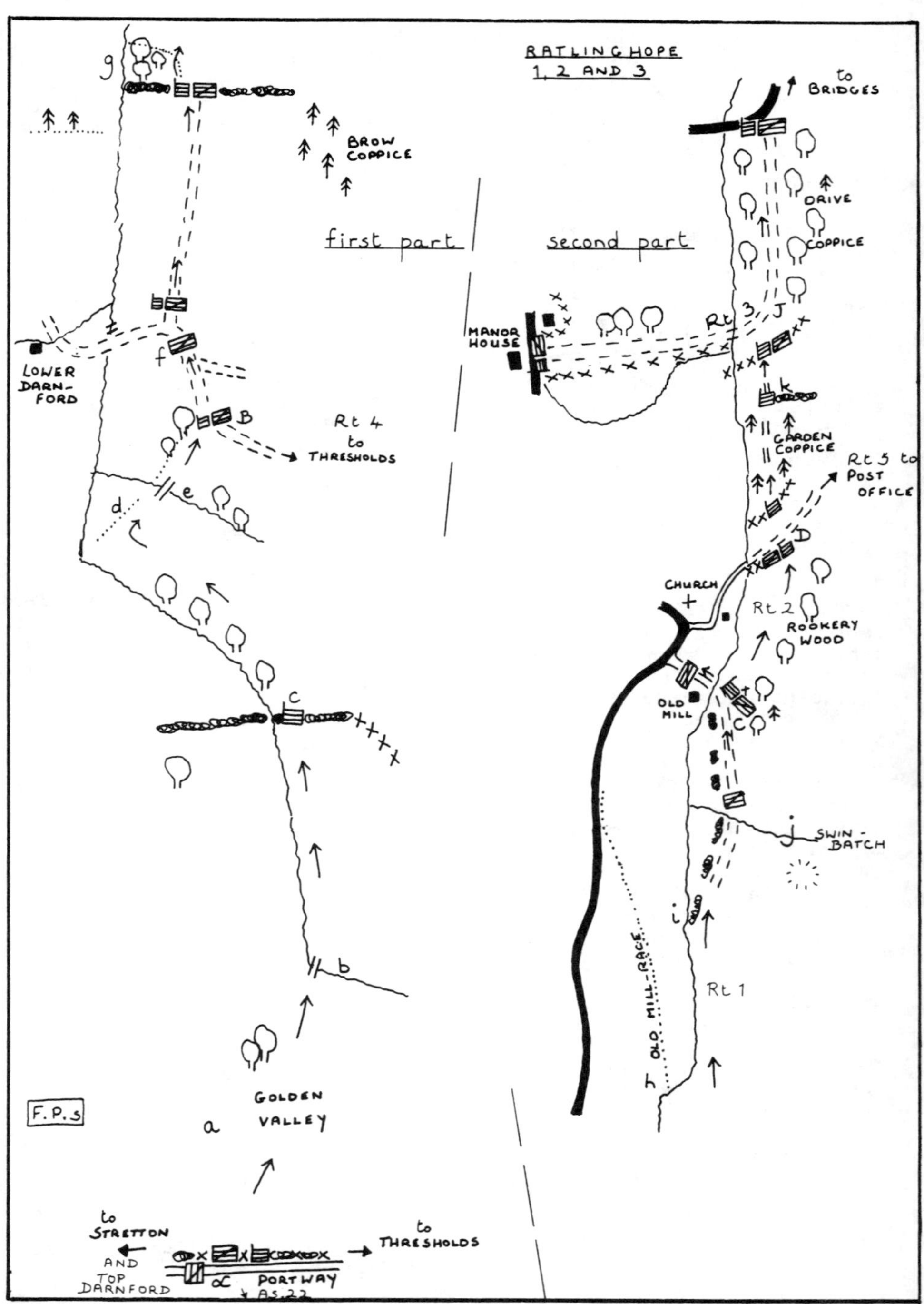
RATLINGHOPE
1, 2 AND 3
first part
second part
g
BROW
COPPICE
LOWER
DARN-
FORD
f
B
Rt 4
to
THRESHOLDS
d
e
c
b
GOLDEN
VALLEY
a
F.P.s
to
STRETTON
AND
TOP
DARNFORD
α
PORTWAY
A5.22
to
THRESHOLDS
to
BRIDGES
DRIVE
COPPICE
MANOR
HOUSE
Rt 3
J
k
GARDEN
COPPICE
Rt 5 to
POST
OFFICE
D
CHURCH
Rt 2
ROOKERY
WOOD
OLD
MILL
C
j
SWIN-
BATCH
i
OLD MILL-RACE
h
Rt 1

RATLINGHOPE 1, 2 AND 3

The Shropshire Way leaves the Portway at α and follows first the Golden Valley and then the valley of the Darnford Brook down to the Bridges. This route probably originated as at least three separate routes, which is how I have described it.

Rt 1 was a link between the Portway (and the habitations such as Top Darnford that lie beside it) and Ratlinghope Church and mill; it also appears to have linked up with a route to Picklescott. From Lower Darnford to Ratlinghope, old trackway is apparent and this was once the only way down the valley (see fig. 12).

Rt 3 is an old trackway running between the Manor House and the Bridges and is likely to have been a private drive; the wood that it passes through is Drive Coppice.

Rt 2 may be a relatively modern link between 1 and 3. It is not shown on old maps; the section through Garden Coppice is shown on the 1904 O/S map.

RATLINGHOPE 1, PORTWAY TO RATLINGHOPE 2.25 Km/nearly 1½m.

Rt 1 leaves the Portway at the end of a surfaced section at α, crosses a stile and descends to the right of a hollow (a). Pass a group of trees and continue down to cross a tiny stream (b), still keeping to the right of the hollow. The slope on the right has numerous gorse bushes, which may be the origin of the name 'Golden Valley' for this area. Gorse appears to have a long flowering season but this is only because there are two species of gorse growing on the Mynd; one flowers in the spring and the other in late summer. **The stream at (b) turns sharply to run down the main valley; follow it to a stile (c), which is in the old hedge that forms the Ratlinghope/All Stretton boundary. The path now runs through an area of bracken and the stream is flanked by many pussy willow trees. At an embankment (d) which is an old hedge/wall, turn right and follow it to cross another small stream (e); a footbridge spans the stream but not the bog! Continue along a line of trees to join a track (Rt 4) at B. Turn left along the track, almost immediately climbing over a stile, and continue along to gate (f). After (f), the track or Rt 4 bears downhill to the left while Rt 1 turns right over a stile; it now follows the Darnford Brook downstream as a grassy track. A slope of grass and bracken ascends to Brow Coppice, a wood largely consisting of old larch trees. A small old plantation is passed at (g) and downstream from this at (h) is the point at which the old mill-stream left the brook; much of its course is still visible but dry. From (i), the track follows hedge to Rookery Wood and then descends to ford the brook by the old mill. Pass through a gate and exit onto lane near the church.**

RATLINGHOPE 2, ROOKERY WOOD TO DRIVE COPPICE 0.5 Km/¼+ m.

As Rt 1 bends to the left at C, Rt 2 enters an enclosed area via a stile and runs beneath a steep slope of mixed woodland (Rookery Wood). Opposite is Yew Tree Cottage and garden where a perforated stone axe-hammer and a lead spindle-whorl were once found. **Leave this area via a stile, cross a track (Rt 5) at D and enter a coniferous wood opposite (Garden Coppice) via another stile. A small path runs through the trees, crossing sections of boardway, and leaves it via a stile (k). Cross the corner of a field, still following the brook, cross stile (k) and enter Drive Coppice to join Rt 3 at J.**

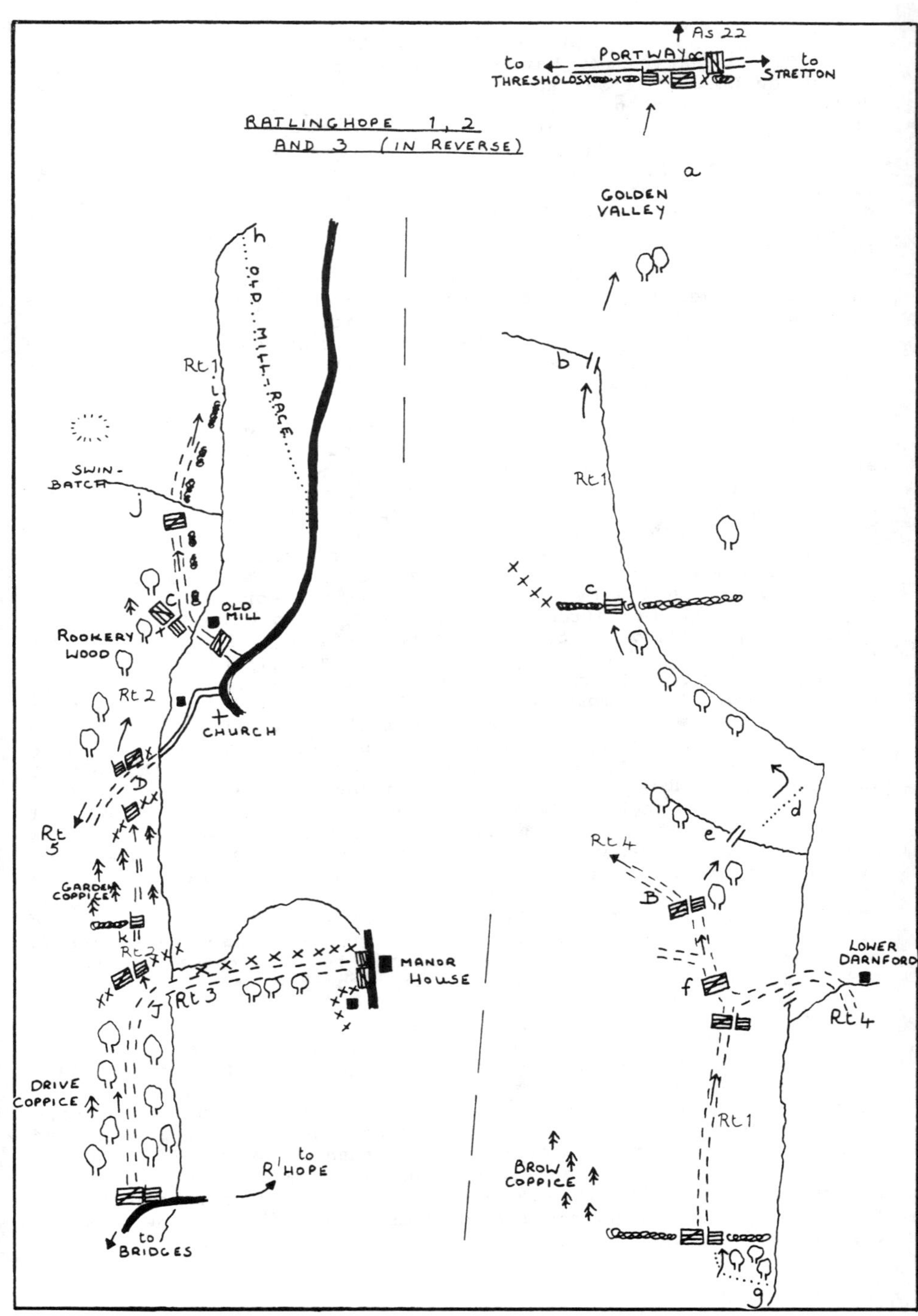
RATLINGHOPE 1, 2
AND 3 (IN REVERSE)
As 22
PORTWAY
to
THRESHOLDS
to
STRETTON
a
GOLDEN
VALLEY
b
Rt 1
c
d
e
Rt 4
B
f
LOWER
DARNFORD
Rt 4
Rt 1
BROW
COPPICE
g
h
OLD MILL RACE
Rt 1
L
SWIN-
BATCH
j
C
OLD
MILL
ROOKERY
WOOD
Rt 2
CHURCH
D
Rt
5
GARDEN
COPPICE
k
Rt 2
J
Rt 3
MANOR
HOUSE
DRIVE
COPPICE
to
R'HOPE
to
BRIDGES

RATLINGHOPE 3, MANOR HOUSE TO BRIDGES 0.5 Km/¼+ m.

(The map for Rt 3 in this direction is on page 157).

Rt 3 forms part of Wild Edrics Way. It starts opposite the Manor House through a gate and follows a fence down to Darnford Brook. It has the appearance of an old track with trees, including horse-chestnuts, along the left-hand side. At the brook, a small stone bridge is crossed and Rt 2 is joined at J. The way continues as a track running above the brook through attractive mixed but mostly deciduous woodland (Drive Coppice). The wood is well-endowed with nesting boxes and this is an ideal habitat for the pied flycatcher and for other more common birds.

RATLINGHOPE 1 (IN REVERSE), RATLINGHOPE TO THE PORTWAY

Take the track past the old mill, ford the brook and follow old trackway along a hedge, passing through a gate and crossing the small stream from Swinbatch at (j). Above, on the left, part of the circular embankment, now thought to have been a Celtic enclosure, is evident. The way from Ratlinghope to Lower Darnford follows Darnford Brook upstream, along the side of slopes of bracken and grass; it passes a small old plantation at (g), runs along under Brow Coppice and joins a stony track (Rt 4) by Lower Darnford. Turn left along the track through gate (f) and continue to a stile and gate at point B. Leave the track and follow a line of trees to a small stream (e). Cross this via a bridge and continue along a small embankment (d) for a short distance before turning left. The path runs through bracken and starts to ascend along the left side of a brook to reach stile (c), and continues up the left side of this small valley to a stile on to the Portway at $\propto$.

RATLINGHOPE 2 (IN REVERSE), DRIVE COPPICE TO ROOKERY WOOD

Leave Rt 3 at J in Drive Coppice i.e. continue on the same side of the brook and bear to the left to exit via a stile into a field. Cross the corner of this field and enter a coniferous wood (Garden Coppice) via stile (k). Follow the small path with sections of boardway and exit via a stile at the far end. Cross Rt 5 (a track) at D and enter an enclosed area via another stile. A wide path runs below a steep slope of trees (Rookery Wood) and joins Rt 1 at C.

RATLINGHOPE 3 (IN REVERSE), BRIDGES TO MANOR HOUSE

Leave the lane by a stone bridge, via a gate into a wood (Drive Coppice), and follow an old grassy track. At J, Rt 3 turns right across a small stone bridge and the Shropshire Way, as Rt 2, bears off to the left. After crossing the brook, follow the fence on the left, with trees on the right, and exit via a gate onto the lane opposite the Manor House.

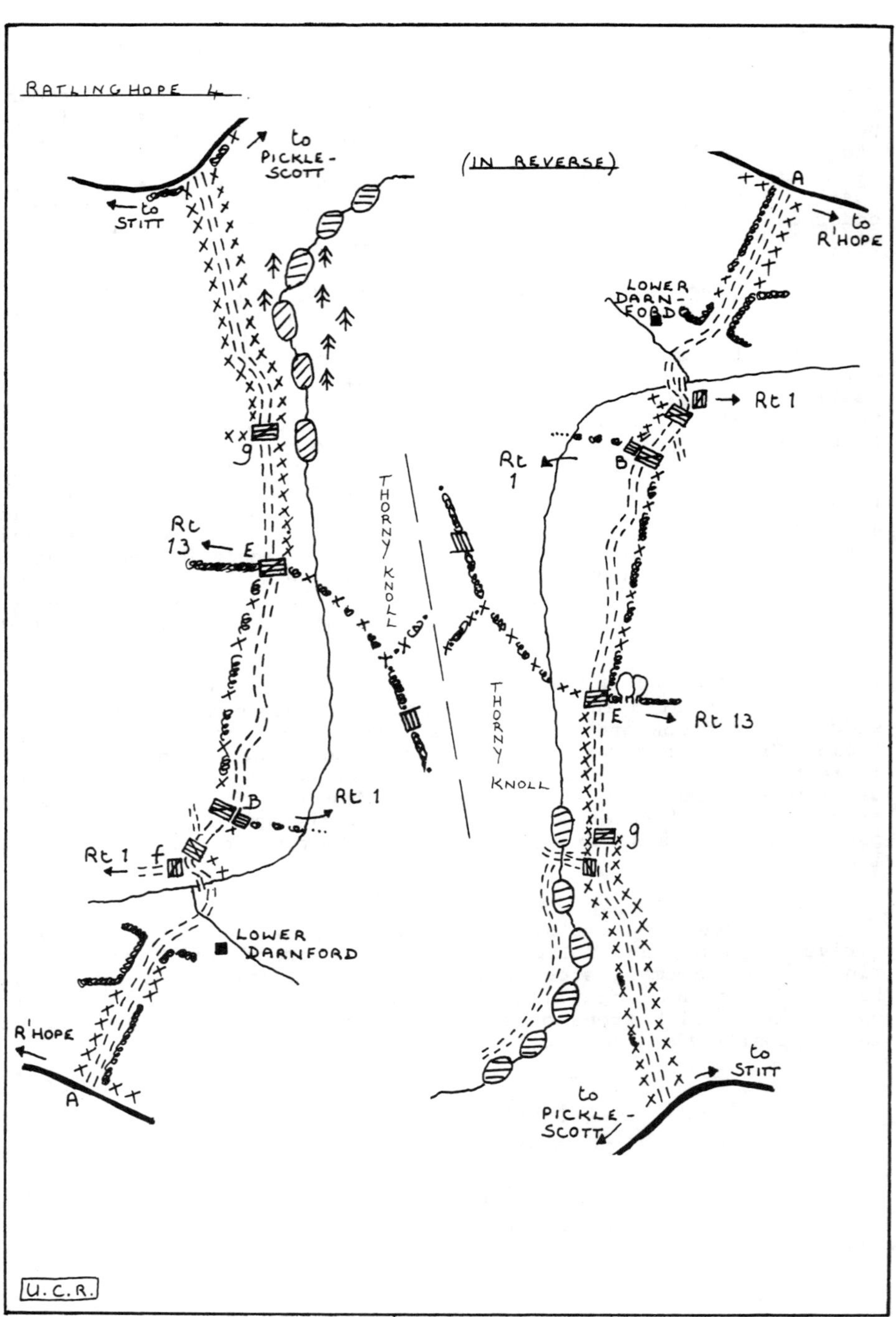

RATLINGHOPE 4
(IN REVERSE)
to PICKLE-SCOTT
to STITT
g
Rt 13
E
THORNY KNOLL
B
Rt 1
Rt 1
f
LOWER DARNFORD
R'HOPE
A
A
to R'HOPE
LOWER DARN-FORD
Rt 1
Rt 1
B
THORNY KNOLL
E
Rt 13
g
to PICKLE-SCOTT
to STITT
U.C.R.

RATLINGHOPE 4, LOWER DARNFORD TO THRESHOLDS 1¼ Km/0.75m.

Rt 4 is an unsurfaced highway and an old track. It would have been used by inhabitants of the Thresholds to get to Ratlinghope, who would branch off it near (f) to follow Rt 1. In reverse it may once have served as an outrack to common land. In the last century the track continued from the Lower Darnford end at A, up onto the hill to join Rt 6 (see fig.12), and this was the way people from Lower Darnford went to Stretton. Ponies and traps were left at pubs while the business in town was done. On one occasion two people who had gone to Stretton from Lower Darnford had left their pony and trap at The Plough (no longer an inn); one decided to come home early on foot and left a message for the other, who assumed she had taken the pony and trap and walked home too. There was no alternative but to walk back and get it (5 miles each way). Today Rt 4 shows no sign of continuation onto the hill but joins the modern Ratlinghope to Woolstaston road at A. As mentioned in descriptions of other routes, parts of this road are relatively new and inhabitants of Lower Darnford would have travelled to Ratlinghope via Rt 1. For most of this century, however, the modern road would have been in use for getting to Ratlinghope or Stretton.

The route starts off the Ratlinghope to Woolstaston road at A, as an enclosed driveway to Lower Darnford. It fords two streams, one of which is Darnford Brook. This may have been the original 'darn ford' or 'hidden ford' as its name means. **Ascend steeply to a gate (f); just before this, on the corner, Rt 1 branches off to the left. Pass through the gate and keep to the right-hand track that follows the fence (the left-hand track only goes to a barn). Pass through another gate at B; Rt 1 branches off to the right along an old wall. Continue up the slope to a gate at E;** this marks the old Stitt manor boundary which runs in an almost unbroken line approximately east/west, from Hillside Farm on the left (west) to Thorny Knoll on the far side of the small valley on the right. Here it joins a hedge, the present-day Ratlinghope boundary, at right angles to it. When Stitt was a manor, this hedge, running northwards over Thorny Knoll, was its eastern boundary. Running southwards it formed the Ratlinghope manor boundary. It is now all the Ratlinghope parish boundary. A feature of Ratlinghope is the presence of many magnificent beech trees particularly along track or hedge; a group of these large trees stands at point E. **The track now runs alongside a fence to another gate at (g). Thorny Knoll is the hill on the right across the small valley.** Its name may derive from the gorse that now only grows on its lower slopes. **Our track runs alongside some relatively new pools and forestry which have refashioned the upper part of the valley and then bears away from them to exit onto the Stitt to Picklescott road.**

RATLINGHOPE 4 (IN REVERSE), THRESHOLDS TO LOWER DARNFORD

Turn off the Stitt to Picklescott road just below the Thresholds and descend along clear track, passing a small beech plantation, to gate (g); this lies to the right of a valley containing pools and forestry. Follow the track along the fence to another gate at E by some large beech trees. Pass through this gate and descend again to another gate and stile at B where Rt 1 joins the track from the left. Continue to gate (f); the track now drops steeply to a ford, with Rt 1 branching off to the right on the corner. Rt 4 crosses two fords, passes Lower Darnford and exits along its driveway onto the Ratlinghope to Woolstaston road.

RATLINGHOPE 5, CHURCH TO POST OFFICE 1 Km/½+m.

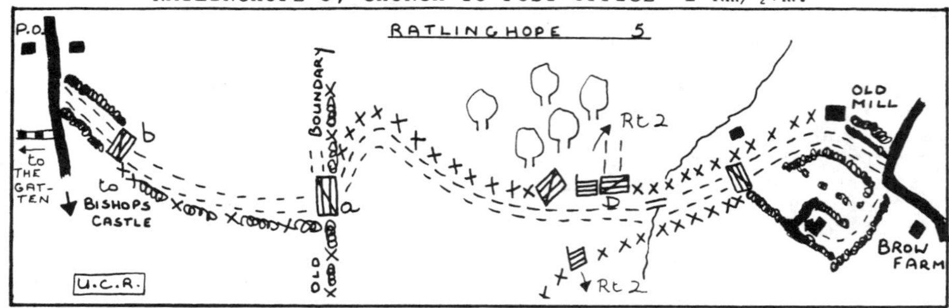

Rt 5 is an unsurfaced highway that links the core of Ratlinghope with the Post Office. In the past it also served as a link with the vicarage (now the Post Office) and the school nearby (now a house). In the latter part of the last century and the early part of this the vicar must have traversed this route many times to take services. The way then became a shoppers' route when (approximately fifty years ago) the vicarage became the P.O. and shop and the site of the bus stop. The P.O. and bus stop remain today.

Ratlinghope school was apparently sited in the present-day YHA building at the Bridges but after a disagreement between the Gatten and Ratlinghope estates a school was built near the vicarage in 1868 for Gatten estate children; later, children of the two communities were reunited in the school by the vicarage and Ratlinghope children would have used Rt 5 until the school closed in about 1960. Teachers going to Church Stretton (e.g. to cash their pay cheques) would have travelled this way. At the Post Office end, Rt 5 links up with another unsurfaced highway that crosses the small range of hills between the Long Mynd and the Stiperstones, via Far Gatten farm; as a continuous route this was a way for people from further afield to get to Stretton.

At its highest point, this track is crossed by an old wall that was the Stitt manor boundary (see Background). A track appears to have run beside it. Both these features are more obvious as they ascend the hill eastwards to an old Celtic enclosure on Stitt hill.

Rt 5 starts as an enclosed track that leaves the road by Ratlinghope church, bending round behind it before descending to the brook. After the brook, the track is crossed by Rt 2 at point D. It then ascends steeply, following a hedge, with Rookery Wood and its fine horse-chestnut trees to the right. At (a), the highest point along the track, pass through a gate in the Stitt boundary wall. The track descends along the right-hand side of a hedge to gate (b). From (b) the track is enclosed. Greater celandine grows plentifully on its verges; it bears little resemblance to the (lesser) celandine that most of us are familiar with. **The track exits onto the main road opposite the Post Office;** the old school is further up the road on the same side as the P.O.

RATLINGHOPE 5 (IN REVERSE), POST OFFICE TO THE CHURCH

Take the track opposite the Post Office and ascend to gate (b). Continue to ascend, following a hedge on your right, and pass through gate (a) at the top. The track now descends along a hedge on your left and, just before the brook, is crossed by Rt 2 at D. Ford the brook or use the footbridge, and follow enclosed track up to the church.

RATLINGHOPE 6, RATLINGHOPE TO WILDMOOR POOL 1¼ Km/0.75m.

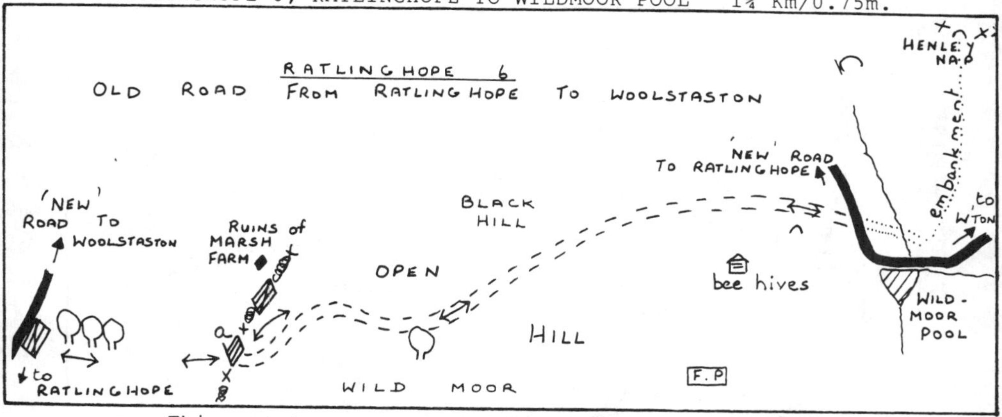

This route was the main 'road' from Ratlinghope to Woolstaston, and was joined by a continuation of Rt 4 from Lower Darnford up onto the hill. Much of the present surfaced road from Ratlinghope to Wildmoor Pool - between the start of Rt 6 and Wildmoor Pool - is not shown on old maps e.g. the 1847 field map. Rt 6 is the way the Reverend Donald Carr travelled 2,500 times, usually on horseback, before his 'night in the snow' in January 1865. How many more journeys he made after his ordeal is unknown, but the last burial in Ratlinghope recorded as being performed by him was only six months later. Ratlinghope people must have used this way too, countless times, as an alternative to Rt 9, to go to Church Stretton and it may have been used by miners, perhaps to get to the Leebotwood coal mines, though this is an assumption based only on the name Colliersford for the old ford by Wildmoor Pool.

Leave the lane between Ratlinghope and the Lower Darnford turn via a gate and follow a line of trees (beeches and ash) initially. Continue straight on up through the green field to a stile (a) onto open hill. This section used to be enclosed track. **Turn left along the fence to the remains of Marsh Farm. Aim up the hill directly away from these ruins along a grassy area between expanses of bracken. There are signs of many tracks here but eventually a clear one evolves; this takes you near to a lone beech tree and then through heather and bilberries to meet the road close to Wildmoor Pool.** Straight across the road, and just below the dam of Wildmoor Pool, signs can be seen of an old track on either side of the brook; this would have been the original route and was the Colliers Ford. Wildmoor Pool must have been created half-way through the last century; it is not shown on the tithe map of 1847 but was specifically mentioned by Rev. Carr as a landmark along his route in 1865. The new road may have been made at the same time, in some places making use of old tracks.

RATLINGHOPE 6 (IN REVERSE), WILDMOOR POOL TO RATLINGHOPE

Leave the road just below Wildmoor Pool and follow the old and clear track over the brow of the hill. Descend to the fence by the ruins of Marsh Farm (the track fades away for the last bit). Follow the fence to the left to get to a stile (a). From (a), walk straight down the green field and join a line of trees, to get to a gate onto the road.

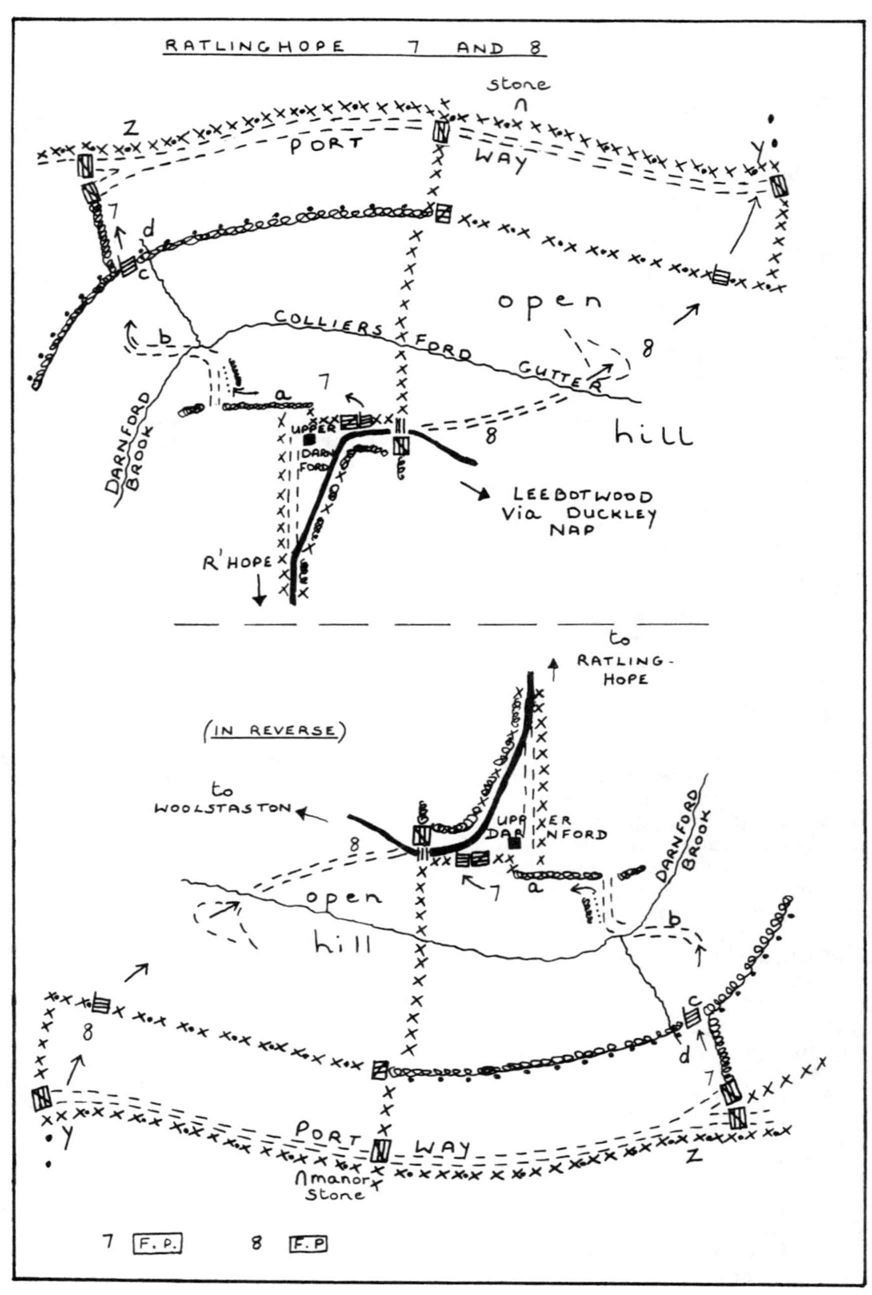
RATLINGHOPE 7 AND 8
stone
Z
PORT
WAY
y
7
d
c
b
COLLIERS FORD GUTTER
open
8
hill
a
7
UPPER
DARNFORD
DARNFORD BROOK
8
LEEBOTWOOD
Via DUCKLEY
NAP
R'HOPE
to
RATLING-
HOPE
(IN REVERSE)
to
WOOLSTASTON
UPPER
DARNFORD
8
open
hill
7
a
DARNFORD BROOK
b
c
d
8
7
PORT
WAY
y
z
manor
stone
7 F.P.
8 F.P

RATLINGHOPE 7 AND 8

Both these routes leave the Ratlinghope to Woolstaston road near Upper Darnford and cross the brook in Colliersford Gutter before ascending steeply to the Portway. Rt 7 shows signs of having been an old cart track and used to be a bridleway, though now downgraded to a footpath. It crosses the brook apparently close to the point at which Colliersford Gutter, which on older maps was the Wildmoor Brook, becomes Darnford Brook. Darnford means hidden ford and is an old name that was in existence long before that of Colliersford. The original hidden ford may have been one of the two present-day fords, either at Lower Darnford or along Rt 7. Colliersford, on the 1847 tithe map, refers to the old ford just below Wildmoor Pool; on another old map (1828) it is Collins Ford.

Upper Darnford, Middle Darnford and Lower Darnford farms and Top Darnford (now in ruins) can be extremely difficult to get to in bad weather. One written account, referring to the winter of 1928, tells of Ratlinghope people making long tunnels through drifts to isolated houses. Upper Darnford that year was cut off for three weeks, by the end of which time furniture was being cut up for firewood. The straw out of mattresses had to be used to feed animals in one of the severe winters, those most usually recalled within living memory being in 1946/47 and 1962/63.

RATLINGHOPE 7, UPPER DARNFORD TO THE PORTWAY AT Z 0.5 Km/¼m.

This route starts just above Upper Darnford. After crossing a stile, follow the fence and hedge that bounds the farm and continue along the hedge (a). At an old gateway and before a break in the hedge on the left, turn right down to the brook. Cross the brook diagonally and ascend an old track (b); this curves to the right higher up and fades out. Aim for the stile (c) which is situated in the Ratlinghope boundary hedge, which also serves as a district boundary. In the boggy area nearby (d) grows the striking bog St.Johnswort (not a common plant). **The path follows a short length of hedge to reach the Portway.**

RATLINGHOPE 7 (IN REVERSE), PORTWAY TO UPPER DARNFORD

Leave the Portway at point Z and follow a short length of hedge to a stile (c). Descend the slope, bearing slightly to the right, to join an old track that bends down to the left to reach the brook. Cross the brook diagonally, turn right and ascend the field to the far hedge. Turn left along it and follow hedge and fence, passing behind Upper Darnford, to exit onto the road via a stile.

RATLINGHOPE 8, CATTLE-GRID BY UPPER DARNFORD TO PORTWAY 0.5 Km/¼m.

This route leaves the road obliquely to the left just after crossing the cattle-grid onto open hill above Upper Darnford. Descend to the brook and after crossing it take a small path leading straight up the slope, not the ones branching off obliquely. A stile is reached at the top of the slope in a fence that marks the Ratlinghope and district boundary. Cross the green field to reach the Portway at point Y.

RATLINGHOPE 8 (IN REVERSE), PORTWAY TO CATTLE-GRID

Leave the Portway at point Y and cross the green field to a stile in a fence that leads onto open hill. Descend the slope along a small path through thick bracken. Cross the brook and ascend to the right along a wider path to reach the road.

RATLINGHOPE 9 AND 11

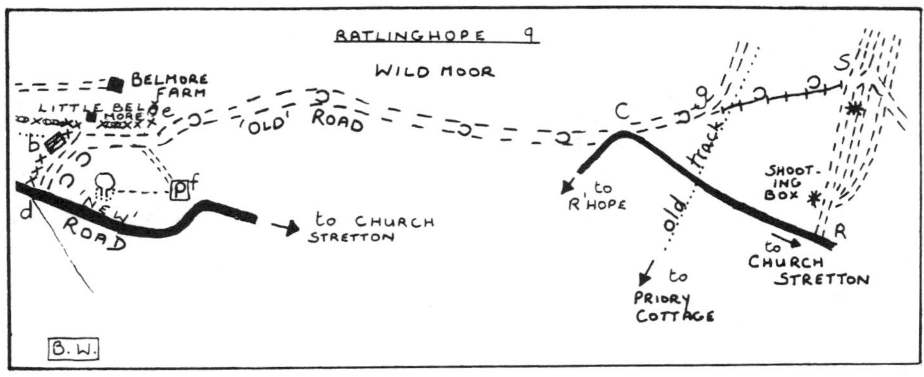

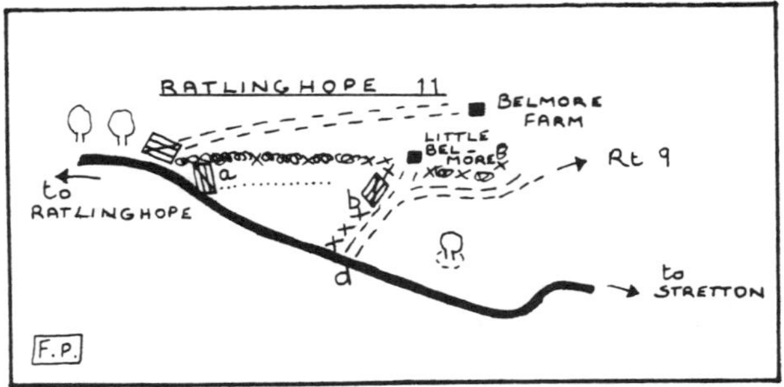

The old route that went over the hill from Ratlinghope to Church Stretton via the Shooting Box and the Burway followed the course of Rt 11 and Rt 9 at least until the 1840s. Ratlinghope people must have used this way countless times to get to Church Stretton, although some used Rt 6. A young teacher at Ratlinghope school once described her experiences of the 1920s; the long journey to and from Stretton just to bank her pay seemed daunting. The new road veers away from the start of Rt 11 at (a) and runs to the south-west of the old route to rejoin it near the Shooting Box at point C; this is the surfaced road of today. One of the distinctive features of Ratlinghope is the presence of beech trees and the road ascending from Ratlinghope passes through an avenue of them as far as the open hill. Rt 11, the old way, has no grand beech trees but an old hedge on one side and an embankment on the other outline a wide straight sweep up to the open hill.

RATLINGHOPE 11, BELMORE FARM TURN TO LITTLE BELMORE

Rt 11 is a public footpath that leaves the Ratlinghope to Church Stretton road as it runs through an avenue of beech trees, close to the driveway entrance to Belmore Farm. Pass through gate (a) and follow the hedge on the left up the field. At the top of the field, exit via a gate onto open hill. Rt 9 continues straight on.

RATLINGHOPE 11 (IN REVERSE), LITTLE BELMORE TO BELMORE FARM TURN

Rt 9 descends the open hill to the entrance to Little

Belmore, where it curves to the left; Rt 11 is the continuation straight on through gate (b) into a field. Follow the hedge on the right down the field to exit onto the road via gate (a).

RATLINGHOPE 9, LITTLE BELMORE TO THE PORTWAY AT S 1.5 Km/lm.

Rt 9 is a bridleway which begins just after the 'new road' crosses a cattle-grid onto open hill at (d); the first part follows the short driveway to Little Belmore, where it is joined by Rt 11. It then turns to the right and for a short distance runs close to a hedge before leaving this at point (e) to run up over open hill. Near (e), tracks and paths lead to the parking area (f) and to Belmore Ring. Belmore Ring is a small enclosed, circular area, probably with an ancient history, which appears to have been planted with trees for a long time; today there are few old trees and it has been replanted. **The track that ascends from (e) through the heather is very clear and easily followed to point C where it rejoins the Ratlinghope to Church Stretton road on a sharp bend. The continuation of this bridleway branches off again from this same corner; it is far more ill-defined, although it starts clearly because the first part is used today by farmers. Start along the used track but as it bends to the left at (g) continue straight on. An old track running from left to right is crossed** (an old route that was in continuity with Rt 10). **The way is vague from here to the Portway at S and appears little used. Aim slightly to the left of straight on and slightly to the left of a faint rise in the ground. It is better to err too much to the right than to the left; Wildmoor, which stretches away to the left, is a bleak and boggy place.**

RATLINGHOPE 9 (IN REVERSE), PORTWAY AT S TO LITTLE BELMORE

This bridleway leaves the Portway via a small path just to the north of a tumulus. The way is vague through the heather; aim slightly to the left of straight on. It is safer to err too much to the left than to the right; Wildmoor, stretching away to the right, is a wild and boggy moor. If your aim has been correct you should meet the Ratlinghope to Church Stretton road on a sharp bend C; if you have erred too much to the left you will still meet this road. An alternative to using this section of Rt 9 is to leave the Portway at R, near the Shooting Box, and use the road to get to the next section of Rt 9 at point C. Rt 9, leaving the road at C, is a clear track that descends the open hill to Little Belmore. Rt 11 continues straight on from here while Rt 9 curves to the left along Little Belmore's driveway to exit onto the road by a cattle-grid.

Focus on birds **Kestrels and sparrowhawks**

The kestrel is the commonest and most widespread bird of prey in Britain and unmistakable when it is hovering, waiting to pounce on its prey. The open hill is good hunting ground and kestrels are a not infrequent sight near such a track as Rt 9. Sparrowhawks are of similar size to kestrels and almost as common but they do not hover and are more likely to be seen on lower ground where there are trees. Sparrowhawks in flight resemble low-flying aircraft (prey is surprised and snatched in flight) and may sometimes be seen speeding along lanes quite close to the ground; eventually they turn off, skimming the hedge and disappearing. Both birds are of similar colouring (brown and grey) but in flight the overall impression of the sparrowhawk is grey while that of the kestrel is brown.

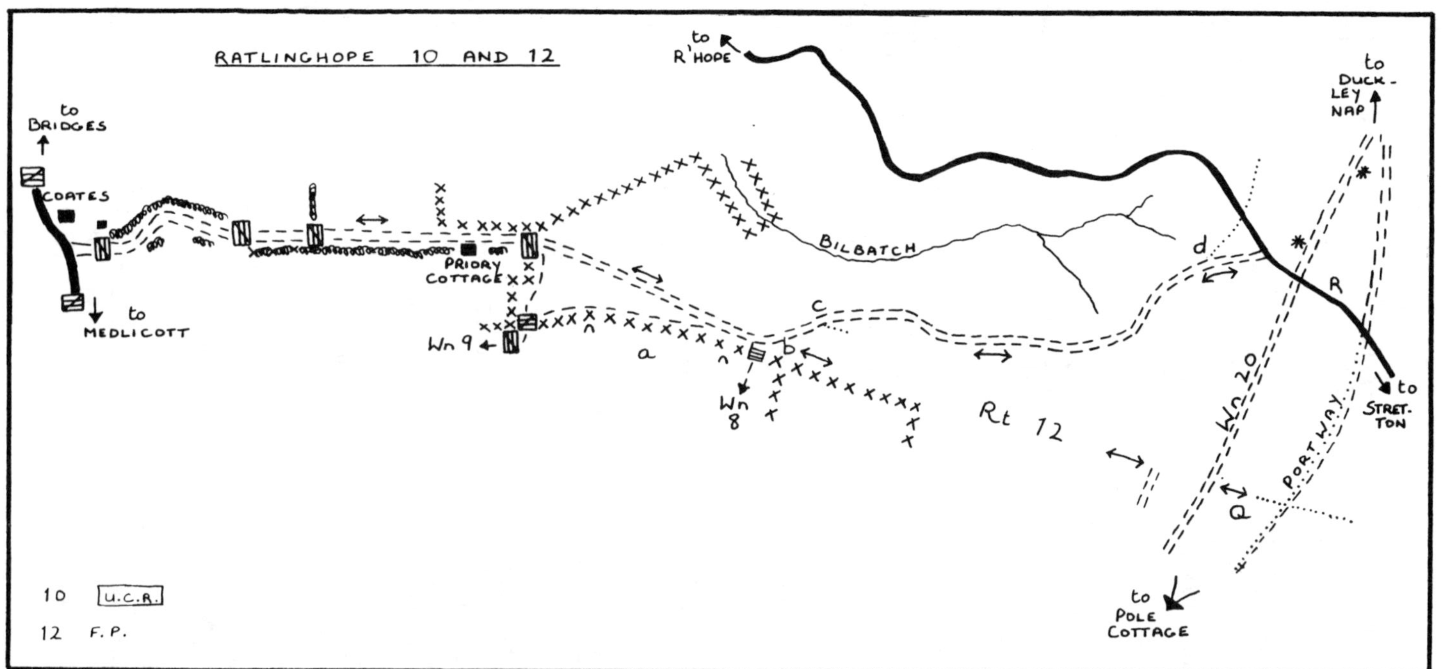

RATLINGHOPE 12 (IN REVERSE), PORTWAY TO Rt 10

This route starts from Wn 20 or the Portway at Q, where the latter crosses a marked embankment that may represent the Ratlinghope parish boundary or old track. Aim down towards the right of a fence in the distance, and along the right of a valley. Follow the fence to join the track (Rt 10) at (b).

RATLINGHOPE 10 AND 12

Rt 10 is an unsurfaced highway from Coates to the Ratlinghope to Church Stretton road near the Shooting Box. By turning onto this road Stretton is reached via the Burway; this way to Stretton would have been the best route for people from Overs, Bridges and Coates as well as being their route onto open hill to tend animals. At (d), a track branched off and continued over the road and on across Wildmoor to Duckley Nap; much of this can still be followed as a heather-clad embankment. The original route to Stretton branched off at (c) and ran up over Pole Bank to join the Burway road. This old way too has disappeared beneath the heather and although it is marked as a public footpath on the O/S map is even harder to follow than the old Wildmoor track; instead, a path (Rt 12) has developed leaving Rt 10 at (b) which runs up to Pole Bank along the National Trust boundary (also the Ratlinghope/Wentnor parish boundary). The majority of 'tumps' that marked the parish boundary have disappeared but two are still discernible at the lower end, just inside the field (a).

Other people to use these routes were those from the area known as The Rock, which lies on Wn 9; Medlicott people had access to these routes via Wn 8 and miners too, when the Medlicott copper mine was in use.

RATLINGHOPE 10, COATES TO SHOOTING BOX 2.75 Km/1.75m.

Leave the gated, surfaced road at Coates and turn up towards the hill via a gate. The track runs on one or other side of a hedge, passing through two gates, as far as Priory Cottage. It runs along a ridge that extends from the west side of the Mynd across to Adstone Hill, creating the head of the valley of Prolleymoor; there are fine views of the western escarpment of the Mynd. Priory Cottage is a deserted hut which replaced Rock Cottage, inhabited until about 1947. The name of Priory Cottage has nothing to do with the fact that Ratlinghope had a priory. It is so called because it was built and used by boys and teachers from the Priory Boys' School (now the Sixth Form College) in Shrewsbury. The hut today may look abandoned but it is actually full of life. The old mattresses that lie amidst rusty bunk-beds make good nesting material for birds. **Beyond the hut a gate leads onto open hill and the grassy track curves with the ridge. There is no difficulty following the clear track from here as it winds around rushy, boggy hollows that are popular with curlews and snipe. Across the valley called Bilbatch is the road running from Ratlinghope to Stretton, which our route joins.**

RATLINGHOPE 10 (IN REVERSE),SHOOTING BOX TO COATES

Leave the Ratlinghope to Stretton road and follow clear track down the left (south) side of Bilbatch. The track leaves open hill via a gate, passes a derelict hut (Priory Cottage) and then runs alongside hedge all the way down to a group of dwellings known as Coates. Coates has existed for centuries and a John de Cotes was beheaded for a felony committed on the Mynd circa 1267.

RATLINGHOPE 12, Rt 10 TO THE PORTWAY 1 Km/½+m.

Rt 12 leaves Rt 10 as a wide track at point (b) and initially follows a fence. It continues in a straight line up the hillside to cross Wn 20 to the north (left) of the highest point of the Mynd, before finishing at the Portway. It does not continue to the Burway road as it once did.

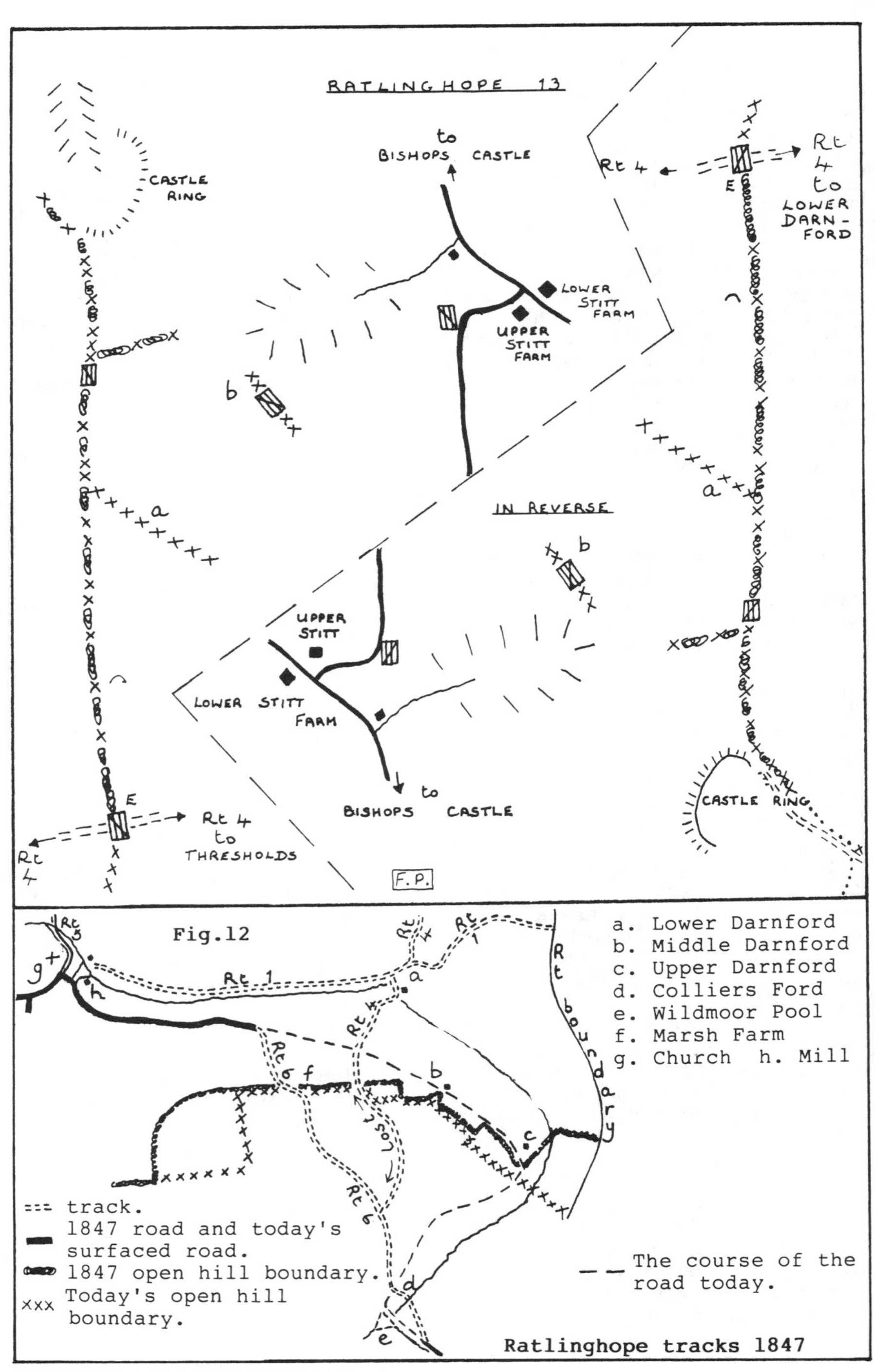

Ratlinghope tracks 1847

RATLINGHOPE 13, Rt 4 TO STITT 1 Km/ ½+ m.

Rt 13 is a public footpath. Leave Rt 4 at point E by some beech trees and follow the old Stitt manor boundary hedge westwards. A tumulus, much diminished by ploughing, is passed; it may once have acted as an ancient route-marker, the route then perhaps continuing along this boundary hedge to the Celtic fort on the skyline ahead. **The route bears to the right to cut off the corner of this field but at present only fence is met and there is no possible detour. The way should continue obliquely across the next field to gate (b) near the head of a small valley. Follow the right-hand side of this valley, keeping along the top of the slope, and then bear away from it slightly to descend to a gate onto the lane. Stitt is the name of the very small hamlet at the end of this walk.** Stitt was a larger hamlet in mediaeval times and had a chapel which was opposite the turning up to the Thresholds i.e. next to Lower Stitt Farm. In the Domesday Book Stitt, as La Scutte, was in the manor of Ratlinghope. Later it became part of Haughmond Abbey's manor of Boveria. It became linked again with Ratlinghope as part of that parish, after the dissolution of the monasteries.

RATLINGHOPE 13 (IN REVERSE), STITT TO Rt 4

Rt 13 starts from the Stitt to Picklescott lane just above Upper Stitt Farm, leaving the lane on a sharp corner to pass through a gate. The way ascends steeply at first and then runs along the upper margin of a small dingle. At the head of this dingle it passes through gate (b) and bears across the field obliquely to the left. At (a), there is at present only fence and no possible detour. The route, however, should cross the corner of the next field to join the old Stitt manor boundary hedge; follow this hedge to get to Rt 4 (a track) at E.

Castle Ring on Stitt Hill

From Rt 4, Rt 11 and Rt 13, the Castle Ring can be clearly seen. It is a semi-circular embankment on the edge of Stitt Hill. As with many of the Long Mynd embankments, this one is also regarded as an ancient animal enclosure. It is however in an extremely good position for seeing approaching enemies, situated at the head of a slope, looking down on the valley of the East Onny, on one side and near the head of a valley (Swinbatch) on another. The lower end of Swinbatch is difficult to see from it but another circle lower down would have given a good view of this and of the Ratlinghope Valley.

The old Stitt manor boundary runs down the side of the Ring as an embankment and bends round to descend to the main road near Hillside Farm. A track once ran beside it and parts of this are still discernible up the hillside and at the Ring; there is a short section of enclosed track at the main road end. This track is believed to be ancient and may have been in use long before any routes up the Ratlinghope valley. A newer track (post 1903) leaves the Ring, cuts through the Stitt embankment and runs along the top edge of Swinbatch onto Ratlinghope Hill (see below).

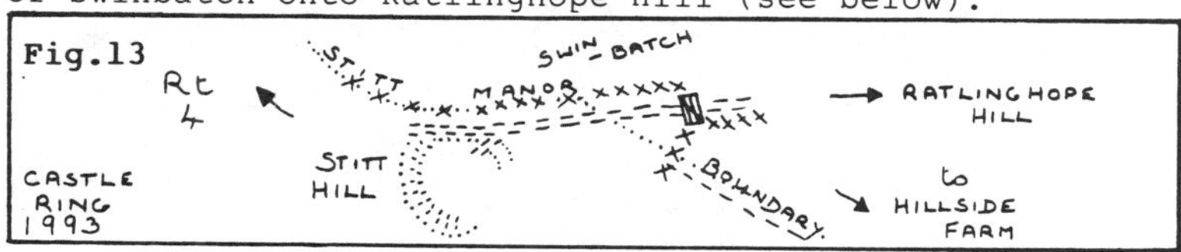

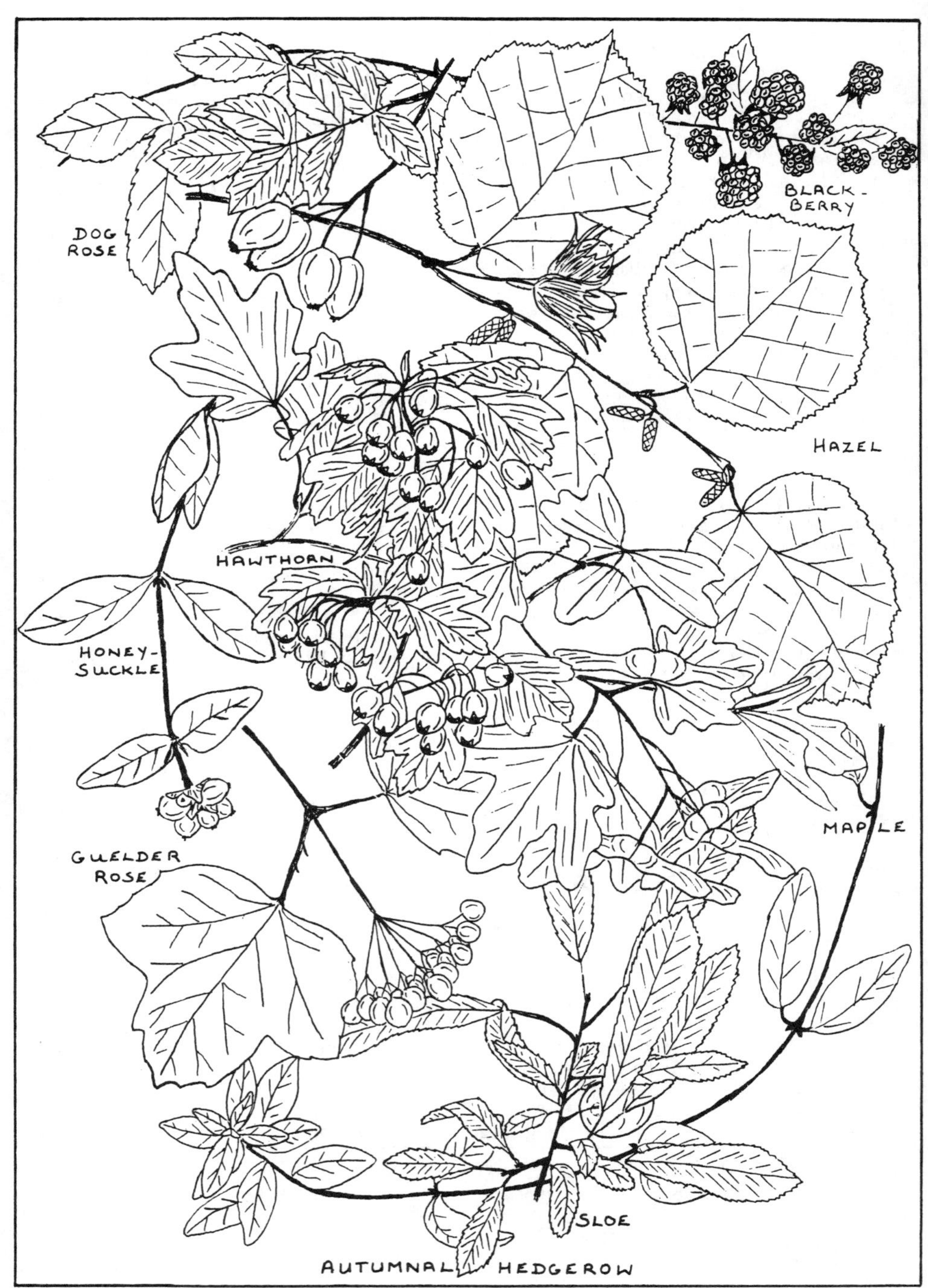

AUTUMNAL HEDGEROW

SMETHCOTT

Smethcott is a parish lying on the north-eastern foothills of the Long Mynd. It is made up of the townships of Smethcott, Picklescott and Betchcott or Batchcott, each having a 'centre' although Betchcott's is very small. Picklescott appears to be the centre for the parish as a whole, having the greatest number of houses in a group, pub and the village hall. The church of St. Michael is isolated but its situation today represents the site of Smethcott hamlet in early mediaeval times, and it lies near the old motte.

Smethcott was the manor of Smerecote in the Domesday Book. A motte was built here and the church was first mentioned in 1341. Picklescott and Betchcott were not mentioned in the Domesday Book but became hamlets at a later date, with their own sets of common fields and common land on the hill. They had a long link with Haughmond Abbey. Betchcott had a mediaeval chapel too, which fell into ruins after the Dissolution. Betchcott's parochial status was uncertain until the last century; some of their dead were buried at Smethcott from the 17th century while pews were apparently reserved for Betchcott people at Leebotwood in the 18th century. It is only because Betchcott became part of Smethcott parish that the latter abuts onto the Portway, Picklescott, but not Betchcott, having lost their rights of common on the hill.

Smethcott, like Woolstaston, used to be covered by a great deal of woodland, of which all that remains is on the slopes of steep dingles. These wooded dingles are Smethcott's greatest natural asset.

From the A49, Picklescott is best reached by the lane up from Dorrington, and Smethcott by a lane up from just north of Leebotwood. Picklescott can be reached from Smethcott either by taking a narrow lane via the church and Smethcott Pool, or by taking a slightly longer and wider route to the north. Betchcott lies close to Picklescott.

Amenities:

Refreshments - The Bottle and Glass at Picklescott with pubs at Dorrington and Leebotwood.
Accommodation - Batchcott Hall near Picklescott - B and B, also two self-catering cottages.
Shop - the nearest shops are at Dorrington.
Bus service - the nearest service is the Midland Red along the A49 (see Church Stretton); these buses pass through Dorrington and Leebotwood.

N.B. Dorrington is 3.75 miles from Picklescott. Leebotwood is 1.75 miles from Smethcott and 3 miles from Picklescott.

SMETHCOTT 1, WILDERLEY HALL TO PEASE LANE 1 Km/½+m.

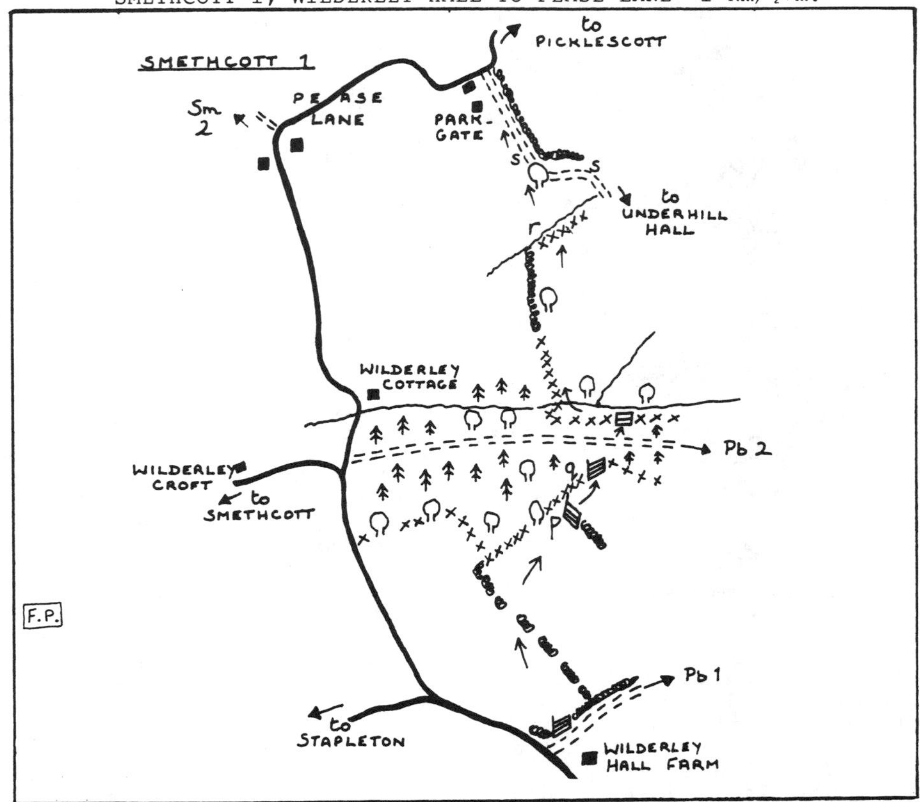

Sm 1 starts opposite Wilderley Hall Farm and crosses a stile into a field (Well Meadow in 1839). **Aim obliquely right across this field to the largest oak tree in the hedge. Pass through a gap in the hedge and aim obliquely left to the left far corner of this second field** (Little Tidders)**, to a stile (p) by the wood. Follow the wood boundary for a short way and then enter the wood via a stile (q).** A small area of this wood was plantation in 1839 while the remainder was fields. **The way to take in the wood is a little unclear; cross a track (Pb 2) and follow a trail marked by tagged trees.** Some of these trees are remnants of the hedge that marked the plantation boundary. **Cross an old stile, follow the brook (Wilderley Brook and also the Pulverbatch/Smethcott parish boundary) downstream to some wire fencing. Cross the stream and follow the fence up the bank. At the top of the bank keep alongside the fence, passing a large beech tree, and descend into a small valley (r). Cross a fence (this is sometimes marked by a plastic sack over barbed wire). Aim straight up the slope towards a tree and join a track (s) running between Pease Lane and Underhill Hall (not a right of way). Exit along this onto Pease Lane, by Parkgate.** Pease Lane appears to have arisen in two or even three parts (see fig.14) unless it represents an ancient through route that had become divided into three fragments by the 19th century.

The original Pease Lane was probably the lower part and may have included Sm 2; the origin of the name is not known.

Although the second half of this walk lies in Smethcott parish, some of this area was in the manor of Wilderley (now a township of Pulverbatch parish), tenants of which had common rights on the neighbouring Smethcott Common. The separate parts of Pease Lane (pronounced Pays Lane) may have acted as outracks to the common; Wilrack Farm, up the lane from Parkgate, is thought to derive its name from being on an outrack of Wilderley manor.

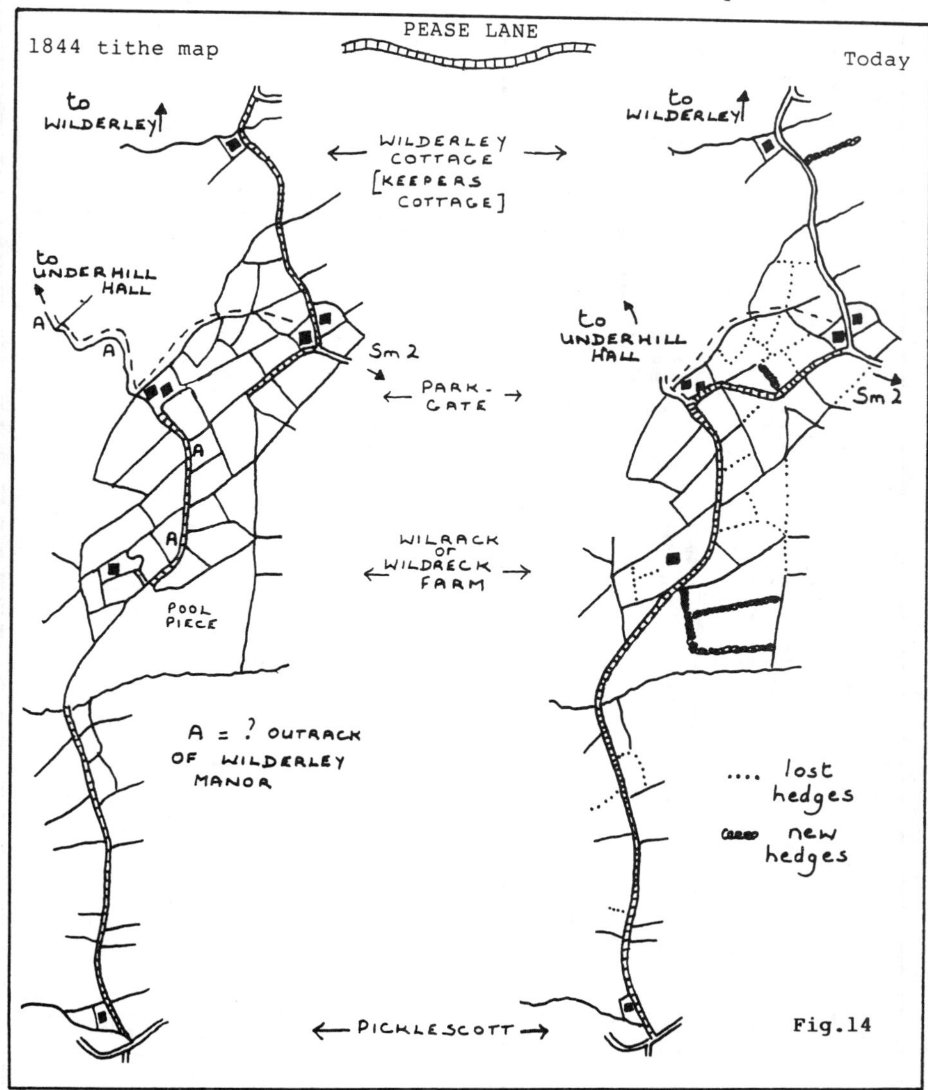

Fig.14

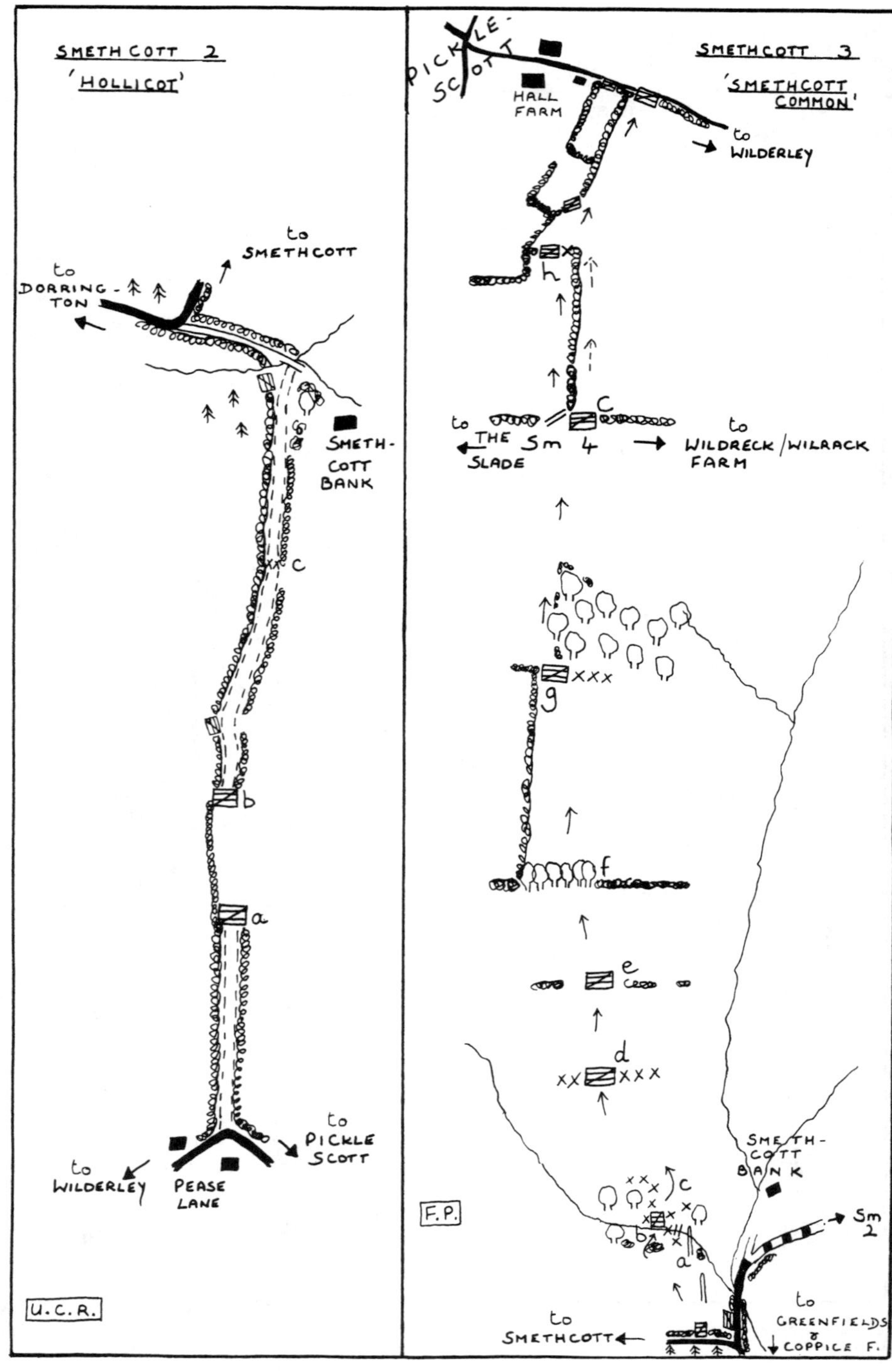
SMETHCOTT 2
'HOLLICOT'
to
SMETHCOTT
to
DORRING-
TON
SMETH-
COTT
BANK
c
b
a
to
WILDERLEY
PEASE
LANE
to
PICKLE
SCOTT
U.C.R.
PICKLE-
SCOTT
HALL
FARM
SMETHCOTT 3
'SMETHCOTT
COMMON'
to
WILDERLEY
h
c
to
THE
SLADE
Sm 4
to
WILDRECK / WILRACK
FARM
g
f
e
d
SMETH-
COTT
BANK
c
b
a
F.P.
Sm
2
to
SMETHCOTT
to
GREENFIELDS
&
COPPICE F.

SMETHCOTT 2, PEASE LANE TO SMETHCOTT BANK 0.5 Km/¼ m.

Sm 2 is an unsurfaced highway but at present is difficult for riders to use, although not impossible. It is an old road linking Pease Lane with lanes to Dorrington and Smethcott, and an old mediaeval area of cultivation called Hollicot lay to the north-east of it. It may once have been a route to and from Smethcott Common and for the few inhabitants in the Pease Lane area it was a way to get to Smethcott church, blacksmith and school.

At a group of buildings on a sharp corner of Pease Lane, Sm 2 starts as a clear track between hedges. At gate (a), it enters open field and follows the right-hand side of a hedge to gate (b). Both gates (a) and (b) are difficult to open at present. From (b), the track is enclosed again and can be exceedingly muddy. At (c), there is sometimes some temporary fencing which is openable but difficult to manage with a horse. From (c), the track descends quite steeply through a tunnel of high hedges and joins the drive to Smethcott Bank at the brook, once known as the Hollicot Brook. Turn left, following the brook downstream, and join a right-angled bend in a road. Turn left, right and left again to get to Dorrington or turn right for Smethcott.

SMETHCOTT 3, SMETHCOTT BANK TO PICKLESCOTT 1.25 Km/0.75 m.

Sm 3 appears not to have been used for a long time because at (f) it is hedge and not fence that blocks the way. This route may have only ever served a few people from places such as Coppice Farm and Greenfields (both of which have been sites of habitation since the late 16th or early 17th centuries), to get to the shops or pub. The path runs across an area that formed part of Smethcott Common (enclosed in 1798). The area including the forest, opposite the start of this walk, is still known as Smethcott Common. It was not marked as such on the 1844 tithe map; there was a smaller plantation then with surrounding fields. The field above the forest was Rabbit Borough (!) which is Rabbit Bury today.

Sm 3 starts at a right angle in the lane where Sm 2, which is also the drive to Smethcott Bank, branches off. At present there is no way through at (f) but hopefully this path will soon be opened up. Pass through a wicket gate and cross a boggy field, aiming obliquely left, to the left of two telegraph poles. Enter the dingle about 30 yards to the left of the second pole (a). Descend to a gate (b) on the far side of the brook. An old bridge exists but it is on the other side of the fence to the right. Ascend a tongue of grassland between areas of woodland. At the top of the bank (c), aim obliquely left across a field, following telegraph poles, to a gate (d). Go straight across the next field to gate (e). Over to the left is Parish House, a new house next to the remains of the old house which was owned by the parish for the use of poor people. **Continue almost straight on to reach a tall hedge (f); there is no way through this at present. Sm 3 continues straight on, following the right-hand side of a hedge to a gate (g). After (g), the way runs along the edge of a wood open to grazing** (an example of a wood leasow, see page 180). **Aim straight on to a hedge running from left to right; this hedge runs with Sm 4 which our route now crosses at C. Cross the drinking trough (or the nearby gate) into a field and follow the hedge to gate (h). From (h), turn half-right and follow the right-hand side of a hedge up to a gate onto the road. This last part, from (h), is a variation on the original route which ran through the farmyard of Hall Farm, and is now the official right of way.**

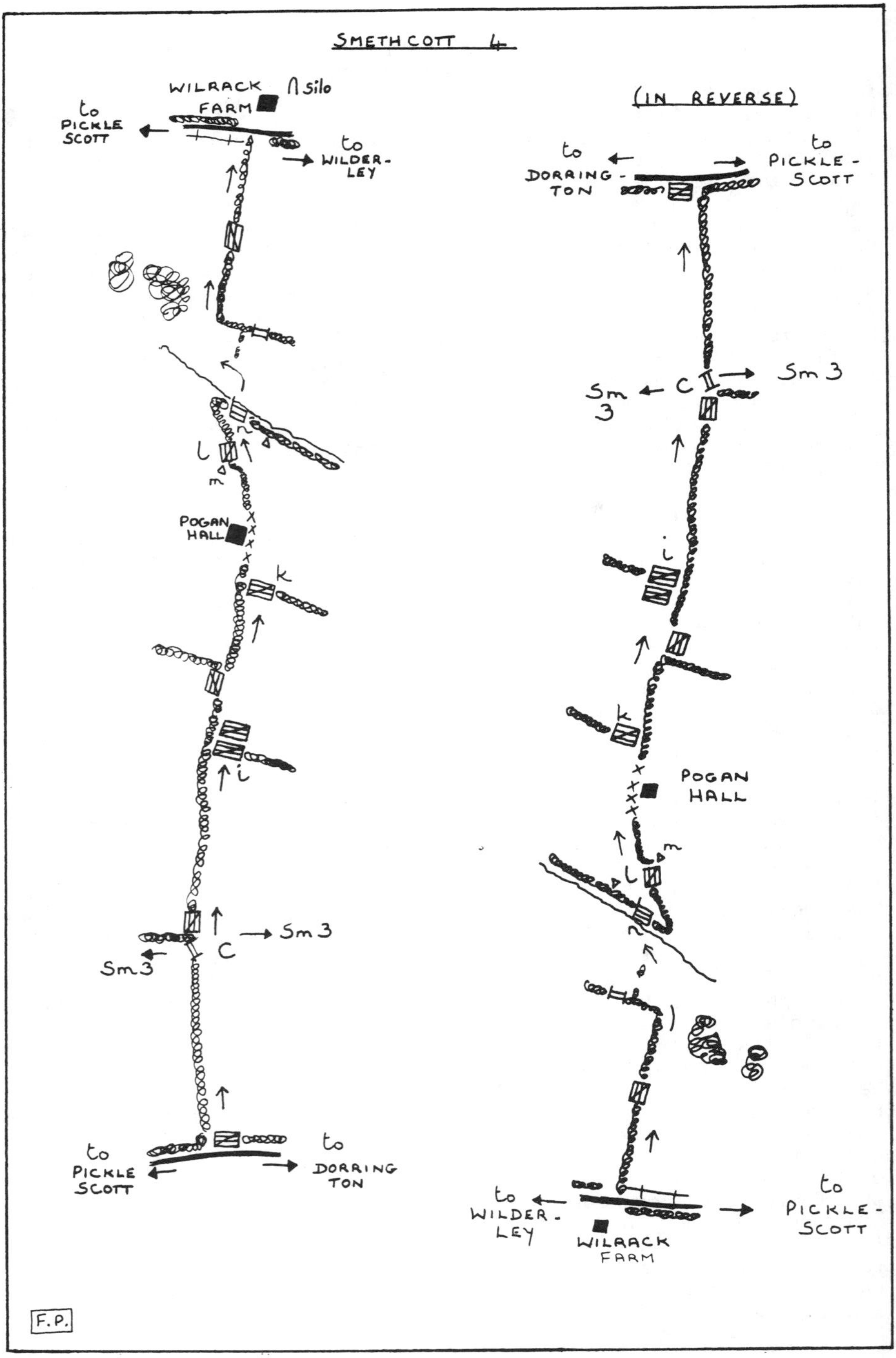

SMETHCOTT 4

WILRACK FARM
silo
to PICKLE SCOTT
to WILDER-LEY
L
m
n
POGAN HALL
k
i
C
Sm 3
Sm3
to PICKLE SCOTT
to DORRING TON

(IN REVERSE)

to DORRING-TON
to PICKLE-SCOTT
C
Sm 3
Sm 3
i
k
POGAN HALL
m
L
n
to WILDER-LEY
to PICKLE-SCOTT
WILRACK FARM

F.P.

SMETHCOTT 4, PICKLESCOTT TO WILRACK FARM 0.75 Km/½ m.

This route may have been used by inhabitants of Wilrack Farm and Pogan Hall to go to church or school, joining Sm 5 or the lane. It may at one time have run along the top (west) edge of Smethcott Common. There are two boundary stones to be seen along this route, one of which (m) appears to be in its original site. These stones were on the common and marked the boundary between the part of the common for tenants of Smethcott manor and that for tenants of Wilderley manor. Each stone bears the initials L.A.P.

The way starts near Picklescott via a gate off the road to Dorrington. It follows the right-hand side of a hedge, crosses Sm 3 at C by a drinking trough, and continues along to a double gate (i). Continue along hedge and pass through another gate (k). After passing to the right of Pogan Hall, the way starts to descend, passing a gate (l) in the hedge on the left. Look over the gate to see the boundary stone (m) in situ at the base of a tree. Continue down the hedge to a stile and gas marker-post (n). To the right is another boundary stone. Cross the stile and brook, then turn left and follow the brook for about 30 yards; this area can be rather overgrown. Turn right up a steep bank of scrubland, a good habitat for wildlife including butterflies. **Follow the left-hand side of a hedge to get to Pease Lane by Wilrack Farm.**

SMETHCOTT 4 (IN REVERSE), WILRACK FARM TO PICKLESCOTT

Sm 4 starts just past Wilrack Farm on the Picklescott side, where the road is open to the field (there is sometimes electric fencing). Follow the right-hand side of a hedge to a brambly bank above a brook. Veer left for a short way and then cross the brook to a stile by a gas marker-post (n). After (n), follow hedge up to Pogan Hall and continue straight on through gates (k) and (i), keeping to the left-hand side of the hedge. Cross Sm 3 at C by a drinking trough and exit onto lane. Turn right and almost immediately enter Picklescott.

Focus on a wood leasow

Leasow (pronounced lezzow) is an old name for pasture land and often features in field names. 'Wood Leasow' is a common field name and indicates a wood that has animals grazing in it. However, by the time of the tithe maps of the 1840s, many of these fields were pasture only, without the trees.

There are still wood leasows to be found scattered around the Mynd. They are most attractive and easy to walk in, unlike some of the ungrazed dingle woods with tangled undergrowth. Their glory unfortunately is relatively short-lived as tree seedlings have no chance to grow in them unless protected. The dingle woods on the other hand not only harbour many species of wildlife but are constantly regenerating themselves.

In the Domesday Book woodland was measured in terms of swine e.g. Smethcott had woodland for 50 swine. Today pigs are not commonly seen in fields or woods and the woodland pastures belong to sheep or cattle.

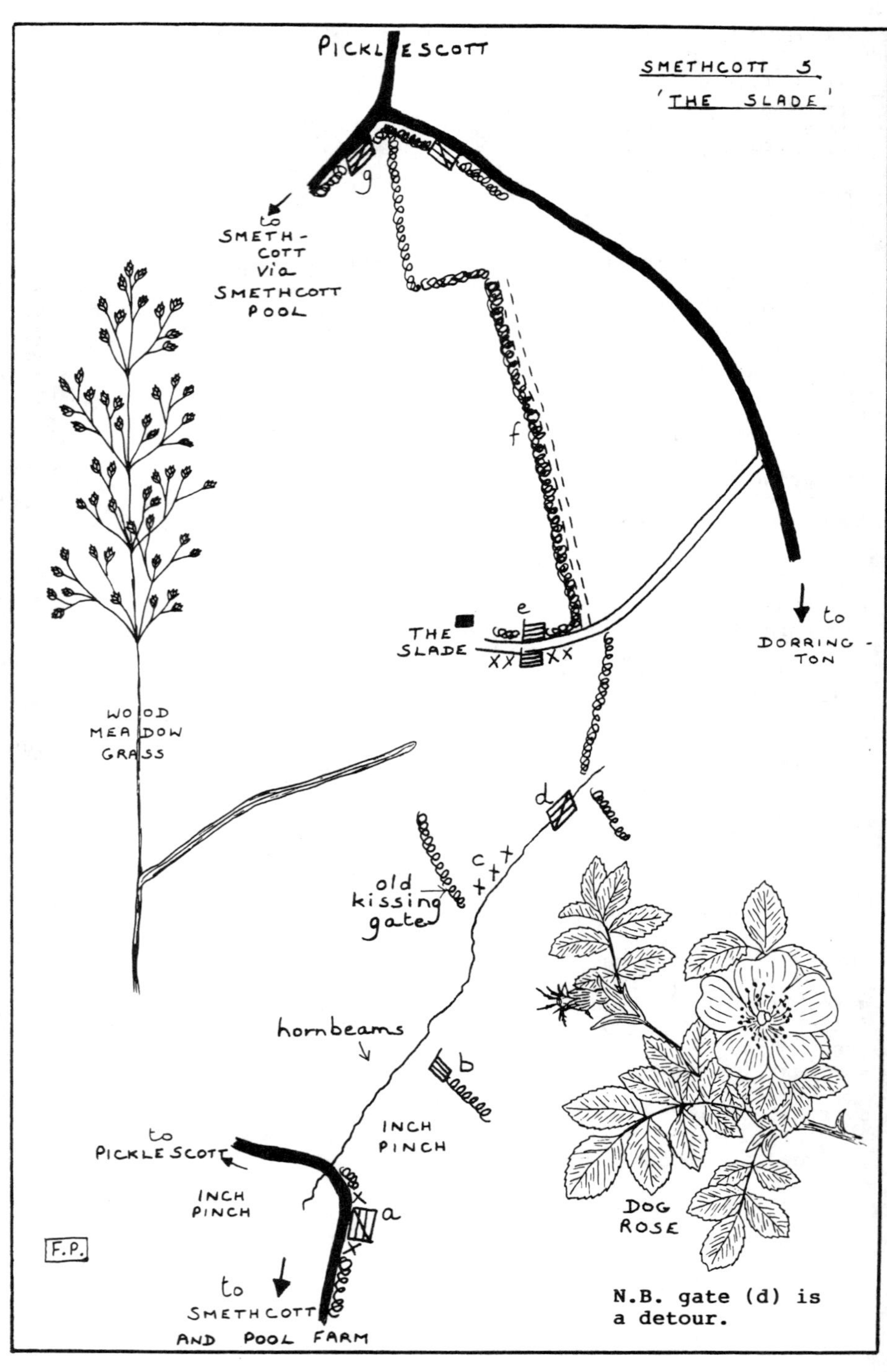
PICKLESCOTT
SMETHCOTT 5
'THE SLADE'
g
to
SMETHCOTT via SMETHCOTT POOL
f
e
THE SLADE
to
DORRINGTON
WOOD MEADOW GRASS
d
c
old kissing gate
hornbeams
b
INCH PINCH
to
PICKLESCOTT
INCH PINCH
a
F.P.
to
SMETHCOTT AND POOL FARM
DOG ROSE
N.B. gate (d) is a detour.

SMETHCOTT 5, SMETHCOTT POOL TO PICKLESCOTT 0.5 Km/¼+ m.

In the 1950s, when paths were assessed for the creation of public rights of way, Sm 5 was one of very few paths in Smethcott that was still in regular use. This was probably because it was a short cut to both school and church; the school closed in 1963. The path also appears on the tithe map of 1844.

If approaching from the church, pass Smethcott Pool and Pool Farm. The lane soon bends into a small dingle; at the start of this bend, leave the lane through a gate into a field (a) that was once called Inch Pinch. Cross this field, keeping to the right of the dingle, to a stile (b) on the left-hand end of a tangled hedge of wild roses (dog roses are pink, field roses are white). In the dingle is an attractive grassy knoll covered in hornbeam trees. **Follow the small stream which should be crossed at (c) but until a stile is placed here it is better to use the gate at (d). The next field to cross was called the Slade (pronounced Slad), as is the house nearby, and means an area too wet to plough.** It is a very boggy field, full of rushes, and illustrates how much of Smethcott Common must have once been. This area previously formed the south-west edge of the Common and the rushes would have been put to good use by local people for thatching cottage roofs or hayricks. They were also used for making candles; the outer green layer was stripped off and the white pith was dipped in fat.

Cross the Slade driveway and enter another field via a stile (e). Follow an old hedge and track (f). There is no reference to a track here on any maps of the last century that are available; the track could predate these and perhaps was a way down to the old common. **Exit from this field onto a Y junction (g) at the edge of Picklescott hamlet.**

Name meaning — **Inch Pinch**

A suggestion for the meaning of this name is that the game of Inchy Pinchy (progressive leap-frog) was played here. Another possible meaning relates to the small, steep dingle since there are two Inch Pinch fields, one on either side of the dip in the road; pinch was an old expression for a steep incline in the road

Focus on trees — **Hornbeams**

The hornbeam is a native tree but in this area it is likely to have been planted. It is an attractive tree, particularly in summer when its winged fruits hang in small chains. Its wood is very hard and difficult to work, and so it has not usually been allowed to grow into a large tree but coppiced (repeatedly cut back to the trunk to obtain straight shoots) and used to supply poles. As firewood too, the hornbeam has been popular; when burnt the wood gives out a great deal of heat. Today hornbeams are being planted to become trees but they are also used as hedging plants.

Focus on maps — **'Foxhall maps'**

H.D.G. Foxhall, author of Shropshire Field Names, painstakingly copied the tithe maps of the 1840s to create one large map for each village. The fields on the tithe maps were numbered and their names listed separately but the Foxhall maps have both the field numbers and names. These maps can be viewed and copied at the Local Studies Library or at the Shire Hall.

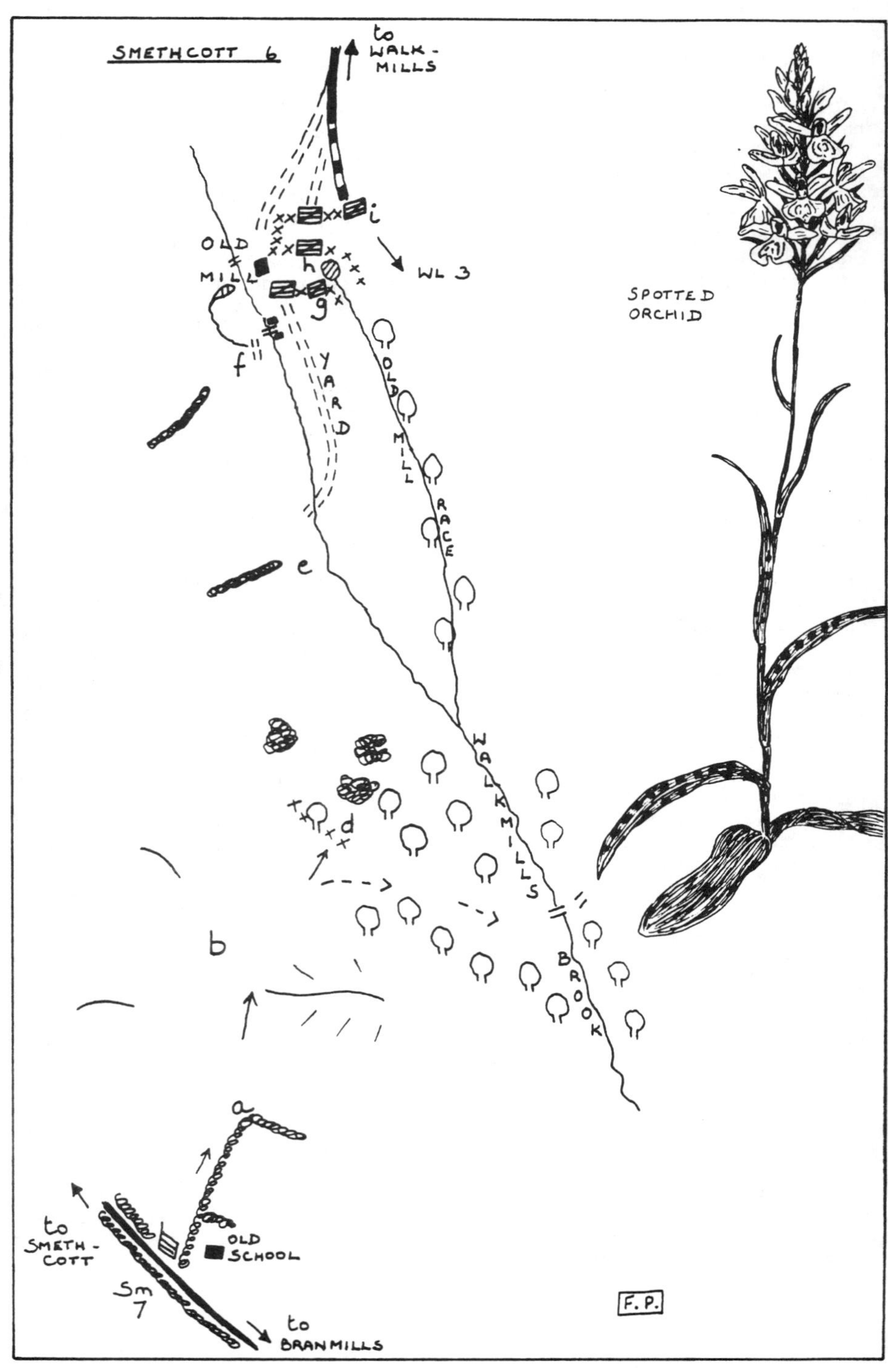
SMETHCOTT 6
to WALK-MILLS
OLD MILL
WL 3
SPOTTED ORCHID
YARD
OLD MILL RACE
WALKMILLS BROOK
to SMETH-COTT
OLD SCHOOL
Sm 7
to BRANMILLS
F. P.

SMETHCOTT 6, SMETHCOTT SCHOOL (OLD) TO OLD MILL FARM 0.75 Km/½ m.

Sm 6 cannot be walked at present. It is an old footpath connecting the Walkmill area with school and church and, in reverse, was a way from parts of Smethcott to the old mill itself and perhaps on to Leebotwood e.g. for the railway station. A further old track to the mill left the lane a short way to the east of the school, on a sharp bend; the only indication of its existence today is the field hedge which ran along one side of it. This old track may have arisen in relation to Smethcott's common fields (see fig. 6).

Leave the lane by the old school (in use from 1867 to 1964) **via a stile. Follow the hedge alongside the garden and then a small field. From the corner of this hedge (a), cross the large field aiming obliquely left and keeping to the right of a distinct hollow (b). This hollow runs with Sm 6 towards an ash tree which is slightly isolated from the nearby wood; the summit of Lawley in the distance is another landmark to aim for. It is at this point (d) that the way is blocked by fencing. If a stile is erected here, it should be just to the right of the ash. From (d), the way goes obliquely left across a bank to the far bottom corner of this field (e), by the brook. The bank is wild and overgrown in places with brambles and bracken and, being situated close to deciduous woodland, is a good habitat for many small birds including marsh tits and warblers.** To distinguish between the several species of warbler here is a difficult task as they are often hard to see and look somewhat alike. (The male blackcap is distinguished by having a black cap). Their songs however, heard in the spring and summer, are easier to pick out. The chiff-chaff sings its own name and the willow warbler has a cascading song. Blackcaps and garden warblers have similar melodious warbles, the garden warbler's particularly beautiful song being more subdued and prolonged.

The bank opens out into a mixture of bog and meadow, with abundant spotted orchids in June, before reaching point (e) where there is a large gap at the bottom end of a hedge. From (e), follow the brook (Walkmills Brook) downstream. At (f), a waterway forms a small loop to the left (this must have been a loop off the brook at some time, perhaps even the original course) **and on the right is a metal bridge; cross this bridge and pass between two old vans into a workyard. Turn left along track towards the old mill but turn up to the right just before a gateway out of the yard. Climb upwards and turn left through a gate (g) to pass behind and above the mill** (in use as a fulling mill or a corn mill from the 17th century until the 1920s and since then for generating electricity) **which is on the left; the old mill-pool is on the right. Pass through another gate (h) into the corner of a field and facing you are two more gates; the correct exit is via the right-hand gate (i). A short section of grassy track leads to surfaced road that continues to Walkmills. The track and gate (i) form the start of Wl 3.**

Another old path, recorded on the tithe map and used by Woolstaston children to get to Smethcott school, began with Sm 6 at the school but left it just before point (d). From here it branched off to the right and crossed the dingle to Woolstaston. Surprisingly it did not become a designated public right of way. Today it is obviously a well-used route and a bridge still spans the brook. It is an attractive route that passes through old woodland and a dramatic stretch of the Walkmills Brook, and should perhaps be added to the definitive map as a right of way when Smethcott's ways are updated.

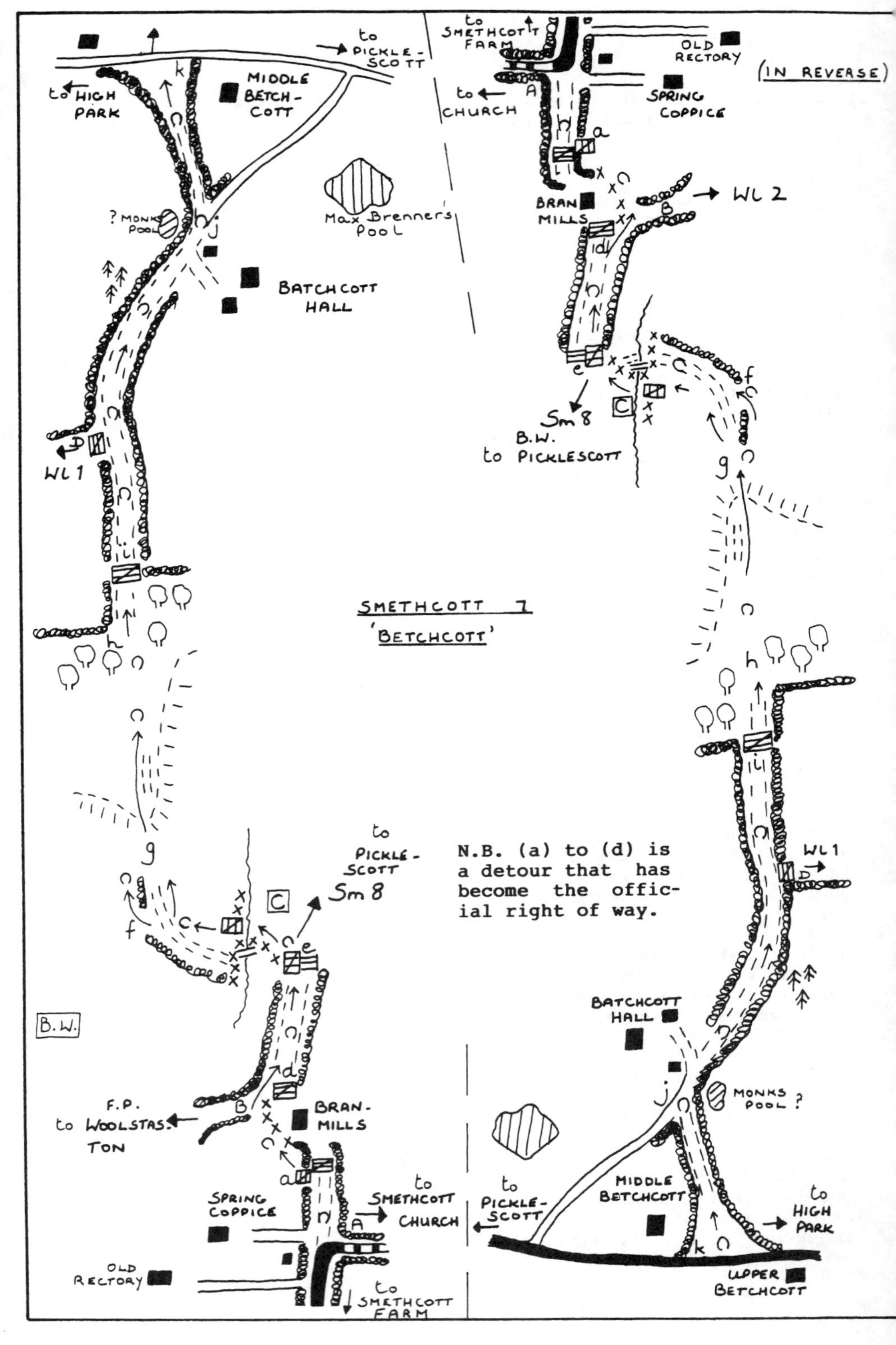

SMETHCOTT 7
'BETCHCOTT'
(IN REVERSE)
to PICKLE-SCOTT
to HIGH PARK
MIDDLE BETCH-COTT
Max Brenner's Pool
? MONKS POOL
BATCHCOTT HALL
WL 1
to SMETHCOTT FARM
OLD RECTORY
SPRING COPPICE
to CHURCH
BRAN MILLS
WL 2
Sm 8
B.W. to PICKLESCOTT
to PICKLE-SCOTT
Sm 8
N.B. (a) to (d) is a detour that has become the official right of way.
B.W.
F.P. to WOOLSTASTON
BRAN-MILLS
SPRING COPPICE
to SMETHCOTT CHURCH
OLD RECTORY
to SMETHCOTT FARM
BATCHCOTT HALL
MONKS POOL ?
MIDDLE BETCHCOTT
to PICKLE-SCOTT
to HIGH PARK
UPPER BETCHCOTT
WL 1

SMETHCOTT 7, SMETHCOTT FARM TO BETCHCOTT 2 Km/1¼ m.

Sm 7 from Smethcott Farm as far as the church turn is surfaced highway and from this point it becomes bridleway. The first section as far as Branmills was a part of the mediaeval road that ran from the Long Mynd via Woolstaston and Branmills, continuing on to Shrewsbury via Dorrington; it was known as the Portway in the 17th century.

Turn off the lane at Smethcott and pass Smethcott Farm. Continue along surfaced road, passing the old school and the old rectory, to reach the church turn opposite Spring Coppice (a house, although it is also the name of the wood nearby). The road continues towards Branmills but is now a bridleway. At (a), the way leaves the road through a gate on the left and passes below Branmills (a house) to rejoin the old road at (d). The section (a) to (d) is a modern diversion. At B, WL 2 and the old Portway from Woolstaston join Sm 7. Branmills is thought to be the site of Smethcott's mediaeval mill, first recorded in the 13th century, and its name means 'burnt mill'. **From (d), continue along enclosed track and pass through gate (e), immediately fording a small stream to reach point C; here Sm 7 and Sm 8 diverge. Turn left across the Walkmills Brook, pass through a gate and ascend straight up the slope to the top (f). There is evidence of old track in this area from the brook to the wood at (h) but at (f) it is easier to curve to the right alongside rather than on the track, which is bounded by trees and shrubs. The track fades out across the field (g) but you will see that the way is now a ridgeway route, albeit a small ridge, that leads to an area of deciduous woodland (h).** The wood is an example of a wood leasow (see page 180) with cattle grazing below (predominantly) oak trees. The cows are also fed in this area and it can be extremely muddy. **Leave the wood via gate (i) and follow the enclosed and stony track, which ascends gradually towards Betchcott. At (j), turn off what appears to be the main track (which has now become the private drive to Batchcott Hall) and follow the grassy track (the original route) out to the road.** On the right side of the open area (k) is an old well; at one time this was decorated annually (May 14th) with flowers. The pool at (j) may once have been a monks' fishpool (see page 190).

SMETHCOTT 7 (IN REVERSE), BETCHCOTT TO SMETHCOTT FARM

Sm 7 begins as a wide grassy area by Middle Betchcott Farm, which is probably the site of the mediaeval manor house.**The hedges of this area converge to form a narrower way that leads to the driveway, coming in from the left, to Batchcott Hall. Turn onto this drive at (j), bearing off to the right away from the entrance to the Hall, down an enclosed and stony track. The way descends gradually until gate (i) is reached. Enter a wood (muddy underfoot), continuing straight on to reach open field (g). There is no clear way here but you will become aware that you are walking along a faint rideway; follow this to reach a section of old track flanked by trees and shrubs at (f). Turn left down the slope, pass through a gate and ford the brook to reach point C. At C, our route is joined by Sm 8. Turn right across another small stream, pass through gate (e) and follow enclosed track once more. At (d), a diversion to the right has been made to circumvent a house (Branmills). Just below the house, WL 2 branches off to the right. Rejoin old track via gate (a). At A, the bridleway becomes surfaced highway that continues to Smethcott via Smethcott Farm. Alternatively, turn left along unsurfaced highway to the church.**

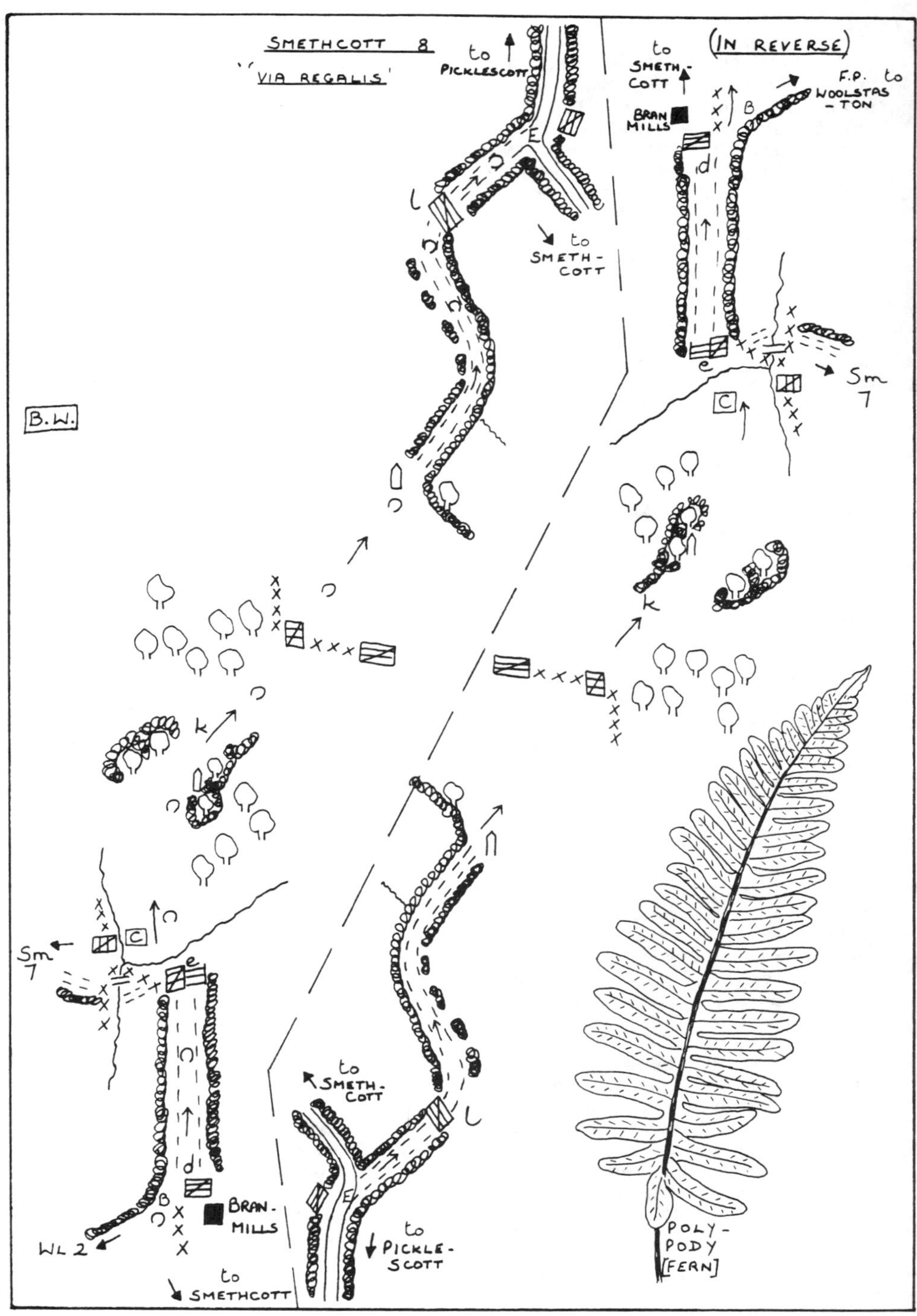

SMETHCOTT 8
'VIA REGALIS'
(IN REVERSE)
to PICKLESCOTT
to SMETH-COTT
BRAN MILLS
F.P. to WOOLSTAS-TON
to SMETH-COTT
Sm 7
B.W.
Sm 7
BRAN-MILLS
WL 2
to SMETHCOTT
to SMETH-COTT
to PICKLE-SCOTT
POLY-PODY [FERN]

Sm 7 and 8 are very obviously old routes and the history of Sm 7 in particular must be bound up with the history of Betchcott. Betchcott and Leebotwood once belonged to a hermit priest called Blethurus who is thought to have built Leebotwood Church and Betchcott Chapel. There appears to be some controversy about the site of the old chapel. In 1183 Leebotwood and Betchcott were granted to Haughmond Abbey; at that time Betchcott was uninhabited forest. For centuries afterwards Betchcott continued to have links with Leebotwood and meanwhile had become a hamlet with its own common fields and a manor house. Monks and others must have journeyed between Betchcott, Leebotwood and Haughmond, as well as other parts of the northern end of the Long Mynd in Haughmond's manor of Boveria, until the 16th century (see Background). Sm 7, by linking Betchcott with the mediaeval Portway to Shrewsbury at Branmills, may have been the route taken to get to Haughmond Abbey. It may also have been the way taken to Leebotwood, perhaps turning off the Portway at Smethcott. After the monastic link ended, Betchcott, still not then part of Smethcott parish, apparently had two pews reserved in Leebotwood church for its inhabitants to worship there. It must have been hard to walk this considerable distance, passing by Smethcott church, and not surprisingly burials took place at Smethcott well before Betchcott was officially in that parish. Betchcott became part of Smethcott parish in the mid 19th century.

SMETHCOTT 8, BRANMILLS TO PICKLESCOTT 0.5 Km/ ¼m.

Starting from the church turn (point A) the first part of this route overlaps with Sm 7. Take the road towards Branmills, passing through gate (a) to circumvent the house and rejoining the old track at (d). Pass through gate (e) and cross a small stream to reach point C. Sm 7 turns to the left at this point whereas Sm 8 bears obliquely up to the right (to the left if approaching from Betchcott). It is a vague route up the slope but in the 15th century Sm 8, in continuity with the present-day lane to Picklescott, was described as a 'via regalis'. The way passes below a knoll of trees and there is a waymarker-post halfway up the slope. At the top of the slope (k) turn left to reach a wicket gate. Aim straight across the next field; another waymarker-post stands at the start of enclosed track. Follow this track, passing through gate (l), to reach the lane. There is a marked contrast in the quality of the track on either side of gate (l). On the field side the route is clear and grazed but erosion is taking place around the base of the hedges and the hedge is getting thin i.e. it is being 'overmanaged'. The road side however is overgrown and undermanaged and these two contrasting sides demonstrate the difficulty of preserving these old tracks.

SMETHCOTT 8 (IN REVERSE), PICKLESCOTT TO BRANMILLS

Take the overgrown track branching off the Picklescott to Smethcott road at E. Pass through gate (l) and follow the track that bears to the left. At the end of the track aim straight across the field to a wicket gate. Turn left and follow the top of the slope for a short distance to (k) before descending obliquely down it to the brook, to join Sm 7 at point C. Turn left, crossing a small stream and immediately passing through gate (e). Continue along enclosed track towards Branmills, making a detour to the right of the house, and rejoining the old track via gate (a). The track leads to Smethcott via the church turn at point A.

SMETHCOTT 9, CHURCH TO SMETHCOTT POOL 0.25 Km.

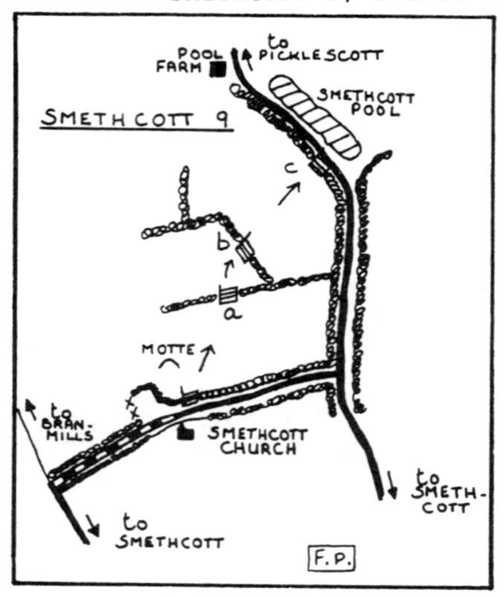

Sm 9 is a public footpath that has almost certainly arisen as a short cut to and from church and school. A stile opposite the church leads into the field with the remains of Smethcott's motte. This motte has contributed towards road repairs and has also been excavated; finds included early 13th century pottery. The field appears to have been nameless on the tithe map but long before that it was part of a much larger open and common field called Castle Field. An older name still (13th century) was Old Field. **Aim obliquely right to another stile (a) and cross a corner of the next field to stile (b). Straight across the third field is stile (c) which leads to the lane by Smethcott Pool.** Smethcott Pool lies in a natural hollow and has probably always been an area of marshland or a pool; in the 13th century it was known as Frogspool. A dyke at the east end suggests that it has at some time been enlarged. It supports several species of coarse fish and some uncommon marsh plants (Veronica scutellata and Peplis portula).

Focus on pools **Fish**

Many pools on and around the Mynd have been created by man. The pools on the hill were made to provide water for animals and to attract water-fowl for sport. The reservoirs in Townsbrook Hollow and New Pool Hollow were created to supply water but have now become homes for the wild trout that frequent the local streams. Other pools have been created specifically for trout and, as with the reservoirs, have to be well-oxygenated for the trout to survive; these pools all lie along the course of a fast-flowing stream. The more stagnant pools have become home to species of coarse fish, which may occur naturally (e.g. a heron travelling between pools may take fish eggs on its feet) or be the result of deliberate stocking. Perch and roach are examples of native fish that may be found in places such as Smethcott Pool. Other species, such as carp and tench, which are not native, are commonly found alongside them in such situations.

Focus on carp

The creation of fish-pools has taken place for centuries and Brockhurst, which was Stretton's mediaeval castle, was surrounded by them. There is a record of bream being ordered to be taken to these, the king's fish-ponds. The bream is another native fish which once formed part of the staple diet of poorer people. The wild carp from Europe replaced it on some tables.

Carp are thought to have been introduced to Britain by the monks and their original home here is likely to have been in a monastery fish-pool ('stewpond') or castle moat. The true wild carp has now become a rarity because of the introduction into pools of other types of carp such as the mirror carp which, by adding its genes to the spawn pool, soon alters the strain. Any search for the true wild carp should perhaps begin in an old monastic pool that has not been restocked. One possible such pool in the Mynd area would appear to be the small pool at Betchcott, which is said to have been a monks' pool, but sadly there do not appear to be any carp in the pool today.

The wild carp and the common carp are regarded as a single species (Cyprinus carpio) but differ in shape from one another. The mirror carp is an example of a variant that has been produced by selective breeding; these strains of the common carp have a faster growth-rate and varying scale patterns, the leather carp having no scales at all and therefore requiring less preparation before eating (one reason for developing such a fish). Wild carp do not reach the great weights that the others do, the record weight for a common carp being 45.75 lbs and for a mirror carp 51.5 lbs. Individual carp are easily identifiable by variations in their scale pattern and some of the larger ones are well-known and have names such as Basil, Heather the Leather and Clarissa (now dead). Carp are thought to be among the longest-lived freshwater fish and may reach 40 years of age or more.

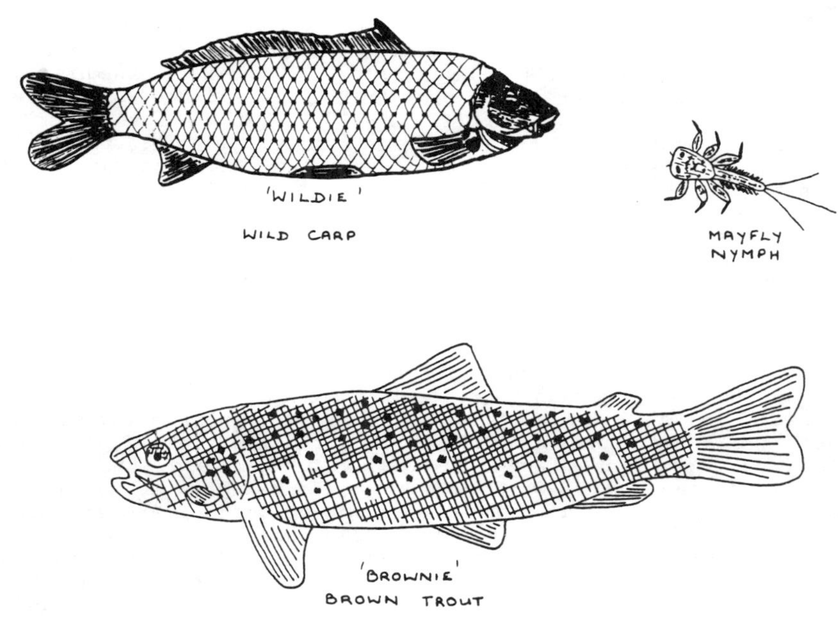

Focus on stream life

Many creatures other than the brown trout and the bullyhead can be found in the small, fast streams of the Mynd area. Several of them form a stage or stages in the life cycle of flying insects, the adult stage often being much shorter. Commonly-found examples are various species of stonefly, mayfly and caddis (sedge) fly nymphs (a nymph is a larval stage); most of these species are only found in clean water and are therefore good indicators of absence of pollution. Caddis-flies are usually encased in sticks or pebbles, attached to the bottom of stones. Mayfly nymphs are often found crawling under stones and usually have three tails, while the stonefly has two. Other creatures easily found under stones are freshwater shrimps and limpets. A catch with a net may reveal various mayfly nymphs and, if taken from a slow-running section, midge larvae (bloodworms) or the fierce-looking alderfly larvae. Any of these creatures and others below the surface may be imitated to create artificial flies for catching trout. Also imitated are the flies themselves that hatch and leave the water as adults or, in the case of the mayfly, as immature adults (subimagos or duns), which 'hatch ' again to become adults (imagos or spinners).

Focus on pools **Dusk in summertime**

Insects can be seen flying around and over pools all day and it is a common sight to see swallows skimming across the water in search of them. It is however at dusk that vast numbers of insects (having spent a large proportion of their life cycle in the water) hatch and leave the water as adults. Many creatures take advantage of this event. Fish, particularly the trout, begin to jump and swifts appear overhead. Carp swim and roll along near the surface of the water, to cool themselves and perhaps also to beat the insects down onto the pool surface for their consumption. Now is a good time for the fisherman, but to outwit the fish, usually trout, he must cast an artificial fly that mimics one of the hatching insects of that particular day. As the light fades further, the swifts leave the pool and bats emerge to take advantage of the end of the hatch. Soon the hatch ends and the bats leave the pool to hunt in the woods. Fish continue to rise to gather casualties fallen on the pool surface. Carp make loud sucking noises as they feed amongst the reeds. There is an occasional birdsong or the flutter of wings as birds roost. Badgers rustle in the undergrowth, owls hoot and voles scuttle after spilled bait; the noises of the night have begun.

Focus on farm animals

It is unnerving to meet a bull, particularly halfway across a large field with a long way to run if the need should arise. A bull is, however, allowed on a right of way if it does not belong to one of the recognized dairy breeds (e.g. the black and white Friesian) and is with cows or heifers (young cows). The red-brown and white Hereford and the creamy-coloured Charolais are the usual bulls in this area, with the occasional shaggy brown Highland bull or 'hookie'. These breeds are acceptable. A bull on its own is only allowed to be on a right of way if it is under 11 months but that is not easy to know. It is wise to be wary of any bull and, if in doubt, keep close to the edge of the field for a possible quick exit. Much more likely to give chase is a herd of young cattle, particularly if you are accompanied by a dog; they will halt if you turn towards them and, if necessary, stamp the ground. Cows with calves are best given a wide berth. Conversely, animals do not like being chased either and it can be dangerous, particularly for sheep in lamb.

SMETHCOTT 10, NEW HOUSE DRIVE TO THE BYNORDS 1 Km/½+ m.

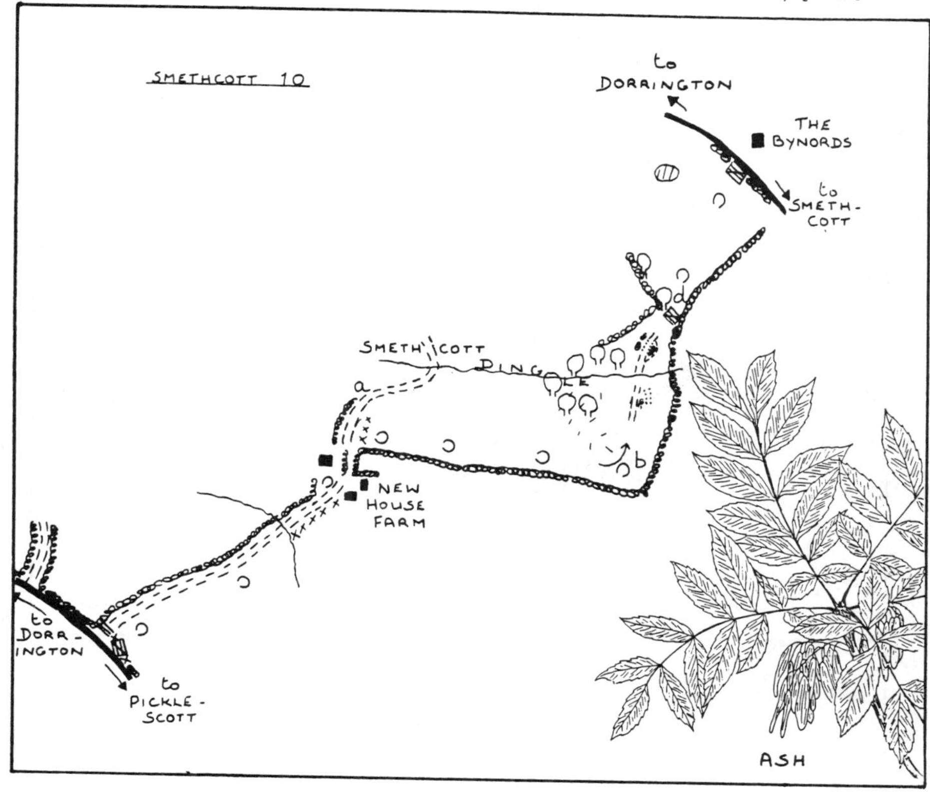

This route is a bridleway which may have arisen as two separate ways for the inhabitants of New House. A section of the way, through Smethcott Dingle, is old track.

Leave the Dorrington to Picklescott road and take the driveway to New House Farm. Pass through the farmyard and start along a track (a). At the boundary hedge of the farm orchard, turn right; if there is a barbed wire fence at this point there is a loop at one end to open it. Follow a straight and long hedge up to the top corner at (b). Turn left and follow hedge (not closely) to the brook. After fording the brook, bear obliquely right up the slope following an old track. Thin and old hedge along the line of the track is just discernible amidst the trees and shrubs of Smethcott Dingle; the track ends at the top of the slope in the corner of a small field. Continue along the hedge which runs on the right-hand side to gate (d) into a larger field. A house (The Bynords) can be seen across this field and is the point to aim for. Exit from the field onto the mediaeval Portway running between Smethcott and Dorrington. In the last field is a small pool which is one of several in the area. They do not appear to be natural and may be clay or marl pits. Field names in the area are Marlpits and Grilpits.

SMETHCOTT 11
THE GREEN LANE
to PICKLESCOTT
to WILDERLEY
3 TURNINGS
Sm 10
NEW HOUSE
SMETH-COTT
DINGLE
to DORRINGTON
NEW HALL
to SMETHCOTT
FACTORY DINGLE
to DORRINGTON
PARK-HEAD
BOOSEY PASTURE
to WALK-MILLS
G.L.

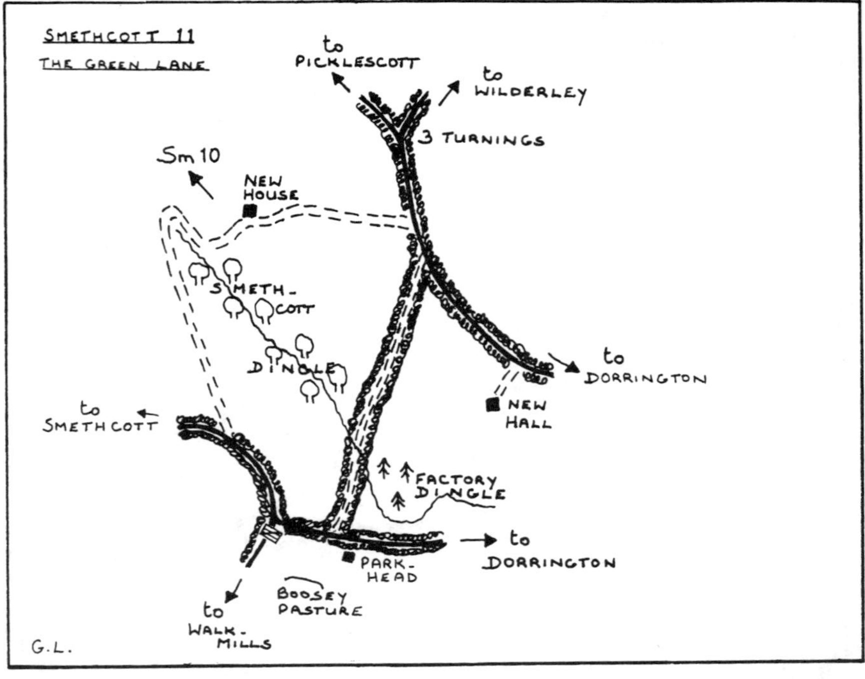

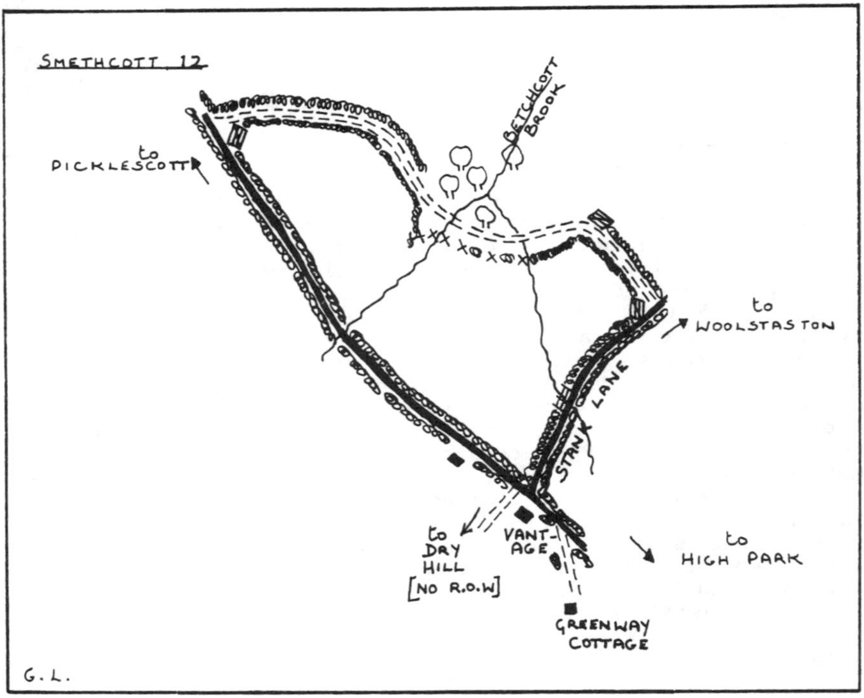

SMETHCOTT 12
to PICKLESCOTT
BETCHCOTT BROOK
to WOOLSTASTON
STANK LANE
to DRY HILL
[NO R.O.W]
VANT-AGE
to HIGH PARK
GREENWAY COTTAGE
G.L.

SMETHCOTT 11, PARKHEAD TO NEW HALL 0.5 Km/¼ m.

Sm 11 appears to be a green lane that belongs to no man and is locally referred to as 'The Green Lane'. It is an attractive, enclosed track that passes through a dingle, known as Smethcott Dingle on the upstream side and as Factory Dingle downstream. An old name for the brook was Tymbrynbesbeches Brook. Smethcott Dingle is a continuation of the valley that begins at Smethcott Pool and, although parts of it are grazed by animals, much of it is overgrown and a haven for wildlife. The lower part of Factory Dingle was Scoltocks Dingle on the tithe map but later became the site of a chicory factory, hence the change of name.

It has been mentioned in the Smethcott introduction that much of Smethcott was woodland and Smethcott Dingle is still well-endowed with trees. Factory Dingle has, for the most part, become a plantation of mixed trees. Two fields adjacent to Factory Dingle were each called Wood Leasow (but were not woodland then) on the tithe map. Woodland flowers along the verges of the track are witnesses to the fact that this has been a woodland track and has suffered little interference. The valley may also have had a fulling mill; a nearby field was called Tainter Yard, which suggests that this was a field where cloth was stretched on tenterhooks. Another interesting field name in the area is that of Boosey Pasture (see next page). Upper Boosey Pasture is a small field that rises to a flat-topped hillock with scattered gorse and blackberry bushes on it; the gated road from near Parkhead to Walkmills runs along the edge of it.

Sm 11 begins almost opposite a house named Parkhead, a name probably related to its one-time position in or near Longnor Park. Upper Boosey Pasture is discernible a short way to the east (behind) as a gorse-covered mound. **Follow a small trail that runs along the centre of the track flanked by meadow plants. As the track descends, crosses the small brook and climbs out of the dingle it is heavily shaded and can seem quite dark; woodland species replace the meadow plants here. The track again becomes more open, the meadow flowers reappear and the way continues to join the lane between New House and New Hall.** New Hall Farm is thought to be one of the earliest sites of settlement outside the old hamlets and may even have been the site of a late mediaeval manor house. New Hall and New House in fact form part of quite a long list of ancient 'new houses' in the Mynd area whose names hint at early replacement of even older dwellings on the same sites.

SMETHCOTT 12, STANK LANE TO BETCHCOTT 0.5 Km/¼ m.

Sm 12 appears to be another unclaimed green lane and although it has not been included in a circuit is an ideal route for horse riders to use to avoid busier lanes.

A narrow unfrequented lane (Stank Lane) runs from near Woolstaston to join a lane from High Park to Picklescott (another mediaeval portway) at Vantage Ironwork (a craft shop worth visiting). Sm 12 turns off this lane a short distance before the above junction and runs as an enclosed track through a dingle. It crosses two small streams which run from High Park Hollow and Hawkham Hollow respectively. These streams join just downstream of the track to form the Betchcott Brook. The track joins the High Park to Picklescott lane near Betchcott.

Name meaning **Boosey Pasture**

A boosey pasture was land on which an outgoing tenant was allowed to pasture his animals for a specified period (Lady Day until the first of May) after the end of his lease. In the Shropshire Word Book, a boosey pasture was described by an inhabitant of Pulverbatch as being a field where cattle were allowed to consume hay, turnips and such produce on the field (during this specified period) as was not allowed to be taken from the farm.

Focus on birds **Dippers and grey wagtails**

These two species share a similar habitat, both being associated with fast-flowing streams. They are not alike in appearance but both bob when perched; the dipper bobs its body while the wagtail bobs its long tail. The wagtail feeds on insects such as the mayfly, which hatch out from the water (see Focus on stream life) while the dipper gets into the water and enjoys a diet similar to that of the brown trout. The dipper can dive and swim using its wings as flippers and even seemingly defy specific gravity by walking along the stream bottom; it is thought to accomplish this by the action of the water tumbling onto its broad back but others would argue that the bird is really swimming. Both birds nest close to water, sometimes making use of the underside of bridges, even close to habitation.

Focus on birds **Woodpeckers and jays**

The colourful woodpeckers and jays are birds associated with mature trees, not necessarily woodland. The green woodpecker, although it does peck wood in search of food, mainly feeds on turf-dwelling invertebrates and has a particular passion for ants. The jay, although it eats a variety of foods, loves acorns and its Latin name means 'chattering acorn-gatherer'. Woodpeckers may be heard more often than seen. The green woodpecker has a distinctive laughing call which has given rise to names such as yaffle, laughing bird and hickle. Rapid tapping of wood or drumming, another not infrequent woodland sound, is likely to be the work of the greater spotted woodpecker. The jay, which is a secretive bird, is most commonly seen at acorn time when a raucous screech and the flash of its white rump is all that is usually witnessed. The jay buries food and this is one way that oaks are propagated.

SMETHCOTT CHURCH LANE

This lane features in several of the Smethcott circuits and is part surfaced road and part unsurfaced. The unsurfaced section runs between Sm 7 at Spring Coppice and the church and is a very narrow (approximately two yards wide) track with steep banks. It would have been an important route in early mediaeval times when the motte by the church was in use and Smethcott hamlet was in this area. (The surfaced section is much more recent, possibly 200 years old and created at the time of the enclosure of Smethcott Common). Rectors must have used this track for 400 years until 1953 on their way to and from the church. The existence of the school would have brought a few generations of children from Picklescott this way until 1964. Today, it provides a way to church for a few.

WENTNOR

Wentnor is a large parish on the west of the Long Mynd, extending from the Portway (including the highest point of the Mynd) on the east to the Stiperstones on the west and including Adstone Hill. It is made up of the old townships of Wentnor, Home, Adstone, Medlicott, Kinnerton and Ritton. Ritton and most of Kinnerton lie outside the area covered in this book. Each of these townships has a small centre of habitation, Adstone's being a single farm. The exception is Wentnor, which has a larger population as well as church, rectory and pub, and is clearly seen to be the centre of the whole parish. Wentnor was the Domesday manor of Wantenouvre, the name meaning Wonta's or Wenta's flat-topped ridge. At that time it also included the Gatten (now in Ratlinghope). Prior to the arrival of the Normans the manor had been held by Edric, possibly that 'Wild Edric', a part-legendary part-historical figure, who rebelled against the Normans; a long-distance route crossing the Mynd has been named after him. Parts of the manor were later granted to Shrewsbury, Buildwas and Haughmond Abbeys. Medlicott was granted to Haughmond but Llewellyn de Medlicott continued to 'hold' it and at some stage it became an independent manor. An embankment crossing the Portway at Q and another between M and N are Medlicott manor boundaries. A Medlicott was to live in the hamlet for 800 years until the 1960s and today some of it is still owned by the family.

There appears to have been a church at Wentnor from at least the 12th century but there were no mediaeval chapels elsewhere in the area of the parish. Kinnerton has a modern chapel.

Wentnor is reached by lane EITHER from the 'main road' (its appearance is that of a main road but it is only classified as a minor road) between Shrewsbury and Bishops Castle OR from the the A489 at Eaton OR from Church Stretton via the Burway road and Asterton. The Inn on the Green is best reached (particularly with a caravan in tow) from the A489, turning off between Eaton and Churchstoke along the 'main road' towards Shrewsbury via Norbury.

Amenities: -

Shop - at the Inn on the Green.

Refreshments - Crown Inn in Wentnor village itself. The Inn on the Green on the 'main road' opposite the turning to Wentnor.

Camping - The Green, adjacent to pub and shop. Cwnd House.

Club camping - in Wentnor village itself.

Riding - Green Farm/Leisure Riding.

Bus service - Horrocks bus runs from Bishops Castle to Shrewsbury on a Tuesday morning via Wentnor, returning at lunchtime. On Fridays a Horrocks bus leaves Bishops Castle in the morning and returns after doing a circuit that takes in Wentnor. Another circuit journey, done in reverse, starts at lunchtime.

WENTNOR 1, BRIDGES TO MAIN ROAD

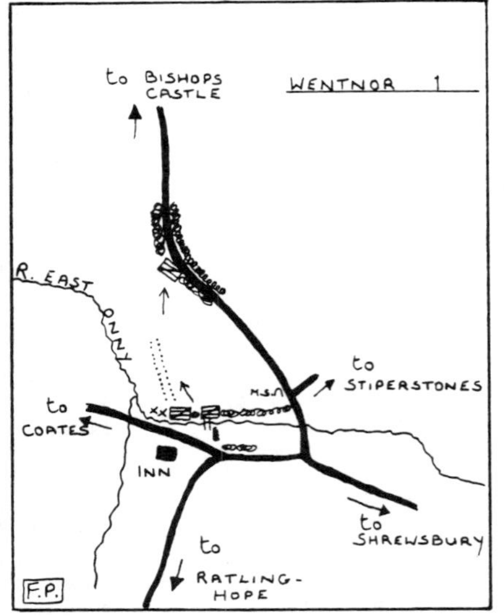

This is the original way into and out of the Ratlinghope valley. At some time a large embankment was constructed to cross the East Onny a short distance upstream from the old ford and this resulted in the main road bypassing the inn at the Bridges. The 'new road' had been built before 1846, when it appears on the tithe map; Wn 1 appears as the 'old road' and was still clearly defined and probably enclosed. Today a faint track only is discernible through open field.

The way starts as a footbridge beside a ford, opposite the front of the Horseshoe Inn. Cross into a field and bear obliquely left along a faint track. Continue in the same direction to join the main road, via a gate, on a sharp corner.

Focus on field names linked with tracks and footpaths

Most tracks were shown on the tithe maps, although not all those over the open hill. While only a few footpaths were shown, some of the field names recorded at that time suggest that footways ran through them or near to them. The list below includes all those fields in the Mynd area that have names linked with tracks or footways and the relevant right of way has been set against each one.

Footway Piece - Wentnor 3. Pulverbatch old path, no right of way. Woolstaston 6.
Sloapway Piece and Upper Sloapway - Wentnor 2.
Outrack - Wentnor 9 and Wentnor 5.
Sheep Rack and Rack Meadow - Church Stretton 19 (Minton).
Footway Hill - Wentnor 12.
Churchway - Wentnor 14.
Way Furlong - Wentnor lane and Wentnor 25.
Halfway End - Wentnor lanes.
Asterton Bridges - Wentnor 31/32.
Bridge Field - Wentnor 35.
Four Wickets - Woolstaston 4.
Rail Leasow - Woolstaston 3.
The Rail - Pulverbatch lane.
Rule - Little Stretton old track, no right of way.
Mapps Ford - Woolstaston 2.
Footway Holdbatch - Minton old path, no right of way.
Four Turnings Piece and Four Turnings Field - Smethcott lanes.
Cross Acre - by junction of lane with Smethcott 8.
Gate Pool and Gate Meadow - by B4370 between Little and Church Stretton.
Hoofway - Minton lane.
Squealing Wicket, Quaking Bridge and Stepping Stone are fields in Church Stretton just outside the area of this book.

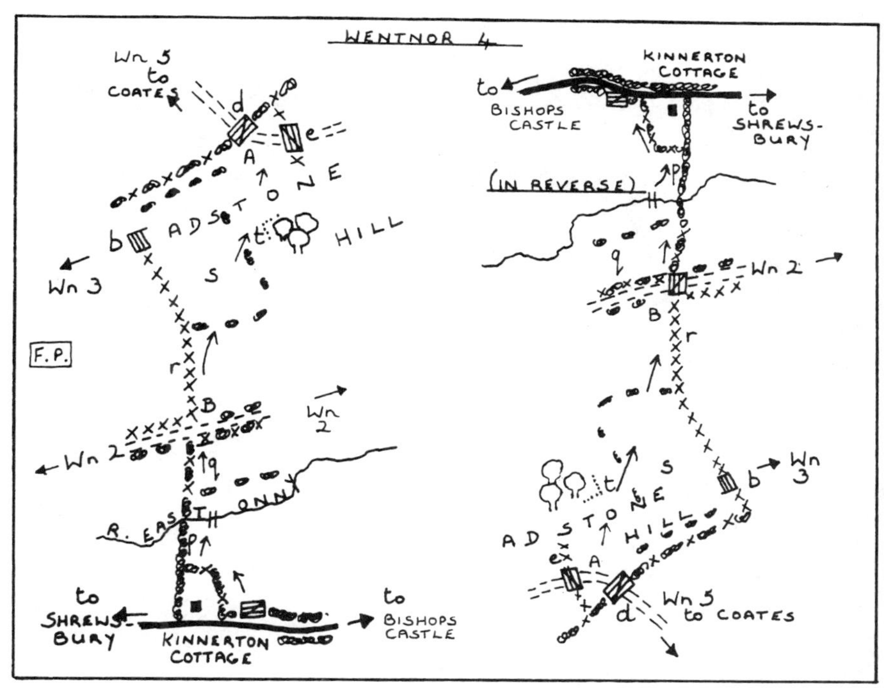

WENTNOR 4, KINNERTON COTTAGE TO COATES 0.5 Km/½+ m.

Wn 4, a public footpath, is shown on the O/S map as starting from the cottage. This is likely to alter and it appears acceptable at present to leave the main road through a gate near the cottage. Follow the new boundary hedge and fence around the cottage and join an old hedge (p), which in turn is followed down to the river. Cross the river (East Onny) via a footbridge and begin the ascent of Adstone Hill, keeping to the right-hand side of a hedge. At the top of field (q), cross a rail in the hedge to reach track (**Wn** 2) at point B. Cross the track and keep going up, bearing slightly to the right away from fence (r). Continue in this direction, crossing the corner of an old field (s) through sparse hedges, and then pass the open corner of a wood at (t). Continue and cross the spine of Adstone Hill to reach track (**Wn** 5) at A.

WENTNOR 4 (IN REVERSE), COATES TO KINNERTON COTTAGE.

Leave **Wn** 5 as it turns between gates (d) and (e) and cross the spine of Adstone Hill bearing obliquely to the right to get to the right-hand corner of a wood at (t). Continue in the same direction, crossing the corner of an old field (s) through sparse hedges and descending to a track (**Wn** 2) by a gate at point B. Cross the track and enter a small field (q) via a rail in the hedge. Follow hedge, keeping to the left-hand side of it, down to the river (East Onny), over which there is a footbridge, and continue along hedge (p) until the new boundary hedge and fence around Kinnerton Cottage is reached; follow this around to the left and exit onto the main road via a gate near the cottage.

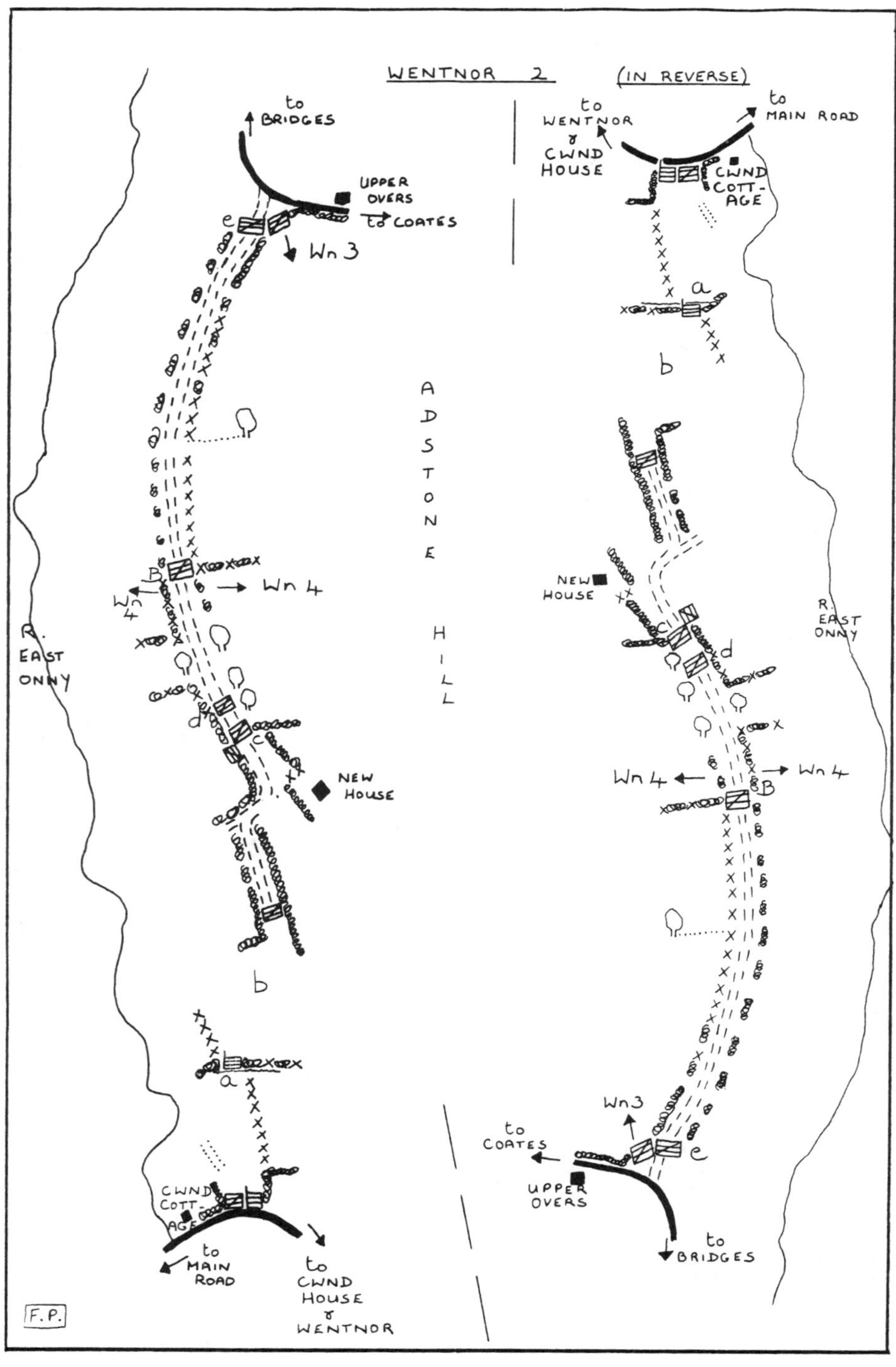
WENTNOR 2
(IN REVERSE)
to BRIDGES
UPPER OVERS
to COATES
Wn 3
Wn 4
Wn 4
R. EAST ONNY
NEW HOUSE
ADSTONE HILL
CWND COTT-AGE
to MAIN ROAD
to CWND HOUSE & WENTNOR
to WENTNOR & CWND HOUSE
to MAIN ROAD
CWND COTT-AGE
NEW HOUSE
R. EAST ONNY
Wn 4
Wn 4
Wn 3
to COATES
UPPER OVERS
to BRIDGES
F.P.

WENTNOR 2, CWND HOUSE TO OVERS 1.25 Km/0.75 m.

Wn 2 is an old route that runs as a public footpath down the valley of the East Onny, keeping to higher ground than the main road. It is likely to pre-date the main road, which passes through what must have been difficult terrain close to the river. For most of its length Wn 2 is obviously a track that has been built up to make a level road along the sloping side of Adstone Hill. Two fields near the track were called Sloapway Piece and Upper Sloapway (examples of some of the interesting and amusing spellings that occur on the tithe maps of the 1840s).

Wn 2 begins off the lane between Cwnd House and Cwnd Cottage, on a sharp bend, and passes over a stile. Do not follow the old track which descends to the river but bear obliquely to the right, keeping parallel to a fence. At (a) a tiny stream is crossed in the corner of the field and then a second stile. In field (b), again bear obliquely to the right; the East Onny river is visible to the left. In the far corner of field (b), the way becomes enclosed track. This next section can be very wet and muddy although the track has been raised up on the left. Continue along the track as it bends to the right to ascend to New House. New House was so called on the tithe map and is certainly not a new house. **Turn to the left by New House and, still following the track, pass through gate (c). A steep bank with some trees, perhaps remnants of an old hedge, forms the right side of the track. Another gate (d) is reached and the track continues under the bank on the right; the left side has been built up. Immediately before the next gate at point B, Wn 4 crosses Wn 2, passing over a stile cum fence on the left to descend to the river. From B, Wn 2 runs for some distance to reach gate (e), which leads onto the road at Overs.** From New House, the track is well above the river and offers attractive views of the valley.

WENTNOR 2 (IN REVERSE), OVERS TO CWND HOUSE

Wn 2 begins just before the lane from Bridges to Coates passes Upper Overs. It branches off as a clear track and almost immediately passes through gate (e). A good track, well above the Onny valley on the right, runs all the way to New House ; at point B, after a second gate, Wn 4 crosses the track. From New House the track descends for a short distance before bending to the left and running in a straight line to end in a field (b). Cross field (b) obliquely right to reach stile (a): the Onny is visible down to the right. From stile (a), follow fence to reach another stile onto the road near Cwnd House.

Name meaning **Onny**

Onny may mean 'ash water';'gwy' or 'wy' is a Welsh word for water often to be seen in river names, either alone, as in Wye, or as an ending e.g.in Onny and many others (Conway,Vyrnwy,etc). 'Onn' is Welsh for 'ash trees'.

Quinney

Quinney Brook is on the east side of the Mynd and runs from Little Stretton southwards via Queensbatch mill. Both 'quin' and 'queen' are likely to have the same origin which is perhaps the Welsh 'gwyn', meaning 'white'. The ending '-ey' may again be derived from Welsh 'wy', i.e. 'white water brook'.'

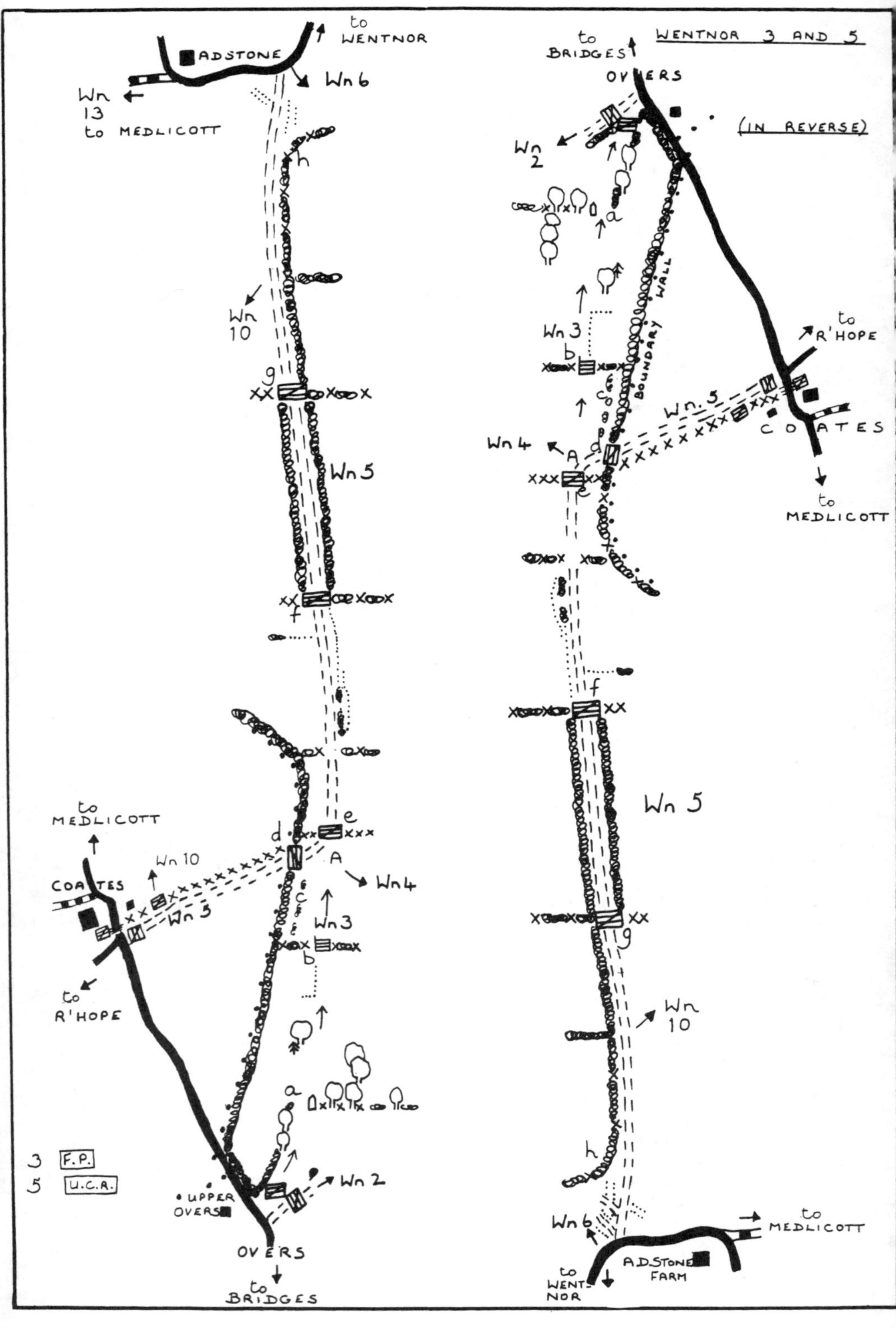

WENTNOR 3 AND 5
(IN REVERSE)
to WENTNOR
ADSTONE
Wn 6
Wn 13 to MEDLICOTT
h
Wn 10
g
Wn 5
f
e
d
A
to MEDLICOTT
Wn 10
COATES
Wn 5
Wn 4
c
Wn 3
b
to R'HOPE
a
Wn 2
UPPER OVERS
OVERS
to BRIDGES
3 F.P.
5 U.C.R.
to BRIDGES
OVERS
Wn 2
a
BOUNDARY WALL
Wn 3
b
c
to R'HOPE
Wn. 5
COATES
Wn 4
A
d
e
to MEDLICOTT
f
Wn 5
g
Wn 10
h
Wn 6
to MEDLICOTT
ADSTONE FARM
to WENTNOR

WENTNOR 3 AND 5

Wn 3 and much of Wn 5, in continuity with each other, form a ridgeway route along the spine of Adstone Hill and may once have been the original route running north-south on this side of the Mynd and continuing along the ridge to Wentnor. As such it may have been used as a link between Ratlinghope's priory and Wigmore Abbey in Herefordshire. A straight road is shown on Robert Baugh's map of 1808 from Bridges to Wentnor, passing near Coat Farm (Coates) and Adstone. On the tithe map, however, Wn 5 is not shown and what appears to be Wn 3 from Overs to Adstone Hill is a track (c) that is running a similar course to Wn 3 but more to the east, off the ridge; this track is easily discernible today and forms the Wentnor/Ratlinghope parish boundary. Other maps of the same period show that Wn 5 did exist in the 1830s; a track ran the length of the hill but was probably Wn 5 with track (c). Enclosure of part of Wn 5 postdates these maps and the appearance of a wide track with predominantly hawthorn hedge is suggestive of a modern addition.

WENTNOR 3, OVERS TO ADSTONE HILL 0.75 Km/½ m.

Wn 3 (a public footpath) begins just before Upper Overs via a gate into a field. Ascend the steep slope, following the right-hand side of a hedge with some beech trees. At (a), keep straight on up the ridgeway, passing the remains of a small mixed wood and continuing to stile (b). Down to the left, the old track (c), mentioned above, runs in the same direction as Wn 3. A short distance beyond stile (b), a stony track (Wn 5), coming onto the hill from the left, is joined on a bend at point A.

WENTNOR 3 (IN REVERSE), ADSTONE HILL TO OVERS.

Wn 3 begins where Wn 5 turns away from the top of Adstone Hill at point A and is a continuation along the top of the hill. The first stile (b) is soon reached. Continue along the spine of the hill, passing the remnants of a small wood, to reach a gateway (a). Follow hedge down to a gate that leads onto the lane at Overs.

WENTNOR 5, COATES TO ADSTONE FARM 1.25 Km/0.75 m.

Coates is an old but very small area of habitation, little more than a farmyard with four dwellings. Wn 5 (an unsurfaced highway) starts by a bungalow just outside the farmyard area. It is a clear stony track that passes through a gate and runs towards Adstone Hill, passing through a second gate (d). As it bends round to the left (point A) it is joined by Wn 3 and Wn 4 before passing through gate (e). The way continues along the spine of the hill, the track becoming grassy. Here there are faint signs of old track and old field boundaries which remain as fragments of old grassland amidst the much greater expanse of improved pasture. These places, along with the steep east slope, hold some interesting small plants e.g. Moenchia erecta. Gate (f) is the beginning of an enclosed section of track which ends at gate (g). From here the track follows hedge to (h), where the hedge diverges and the track crosses a rough area of heathland to reach lane near Adstone Farm.

WENTNOR 5, ADSTONE FARM TO COATES

Leave the lane to Adstone Farm, crossing a small area of heathland to follow a hedge to gate (g). Continue along an enclosed section of track to gate (f) and on again to gate (e). The track then bends to the right, passes through gate (d) and descends to Coates.

WENTNOR 6

In places it is still evident that Wn 6 was an old track to Adstone Hill but today it is only classified as a public footpath. Wn 6, in continuity with Wn 13 and Wn 7, may have been the way inhabitants of Ashgrove and Cwnd House reached the Mynd to tend their animals; both these farms have common rights on the hill, although these rights have not been exercised for two generations or more.

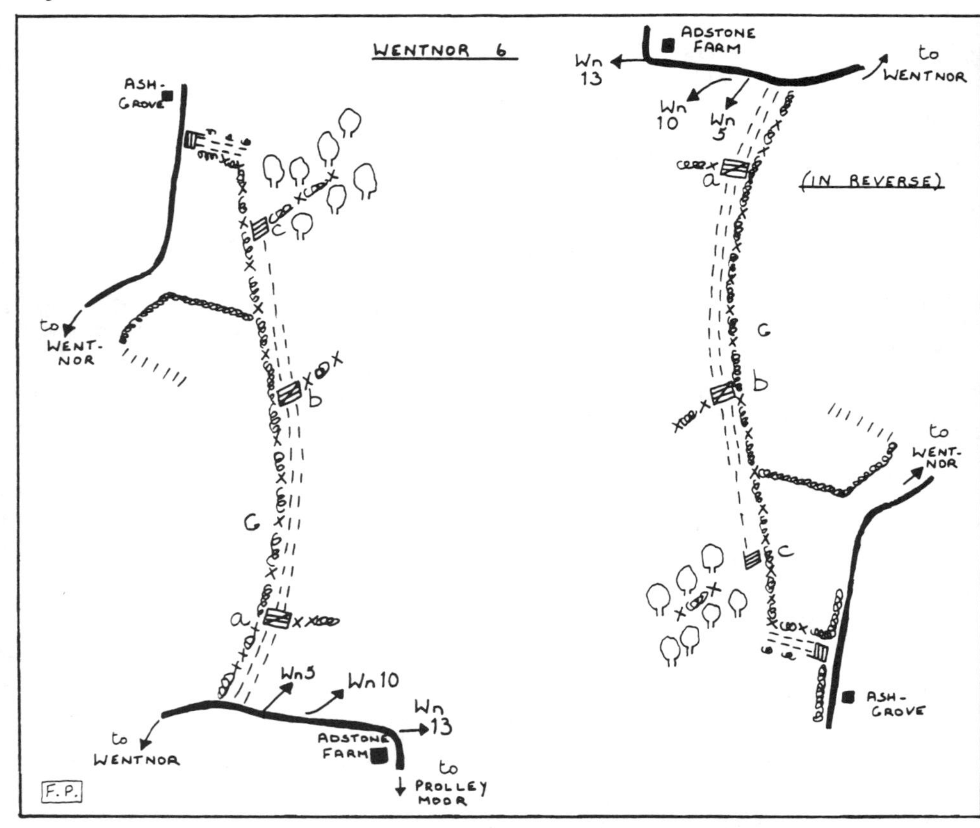

WENTNOR 6, ADSTONE TO ASHGROVE 0.75 Km/½ m.

The way starts just after the Wentnor to Adstone road passes through a gate onto the end of Adstone Hill. Follow a faint track obliquely left along the right-hand side of a hedge to gate (a). Continue following the hedge. Just before gate (b), old track is evident again and there is a spring beside it. From (b) continue along the hedge under a slope covered by bracken and gorse. A wood is entered just before crossing stile (c) and the wood extends along the hillside beside our route and beyond; it is a good example of a wood leasow (see page 180). Follow the hedge, which turns away from the wood, down to the left and descend to a stile onto Ashgrove Lane nearly opposite Ashgrove.

WENTNOR 6 (IN REVERSE), ASHGROVE TO ADSTONE

The way starts at a stile nearly opposite Ashgrove. Follow hedge up to the bottom of a wood where the hedge and path turn sharply to the right. Hedge and, in places, old track lead you up the slope; cross stile (c) and gates (b) and (a) to reach the lane near Adstone Farm.

WENTNOR 7

Wn 7 is a stony track (the lower part is surfaced) along which generations of Medlicott people, with or without animals, on foot or by pony and trap, have travelled to get to Stretton. The advent of buses, providing transport to Bishops Castle and Shrewsbury, resulted in many people on the west of the Mynd going elsewhere to shop. As more people acquired cars this trend continued and therefore this track to Stretton became used less. It has remained an unsurfaced highway and locally is known as High Arkoll.

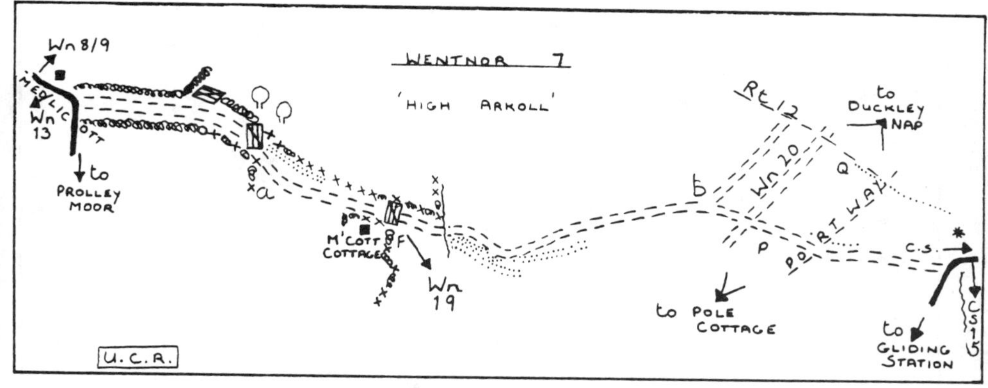

WENTNOR 7, MEDLICOTT TO BOILING WELL 2 Km/1¼ m.

Wn 7 turns off the Bridges to Prolley Moor road by Medlicott Manor Farm and ascends as an enclosed track. At gate (a) the track becomes open and climbs to Medlicott Cottage. One of the fields to the right was called Batted Piece which suggests that it has been 'betted' at some time; this means that the turf was cut in strips, burnt and dug in, as a way of improving the rough grassland. **At the cottage, pass through a gate onto open hill; Wn 19 branches off to the right by a pile of stones. Wn 7 continues as a clear track. The land on the left is soon unenclosed but is privately owned by Medlicott farmers, while on the right they have common rights on the common land owned by the National Trust.** Old tracks are apparent near today's route. At point (b), a grassy track branches off to the left which joins Rt 12. Wn 7 continues and crosses first Wn 20 and then the Portway at P before descending to the Stretton to gliding station road opposite the Boiling Well.

WENTNOR 7 (IN REVERSE), BOILING WELL TO MEDLICOTT

Take the stony track opposite the Boiling Well (near the Y junction of the surfaced roads) and follow it over the hill and down the west side of the Mynd to Medlicott Cottage. Leave the open hill via a gate and cross a field to gate (a). Descend enclosed track to Medlicott itself.

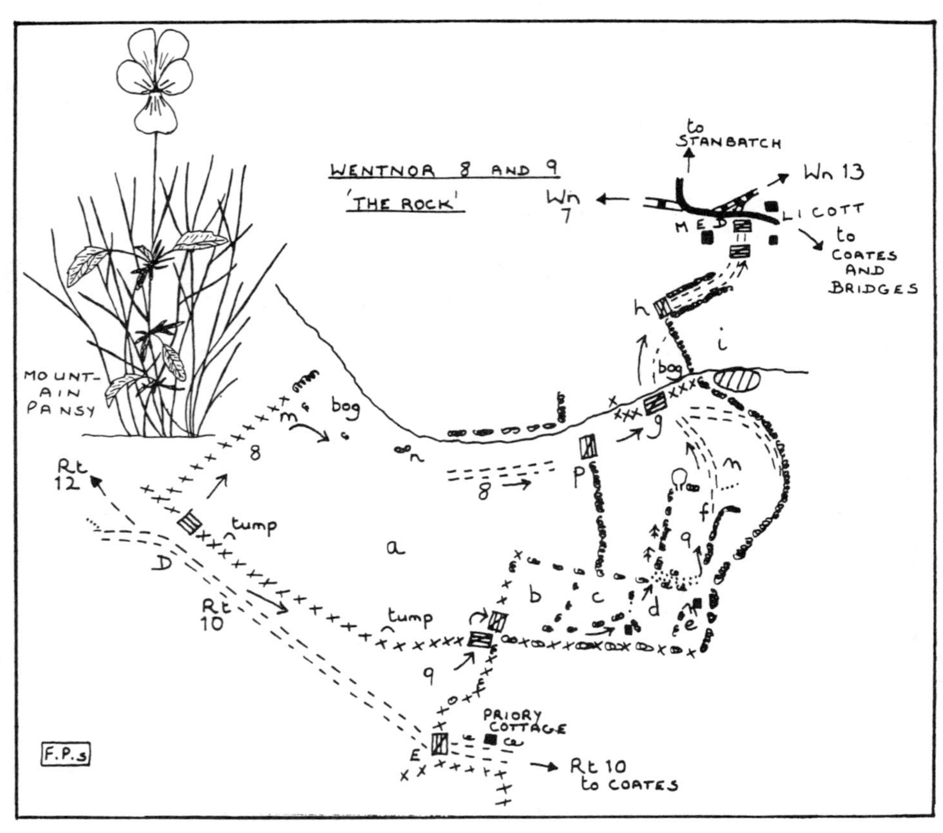

WENTNOR 9, Rt 10 AT D OR E TO MEDLICOTT VIA THE ROCK 1.5 Km/1 m.

Much of this footpath runs through an area known as The Rock (see page 207). **Leave Rt 10 where it runs close to the fence at D or where it enters/leaves open hill at E and follow fence to a gate in the corner.** In field (a), tumps marking the Wentnor/Ratlinghope boundary can be seen. **Pass through the gate into field (a) and immediately turn right through another gate into a group of small fields. Fields (b), (c) and (d) were each called Croft, a name often given to a small field.** These fields have been created in the past from the moorland and are now good examples of old hill pasture; the grass is short and springy to walk on and is full of small flowers. In May and June heath bedstraw gives the appearance of snow-covered ground and at the same time mountain pansies can be seen in field (d). These used to be a common sight over the area west of the Mynd but today the number of places where they are found has fallen dramatically. Their yellow heads look sturdy enough but the plants are in fact very frail, so be careful where you walk. Field (d) also has a boggy area in which, at mountain pansy time, are plenty of cuckoo flowers (lady's smock) which attract orange-tip butterflies. Look carefully on the thin stalks bearing the flowers (not the main stem) and you may find minute single orange eggs left by the orange-tip butterflies; later these will have become green caterpillars which eat the young fruits. Sedges typical of many Mynd bogs and the less common pill sedge grow here too and the abundance of plant species attracts many other insects.

Much therefore can be seen along the way as it descends through these fields, passing to the left of some ruins. Cross field (d) obliquely to the left to reach the left side just short of the far left corner. Leave the field by some larch trees, turning sharply to the right to descend past a rock face and the ruins of Rock Farm (e) on the right. Turn left but keep up, following a line of trees rather than the lower stone wall. The bracken can be thick here but a small path (probably made by animals) is soon evident which continues straight on away from the trees at (f). It ascends slightly to a brow above another rock face on the right which looks out on Sorrowful (see next page). The way now descends as a track to a gate (g) close to the brook, at this point joining Wn 8. Pass through the gate, cross the brook and aim obliquely right up to a gate (h). On the right is a field (i) that shows signs of past mining activity. Little is known about the mines except that they were for copper. There is nothing on the tithe map to suggest activity then but another map of that era shows a 'Wheelpit Bank' in the vicinity and local tradition still recalls - rather unnervingly! - how one family there could hear sounds of mining activity and voices underground inside their own farmhouse. **Pass through the gate and follow old track which runs between farm buildings to the right of a house, passing through two gates to exit onto the Bridges to Stanbatch road.**

WENTNOR 9 (IN REVERSE), MEDLICOTT TO RT 10 VIA THE ROCK

Turn off the lane at Medlicott and go through two gates between farm buildings to the left of a farmhouse. Follow an old track down to gate (h) and then aim obliquely left around the bog down to the brook. Ford the brook and pass through gate (g). Take the track to the left, up the hill to the brow. Descend slightly to follow a line of trees (one tree is dead and therefore distinctive) from (f). At the end of this line, at the rocks (e), turn up to the right and then turn left by some larch trees into field (d). Cross this field aiming obliquely up to some ruins, passing them and then following a hedge straight up to a gate. Pass through this gate into field (a) and immediately turn left through another gate onto open hill. Cross to Rt 10 (a track).

WENTNOR 8, RT 10 TO MEDLICOTT 1 Km/½+ m.

Wn 8 leaves Rt 10 at D via a stile into field (a). Note the boundary tump near the stile. Follow fence down the steep slope. At the bottom of the slope, follow a sparse line of small trees (old hedge) which at (n) meets a brook. Follow the tree-lined brook along a new track, passing through an old gate (p). Continue along the brook to gate (g). This area along the right-hand side of the brook was called Outrack, linking open hill with the track that now stops at (h), and would have been where the sheep were gathered off the hill and sorted between their various owners. **Wn 9 is joined at (g). Turn left through the gate and ford the brook. Aim obliquely up to gate (h) and go along track. Exit onto lane via two gates between buildings and a farmhouse.**

WENTNOR 8 (IN REVERSE), MEDLICOTT TO Rt 10

Turn off the lane at Medlicott and pass through two gates

between farm buildings to the left of a house. Follow track down to gate (h). Aim down to the brook and pass through gate (g). Turn right and follow the brook and trees to (n), passing through gate (p) and making use of a stretch of new track. A sparse line of small trees (an old hedge) leaves the brook at this point; follow this above an area of rushes until a fence is reached at (m). Turn left to follow this up the slope to a stile which leads onto open hill to join the track of Rt 10.

THE ROCK

The Rock is a corner of the Long Mynd near Medlicott that was probably taken over by squatters at some time and changed into an area of small fields above and around rock faces. The boundaries of the fields can still be seen as old grassy embankments or lines of trees and the ruins of two habitations are also still evident. In 1831 these were referred to as Bishops Cottage and Everalls Cottage. The lower site was called Rock Farm latterly and lies under a rock face. An old track leads away from it and follows the contour of the hill to get to Medlicott, passing under another rock face. The income of some of the inhabitants of The Rock may have been supplemented by working at Medlicott's mine but life here must have been hard. One of their fields was called Sorrowful and it is difficult not to feel a little sad at the sight of past endeavours.

The Rock lies just within the parish of Wentnor, the boundary with Ratlinghope running down from the hill beside the upper ruins. Some of the inhabitants were buried at Ratlinghope rather than Wentnor.

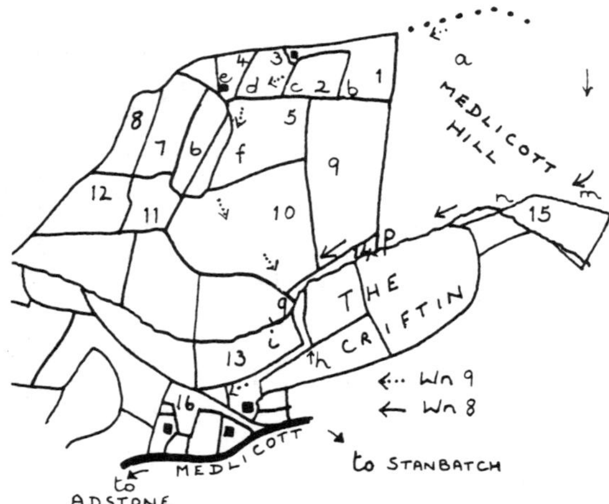

The Rock area in the 1840s
1. The Croft. 2 & 3. Crofts.
4. Close and Rock House.
5. Rock Leasow.
6. Rock Ground.
7. Middle Rock Piece.
8. Lower Rock Piece.
(6, 7 and 8 are now one meadow).
9. Hill Leasow. 10. The Bank.
11. Sorrowful (bog).
(11 and 12 are now one field).
13. Bank Leasow. 14. Outrack.
15. Upper Criftin.
16. The present-day road from Medlicott to Coates apparently did not exist and ended here in 'open waste land'.

WENTNOR 10

Wn 10 is a public footpath but at present it is not possible to use it. As an entity it is an odd route, ascending the hill as it does to join Wn 5, immediately leaving it to part-descend the hill again and then curving round the end of the hill to rejoin Wn 5 once more. It has probably arisen as two separate short cuts, one from Coates to Wn 5 on the hill and thence on to Wentnor and the other from Adstone to Wn 5 on the hill and thence on to the Bridges.

WENTNOR 10, COATES TO ADSTONE 1.5 Km/nearly 1 m.

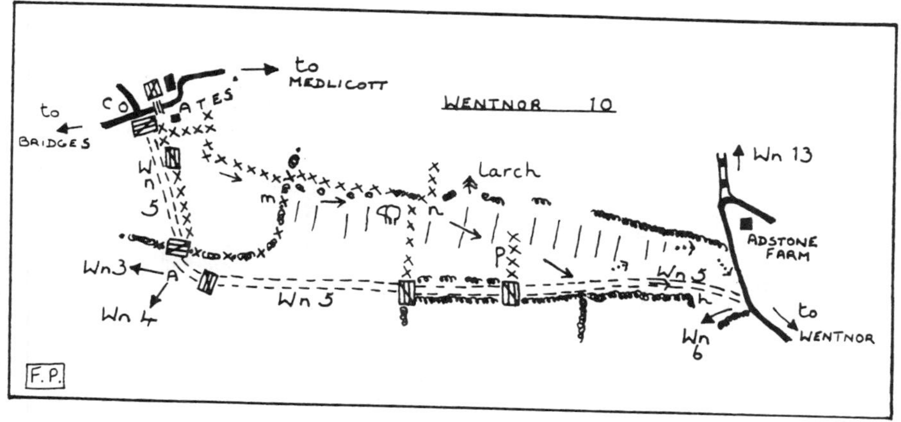

Start along the track (Wn 5) that turns off the lane just before the farm area of Coates, by a bungalow. Pass through a gate and then almost immediately go through a gate on the left into a field. Cross part of the field to come in line with a fence which is then followed to the far side of the same field. The hedge here (m) is the Wentnor/Ratlinghope boundary; it is supplemented by fencing and at present there is no way to cross it. The way continues straight on, following the line of an old hedge at the bottom of the slope of Adstone Hill. A few mature trees are passed on the slope and a short distance beyond these, the hedge and fence being followed turn away at a right angle (n). From here the slope must be ascended obliquely to the right but it is impossible to know the exact right of way. An old hedge running along the bottom of the slope has an old larch tree in it; when in line with this you should be approximately half-way up the slope. Continue obliquely upwards. At the top of the slope is another fence (p). From here the old and correct way is to aim obliquely right from the fence until Wn 5 is joined; as Wn 5 is following a line of trees it is easy to aim for. It is probably simplest then to continue along Wn 5 and not attempt to follow the rather pointless last section of Wn 10.

WENTNOR 10 (IN REVERSE), ADSTONE TO COATES

The first part of this path as shown on the O/S map is almost impossible to follow accurately and of no benefit distance-wise. Therefore start along Wn 5, reaching hedge at point (h) and following this until in line with a field boundary on the left. At this point aim obliquely right and keep along the same line all the way down the slope. There is a fence at (p) and about half-way down the steep slope you should be in line with an old larch tree down to the right. Hopefully you will reach the bottom of the slope at a right angle in a fence at point (n). Follow this fence and hedge (later old hedge alone) to cross the Wentnor/Ratlinghope boundary hedge at (m); this is not possible at present. Follow fence to a right angle and continue in the same line to a gate onto track (Wn 5). Turn right and pass through a gate onto lane by Coates.

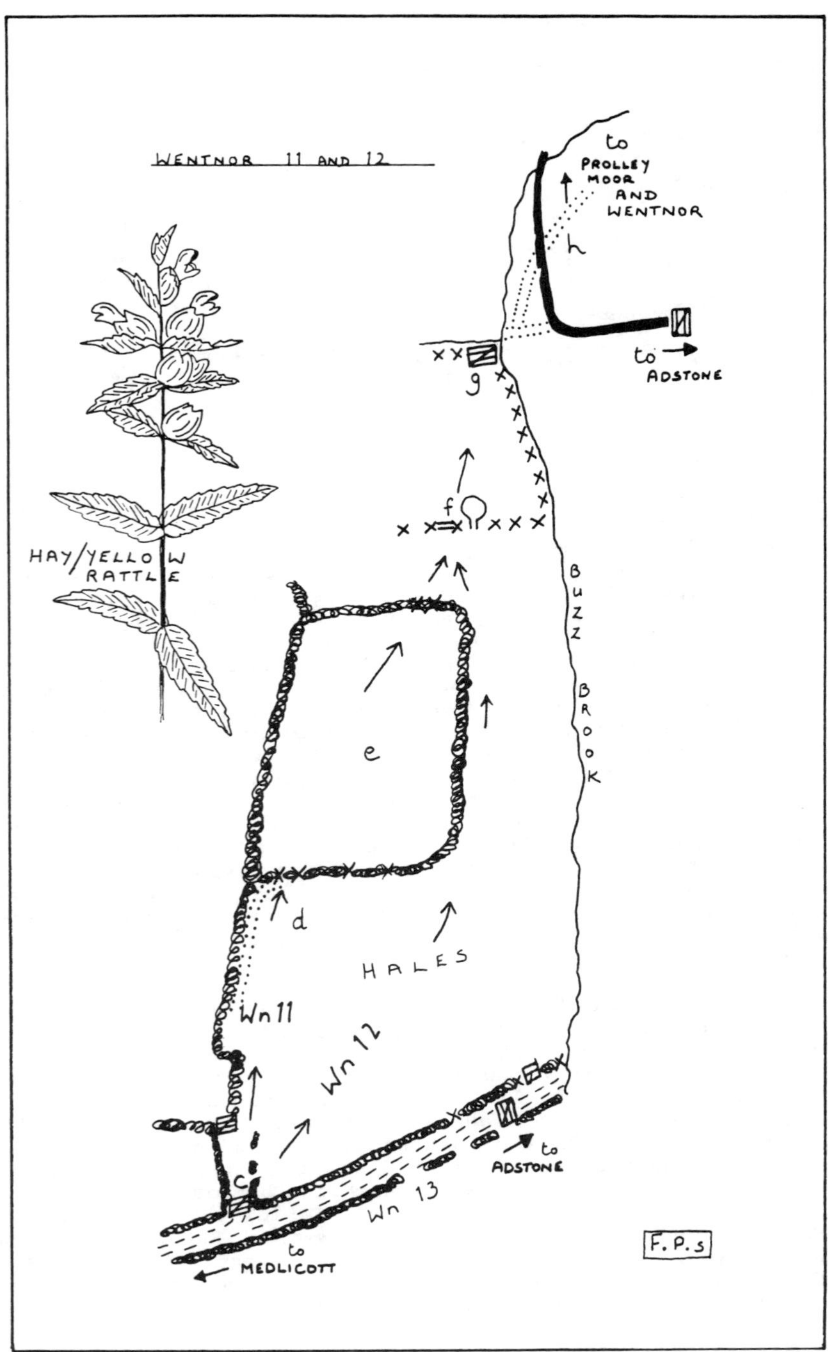
WENTNOR 11 AND 12
HAY/YELLOW RATTLE
to PROLLEY MOOR AND WENTNOR
h
to ADSTONE
g
f
B U Z Z B R O O K
e
d
HALES
Wn 11
Wn 12
c
to ADSTONE
Wn 13
to MEDLICOTT
F. P. s

WENTNOR 11 AND 12

These are the routes by which Medlicott inhabitants went to Wentnor for church, school, shop and spa-well amongst other reasons. Wn 11 must be an old route since one of the fields it passes through was called Footway Field on the tithe map and at the Medlicott end faint traces of it running as an old track as far as field (d) can still be seen. However, it is impassable at present and as it runs in such close proximity to Wn 12 it seems unnecessary for it to be put into use. Both are public footpaths.

WENTNOR 12, MEDLICOTT TO PROLLEY MOOR 0.5 Km/¼+ m.

Take the 'Front Road' (Wn 13) from Medlicott, passing below two farms and continuing along well-used track. Other tracks branch off into fields as Wn 11/12 does at (c) but this is the only branch track that shows signs of a hedge each side, albeit for a short distance, before it leads through a gateway into a field. This field is still called Hales today (it was three fields on the tithe map - Upper Ale, Lower Ale and Little Ale - with neighbouring Big Hale and Hale Meadow); Hales was a name for a water-meadow, remote valley or a corner of land, all of which can apply here. **Wn 12 bears off to the right, descending slightly before following the contour of the bank round until it is running with the hedge. Continue to follow the hedge and the contour of the slope. Wn 11 passes through the field (e) on the left, formerly Footway Field, which is an example of one of Medlicott's attractions, a traditional old hay meadow;** in June and July this field is a warm, orange colour due to sorrel flowers and foxtail grass, with an abundance of other shorter flowers and grasses growing underneath. **At the corner of this meadow Wn 11 and Wn 12 unite; continue straight on and cross a wooden bar by an oak tree (f). Cross the next field bearing obliquely right to a gate (g) in the far right-hand corner. After the gate, turn right across Buzz/Criftin Brook to reach the Adstone to Prolley Moor gated road. Turn left to go towards Wentnor.**

Bird Cherry can be seen beside the brook here and along Wn 13 near Medlicott. It is a small tree with white blossom hanging in small chains and leaves that later become literally moth-eaten (green caterpillars can be seen at flowering-time). It is a tree usually associated with hill country and is of very limited distribution in Shropshire. In the Long Mynd area it is confined to the vicinity of Medlicott and Prolley Moor and it was therefore chosen as the emblem for Wentnor in this book. One Medlicott inhabitant recounts taking specimens of bird cherry to the pub for quizzes of plant names; no one ever knew what it was.

There are signs of old tracks in relation to the road at the end of Wn 11/12. Track (h) runs for some distance and appears to finish at a field that was called Outrack on the tithe map, although the track was not shown then. Its use must pre-date this and it is difficult to work out where it was leading from. It may have been a track and outrack (sorting area) used by Wentnor inhabitants from Prolley Moor or even from the Mynd. Perhaps the old track at the start of Wn 11/12 was once in continuity with it.

WENTNOR 13

Wn 13 is an unsurfaced highway and is an old road that links Adstone with Medlicott. In continuity with Wn 6 at one end and Wn 7 at the other, it provided a route from Ashgrove and Cwnd House to the Mynd (both have common rights on the hill) as well as to Stretton. The road has been little used within living memory except at the Medlicott end which is in regular use for gaining access to fields. It is difficult for riders to use in its present state.

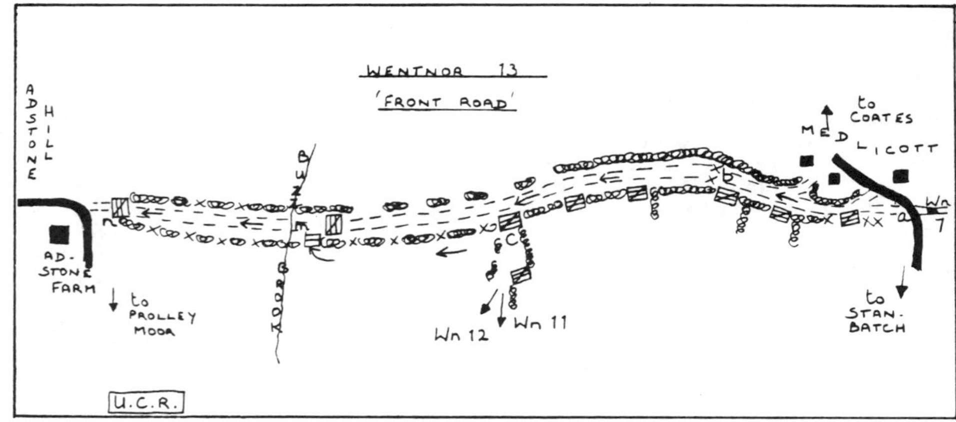

WENTNOR 13, MEDLICOTT TO ADSTONE 1 Km/½+ m.

Take the enclosed track branching off at Medlicott and pass below two farms. Continue along the track, well-used here, and pass through hurdles (?temporary) at (b). Pass the short track (c) on the left that is the start of Wn 11/12 and continue down the somewhat overgrown track (an alternative is to enter the field on the left at (c) and descend along the outside of the track). At the bottom, pass through an old gate to reach point (m) which is where the track is rejoined if you have used the field route. Although the track is no longer overgrown from here, the area on either side of the brook is boggy. Once through bog and brook, ascend the track and exit via a gate (n) by Adstone Farm.

WENTNOR 13 (IN REVERSE), ADSTONE TO MEDLICOTT

Wn 13 starts by Adstone Farm through a gate (n). The track is enclosed and grassy and descends to a boggy area by Buzz/Criftin Brook. There are several bird cherry trees in the hedge on the right just before the brook. Pass through an old gate and continue up the track (or go into the field on the right at (m) via a stile and follow the outside of the track). The track is still enclosed but the left-hand hedge is patchy and open to the field as it ascends. Bird cherry trees occur intermittently all along the way. **At (c), a short track branches off to the right; this is the start of Wn 11/12 and is also the point at which the track is rejoined if you have used the field route. Continue along the track to the hurdles (not always up). The track passes below two of Medlicott's three farms (hence the name 'Front Lane'), divides into two and joins the Bridges to Stanbatch road. On the tithe map, Wn 13 (a) in continuity with Wn 7 was the main route and tracks to Coates and Stanbatch were branches off it.**

WENTNOR 14, ADSTONE TO HALFWAY END

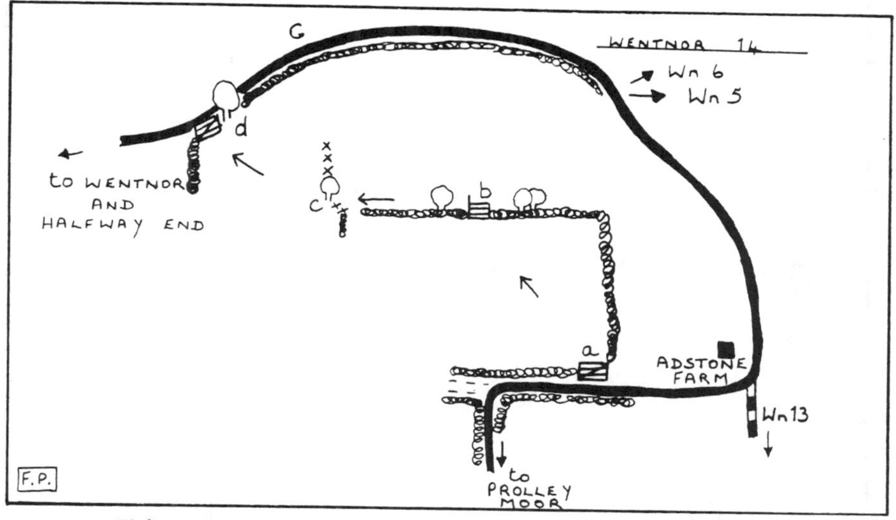

This short route begins at gate (a) off the gated road between Prolley Moor and Adstone Farm and is a public footpath. The first field was called Church Way, suggesting that this path was a way to church for someone at some time. **Aim obliquely across the field to approximately half-way along the far hedge, or follow the hedge round to the same point if the grass is long, to a stile (b). Turn left over the stile and follow the hedge;** a few woodland flowers have survived on the bank under the hedge. **The way is blocked at (c) by a fence at present but it is one that can be crawled under, near the ash tree. Aim towards the far right-hand corner of the next field (d) to a tree next to a gate onto the Adstone to Wentnor lane near Halfway End.**

Focus on field names

Field names in the text of this book are historical names as the only comprehensive records of them are in the tithe maps and apportionments of the 1840s. Today, some fields still have names but, as there is no public record of them to refer to, there is no way of knowing which names have survived other than by asking all the landowners. The conclusion that can be drawn from studying limited areas is that some field names have survived just as they were in the 1840s. Others have altered but are still recognizable e.g. one of the Holy Wall fields is now known as Willy Walls (see W on Wn 22), Killuluddy is Cloddy Well (see K on Wn 23) and several fields near Halfway End, known as Upper or Lower Wentnor or simply Wentnor, are The Wenners. Many fields have acquired new names, sometimes related to their acreage, crop or quality. An interesting field name surviving in Wentnor is that of Black Graves (see G on Wn 14); it was Black Greaves on the tithe map, with adjacent Black Furlong and Black Graves Wood (see G on Wn 6). It is believed that victims of the Black Death were buried here, in which case these particular field names are centuries old. Many others may be equally ancient and some provide the only clue to the past of each small patch of land.

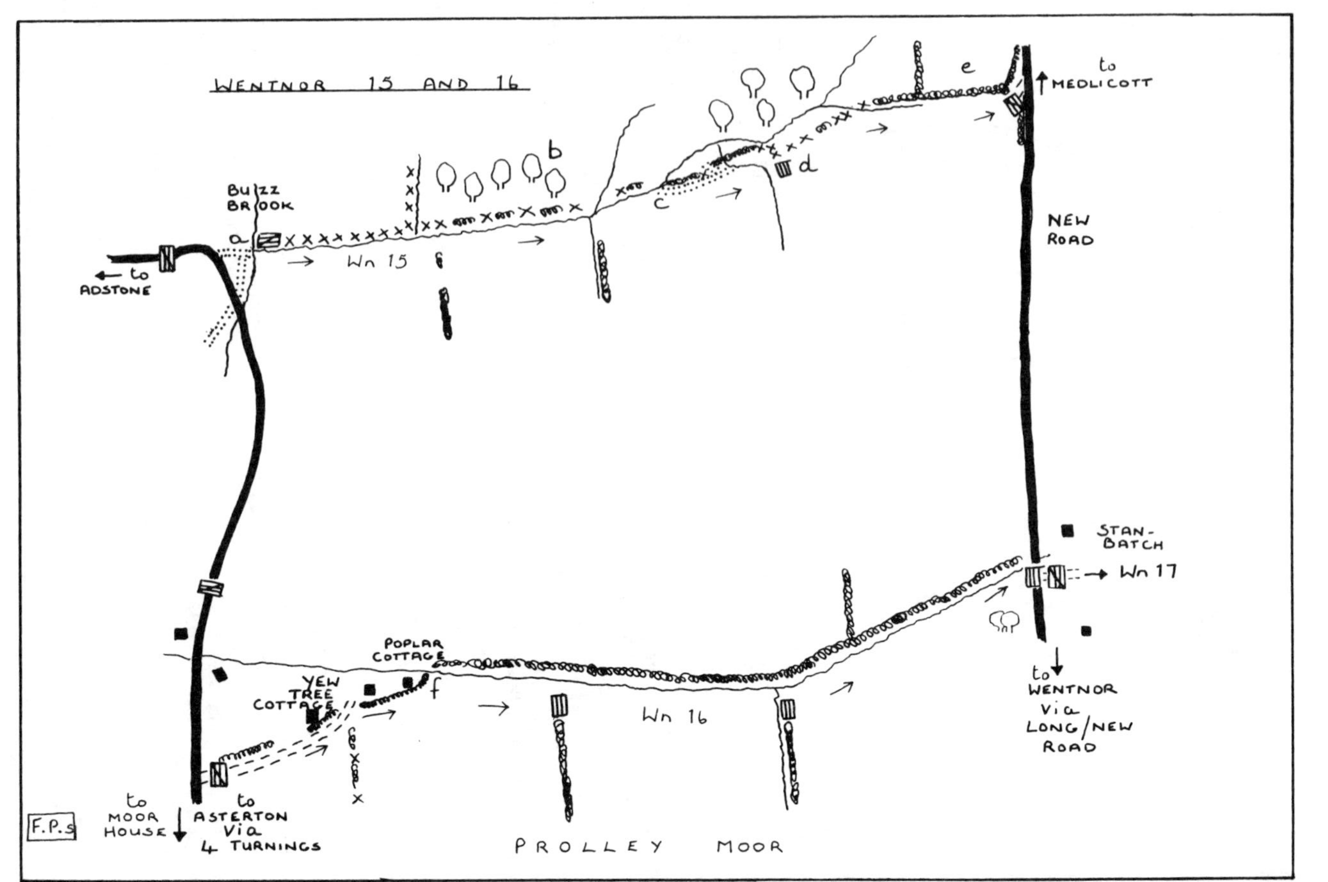
WENTNOR 15 AND 16
BUZZ BROOK
a
b
c
d
e
f
Wn 15
Wn 16
Wn 17
to MEDLICOTT
NEW ROAD
to ADSTONE
STAN-BATCH
POPLAR COTTAGE
YEW TREE COTTAGE
to WENTNOR Via LONG/NEW ROAD
to MOOR HOUSE
to ASTERTON Via 4 TURNINGS
PROLLEY MOOR
F.P.s

WENTNOR 15 AND 16

Wn 16 runs along what was the northern edge of an open Prolley Moor on the tithe map; it was not shown on that map but is on another map of the same period, where it is joined by a branch from Moorhouse and is in continuity with Wn 17 onto the open hill. Wn 15 may represent an older boundary of Prolley Moor and the houses near the end of Wn 16 may have been built originally by squatters on the moor.

Wn 16 is part of the Shropshire Way.

WENTNOR 15, ADSTONE TO NEW ROAD 0.75 Km/½ m.

Wn 15 begins off the gated road running between Prolley Moor and Adstone Farm. An old track (a) is followed down to the brook; this is the way the road once ran, turning right after the brook to go towards Prolley Moor. **Cross Buzz Brook and follow a tributary of it upstream that runs with fence and/or hedge.** This is a walk where several bird cherry trees can be seen (see Wn 11 and 12). **An area of deciduous woodland (b) is passed on the left while the path crosses through two old hedges.** It is an ideal habitat for the redstart, a summer visitor which is not unlike a robin in appearance but has a red tail that is often the first feature to catch the eye as the bird flies off. **The path veers away from the brook slightly at (c) but continues to follow an old hedge and the woodland continues on the left.** There is more woodland in this area today than was present at the time of the tithe map, when there were five fields with names suggestive of woodland but only one area was actually a wood. Today, three of these fields (Lower Wood, Wood and Upper Wood) are woodland or, to be more precise, wood leasows (see page 180). **A boggy area has to be crossed to reach a new stile at (d). The path then follows hedge to a gate onto the road.** The rushy field on the left (e) was Medlicott's Meadow.

WENTNOR 15 (IN REVERSE), NEW ROAD TO ADSTONE

The way begins between Stanbatch and Medlicott off the New Road. Pass through a gate and follow the left-hand side of a hedge to a new stile (d). Continue in the same line after the stile following initially old hedge and then hedge and brook. There is woodland on the right for much of the way. Pass through two old hedges and continue along the brook until it joins the larger Buzz Brook. Cross this brook and ascend to the lane between Prolley Moor and Adstone Farm.

WENTNOR 16, YEW TREE COTTAGE TO STANBATCH 0.75 Km/½ m.

The first part of this public footpath is also the driveway to some dwellings which, like so many Prolley Moor homes, are named after trees. Follow the boundary hedges of these houses to reach a small stream at (f). This stream and its accompanying hedge are followed all the way to Stanbatch, where the path exits onto the New Road opposite the start of Wn 17.

WENTNOR 16 (IN REVERSE), STANBATCH TO YEW TREE COTTAGE

The path begins off the New Road opposite Wn 17, crossing a stile and continuing alongside a small stream for most of its length. At (f), the stream disappears to the right and the path follows the boundaries of some houses, soon becoming driveway, and exits onto the road via a gate.

WENTNOR 17 AND 18

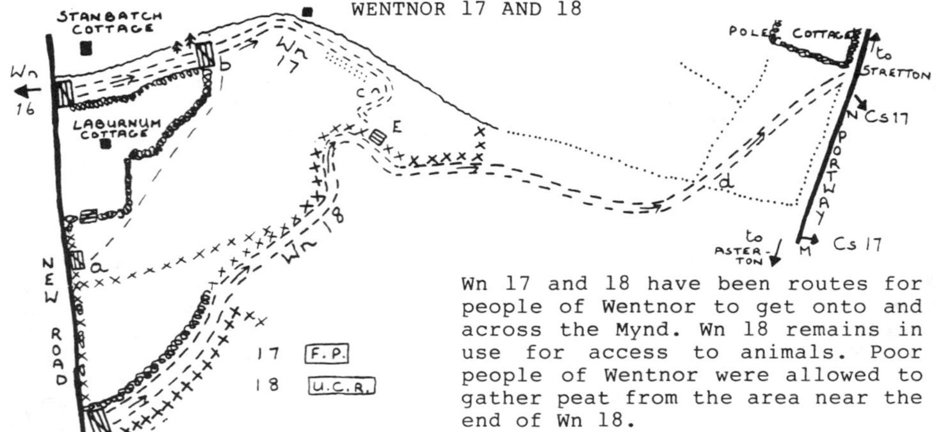

Wn 17 and 18 have been routes for people of Wentnor to get onto and across the Mynd. Wn 18 remains in use for access to animals. Poor people of Wentnor were allowed to gather peat from the area near the end of Wn 18.

WENTNOR 17, STANBATCH TO Wn 18 0.5 Km/¼+ m.

Wn 17 is a public footpath that leaves the New Road by Stanbatch Cottage as a track. Pass through two gates to reach point (b). (Alternatively there is a public footpath between (a) and (b) that follows the boundary of Laburnum Cottage). Follow old grassy track from (b) up a small valley, passing a cottage. At (c), the track bends sharply to rise out of the valley. At this point there is a large rock; this may be the White Woman that appears on one old map (1831). At E, join Wn 18 via a stile.

WENTNOR 17 (IN REVERSE), Wn 18 TO STANBATCH

Leave Wn 18 at E via a stile and descend steeply along a deep-cut grass track down to a rock (c). The track bends round to the left and runs down a small valley, passing a cottage. At (b), either pass through a gate and reach the road by Stanbatch Cottage or turn left and follow the boundary (an old hedge with many plant species including laburnums) of Laburnum Cottage to reach the road at (a).

WENTNOR 18, NEW ROAD TO POLE COTTAGE 1.25 Km/0.75 m.

Wn 18 is an unsurfaced highway and is a clear, stony track. It branches off from the New Road, passes through a gate and ascends the hillside. The first part is enclosed and the track then becomes open on one side. It makes a loop round the hillside and Wn 17 branches off it at point E. Continue along the track which soon becomes open and runs through thick heather. At (d), Wn 18 cuts through an embankment which runs from the Portway across to the head of the small valley of Stanbatch; this is an old Medlicott manor boundary. Other embankments in the area may be related to peat-cutting. The surfaced hilltop road is reached just south of the Pole Cottage enclosure.

WENTNOR 18 (IN REVERSE), POLE COTTAGE TO THE NEW ROAD.

Take the clear, stony track that leaves the surfaced hilltop road just south of Pole Cottage. It crosses an area of thick heather and descends the west side of the Mynd as a good track, the last section being enclosed. Wn 17 branches off to the right on a long bend at point E.

WENTNOR 19

Wn 19 branches off from Wn 7 at Medlicott Cottage and is the way that was used to get from Medlicott to Little Stretton or Minton by linking up with Cs 17 or Cs 19 at the Portway. It would also have been a path used by the isolated inhabitants of Pole Cottage. Pole Cottage, with its surrounding little fields, must have been a home at times to gamekeepers and shepherds and has been called Shepherds Lodge in the past. The shepherds may have been paid to look after other people's sheep as well perhaps as having a few of their own. Jackie was one such shepherd (see Cs 17) on the Mynd. The last inhabitant to have the right to turn out sheep (30) was a Mr Crebbin; the right ceased after his death in the early part of this century. The last inhabitant was one of two brothers (owners of Walcot Hall) who left in the 1950s. He was interested in falconry, a fact that many people recall. This was not the end of Pole Cottage, however, as it continued to be or became the focal point in the annual event of sheep dipping. All the sheep had to be taken off the hill to be dipped and their owners would then trudge back up to Pole Cottage and have a good time there while the police, in uniform, checked the hillsides for any remaining sheep. Their work done, they would join in the party too. After some years the police were relieved of this duty and the event died out. Pole Cottage, although no longer a cottage but just an enclosed area, remains a focal point as a landmark for walkers and riders and continues to offer a little shelter in the midst of what can seem a bleak and wild expanse of moorland.

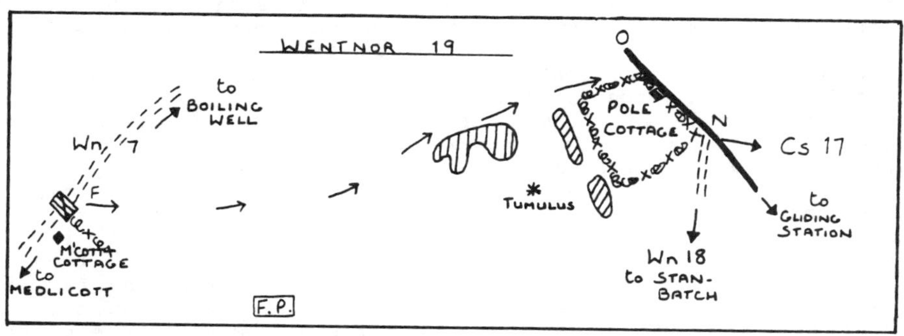

WENTNOR 19, MEDLICOTT COTTAGE TO POLE COTTAGE 0.75 Km/½ m.

Leave the track (Wn 7) just above Medlicott Cottage, after reaching open hill, and bear off obliquely right by a pile of stones. A small path ascends across an area of heather and bilberries, which is common land. The path divides into two; take the left branch and pass two pools, keeping to the left of them. Over to the right is a tumulus. The way, which may at times seem rather vague and boggy, runs along the left-hand side of the Pole Cottage enclosure to reach the surfaced hilltop road (the Portway here) near point O, where the Portway and the road diverge.

WENTNOR 19 (IN REVERSE), POLE COTTAGE TO MEDLICOTT COTTAGE

Leave the Portway on the Stretton end of the Pole Cottage enclosure and walk along to the right of this, continuing along the right-hand side of two pools. Descend along a small path through heather to Medlicott Cottage, where a good track (Wn 7) is joined and the open hill is left behind.

WENTNOR 20

Wn 20 is the wide and well-used path that runs across Pole Bank, passing the summit of the Long Mynd. The route is an alternative to the Portway between points O and S and has therefore been described together with the Portway on pages 21 to 24. In reverse, from S to O, it is described on pages 27 to 30. At the summit a toposcope indicates the names of many of the surrounding hills and the view to the west covers a large area of Wales.

The view to the west from the summit

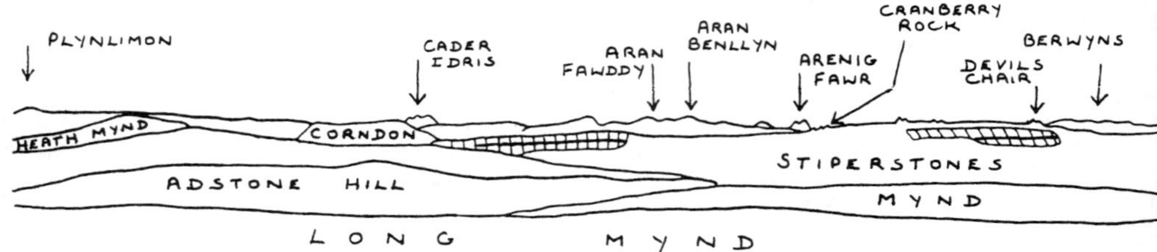

Of the hills visible in all directions from the summit the highest and most numerous are to the north-west and this view is explained in more detail here:

Plynlimon or Pumlumon Fawr, meaning 'the five hills', seen to the left of Corndon, is actually situated quite near the Welsh coast east of Aberystwyth and Borth. It is the source of many rivers including the Severn (into which the Mynd drains via the Onny or the Cound Brook), the Wye and the Rheidol.

Cader or Cadair Idris, meaning Idris' Chair, immediately to the right of Corndon, is further away than Plynlimon and is situated south-east of Barmouth. Idris was a giant or a scholar.

Aran Fawddwy and Aran Benllyn are about the same distance away as Plynlimon and are situated to the west of Lake Vyrnwy and to the south of Bala Lake. Aran Fawddwy is the source of the River Dovey or Afon Dyfi; Fawddwy may mean 'great water'. Fawddwy is the name on the O/S map, Mawddwy is on the toposcope. Mawr and fawr are different gender-forms of the same word which means 'great'. Aran Benllyn contributes to the upper reaches of the River Dee or Afon Dyfrdwy; Benllyn means 'head (of the) lake'.

Arenig Fawr is north-east of the Arans and is about the same distance away as Cader Idris. Aran and Arenig may mean 'kidney-shaped'. It can only be seen on clear days as two bumps on the horizon to the left of Cranberry Rock. Another bump on the horizon, again only seen on clear days and to the left of Arenig Fawr, may be Moelwyn Mawr near Blaenau Ffestiniog.

Snowdon or Yr Wyddfa (Fawr), meaning 'the great tomb' (there was once a large cairn on the summit that was believed to be a giant's tomb), is considerably further away again beyond the Arenigs and is nearly 800 feet higher.

The Berwyns are the nearest of the hills along the horizon, extending well to the right from behind the Stiperstones. They are situated to the north-east of Lake Vyrnwy.

The Stiperstones lie in the near distance. One of the rocky crags is called the Devil's Chair and resembles a throne from certain aspects but not from the Mynd.

WENTNOR 21, HALFWAY END TO MOORHOUSE 0.75 Km/½ m.

Halfway End is the point at which a small lane branches off to Adstone from the Wentnor to Main Road lane. It is about half-way between Wentnor village and the end of Adstone Hill and also between Wentnor and Prolley Moor if using Wn 21; Wn 21 was once a track. Four fields surrounding the junction were called Halfway End. Another feature of this area, but to the east of the road, must have been a holy well since three fields bore the name of Holy Wall and one was called Halfway Well. **Leave the road junction via a gate that leads into a field on the left-hand side of a hedge. The second half of this field (a) was the old field called Halfway Well. Follow the hedge to gate (b) and then follow a track running along the right-hand side of a hedge.** The field on the left (c) was Holy Wall. **Pass through gate (d) and follow the left-hand side of a hedge to gate (e). The track bends down to cross Buzz Brook close to Moorhouse and continues as the driveway of Moorhouse, to exit onto the road.** By the exit are some bay willow trees.

WENTNOR 21 (IN REVERSE), MOORHOUSE TO HALFWAY END

Leave the lane via a gate, along the driveway to Moorhouse. This becomes track that skirts the farm, crosses Buzz Brook and ascends to gate (e). From (e), continue along the track, which runs along the right-hand side of a hedge, to gate (d). From (d), follow the left-hand side of a hedge to gate (b) leading into field (a). Turn left to walk along the right-hand side of a hedge that leads you to the road at Halfway End.

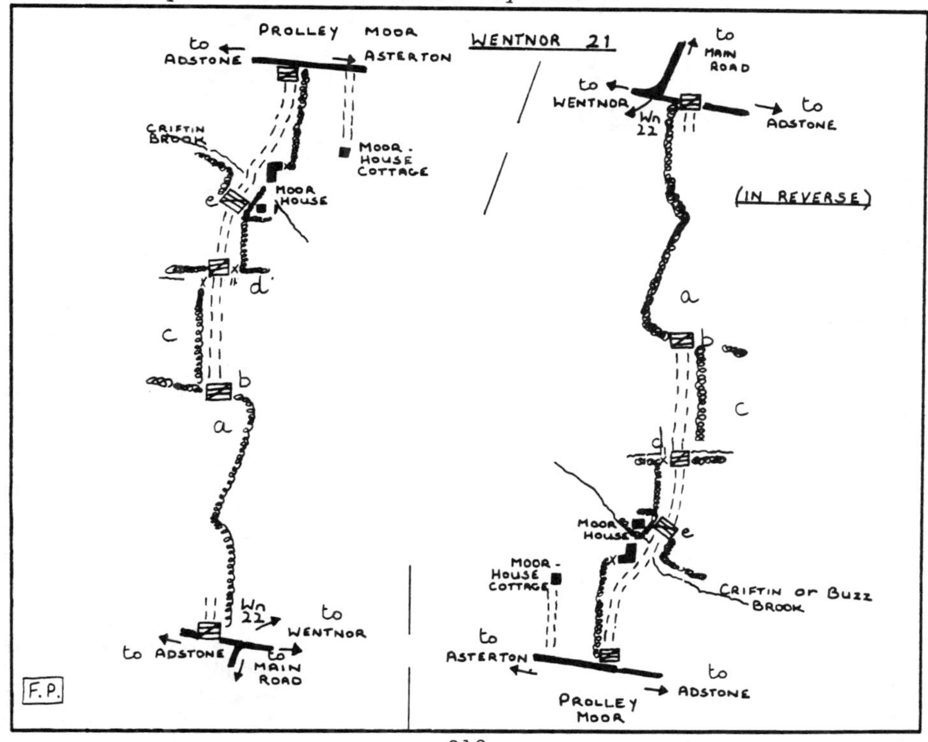

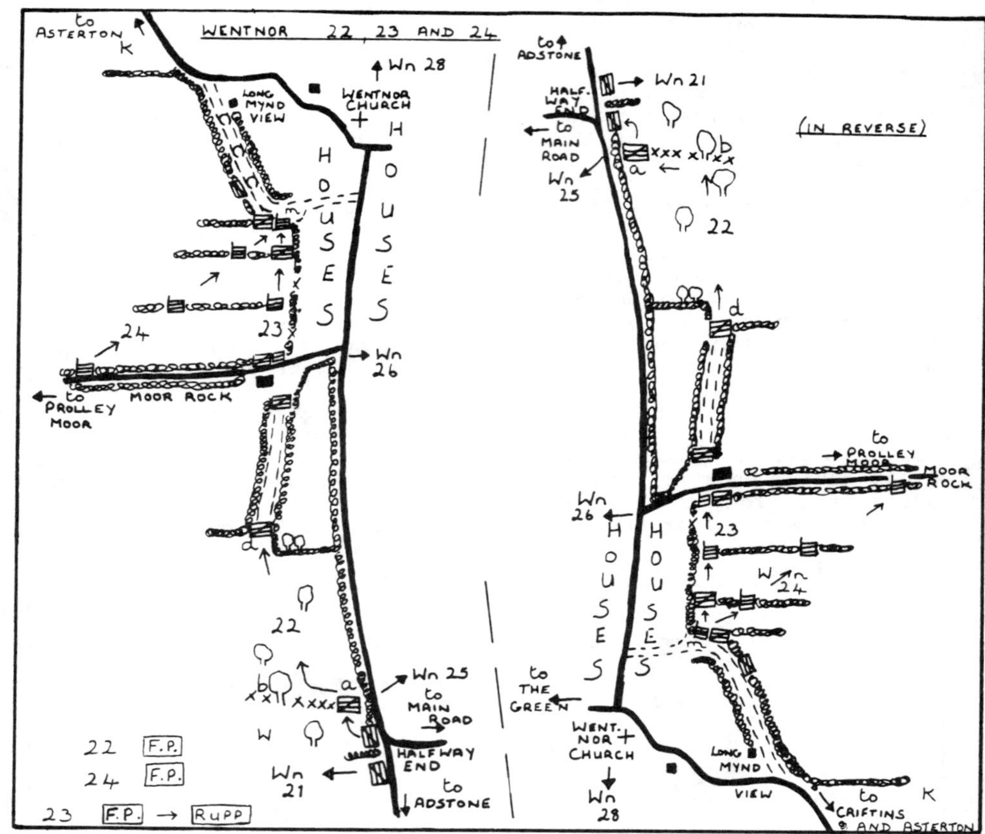

WENTNOR 22, HALFWAY END TO WENTNOR 0.5 Km/¼+ m.

Wn 22 is a public footpath. Leave the road junction at Halfway End, entering a field on the right-hand side of a hedge. Bear right and pass through gate (a). Turn left for a short distance and then turn right and cross the field along the faint ridge to reach gate (d). From (d) the route is an enclosed track that runs almost out to the lane by a building.

WENTNOR 22 (IN REVERSE), WENTNOR TO HALFWAY END

Turn off the Wentnor/Prolley Moor road by some buildings and follow enclosed track to gate (d). Enter a field and continue in the same direction across it to reach an ash tree (b) in a fence. Turn left along the fence and pass through gate (a). Cross the corner of the field and exit onto the lane.

WENTNOR 23, MOOR ROCK TO LONG MYND VIEW 0.25 Km.

This way runs behind the houses along the main street of Wentnor. The first part is footpath and the second part track and RUPP. Pass through the gate opposite the building at the end of Wn 22 and keep in a straight line, crossing stile or gate in three hedges before joining a track from the pub at (m). Follow this old

enclosed track to the left and exit onto lane by Long Mynd View (a house).

WENTNOR 23 (IN REVERSE), LONG MYND VIEW TO MOOR ROCK

Leave the Asterton to Wentnor road just before entering Wentnor, by Long Mynd View, and follow old and enclosed track until it turns to the left at (m) to run alongside the pub. Bear off to the right over a stile and walk in a straight line behind buildings and along the top of three fields to join the Wentnor to Prolley Moor lane. The fields crossed on this route and those to the east of Wn 22 are the narrow strip-like fields that run from Wentnor down the slope to the Criftin/Buzz Brook and appear so striking when seen from the Mynd. This pattern may represent the mediaeval strips of Wentnor's common fields (see page 10), the hedges being a later addition.

WENTNOR 24, MOOR ROCK TO LONG MYND VIEW 0.5 Km/¼+ m.

Wn 24 is likely to have arisen as a short cut to the village, turning right at (m) to exit alongside the pub. It is a **public footpath. Leave the Wentnor to Prolley Moor road on the steep hill (sometimes known as Moor Rock), crossing three fields obliquely to the right up the hill. There are stiles in each hedge, the topmost stile being in the top far corner of a field; this leads onto track at (m). Bear left along the track and exit onto lane by Long Mynd View.**

WENTNOR 24 (IN REVERSE), LONG MYND VIEW TO MOOR ROCK

Leave the Asterton to Wentnor road by Long Mynd View and follow enclosed track to (m), where it bends to the left. Turn to the right, crossing a stile into a field. Aim obliquely to the right down and across three fields to join the Wentnor to Prolley Moor lane on a steep bank (Moor Rock). There are stiles in every hedge.

WENTNOR 25, THE GREEN TO HALFWAY END

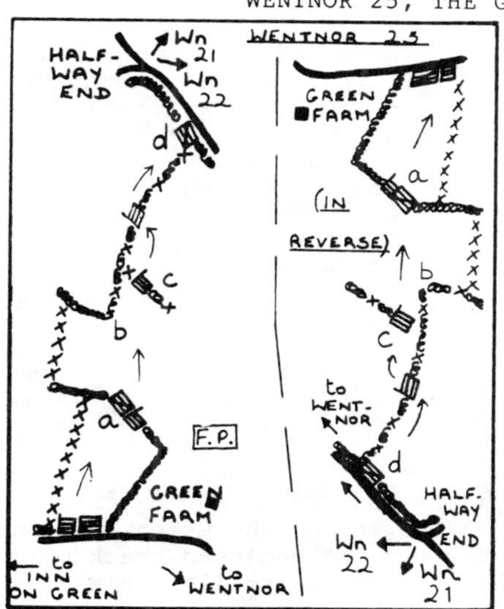

Leave the Green Rock road between the Inn on the Green and Green Farm (Leisure Riding) via a stile or gate. Follow fence to gate and stile (a). Cross the next field to a right angle in a hedge (b) and then follow the hedge to stile (c). From (c), walk along the right and then the left-hand side of a hedge to reach gate (d) onto the road near Halfway End.

Wn 25 (IN REVERSE)

Leave the road near Halfway End via gate (d). Follow the right and then the left-hand side of a hedge down to stile (c). From (c), walk alongside hedge to (b) and then continue almost straight on across the field to gate and stile (a). From (a), follow fence to a gate and stile onto Green Rock road.

WENTNOR 26

Wn 26 was the old road from Wentnor down to Walkmills and thence to Bishops Castle, the way from Walkmills being different from today's route. The present-day main road running between the turning to Cwnd House, over a mile to the north of the Inn on the Green, and Walkmills did not exist on the tithe map of the 1840s, the route from Shrewsbury to Bishops Castle going directly to Norbury along what is now a small lane passing Gravenor (route 1 in figure 15). The main road of today south of Walkmills to just beyond Norbury also did not exist in some parts, although others have been derived from old lanes. From the end of Wn 26 (route 5 in the figure) at Walkmills the old road to the south divided into two. The left-hand turn (route 7) ran to Whitcot and the right-hand turn (route 6) to Norbury, joining route 1 and continuing on to Bishops Castle. Today the north end of route 7 is main road while the south end is bridleway. Route 9 and part of route 14 with route 1 south of Norbury, form the main route through Norbury. The lane from Wentnor via Halfway End and Cwnd House (route 2) must have been the way to Shrewsbury from Wentnor. The two other lanes (routes 3 and 4), now the most used routes from Wentnor to the main road, existed on the tithe map; route 3 would have been the way to the mill, still called Upper Mill. Route 4, the lane down to the Inn on the Green, was an open track crossing an area called Wentnor Green. These routes appear to have linked up with tracks 11 and 12 on the other side of the valley; these are now public footpaths across to route 1. Route 10 is also a footpath while route 8 has become a bridleway. The small section of lane near Norbury (route 13) is only a hedge.

The roads of the tithe map (1840s) near Wentnor and Norbury

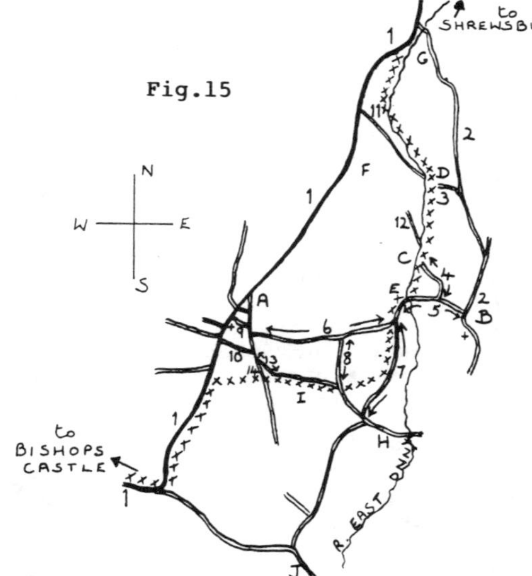

xx. The course of today's main road near Wentnor.
A. Norbury. B. Wentnor.
C. Inn on the Green.
D. Mill. E. Walkmills.
F. Gravenor. G. Cwnd House.
H. Whitcot. I. School.
J. Hardwick.

WENTNOR 26, WENTNOR TO WALKMILLS 0.25 Km.

Descend from Wentnor towards the Inn on the Green, leaving the road on a sharp corner. Follow the old and enclosed track which continues straight down to the main road at Walkmills. This route appears to be simply a green lane.

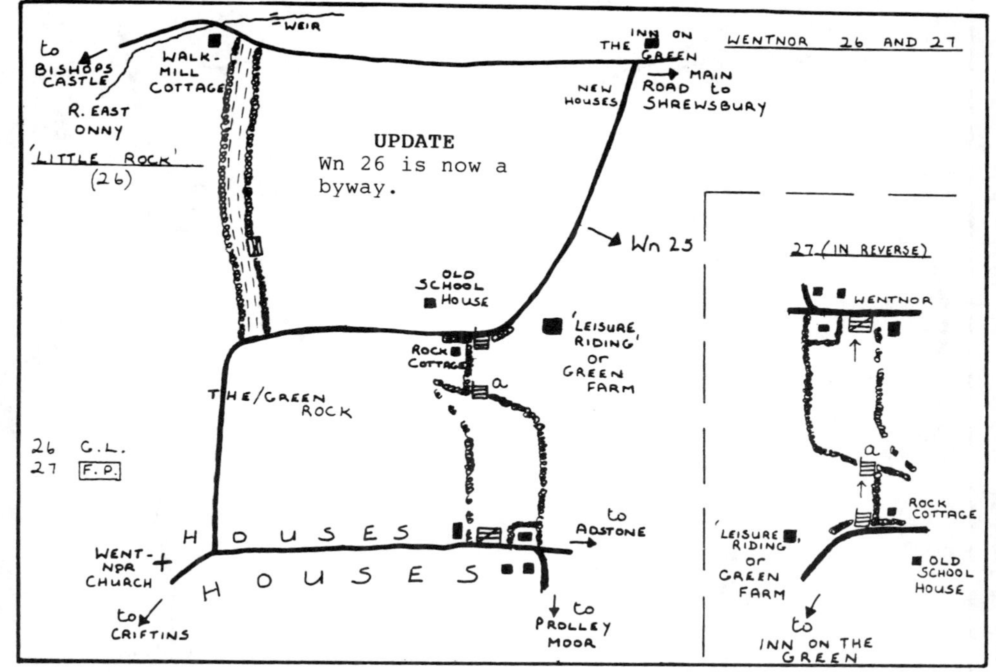

WENTNOR 27, WENTNOR TO THE GREEN

Wn 27 is a short steep public footpath, a useful short cut for anyone living at the north end of Wentnor village. Leave the road through Wentnor village at its north end and enter a field via a gate between a bungalow and buildings. Go straight on to reach stile (a). From (a), descend steeply along the boundary hedge of Rock Cottage and join the Wentnor/Green road via a stile beside the cottage. Opposite and below is the Old Schoolhouse (thought to belong to the parish) which ceased to be a school near the end of the last century but continued as the venue for village functions before becoming the sexton's home (see page 121).

WENTNOR 27 (IN REVERSE), THE GREEN TO WENTNOR

Leave the Wentnor/Green road just below Rock Cottage via a stile. Ascend steeply along the boundary hedge of the cottage to stile (a). From (a), continue upwards in the same direction, soon coming alongside an old hedge. Exit via a gate onto road at the north end of Wentnor.

Focus on Walkmills

There are two areas known as Walkmills in the area covered by this book; that mentioned on the preceding page is just in Norbury while the other lies in Woolstaston. The name indicates the past existence of mills used for waulking cloth, a process whereby cloth was worked up and down a board to clean and thicken it, also known as 'fulling'. The presence of fulling mills along the Walkmills Brook in Woolstaston has been documented since the 17th century; there were much earlier fulling mills in neighbouring Longnor and Leebotwood. Perhaps the cloth waulked was Welsh cloth, (for which Shrewsbury provided an important market) which may have reached here via some of the Mynd routes.

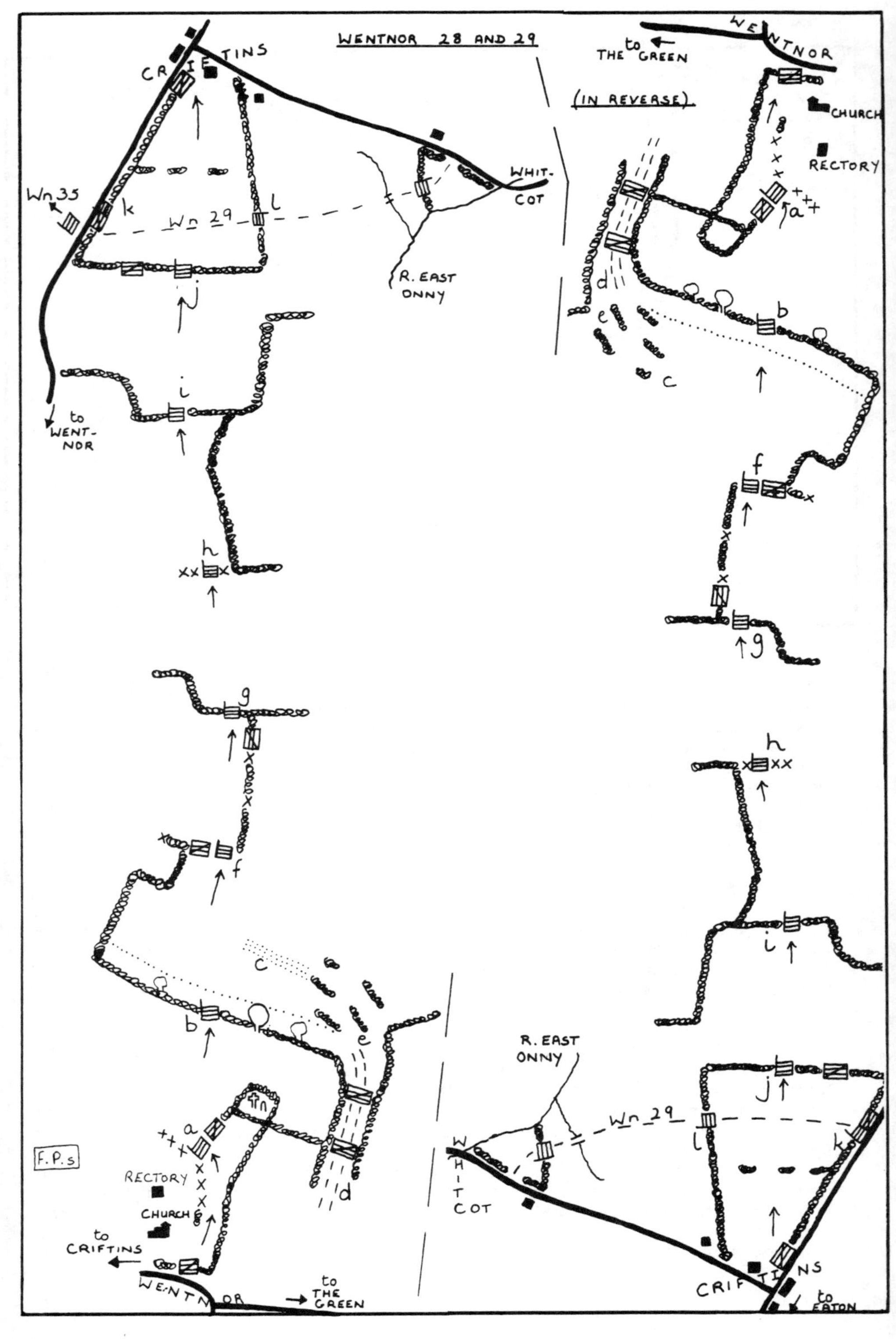
WENTNOR 28 AND 29
(IN REVERSE)
CRIFTINS
Wn 35
Wn 29
WHITCOT
R. EAST ONNY
to WENTNOR
to THE GREEN
CHURCH
RECTORY
a
b
c
d
e
f
g
h
i
j
k
l
to CRIFTINS
to EATON
F.P.s

WENTNOR 28, WENTNOR CHURCH TO THE CRIFTIN 1 Km/½+ m.

Wn 28 is a public footpath that runs between Wentnor village and the Criftin. As it offers only a slightly shorter route than the road, it has probably not had much use within living memory. It may, however, have formed part of the original route down this valley since it runs along the south end of the ridge which extends from Overs via Adstone Hill and Wentnor to point (b) along its course; ridgeways were the best ways to travel in early times (see Background).

The way starts at the church, skirting the right-hand side of the churchyard. It runs to the right of the Rectory and curves round to cross stile (a). Bear obliquely right to stile (b), which is to the left of a tree in the hedge, and enter field (c). At the top of this field, running from left to right, is an embankment that may once have been a track, although on the tithe map the area is called Field Piece and is one of several sections, not separated by hedges, in this field. If it was once a track, it must have been in continuity with the enclosed track (d) that still runs from the village to this field. Track (d) appears to have fanned out at (e) into about three tracks. **Cross the embankment and descend a steep slope; the field then flattens out and the way crosses to stile (f). From (f), follow the left-hand side of a hedge to stile (g) and from there continue straight across the next field to stile (h) in a fence. Again follow the left-hand side of a hedge, bearing away from it slightly at the far end to reach stile (i). The way continues straight across the next field (Heath Field, now arable) to stile (j) and on again to the Criftin/Criftins, where the road is reached via a gate in the far corner of the left-hand hedge. Alternatively, turn left soon after stile (j) and reach the road via stile (k) on Wn 29.**

WENTNOR 28 (IN REVERSE), THE CRIFTIN TO WENTNOR CHURCH

Wn 28 begins at a gate just past the Criftin (going towards Wentnor). From the gate, turn right and cross the length of the field to stile (j). Alternatively, start from stile (k), nearly opposite the end of Wn 35, cross about half the width of the field and then turn right to reach stile (j). Continue straight across the next field to stile (i). From (i), follow the right-hand side of a hedge to stile (h) in a fence. Cross the next field, still travelling in the same direction, to reach stile (g). From (g), follow the right-hand side of a hedge to stile (f). From (f), aim straight on, climbing a steep slope to stile (b) and then on across the next field to stile (a) by the Rectory. Skirt the Rectory garden and the left-hand side of the churchyard to exit onto the road.

WENTNOR 29, WN 35 TO WHITCOT 0.25 Km.

Wn 29 would have been used in continuity with Wn 35 for access to Grove Cottage. Wn 35 was in turn linked with Asterton via the lane or MY 11. Its use has been discussed under MY 11 on page 137. **This public footpath begins nearly opposite Wn 35, leaving the road via stile (k). Cross the width of the field (once Gorsty Meadow) and enter the next field (Whitcot Cow Pasture) via stile (l). Continue in the same direction, crossing a tiny stream just before a stile** (in the Wentnor/Norbury parish boundary) into a small shady enclosure beside the East Onny. **Reach the road on the left via a gap in the hedge and exit opposite the old Whitcot smithy.**

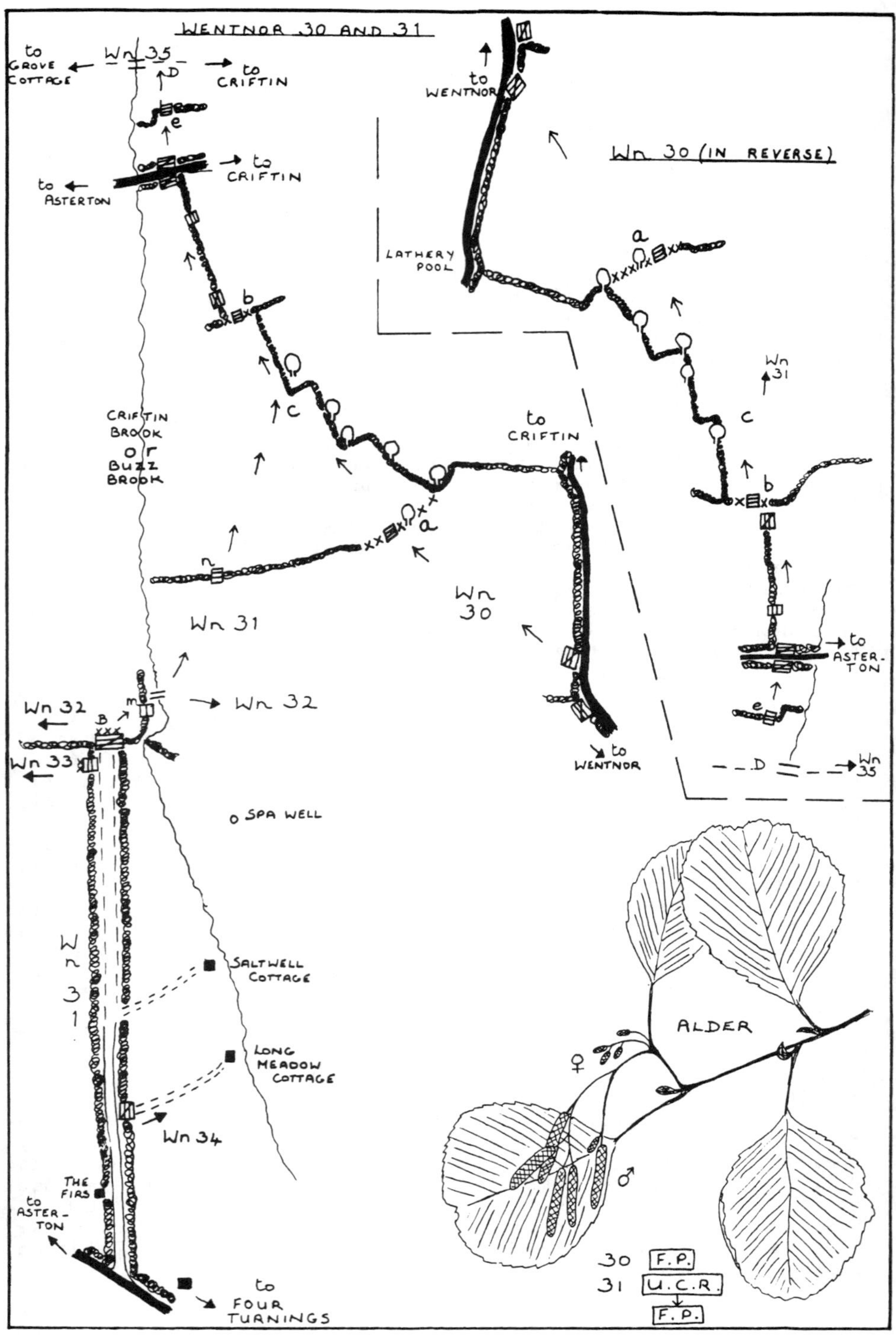
WENTNOR 30 AND 31
to GROVE COTTAGE
Wn 35
D
to CRIFTIN
e
to CRIFTIN
to ASTERTON
b
c
CRIFTIN BROOK or BUZZ BROOK
to CRIFTIN
a
n
Wn 31
Wn 30
Wn 32
m
B
Wn 32
Wn 33
to WENTNOR
o SPA WELL
Wn 31
SALTWELL COTTAGE
LONG MEADOW COTTAGE
Wn 34
THE FIRS
to ASTER-TON
to FOUR TURNINGS
to WENTNOR
Wn 30 (IN REVERSE)
LATHERY POOL
a
Wn 31
c
b
to ASTER-TON
e
D
Wn 35
ALDER
♀
♂
30 F.P.
31 U.C.R.
F.P.

WENTNOR 30, WENTNOR TO WN 35 AT D 0.75 Km/½ m.

Wn 30 from near Upper Criftin may have been a route used by inhabitants of Asterton or Grove Cottage as a short cut to Wentnor, although within living memory Asterton people have favoured Wn 32. Earlier O/S maps show a path running from Barnes Farm (south of point D) to Wentnor i.e. there was a section of path running between point D and the farm which has been lost.

There are two gates quite close together off the Wentnor to Criftins road as it descends from the village; take the lower one for the start of Wn 30 and go almost straight across the first field to reach stile (a) in a fence. A small part of this field was Lathery Meadow and the pool (now bog) on the other side of the road was called Lathery Pool. Follow the hedge on the right approximately (it tends to dog-leg). Wn 31 joins this path at point C.

From point C, continue along the hedge to stile (b). The hedge running down to the left bounded a small field by the brook called Purgatory. **From (b), almost immediately turn left through a gate then turn right and follow the hedge to a gate onto the road near Upper Criftin. The path crosses the lane and enters the opposite field via a gate. Continue straight on, crossing stile (e). Just beyond this stile, Wn 35 is reached at point D. A bridge across Buzz/Criftin Brook is down to the left on the course of Wn 35.**

WENTNOR 30 (IN REVERSE), D ON WN 35 TO WENTNOR.

This path starts at point D on Wn 35 near Buzz/Criftin Brook. Follow the approximate course of the brook upstream, crossing stile (e) and a gate to get to the road near a bridge. Pass through the gate on the other side of the road into the field once known as Piece by Buzzy Brook **and follow the right-hand side of a hedge to the far end. Turn left through a gate and then immediately right to cross stile (b). Follow the right-hand side of the hedge again. Point C is at the first dog-leg in this hedge; Wn 31 (in reverse) branches to the right here. Continue along the hedge to reach stile (a) in a new fence. Continue straight across the next field to exit onto the lane via a gate.**

WENTNOR 31, PROLLEY MOOR TO POINT C ON Wn 30 1 Km/½+ m.

Wn 31 from Prolley Moor is a partly surfaced highway as far as point B and from there is a public footpath to point C. The highway part was perhaps created to reach the spa well but the intention may have been to continue further down the valley. **The road begins near Four Turnings on Prolley Moor, off the lane to Asterton. It almost immediately passes The Firs and continues as a straight, wide-verged road passing the driveways to two cottages, Long Meadow and Saltwell.** Saltwell is named after the nearby spa well. Long Meadow may be named after the road, as verges (in this case wide ones) were sometimes referred to as 'the long meadow' and were available for anyone to graze their animals. **The road ends in a gateway (at present fenced along the top). Wn 33 branches to the left just before the gate and Wn 32 just after it at point B (in practice Wn 33 has to be started from Wn 32 after the gate). From B, follow the hedge round to the right to a small 'stile' (m), cross Buzz Brook via a bridge and turn obliquely to the left to cross the field** (Asterton Bridges) **to stile (n). From (n), aim obliquely to the right up to the top hedge at point C, thereby joining Wn 30.** Two less common trees to look out for by Buzz Brook, in the area near B, are aspen and bird cherry.

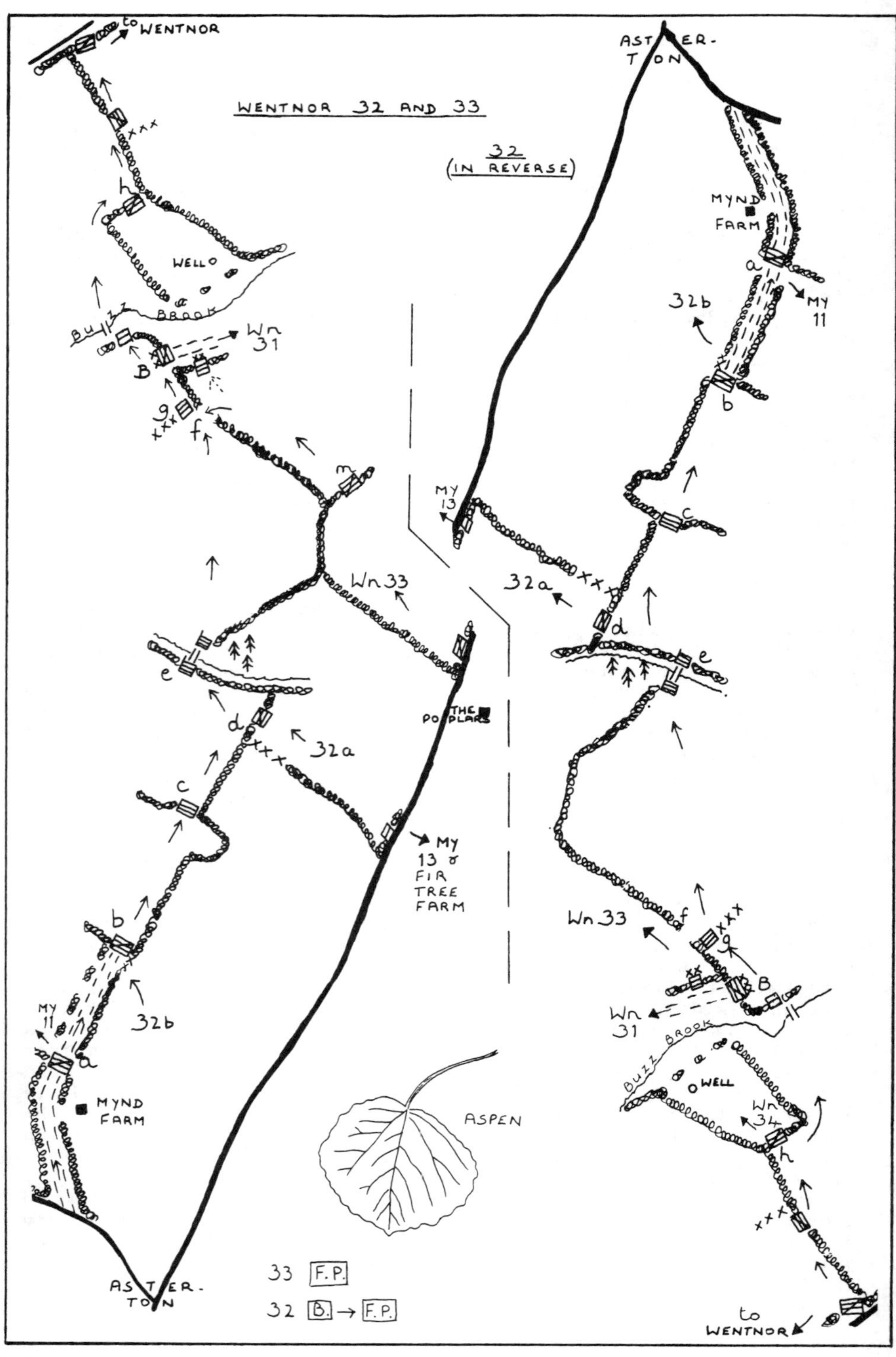
WENTNOR 32 AND 33
32
(IN REVERSE)
to WENTNOR
WELL
BROOK
BUZZ BROOK
Wn 31
Wn 33
Wn 34
32a
32b
MY 11
MY 13
MY 13 or FIR TREE FARM
MYND FARM
THE POPLARS
ASTERTON
ASPEN
33 F.P.
32 B. → F.P.

WENTNOR 32, ASTERTON TO WENTNOR 1.5 Km/ 1 m.

Wn 32 was the route favoured by Asterton people for getting to and from Wentnor for shop and pub. They did not attend Wentnor church and there has been no school at Wentnor for 100 years.

Wn 32 is an enclosed track and an unsurfaced highway as far as gate (a). It passes a rather derelict but still inhabited Mynd Farm. At (a), MY 11 branches off to the left. The way continues as a public footpath but is still obviously old track whose left-hand hedge has become somewhat sparse. At gate (b) the track ends and Wn 32 is joined by 32b, another short link with Asterton, which it is not possible to use at present. Continue straight on, initially alongside hedge, to a wooden fence (c). Follow the hedge to (d) where Wn 32 is joined by 32a (which begins almost opposite the driveway to Fir Tree Farm, leaving the lane via an old stile and following hedge across to a gate at point (d), where it joins the main Wn 32 route). Wn 32 now cuts across the corner of the field, aiming towards a white stile (e) which leads onto a rather dilapidated, although once obviously substantial bridge over a tiny ravine. There is a small plantation to the right and a stile at the far end of the bridge. The large field now entered is crossed by aiming obliquely to the left to reach the far left-hand corner (f); this is the point at which Wn 33, in practice, joins Wn 32. An old stile (g) in a fence leads into Lower Lawns. Follow the hedge on the right (with aspen trees in it) down to a gate at point B, where Wn 32 is joined by Wn 31. Continue round along the hedge to a small 'stile' which leads to a bridge over Buzz/Criftin Brook into the field called Asterton Bridges. Walk obliquely to the right up this field, passing the corner of another small field (Saltwell), to reach the right-hand hedge. Follow this hedge to the road, first on the left-hand side of it and then on the right.

WENTNOR 32 (IN REVERSE), WENTNOR TO ASTERTON

Leave the Wentnor to Criftins road on a bend, via a gate, and follow the left-hand and then the right-hand side of the same hedge down to a small field (Saltwell). Wn 34 branches off at this point (h) to enter the field. Wn 32 turns right and from the corner of Saltwell runs obliquely down to the brook. Cross the brook via a bridge and pass over a small 'stile'. Turn left along the hedge to reach point B, where Wn 31 branches off to the left. Continue along the hedge, cross stile (g) and aim obliquely right to the far right corner of the field, by a small plantation. Cross a dilapidated bridge with a stile at each end (e) and cut across the corner of the next field to (d). Wn 32a here passes through a gate and follows hedge up to the lane. Wn 32 turns right along the hedge to get to a wooden fence (c). Walk straight on to gate (b) and continue along old track through gate (a) and on past Mynd Farm to reach the lane at Asterton.

WENTNOR 33, THE POPLARS TO B ON Wn 31 0.5 Km/¼+ m.

Wn 33 follows the old Prolley Moor boundary. Leave the lane opposite The Poplars via a gate and cross the field by aiming slightly to the right. Pass through gate (m) and then follow the right-hand side of a hedge, in theory all the way to the far end but in practice to a point short of that; the correct exit from this field is obstructed but a gateway at (f) provides access to Wn 32 and point B can then be reached via stile (g).

Focus on the spa well at Wentnor

Large numbers of people partook of the salty water in this little brick-lined well. An account written at the turn of the century describes as many as 100 people taking a tot in the early morning. The water was claimed to be good for rheumatism and there were plans to pump it (the well yielded hundreds of gallons a day) across to Stretton. It was also an effective aperient i.e. it 'went through you like a dose of salts' and was therefore best drunk not too far from home. Use of the well continued for most of the last century and seems only to have tailed off before World War I. Such prolonged use seems remarkable given that Asterton alone was visited by a chemist twice a week.

WENTNOR 34, WENTNOR TO PROLLEY MOOR VIA THE SPA WELL 0.75 Km/½ m.

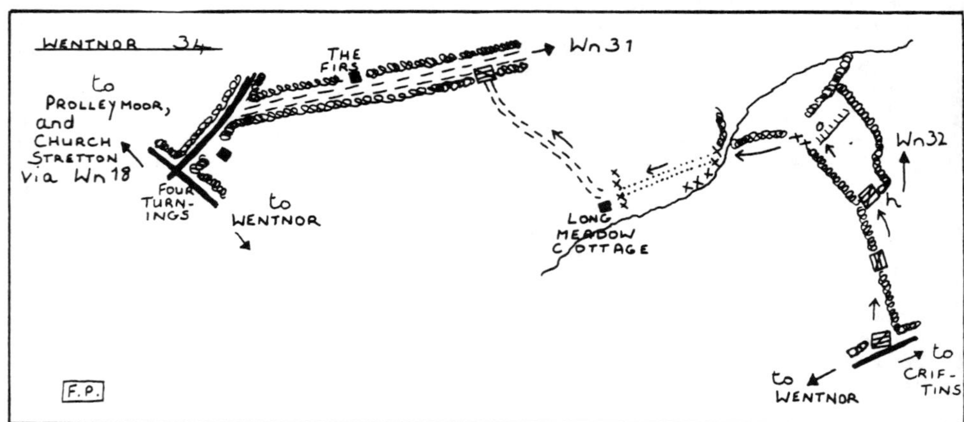

At present it is not possible to use this public footpath as a through route but the first part, providing access to the spa well, can be walked. This footpath must have been used by people visiting the well and in reverse was probably the way Stretton people reached it having come across the hill via Wn 18. **Leave the Wentnor to Criftins road via a gate and follow hedge, first on the left-hand side and then on the right, down to a gate (h) into a small field (this first bit of footpath is also Wn 32). Walk down the field; the well is situated at the foot of a short, steep bank in marshy ground and is covered by a sheet of corrugated iron.** The field must have remained almost unchanged since the time of its countless visitors and is an attractive corner of old grassland and bog. **If this footpath were to be cleared, the way would follow the left-hand hedge, first passing through it, down to the brook. The brook would then be crossed and an old faint track followed towards Long Meadow Cottage. The driveway of this house leads out to the unsurfaced highway (Wn 31) that in turn runs out to Four Turnings.**

Focus on Buzz Brook

Buzz Brook is the name used locally for the brook that runs from near Coates (one tributary) and Medlicott (a second tributary) in the north, to Eaton in the south where it runs into the River Onny. On the O/S maps it is labelled as the Criftin Brook, a name that has probably arisen because the brook runs near the Criftin south of Wentnor; there are also two fields by the Medlicott tributary that were called The Criftin and Upper Criftin. The name 'Criftin' perhaps sounds more convincing than 'Buzz' but the latter has in fact a very long history; in the 13th century Bassebrok rivulet is recorded as forming part of the Wentnor/Lydbury North manor boundary while on the tithe map a field near the Criftin next to the brook was called Piece by Buzzy Brook and another field downstream was Bosbrook Meadow. Downstream again, in Myndtown, was a field called Bush Brook. The name may be derived from the Welsh 'bas' meaning 'shallow'.

WENTNOR 35, THE CRIFTIN TO GROVE COTTAGE 0.75 Km/½ m.

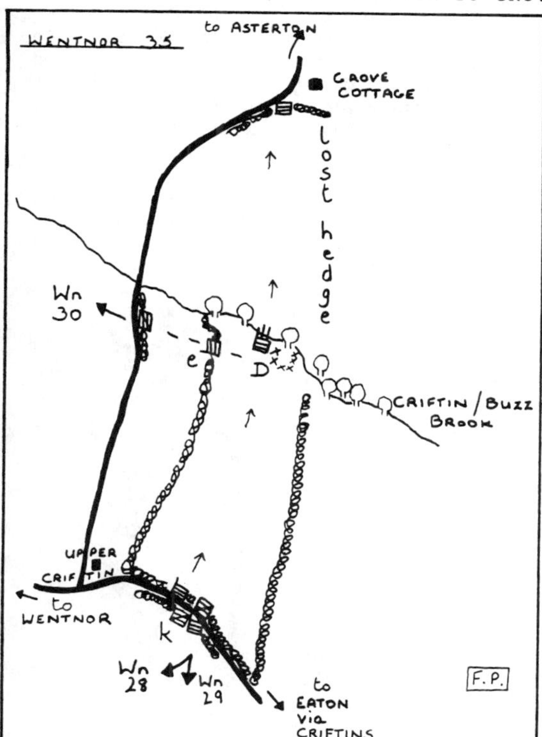

The use of Wn 35 in conjunction with Wn 29 and MY 11 has been discussed under MY 11 on page 137. **Wn 35 is a public footpath which is usable and has a substantial bridge along its course but is difficult to walk because it crosses arable land. It starts nearly opposite the end of Wn 29, leaving the road via a stile. The way then runs straight ahead through the middle of an arable field (since it runs the length of the field it is possible to walk between the rows of crops). At D, Wn 30 branches off to the left and Wn 35 continues over a stile, crosses the brook via a footbridge and ascends a short steep bank. At the top of the bank difficulties arise where, faced with a large arable field and no view of Grove Cottage, it is difficult to strike a consistent route. Until recently it was possible to skirt round the edge of the field by following a hedge on the right but this has now disappeared. Aim initially towards the second, and more prominent, hollow to the left of the forest on the west face of the Mynd and then just to the left of Grove Cottage, when it comes into view. Exit onto the lane via a stile by the cottage.**

Focus on trees

Aspens

The aspen is one of only three native poplars and is often to be found in damp habitats e.g near point B on Wn 31. When in leaf, it can be distinguished at some distance by the delicate shaking of its leaves and the Latin name for this tree means 'trembling poplar'. Aspen trees are often in a group as they spread readily by suckers. The attractive grey woolly catkins are an early sign of spring.

Focus on bells

All the churches around the Mynd have bells in varying numbers. Most of them have had bells for hundreds of years; some of these have been replaced, recast or rehung at some time and new bells have been added. Mediaeval bells remain at Ratlinghope, Leebotwood and Myndtown churches. Wentnor's four bells are thought to have been recast wholly or in part from the mediaeval bells there, that may have been made by the monks of Haughmond Abbey. Smethcott and Woolstaston, both recorded as having two bells in 1552, had theirs recast in the 18th century. Pulverbatch, Church Stretton, Lydbury North and Wistanstow churches all have a greater number of bells, which are hung in such a way that the art of true bell ringing, as we know it today, can be pursued; they too, will have started simply.

Many of the bells bear inscriptions, which usually provide information on the bell foundries involved with recasting, rehanging or with providing new bells. These include Rudhalls of Gloucester, Barwells of Birmingham, Taylors of Loughborough and Mears and Stearbank (Whitechapel Bell Foundry); the last two are the only surviving bell foundries today.

Other inscriptions include names of church wardens or rectors (Church Stretton 8, Pulverbatch 1, Wentnor 2, Myndtown 2 and Wistanstow 7 and 1, the last being a donation) and of local gentry who have donated bells (Lydbury North 1 - 5, Church Stretton 4). One bell was donated in gratitude for the return of a son from war (Wistanstow 2). Two inscriptions refer to the king or queen ('God save his church, our queen and realm' on Lydbury North 6 and 'Fear God, honour the King' on Pulverbatch 3) and four bells bear 'Peace and good neighbourhood' (Church Stretton 7, Wentnor 3, Pulverbatch 2 and Wistanstow 3). Some have inscriptions in Latin; 'Te Deum Laudamus' (We praise thee, O Lord) on Church Stretton 1, 'Laudate eum in excelcis' (Praise him in the heights) on Church Stretton 2 and 'San(c)te petre ora pronobis' (St Peter pray for us) on Myndtown 2; the last inscription may indicate dedication of the bell to St.Peter. Other inscriptions in English are 'Prosperity to this Place' (or 'parish' or 'our benefactors') on Church Stretton 5 and Wistanstow 4 and 5, 'Come at my call and serve God all' on Pulverbatch 6 and 'God preserve the Church of England' on Wentnor 4. An inscription that is on Pulverbatch 4, but hopefully pertains to all the bells in the area, is 'When you ring us we'll sweetly sing'. A message to remind us of the function of the bells is on the tenor (lowest) bell at Wistanstow - 'I to the church the living call and to the grave do summon all'.

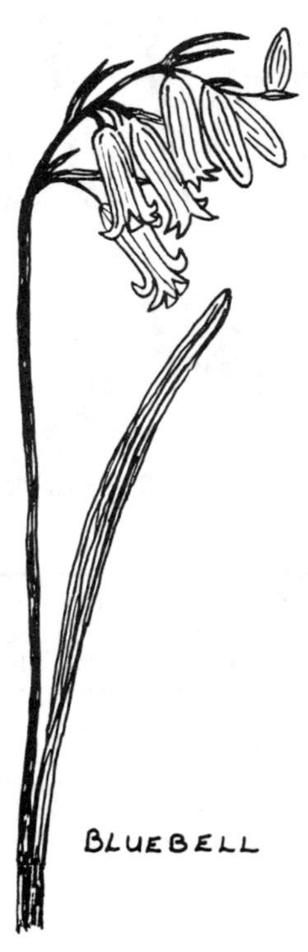

WISTANSTOW

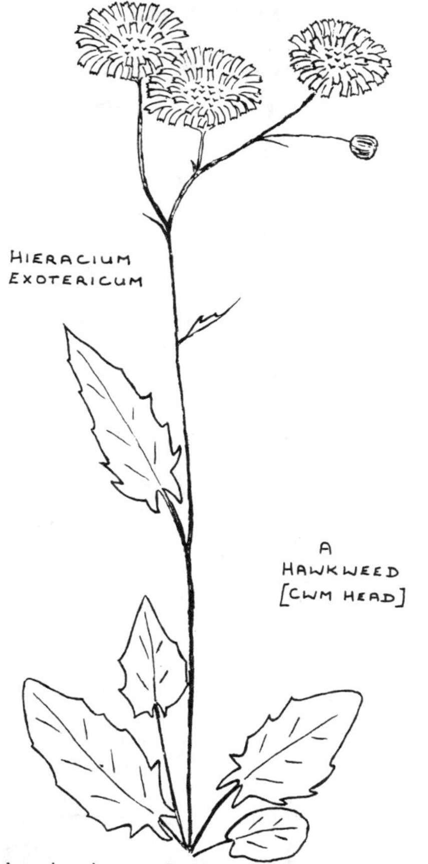

Wistanstow is a parish situated to the south-east of the Mynd and includes a small area on the edge of the Mynd itself. This area lies in the old townships of Woolston and Whittingslow, two of several hamlets and townships that make up the parish. Wistanstow itself is the largest of these and has the old church. Several of the old townships were manors in the Domesday Book. Whittingslow was the manor of Witecheslawe and once lay in Church Stretton parish. The hamlets of Marshbrook and Cwm Head lie along the B4370, the boundary line for the area covered in this book; Cwm Head has a modern church. Hawkhurst and Bushmoor were royal hayes in the Long Forest and the tenant of Minton, which had itself been a manor but was allocated to Stretton manor at the time of the Domesday Book, became their guardian. Bushmoor (outside the area of this book) was once Bissemoor, 'bissa' meaning 'doe'. Hawkhurst (or Haycrust) ultimately became a common, some or all of which belonged to the lord of Stretton manor at the time of enclosure at the beginning of the last century; the few routes described under Wistanstow are ways across this old common.

Amenities near the Mynd:

Refreshments - The Wayside Inn and The Lazy Trout, both at Marshbrook.

Accommodation - The Wayside Inn, Marshbrook.

Camping - The Wayside Inn.

Club camping - near Hamperley.

Bus service - Midland Red buses run between Ludlow and Shrewsbury via Marshbrook (see Church Stretton).

On Saturdays, an early bus (Horrocks or Shropshire Bus) runs from Bishops Castle to Shrewsbury via Marshbrook, two later buses running only from Acton Scott to Shrewsbury via Marshbrook. There are also three return journeys but again only the first bus goes on to Bishops Castle.

An infrequent bus service also operates along the A489 between Craven Arms and Bishops Castle, passing the south end of the Mynd (see Lydbury North).

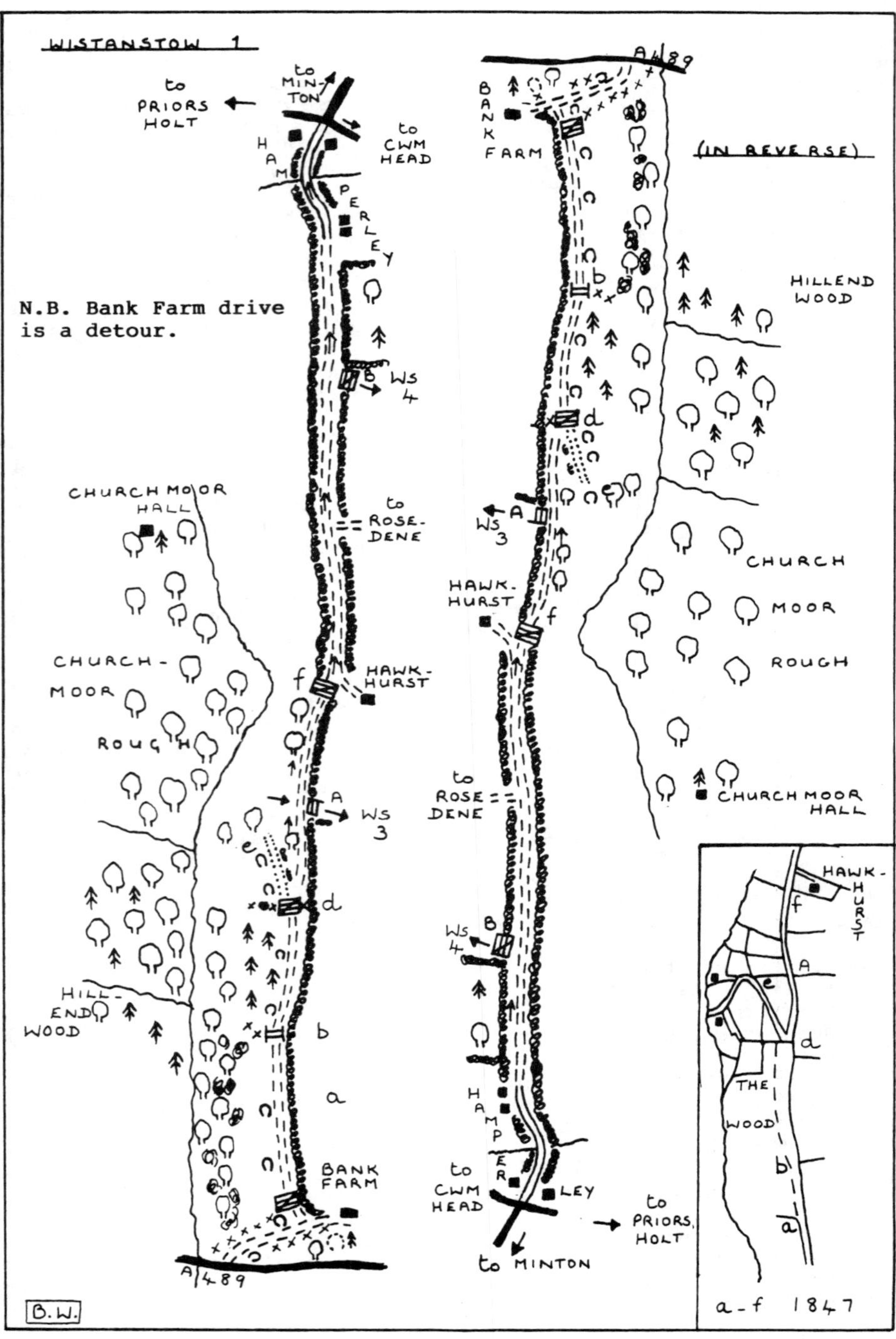
WISTANSTOW 1
N.B. Bank Farm drive is a detour.
to MINTON
to PRIORS HOLT
to CWM HEAD
HAM
PERLEY
WS 4
WS 3
to ROSE-DENE
HAWK-HURST
CHURCHMOOR HALL
CHURCH-MOOR ROUGH
HILL-END WOOD
BANK FARM
A 489
(IN REVERSE)
HILLEND WOOD
CHURCH MOOR ROUGH
HAMPERLEY
THE WOOD
a-f 1847
B.W.

WISTANSTOW 1 AND 2

Ws 1 from (d) to Hamperley and Ws 2 were green lanes only until recently. Both must have been regarded as rights of way for some time since Ws 4 and a branch of Ws 3 cannot be reached without using them. They have now acquired bridleway status. One factor that can contribute today towards the conversion of a route into a public right of way is evidence of antiquity and both these tracks are recorded on the tithe map of 1847.

WISTANSTOW 1, BANK FARM TO HAMPERLEY 2.25 Km/1¼+ m.

The first part of this route, as far as (e), was a bridleway when the second part was still only a green lane. The initial part, as shown on the map and as it was in the past, is now impossible to use and the driveway to Bank Farm has to be used instead. Just before reaching the farm itself, turn left and enter a field via a gate. Continue along a track which runs on the left-hand side of a hedge; it can be extremely muddy. The far left side of this field slopes steeply down to a brook (the Wistanstow/Lydbury North boundary); the bank is an attractive area of trees and scrub. The first half of this field was once two fields called Tinkers Piece and Little Tinkers Meadow. On the opposite side of the brook is Hillend Wood, mostly coniferous. **At (b), a wood is entered via slip-rails and the way continues along the left-hand side of the hedge to exit from the wood at gate (d). A track continues straight on as the former green lane (now bridleway) mentioned above, but the original bridleway turns down to the left along an old grassy track and ends rather oddly at the bottom of the slope.** Some explanation can be gained from the tithe map (see inset on facing page); Ws 1 was an enclosed track for most of its length except between (a) and (d), a section which passed through an area labelled 'The Wood with Outrack open to it'. The term 'outrack' associated with this route suggests that Ws 1, possibly only as far as here, was a way to get to and from the old Hawkhurst Common. From (d), Ws 1 on the tithe map was again enclosed and a small branch track descended to an area of small fields around two homes beside the brook; the short stretch of bridleway between (d) and its end at (e) is part of that branch route. **To continue to Hamperley keep to the former green lane from (d), now open to field on the left. Ws 3 branches off to the right at A. Across the valley to the left is Churchmoor Rough,** an attractive area of mostly deciduous woodland that extends up the valley to and around Churchmoor Hall; behind the wood, Churchmoor Hill and Priors Holt Hill rise to the Mynd plateau. Buzzards soar and call above the wood. **At (f), a gate leads onto enclosed track where the driveway to Hawkhurst (a farm) branches off.** The name 'Hawkhurst' is thought to mean a 'wooded knoll (hurst) for hawks' and has been recorded for centuries for this area, as has its alternative name of 'Haycrust'. Some of the field names on the tithe map incorporate the name of Hawkroost. **Follow the green lane all the way to the hamlet of Hamperley.**

WISTANSTOW 1 (IN REVERSE), HAMPERLEY TO BANK FARM

Take the road, initially surfaced, through the farm at Hamperley opposite the end of the lane towards Minton. Follow this green lane some distance to reach gate (f) near Hawkhurst. Continue along the right-hand side of the hedge from (f), passing point A, through gates (d) and (b) and on to the gate near Bank Farm. Exit through the gate, turn right and descend to the main road via the driveway of Bank Farm.

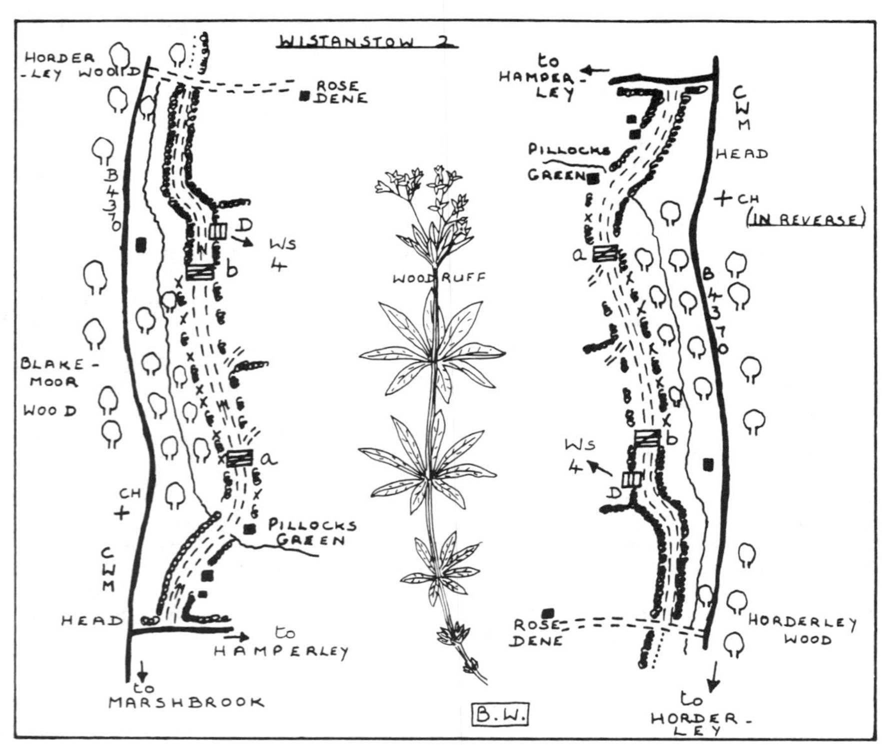

WISTANSTOW 2, PILLOCKSGREEN TO HORDERLEY WOOD 1 Km/½+ m.

Ws 2 is an enclosed track, although the hedges are sparse in places. Leave the Cwm Head to Hamperley road near Cwm Head and descend the west side of the cwm or valley while the B4370 descends the east side. The early part of the track passes three houses; this is Pillocksgreen. It continues above a wood, passing through gates (a) and (b). Wn 4 branches off to the right via a stile after gate (b), just before the road bends to the left. On this bend part of the hedge has slipped away in a small landslide that must have occurred as a result of the persistent rain in 1991. The lane finishes at the driveway to Rosedene. It also finished at this point on the tithe map (but by a cottage and Rosedene did not exist); there are signs to show that the track continued further at some time. **Exit along a short section of Rosedene driveway.** There used to be stone quarries above the exit point and the woodland here appears on maps as Brokenstones Plantation. This does not seem to be its local name but Brokenstones is the name of a place above the wood on the way to Woolston.

WISTANSTOW 2 (IN REVERSE), HORDERLEY WOOD TO PILLOCKSGREEN

Take the driveway towards Rosedene, soon turning right to go along an old and enclosed track. At the top of a bend Ws 4 branches off to the left. Continue, passing through gates (b) and (a) and on past three houses, to exit onto lane near Cwm Head.

WISTANSTOW 3, HAWKHURST TO HORDERLEY WOOD 0.5 Km/¼ m.

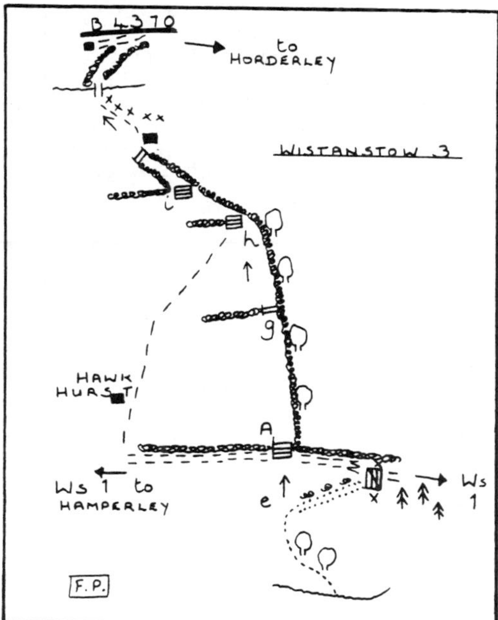

Ws 3 begins at point (e) on Ws 1, at the end of an old track which once continued a little further to some houses by the brook. The path must have been created by inhabitants of these houses (now gone) to get to the Cwm Head valley, where at one time there were church, pub (Red Lion), school, stone quarries and a cider mill; only the church remains today but the old pub and school still exist as houses. **From (e), climb a steep bank and cross the Ws 1 track at point A (a more likely situation is that you will be starting along Ws 3 from this point). Cross a stile and follow the left-hand side of a hedge to wooden fencing (g). From (g), continue along the hedge to a small stile (h). At this point a public footpath from Hawkhurst (Farm) joins Ws 3.** Hawkhurst inhabitants therefore also contributed to the creation of Ws 3 and children from there appear to have been the last regular users of this route. **From (h), continue along old hedge to stile (i). The next section is an old and enclosed track** which suggests that part of this route was once more than just a footpath. Perhaps it was a track to the old Hawkhurst Common; if so, it had gone out of use by the mid 19th century as it is not shown on the tithe map. **The track runs down the slope behind a cottage, finishing at a wooden rail near the end of the house. Pass the end of the house and go down a small garden path which soon turns left and descends to the brook. Cross the brook by a footbridge and continue up an enclosed path** (possibly another section of the old track running up behind the house) and exit onto the main road.

Focus on birds

Nightingales

The nightingale is very scarce in Shropshire although it used to breed regularly in the eastern part of the Severn valley. The scattered and sporadic recordings of it in the south and east of Shropshire represent its north-western limit in Britain. The valley of Cwm Head has been the site of sporadic visits, each visit being an event remembered long afterwards by local people, the influx of visitors as much for the song. Inhabitants of Little Stretton recall being amongst the crowds that went to hear the nightingale on one of its visits in the 1950s and a local inhabitant remembers its last visit about 15 years ago when 20 or 30 cars at a time were parked along the road.

WISTANSTOW 4, Ws 2 AT D TO Ws 1 AT B 0.5 Km/¼ m.

Ws 4 and the other three Wistanstow routes described offer views of several woods and are particularly attractive to walk in autumn. To the west of the routes are Hillend Wood and Churchmoor Rough while to the east are the woods enveloping the valley of Cwm Head. Looking south-east across the valley from any of the routes, the woodland on the left is Blakemoor Wood, that on the right (downstream) is Horderley Wood, which includes Brokenstones Plantation. Between the two is an area known as The Smouts (fields on the tithe map were called Smouts Ground) and the old school (a round house) is nearby.

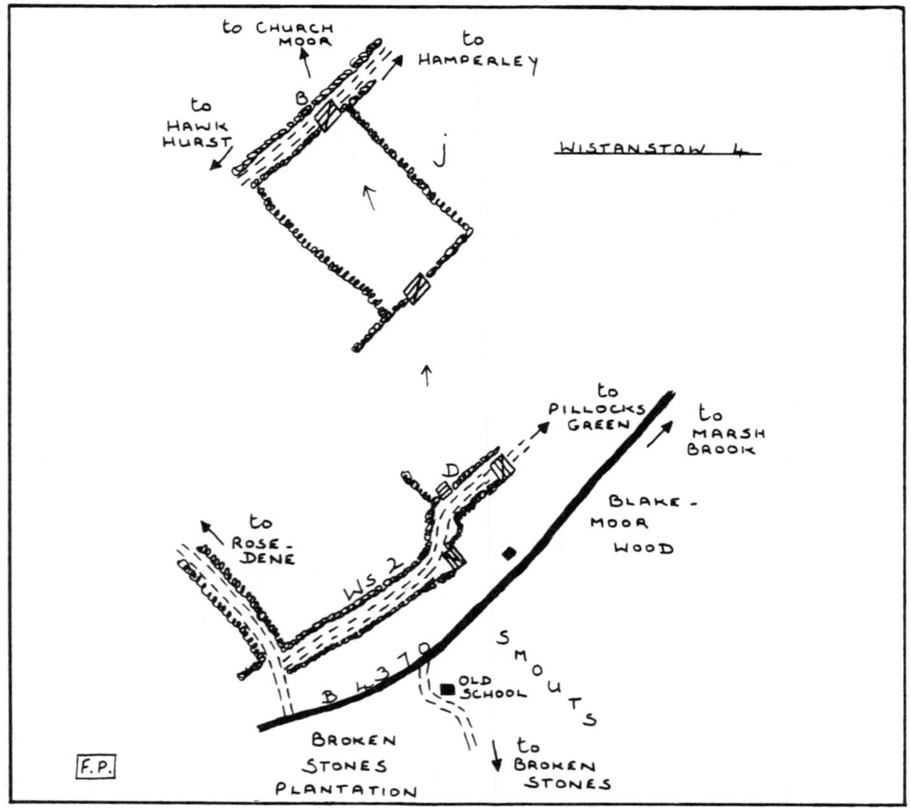

Ws 4 must have provided access to the school as well as to the quarries or pub. More recently it was a way for several children from Churchmoor to go to school at Wistanstow; from the Cwm Head valley their way led past the old school, up the Smouts, over to Woolston and on, a journey of about two miles. **Ws 4 is a public footpath which begins from Ws 2 at the top of a marked bend, at point D. Leave the track via a stile. Aim obliquely right up and across a field to a gate. From this gate, cross to the gate in the far right-hand corner of the field, joining Ws 1 at B.** The field (j) alongside contains a number of trees growing in a rather orderly fashion; this is Hamperley Plantation.

WOOLSTASTON

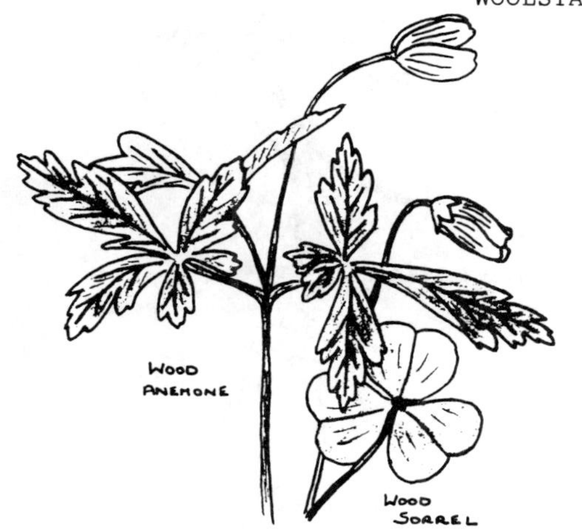

Woolstaston is a small parish lying on the north-eastern foothills of the Long Mynd. It was the manor of Ulestanestune in the Domesday Book, a name that is thought to mean 'Wulfstan's estate'. A motte was built here and a church was first mentioned in 1272. Much of the parish was woodland in the late 17th century but little of this remains. The inhabitants had common rights on the Mynd extending up towards Duckley Nap but these were lost in 1743, leaving Woolstaston as the only parish around the Long Mynd not to abut onto the Portway.

Woolstaston is centred on the church, with only scattered habitations or small groups of houses elsewhere. This 'centre' is best reached by the lane leaving the A49 nearly opposite the Pound Inn at Leebotwood. It is interesting to note that this route was once of far less importance than others radiating from Woolstaston and it illustrates well how the relative importance of different routes alters over the centuries. In former times the drovers used this way to descend from the Long Mynd to Leebotwood and thence to Wednesbury, avoiding the toll roads (see Background).

Woolstaston, perhaps as a name only, has become familiar to many as the former home of the Reverend E.D. Carr who wrote 'A Night In The Snow'. Rev.Carr died and was buried here in 1900. There is a tablet to his memory inside the church and he is buried alongside his wife between the end of the church and the old vicarage, the crosses at their heads facing the house where they lived for so many years.

Amenities:-

Refreshments - the nearest places are at Leebotwood, 1½ miles from the church; The Pound Inn and The Copper Kettle cafe. The Little Chef lies on the A49 south of Leebotwood.
Accommodation - Rectory Farm (award-winning Bed and Breakfast).
Also B and B at Batchcott Hall in Smethcott.
Club camping - Castle Hill Farm.
Bus service - Midland Red buses, running between Shrewsbury and Ludlow, pass through Leebotwood (see Church Stretton).
Boulton's also operate a bus service, between Shrewsbury and the south via back lanes, that passes through Leebotwood.

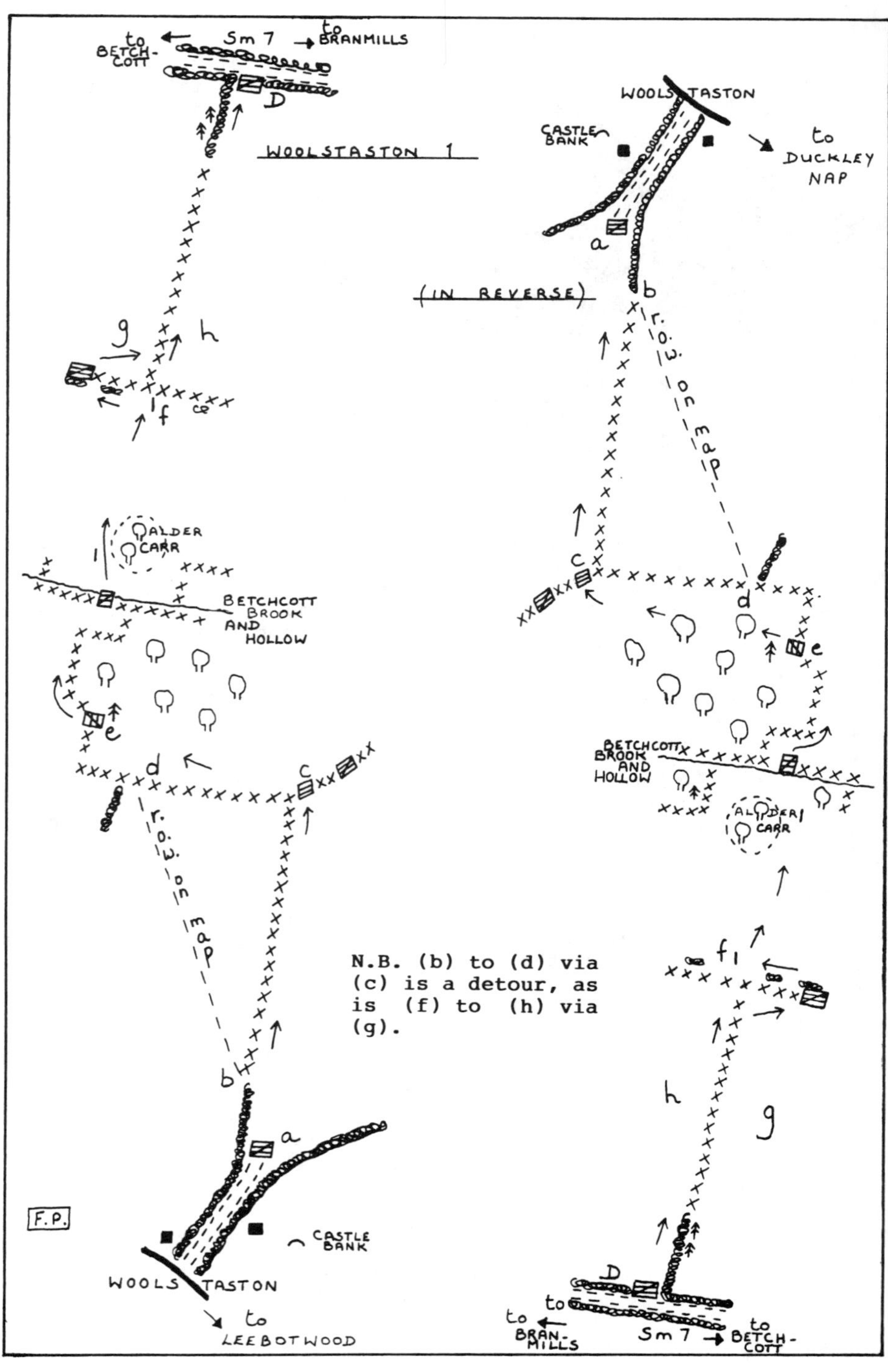
to
Sm 7
to
BRANMILLS
BETCH-
COTT
D
WOOLSTASTON 1
g
h
f
WOOLSTASTON
CASTLE BANK
to
DUCKLEY
NAP
a
(IN REVERSE)
b
r.o.w. on map
ALDER CARR
BETCHCOTT BROOK AND HOLLOW
e
d
c
b
a
CASTLE BANK
WOOLSTASTON
to
LEEBOTWOOD
F.P.
N.B. (b) to (d) via (c) is a detour, as is (f) to (h) via (g).
D
to
to
BRAN-
MILLS
Sm 7
to
BETCH-
COTT

WOOLSTASTON 1, WOOLSTASTON TO Sm 7 AT D 0.75 Km/½ m.

WL 1 is a public footpath that cannot at present be followed exactly as recorded on the O/S map but is usable by taking slight detours. Leave Woolstaston just above Castle Bank, the site of Woolstaston's Norman motte. Follow an enclosed track (part of the mediaeval Portway running from the Mynd to Shrewsbury) **for a short distance to (a) where it opens out into a field. At this point the Portway continued straight on but WL 1 turns left to follow a fence across to the wooded dingle (Betchcott Hollow), which is entered via stile (c).** This wooded dingle, like similar ones nearby, is a remnant of ancient woodland, somewhat modified with time but still containing many species of woodland plants and trees and providing a good habitat for wildlife. The wood was Dickens Coppy on the tithe map. **From (c), turn left and walk along near the top of the wood passing point (d). (The official right of way passes directly across the field from (b) to (d) but is unusable). Continue in the same direction and leave the wood via a wicket gate (e) near a large Scots pine tree. Turn right and follow a fence down to the brook, passing through another wicket gate. Ford Betchcott Brook and climb up the opposite bank, which can be muddy. Aim up to the top of the field, passing to the left of a clump of alders in a boggy area (alder carr).** This steep field is old pasture but stunted bluebells in the grass are reminders that this bank, like many of the nearby slopes, was once woodland.**At the top of the bank are remnants of an old hedge running from left to right and an old post (f) in it acts as a route-marker. The fence just beyond it unfortunately offers no stile and a gate to the left has to be used. This leads into field (g) rather than field (h) but incomplete fencing between the two fields means that the correct route can be rejoined. Follow the fence, subsequently hedge and coniferous plantation, to exit via a gate onto a track (Sm 7) at D.**

WOOLSTASTON 1 (IN REVERSE), Sm 7 AT D TO WOOLSTASTON

Leave Sm 7 at point D and enter a field via a gate. The path runs along a hedge and small coniferous plantation that subsequently become a fence. The correct way continues along the left-hand side of this fence but you should pass through a gap to follow the right-hand side on a slight detour. Where this fence meets another fence at right angles the gate to the right has to be used to get to post (f). From here descend the steep field, passing to the right of a group of alder trees, cross the brook and go through a wicket gate. Follow a fence up the slope and turn left into the wood via a wicket gate (e) close to a large Scots pine. Walk across the top of the wood, passing point (d). The wood opens out and a gate out of the wood lies ahead; use the stile (c) up to the right. From (c), follow the fence across to the end of a track; turn right along this and follow it to the road.

Focus on mink

The mink was brought to Britain this century to be bred for its fur. Following a series of escapes it has become established in the wild, frequenting streams and pools. As an alien it is regarded with dislike and distrust, particularly as it has a liking for trout and poultry, but it is a beautiful and clever creature, wily enough to creep up behind the fisherman and steal his catch off the bank.

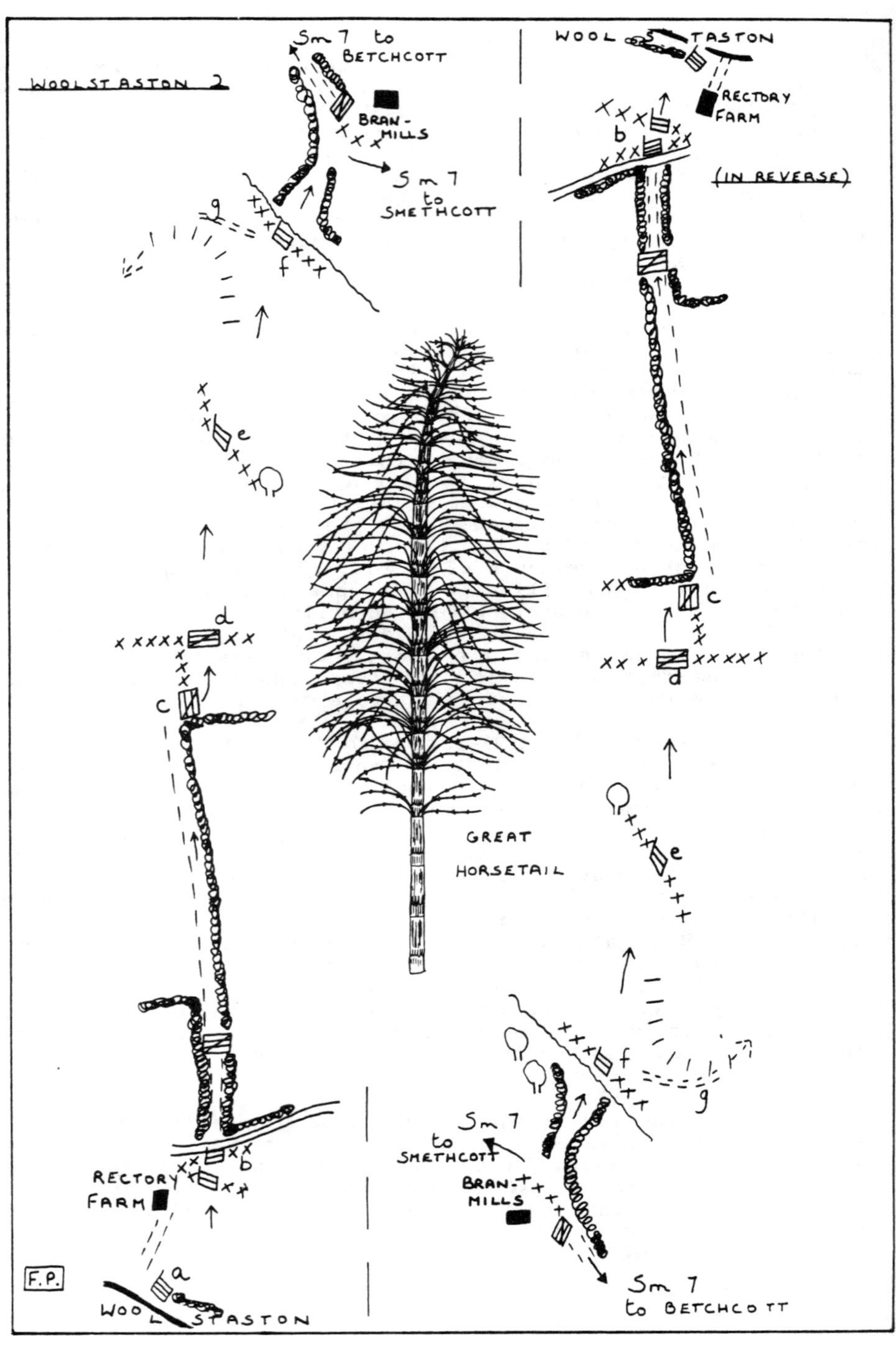

WOOLSTASTON 2
Sm 7 to BETCHCOTT
BRAN-MILLS
Sm 7 to SMETHCOTT
g
f
e
d
c
b
a
RECTORY FARM
WOOLSTASTON
F.P.
GREAT HORSETAIL
(IN REVERSE)

WOOLSTASTON 2, WOOLSTASTON TO BRANMILLS 0.75 Km/½ m.

There were at one time at least three routes running between Woolstaston and Smethcott but only one of them became a right of way. The mediaeval Portway which ran past the motte and down to Branmills and was part of the way from the Long Mynd to Shrewsbury, is sadly almost lost but can still be traced along the dingle slope. WL 2 runs from the church to Branmills and is a much wetter route. The third route crossed through Spring Coppice and led to Smethcott school, with a branch off it to Smethcott Farm. This route is obviously well used today and even has a footbridge; it is not a public right of way (see also under Sm 6) yet it must have been the best route for Woolstaston schoolchildren who went to Smethcott school (functioning between 1867 and 1964) and for the rector of Smethcott, who looked after the two churches between 1929 and the 1950s.

WL 2 starts above the church at the uppermost of two stiles that leave the lane and enter a garden in front of the black and white Rectory Farm. Cross in front of the house to two consecutive stiles (b) separated by a small corner of field. Opposite the second stile is a track, at first enclosed and then open on one side, that leads to a gate at (c). Turn right through this gate, then left to reach gate (d). Cross the field, aiming to the left of a tree, to get to stile (e). Ahead is a sloping, boggy field with alder trees (often referred to as alder carr). There is no way of avoiding the bog. This area was called Mill Ground and on the other side of the brook is a house called Branmills. A mediaeval mill existed here but the exact site is unknown. The miller certainly did not have a very good piece of land nor was this ever a way to walk in your Sunday best. **Aim diagonally leftwards and down from stile (e) into the bog.** Bogs are always interesting places to look for plants and insects; a prominent plant of this bog is the great horsetail. **A fence runs along the bottom of this field above the brook and it can be followed to stile (f) if your aim has brought you to the bottom of the slope too soon.** Just before (f), on the left, is an old crab-apple tree and beyond this can be found traces of the mediaeval track (g) mentioned above, which would have crossed the brook at the same place as WL 2 does now. The brook is called the Walkmills Brook and the ford may once have been Mapps Ford (the name of a neighbouring field on the tithe map). **After fording the brook, follow the right-hand side of a hedge up to join Sm 7 just below Branmills (a house) in the area of the original mediaeval settlement of Smethcott.**

WOOLSTASTON 2 (IN REVERSE), BRANMILLS TO WOOLSTASTON

Leave Sm 7 just below Branmills and follow the left-hand side of a hedge down to the brook. Ford the brook and cross stile (f). Aim obliquely left, up and across a very boggy slope to stile (e) at the top. Again aim diagonally left to gate (d), continue straight on, turn right through gate (c) and then left along a track. This track joins another which is crossed to reach two stiles (b) separated by a small corner of field. Pass in front of the black and white Rectory Farm across a lawn and exit onto the lane at (a).

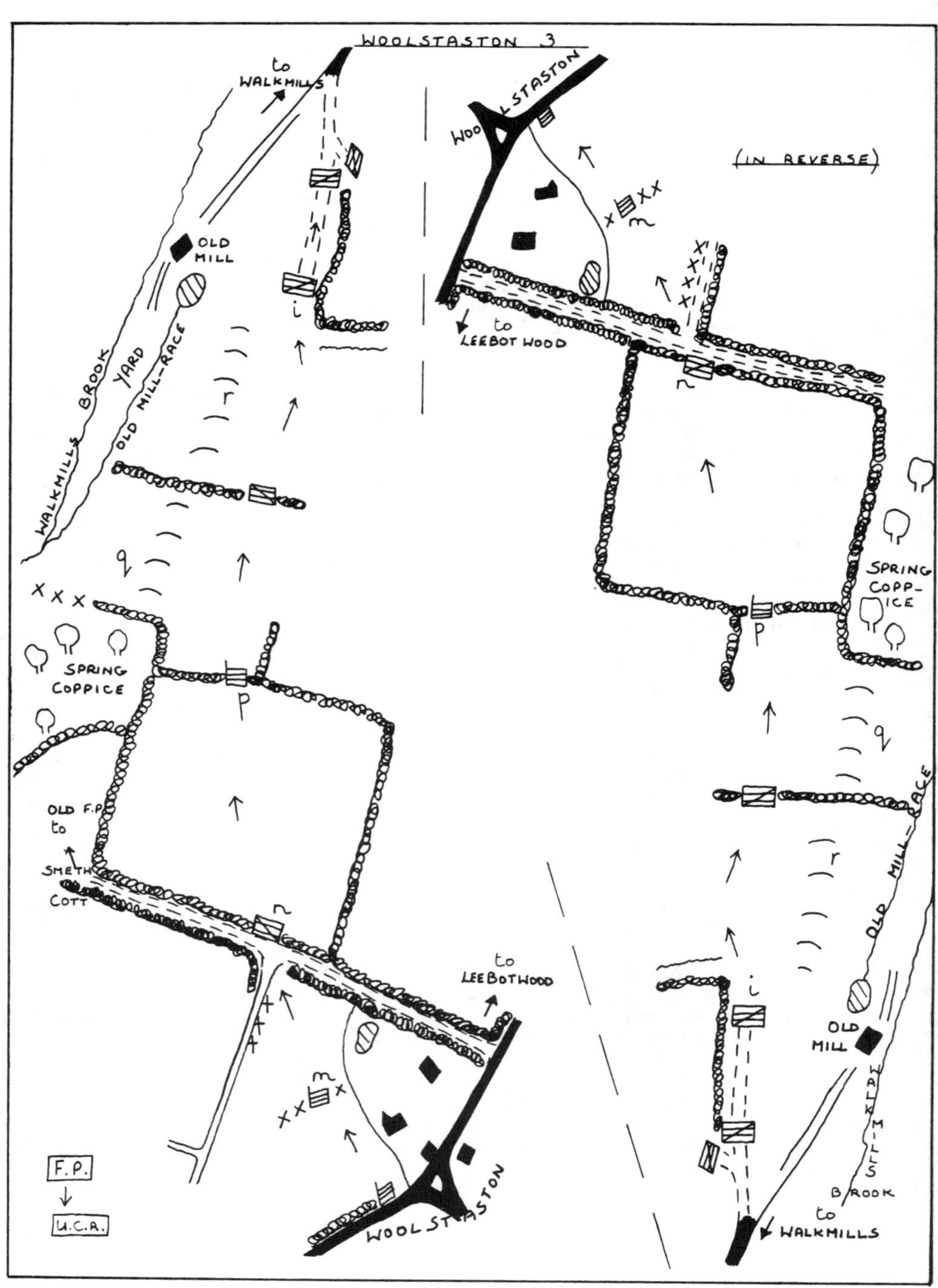
WOOLSTASTON 3
(IN REVERSE)
to WALKMILLS
OLD MILL
WALKMILLS BROOK
YARD
OLD MILL-RACE
WOOLSTASTON
to LEEBOTWOOD
SPRING COPPICE
OLD F.P. to SMETHCOTT
F.P.
U.C.R.
SPRING COPPICE
to LEEBOTWOOD
WOOLSTASTON
OLD MILL-RACE
OLD MILL
WALKMILLS BROOK
to WALKMILLS

WOOLSTASTON 3, WOOLSTASTON TO THE OLD MILL 1 Km/½+ m.

WL 3 is a public footpath. It must have been a way for Woolstaston people to get to the mill and for inhabitants of the mill and the Walkmills area to get to church. **It leaves the road above the small village green via the lower of two stiles onto a large lawn. Walk past the church to another stile (m) and cross a field to the far corner where a track is joined near a T junction. Opposite is a gate (n) into an arable field. Aim slightly to the left of straight ahead across this field to a stile (p) by some trees; if there is no trail through the corn it is better and easier to walk astride the rows and turn left at the end to get to stile (p). From (p), walk straight on. To the left the field drops steeply down (q) to an old mill-race and the next field (r) is similar.** The whole length of the bank is an amazing sight in June with meadow flowers and countless spotted orchids (**do not pick). Towards the end of the second field descend the bank obliquely to gate (i).** On the left the mill-race has reached a mill-pool and beyond it is the mill-wheel on the side of a house (Old Mill). **Pass through gate (i) and follow a short section of grassy track (unsurfaced highway) to join surfaced road to Walkmills.**

WOOLSTASTON 3 (IN REVERSE), OLD MILL TO WOOLSTASTON

Turn off the Walkmills to Old Mill road just before it enters the yard of the latter. Follow a short section of unsurfaced grassy highway to reach gate (i). Aim obliquely left up a bank and turn right at the top to walk parallel to the top of the bank (r) but not actually along it. Pass through a gateway and continue straight on to stile (p). From (p), cross the arable field obliquely to the left to get to gate (n); it is easier and does not damage the crop if you can keep astride of the rows but it will lead you a little off course. Gate (n) opens onto a track at a T junction; cross it and enter a field at its corner. Aim obliquely across this field and enter a garden via stile (m). Follow the churchyard boundary and exit via a stile onto the road.

Focus on flowers **Orchids**

Orchids are always rather special plants to find, particularly as some species are so rare. The Mynd area only provides a suitable habitat for spotted orchids (two species) but woodland on its fringes contains early purple orchid and broad-leaved helleborine. Although spotted orchids are not uncommon it is an unusual sight today to find such a spread of them as can be seen near WL 3. The number of orchids flowering each year may vary enormously, one reason being that seedlings can take years to produce leaves and even longer to produce flowers. Some species of orchid will only flower for one year but the spotted orchid (one of the tuber-bearing species) is among those that can flower from the same tuber for several years. Orchids, like many other species of plants, should never be picked. It is pointless, too, to gather their seeds since it is very difficult to get them to grow; orchid seedlings need the help of a fungus to grow, in a relationship which is mutually beneficial. This association, which also occurs with other plants in differing ways, is termed a mycorrhiza.

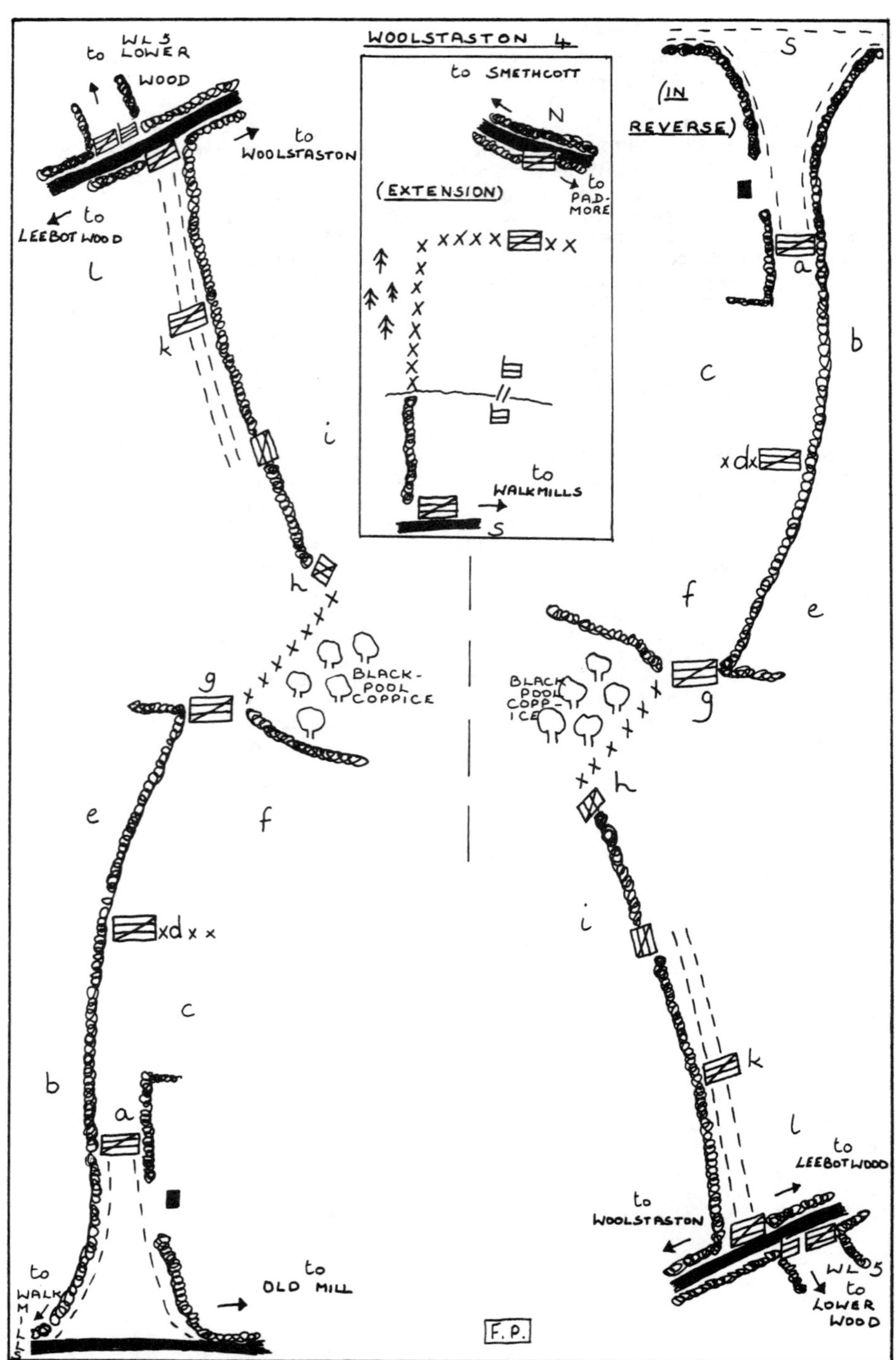
WOOLSTASTON 4
to WL5 LOWER WOOD
to WOOLSTASTON
to LEEBOTWOOD
l
k
i
h
g
BLACK-POOL COPPICE
f
e
xd x x
c
b
a
to WALKMILLS
to OLD MILL
to SMETHCOTT
N
(EXTENSION)
to PADMORE
to WALKMILLS
S
S
(IN REVERSE)
a
b
c
xdx
f
e
g
BLACK POOL COPPICE
h
i
k
l
to LEEBOTWOOD
to WOOLSTASTON
WL5 to LOWER WOOD
F.P.

WOOLSTASTON 4, OLD MILL TO WOOLSTASTON LANE 0.75 Km/½ m.

WL 4 is an old track that would have been the best route to the mill from Woolstaston. The footpath extending northwards at S (see extension on route map) is also likely to have been a way to the mill, but there is no evidence that it was ever a track. WL 4 is shown on the tithe map almost as it runs today, passing a field called Four Wickets. At its north end, however, it curved round to run to the mill and there was no track from Walkmills as there is today.

Leave the surfaced Walkmills to Old Mill road near the Old Mill and follow enclosed track past a house. Go through gate (a) and follow the right-hand side of a hedge to gate (d) and on to gate (g). Field (e) on the left was called Four Wickets. From (g), follow the fence along the edge of Blackpool Coppice, presumably so called because of the pool in the wood. It is a deciduous wood and the tithe map indicates it as such in the 19th century though the names of the nearby fields suggest that the woodland had been more extensive; (b) was Upper Wood Piece, (c) was Wood Piece, (i) was Coppy Leasow and (l) was Holly Piece. **At the corner of the wood (h) turn left and follow the hedge, joining used track, passing through gate (k) and continuing along hedge out to the road.**

WOOLSTASTON 4 (IN REVERSE), WOOLSTASTON LANE TO OLD MILL

Leave Woolstaston Lane via a gate and follow a track along the right-hand side of a hedge, passing through gate (k). Continue along the hedge to the corner (h) and turn right to follow the fence that bounds Blackpool Coppice. Pass through gate (g) and follow the left-hand side of a hedge, passing through gates (d) and (a). A short section of enclosed track leads out to the Walkmills to Old Mill road.

A public footpath, not included in any circuits in this book, begins opposite the end of WL 4 at S, crosses the valley and ascends to the Padmore to Smethcott road road at N (see inset on the facing page).

Focus on flowers **Bluebells**

The bluebell is a typical plant of the woods and some of the shaded hedgerows around the Mynd but there are also some fine stands on unwooded slopes. It is likely that such stands are indicators of past woodland and there would probably be many more if the land had not been further disturbed after the removal of the trees. Many of these sites have, however, been woodland until within the past 150 years, and it is perhaps debatable whether bluebells can continue indefinitely without trees though they appear to coexist very well with bracken which, by creating shade in summer and autumn, is providing a similar pattern to that of deciduous trees.

Bluebells will also colonize new woodland, though the time needed for this is uncertain. It is dependent presumably on the proximity of established woodland with bluebells in it and it would be interesting to time their arrival in a new plantation, such as at Womerton, where there is no adjacent woodland and the plantation is on grassland with no woodland flowers. A plantation in Wilderley which is little more than 100 years old, is full of woodland flowers; it was recorded as being an arable field in 1839 and is therefore unlikely to have had woodland flowers when it was first planted.

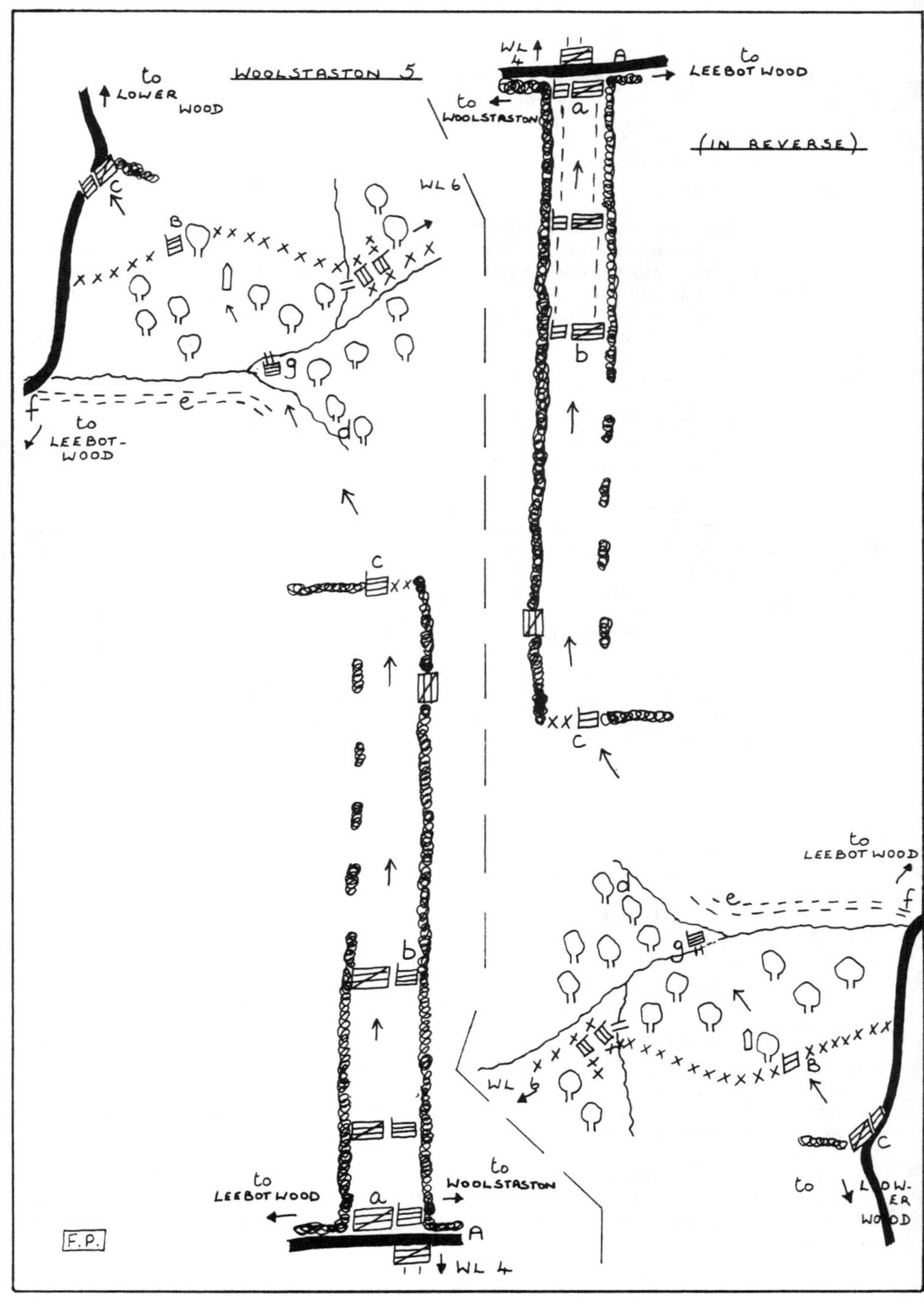
WOOLSTASTON 5
(IN REVERSE)
to LOWER WOOD
to LEEBOTWOOD
to WOOLSTASTON
WL 4
WL 6
A
a
b
c
B
d
e
f
g
to LEEBOT-WOOD
to LOW-ER WOOD
F.P.

WOOLSTASTON 5, WOOLSTASTON LANE TO LOWER WOOD 0.75 Km/½ m.

WL 5 appears to have been an enclosed track to (c) and one would suspect that it was once in continuity with WL 4. However, on the tithe map the first section from (a) to (b) did not exist. Instead, a track from further up the Woolstaston lane was in continuity with the second section from (b) to (c), where it ended in a field called Green Park. The track may once have continued and linked up with track (e) and thence to Lower Wood (there was no road to the left at (f), see WL 7) and on to Stretton. Alternatively, it may have continued as a footpath, as it does today. This route was not used exclusively by Woolstaston people; the children of Lower Wood once used it as a way to Mrs Carr's Sunday school.

WL 5 is a public footpath that leaves Woolstaston Lane opposite the end of WL 4. Pass over gate or stile (a) and descend along enclosed track via a second gate and stile to reach a third gate and stile at (b). From (b), continue straight on along the older section of this track whose left-hand hedge has become somewhat sparse. At (c), change direction, aiming obliquely left across the field towards the wooded dingles. Follow the margin of the small dingle (d) downstream and cross its brook and another just before they join up. The second brook is spanned by a bridge after stile (g). From (g), climb the steep and wooded bank, aiming straight on. Try not to be led astray by the better-used animal tracks; there is a marker-post to guide you. Cross stile B at the top and walk across to the far right-hand corner of the field to join the road by a tree.

WOOLSTASTON 5 (IN REVERSE), LOWER WOOD TO WOOLSTASTON LANE

Leave the Lower Wood to Leebotwood road on a sharp corner, via a stile or gate, and cross the field, aiming obliquely away from the left-hand hedge. Cross stile B into a wood and descend a steep bank directly down to a brook. Cross a bridge over the brook and then stile (g). Ford a second brook and then climb up a slope. Follow the top of the small dingle (d) for a short distance upstream before bearing away from it obliquely to the right to reach stile (c). From (c), the way is straight and follows an old track via three gates or stiles to get to Woolstaston Lane.

Focus on flowers **Brambles**

There are many species of blackberry in Britain. If you have picked blackberries, you may have noticed that those on the roadsides are often early and have large, irregular and tasty fruits, whereas later blackberries, often to be found on the dingle slopes, have neater fruits, grow in more profusion and are therefore better to pick if a large quantity is needed. The earlier species described is Rubus tuberculatus, a species typical of this area whose large white flowers in June are seen along all the Mynd hedgerows. The other species of blackberry in this area, mostly flowering a little later, are less easy to distinguish. A particularly attractive one is to be seen in woods e.g. in the dingles along WL 5; the large pale pink flowers are each made up of several slender petals. Brambles rarely have common English names and all are known botanically by the Latin name of Rubus along with a second name, usually also in Latin, but this woodland blackberry has a Greek second name ('hylocharis') which means 'woodland grace'. There is also a 'grace of the shade' and over 300 other species for anyone interested in the study of brambles (batology).

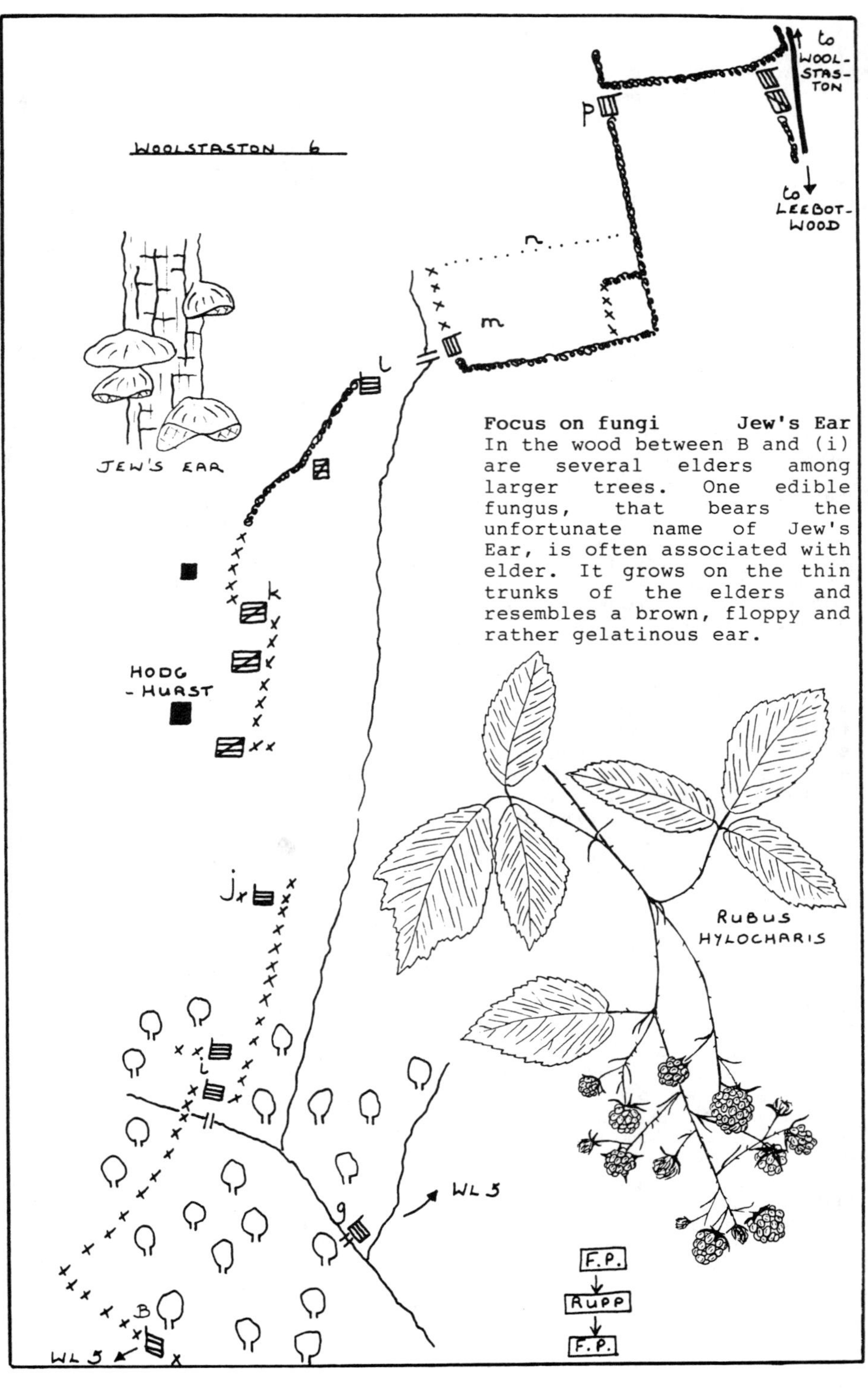

Focus on fungi **Jew's Ear**

In the wood between B and (i) are several elders among larger trees. One edible fungus, that bears the unfortunate name of Jew's Ear, is often associated with elder. It grows on the thin trunks of the elders and resembles a brown, floppy and rather gelatinous ear.

WOOLSTASTON 6

WL 6 is part RUPP and part public footpath. RUPP stands for 'road used as a public path', a term which does not explain who or what exactly can use it. RUPPs are gradually being reclassified and it is likely in this case that the RUPP section will become a footpath as it is isolated between two stretches of footpath and could never be used by anyone other than a walker. It is difficult to understand how this section became a RUPP unless possibly it was the old way to and from Hodghurst. If so, there is no evidence of it on the tithe map and, looking at the dingle itself, there does not appear to have been a track through it.

WL 6 begins at the top of a wooded dingle, leaving WL 5 at stile B. Follow the boundary fence round and descend to the bottom of the slope through bog. Cross a brook and two stiles at (i) and ascend into open field. The field is surrounded by trees, giving the effect of a clearing in a large wood. Follow the left-hand side of a fence to stile (j), the top of Caradoc to the east coming into view as the way climbs. A brook runs on the right of the fence, serving as a boundary between Stretton and Woolstaston parishes. This brook originates from High Park, the first part of its journey passing through Dead Mans Batch, whose name may have arisen when Woolstaston failed to bury the body of a man who died in this area; this episode contributed towards Woolstaston's loss of common rights on the Mynd. Downstream the brook joins the Quaking Brook from Stretton to form the Broad Brook which runs through Leebotwood and further north becomes the Cound Brook. **From (j), aim obliquely left up to Hodghurst (a farm) and pass through some gates close to the right of the farm and a new house. From the last gate (k), follow the right-hand side of a hedge, passing through a wicket gate and along an old track to stile (l). Cross the brook via a bridge and enter field (m).** This is composed of two old fields called Hop Yard and Barn Moor, ('hop' in this case meaning 'valley') which even today are fields of the past. Rabbits run across old rough grassland amongst scattered bushes and the bog higher up is full of interesting plants. Purple moor-grass, a grass normally only seen now on moorland, still grows on Barn Moor. **From the stile by the brook aim obliquely left across rough grassland, crossing an old field boundary at (n) and continuing in the same direction across modern grassland to stile (p). From (p), follow the right-hand side of a hedge and exit onto the road via gate or stile near Woolstaston village.**

Focus on sedges

Sedges are a group of grass-like and rush-like plants, often to be found in wet ground. Several species can be seen in the Mynd area. In the summer look in bogs for small green plants bearing clusters of little green fruits. Sedges are often named according to the shape of the individual fruit or the shape of the cluster. The two commonest sedges locally are star sedge (the cluster is in a tiny star shape) and low sedge, which lies almost on the ground. Pill sedge is a taller and uncommon sedge which has small round clusters of fruits. Bottle sedge is the tallest sedge in the area and almost fills Wildmoor Pool; the individual fruits are bottle-shaped. Another common small sedge is black sedge, whose green fruits are interspersed with black scales (glumes).

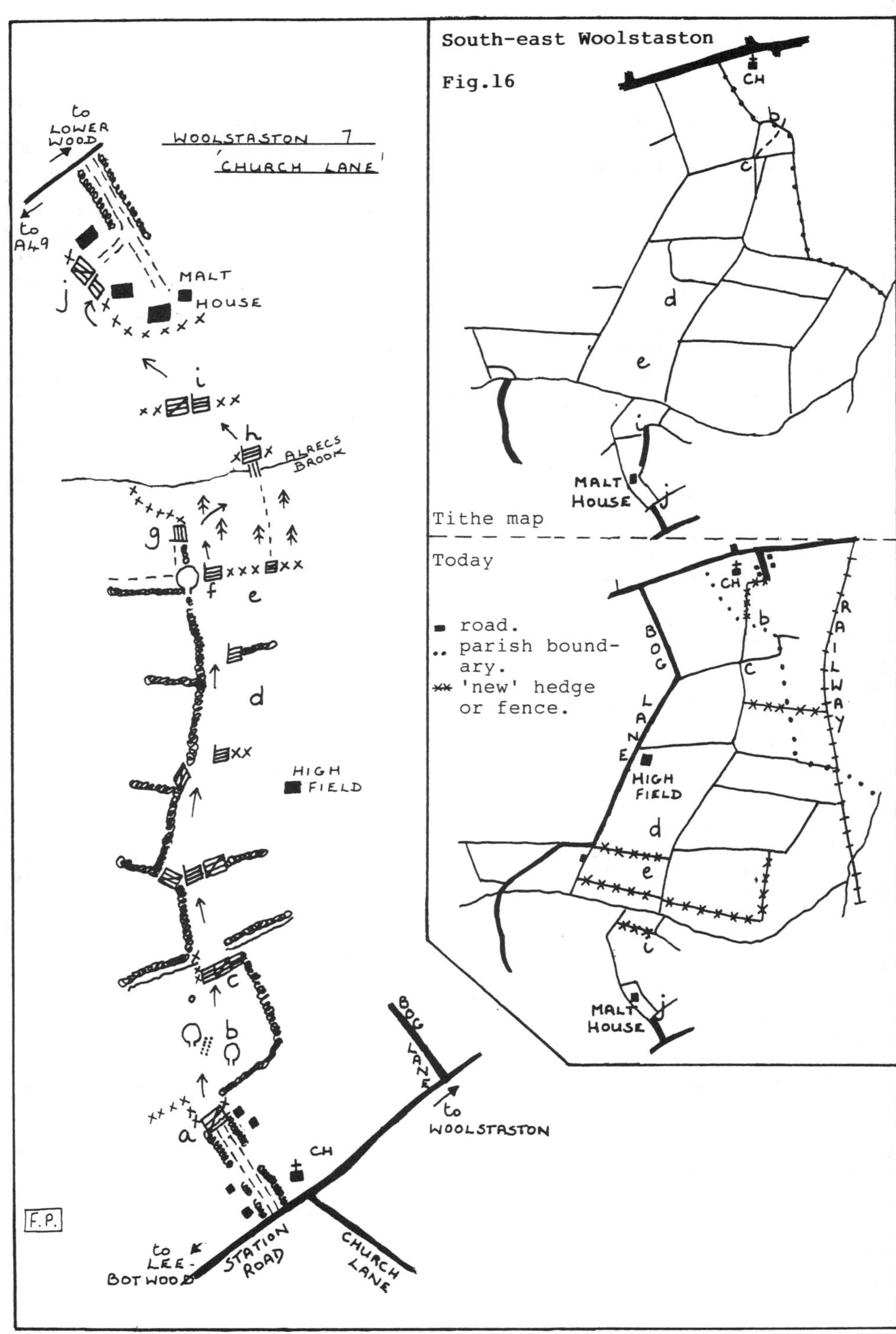

to LOWER WOOD
WOOLSTASTON 7
'CHURCH LANE'
to A49
MALT HOUSE
j
i
h
ALRECS BROOK
g
f
e
d
HIGH FIELD
c
b
a
BOG LANE
to WOOLSTASTON
CH
STATION ROAD
CHURCH LANE
to LEE-BOTWOOD
F.P.
South-east Woolstaston
Fig.16
CH
Tithe map
Today
RAILWAY
■ road.
•• parish boundary.
✕✕ 'new' hedge or fence.

Focus on the eastern boundary of Woolstaston

On a modern map the eastern boundary of Woolstaston, running between Walkmills Brook and Broad Brook, appears to run a meandering course unrelated to any land features. On the tithe map, however, it was following field boundaries, all of which have disappeared. This boundary is an ancient one which was fixed in the 13th century; at that time it was the eastern boundary of Woolstaston Wood which covered a large area of the parish (half of the parish was still woodland until the late 17th century). Latterly, Woolstaston Wood lay only on the lower ground in the east of the parish.

WOOLSTASTON 7, LEEBOTWOOD CHURCH TO MALT HOUSE 1 Km/½+ m.

WL 7 was at one time a track running between Leebotwood and Lower Wood. It is an ancient link between the two places, Lower Wood (Lower pronounced as in 'four') having once been in the manor of Leebotwood. Until the 1940s it was a track used by walkers, packhorses and cattle, particularly from the Malt House, for getting to church or railway station. The last field extending down to the brook was called Outrack and Rough on the tithe map. An outrack tends to be associated with common land and this area once lay in Woolstaston Wood, in which people had common rights, but there appears to be no record of common land here since the wood was felled. Another noticeable feature missing on the tithe map is Bog Lane, the present-day road between Leebotwood and Lower Wood; only the section south of the brook (the Lower Wood end) existed then (see fig.16 on the facing page). The name Church Lane, now used for the lane running between Castle Hill Farm and the church, may also have applied to WL 7. Station Road was once Church Road.

WL 7 is a public footpath that begins between Leebotwood Church and the Old Vicarage and runs as an enclosed track, passing a few houses, to gate (a). From (a), cross the field obliquely to the right to the far corner (c), passing between two mature trees (b); these trees may be Woolstaston/Leebotwood parish boundary markers and once formed part of, or lay close to, a hedge to Little Church Piece (a field). **At (c), cross a gate or stile and then a small stream.** One of the fields drained by this stream was called Seeding Wall, which is thought to have originally been Seething Well. **Continue along the right-hand side of a hedge all the way to the dingle (f) via three stiles alongside gates or gateways. High Field (Farm) lies to the right of the path and close to Bog Lane.** The old Outrack and Rough equates approximately with fields (d) and (e) and the wood down to the brook. High Field lies in a corner of it. **At the dingle enter a largely coniferous wood via stile (f) and follow the wood boundary down to stile (g). A public footpath branches off to the left via stile (g). WL 7 does not cross this stile but turns to the right to follow (approximately) the brook upstream for a short distance. A log bridge spans the brook (once known as Alrec's Brook) and leads to stile (h).** Broad Brook, which this brook soon becomes, was the site of Woolstaston's first fulling mill. **From (h), bear obliquely left up a slope to a stile and gate (i) and then continue in the same direction to a gate and stile (j) on the left-hand side of Malt House and its buildings. From gate (j), pass between two sets of buildings and turn left to follow the Malt House driveway (old enclosed track with RUPP status) out to the road.**

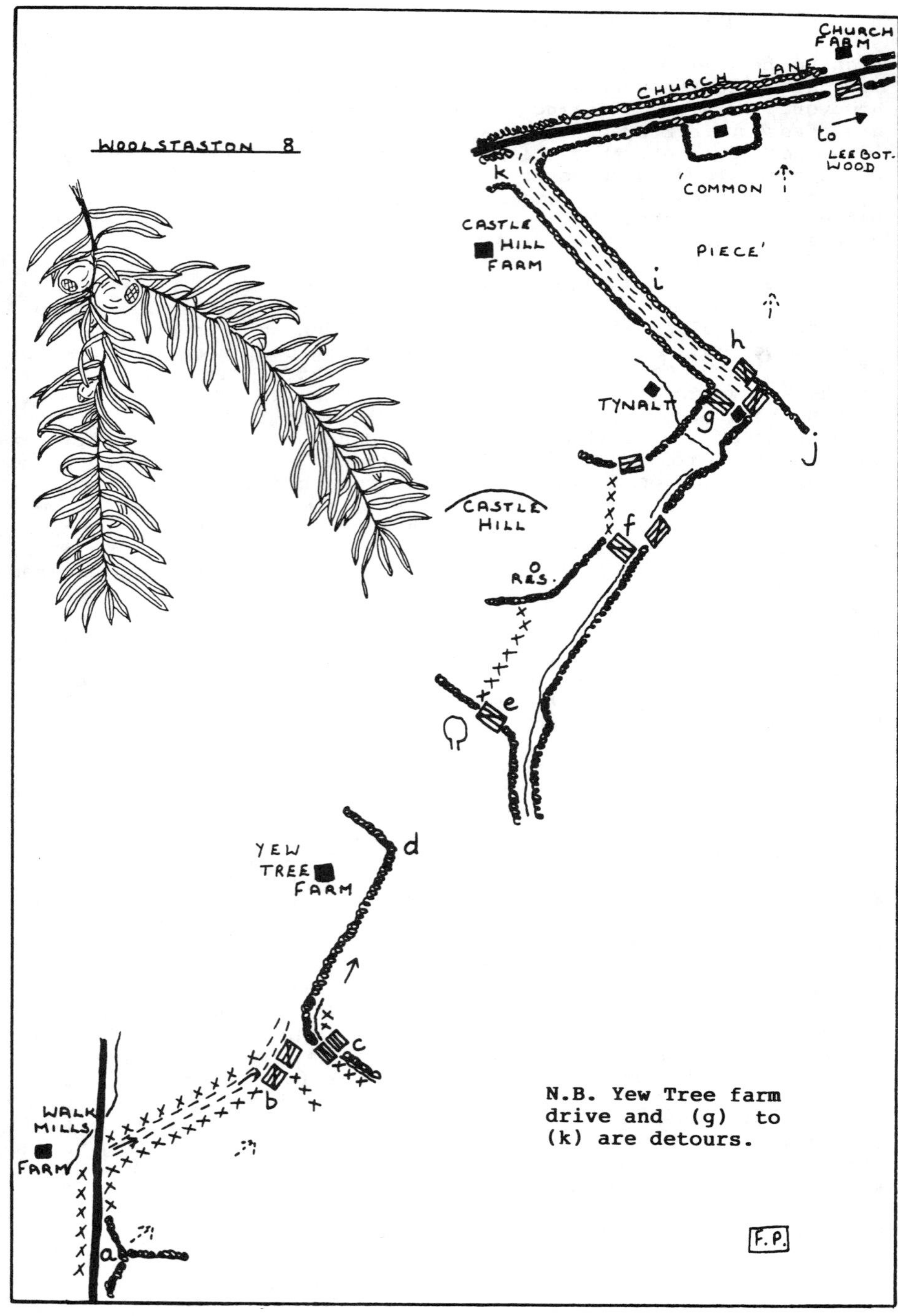
WOOLSTASTON 8
CHURCH FARM
CHURCH LANE
to LEEBOT-WOOD
'COMMON
PIECE'
CASTLE HILL FARM
TYNALT
CASTLE HILL
RES.
YEW TREE FARM
WALK MILLS FARM
a
b
c
d
e
f
g
h
i
j
k
N.B. Yew Tree farm drive and (g) to (k) are detours.
F.P.

WOOLSTASTON 8. WALKMILLS TO CASTLE HILL FARM 0.5 Km/¼ m.

WL 8 is a public footpath that begins near Walkmills Farm. A slight detour has to be taken initially which involves setting out along the driveway towards Yew Tree Farm. Leave the driveway via gate (b) on the right. From (b), immediately turn left and cross two sets of wooden rails at (c). The official right of way is from (a) to (c) but this cannot be walked at present. Follow the right-hand side of a hedge and pass Yew Tree Farm. At (d), where the hedge turns to the left, continue straight on across the field to a tree and gate (e). From (e), the way continues as a wide strip of land. Ahead and to the left is Castle Hill, a natural mound, which was one of the first areas in Woolstaston Wood to be cleared and the site of a mediaeval settlement. **Pass through gate (f) and continue along a wide enclosed track to gate (g) by a garage.** On the tithe map the strip of land between (e) and (g) was marked as a road; it is likely to have been so all the way to Walkmills at some time. **From (g), another detour has to be made. The official route is through gate (h) and across the field to exit nearly opposite Church Farm but this cannot be done. The detour involves turning left to follow the old enclosed track (i) to the road. Track (i) appears to be a green lane and is an ancient route.** On the tithe map it ran from Castle Hill Farm across to Woolstaston Lane to the west of Leebotwood Church, surviving today, from (g), as a long stretch of hedge (j) only. From (g) northwards track (i) today runs to the road but the arrangement of the hedges at (k) suggests that it used to swing round to Castle Hill Farm. This track may have been the older route across the area between Castle Hill Farm and Leebotwood Church, which was a small common; today's road, Church Lane, bears a resemblance to other roads through old commons and may have been created at the enclosure of the common. The common existed near the end of the 18th century but by the 1840s it was enclosed and Church Lane, as it is today, was present; three of the new fields were each called Common Piece (see fig.17 below).

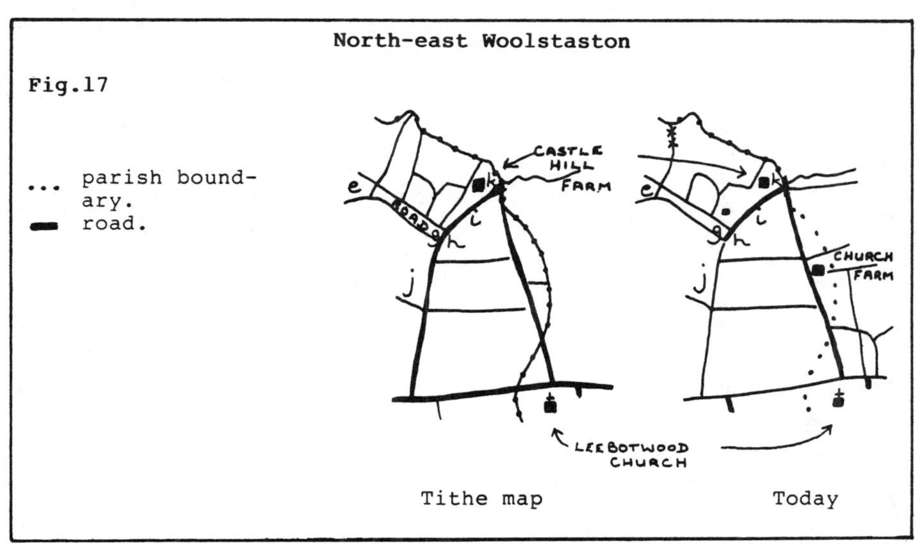

Focus on pools **Insects and snails**

Pools, like streams, are home to nymphs (larvae) of flying insects but many of the stream nymphs cannot tolerate still water. Pool nymphs include those of dragonflies and damselflies, fierce-looking underwater creatures with a hinged mask that can flick open to present strong claws on the front end that will catch even small fish. Damselfly nymphs have three 'tails' and thus bear a superficial resemblance to mayfly nymphs but the 'tails' are leaf-like and are actually gills. An imitation of a damselfly nymph makes a good artificial fly for catching trout. The colourful adults can be seen around pools, the damselflies being much more slender than the dragonflies. Damselflies found in the Mynd area include the common blue damselfly (blue and black), the blue-tailed damselfly (a mostly black body with blue near the tail end), the large red damselfly (red and black), the azure damselfly (also blue and black) and the emerald damselfly (metallic green). The eyes often match the main colour scheme! There are some magnificent dragonflies too, including the common and the southern aeshna (black, yellow and blue) and the black and gold-ringed dragonfly (black and yellow with green eyes); the latter prefers a stream habitat but it can be seen at Wildmoor Pool, which has two inflowing streams. The broad-bodied and the four-spotted chaser are shorter & stouter than the species just mentioned and are dull-coloured apart from the male of the former, which is blue. The black darter is another smaller species that frequents Wildmoor Pool.

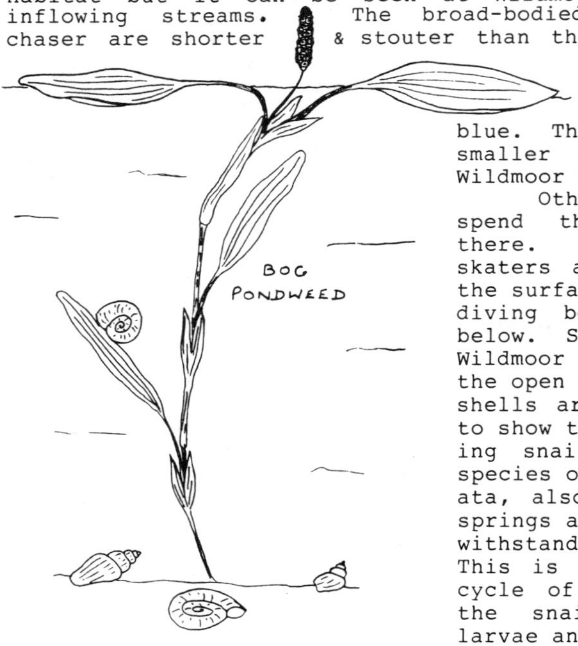

BOG PONDWEED

Other creatures in the pool spend their whole life cycle there. Insects include pond skaters and whirligig beetles on the surface with water boatmen and diving beetles and their larvae below. Snails, too, abound and Wildmoor Pool (the largest pool on the open hill) has plenty of empty shells around its shallow margins to show that ramshorn and wandering snails are present. Another species of snail, Limnaea truncul-ata, also frequents the hillside springs and pools, although it can withstand drought for some time. This is associated with the life cycle of the sheep liver fluke; the snails harbour the fluke larvae and the sheep the adults.

Focus on maps **Tithe maps**

Tithes, taxes for the support of clergy and church, were reassessed around 1840. The maps drawn up then, along with lists of apportionments, tell us in great detail about the buildings and fields (including the field names) at that time, and about land ownership. The old tracks are shown and some footpaths but sometimes it is only the field names that suggest the passage of a path through or near them.

SOME BOUNDARY STONES

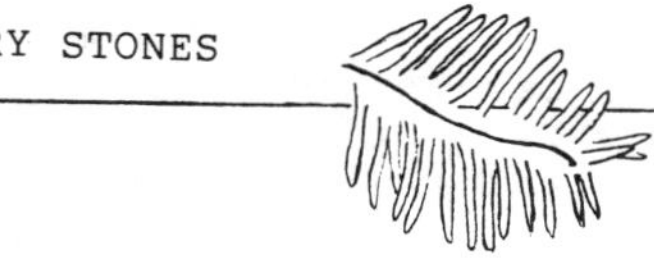

BOUNDARY STONE ON THE OLD SMETHCOTT COMMON, see Sm 4.

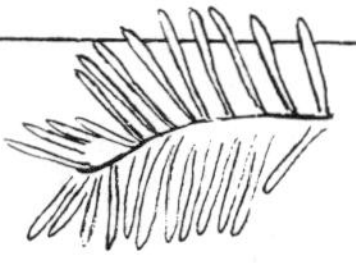

THE BOTLEY STONE, see MY 3.

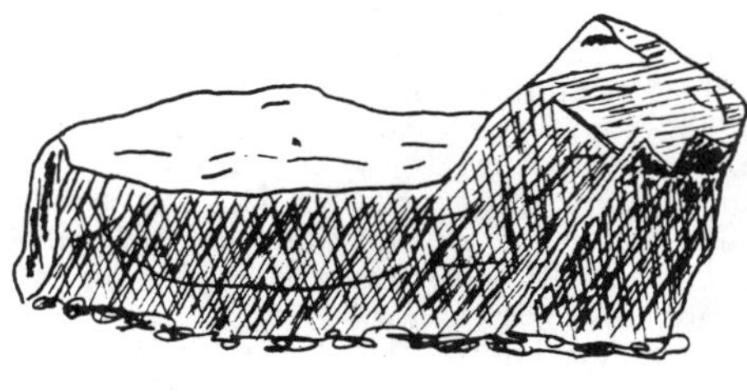

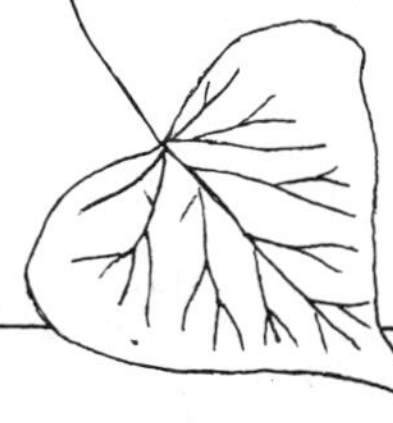

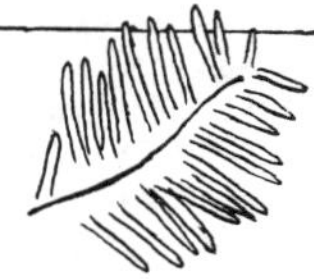

BOUNDARY STONE ON COTHERCOTT HILL, see Pb 8.

Focus on patron saints.

Each church around the Mynd is dedicated to a particular saint and each parish, in some way, commemorates its patron saint's day e.g. Church Stretton usually has a special day of prayers and gifts. In the past, the saint's day or the nearest Sunday to it, and even the eve and the day after, were celebrated with much festivity, known as a wake. Pulverbatch had a three-day fair but it was unusual for an annual fair to be held in relation to the patron saint.

Smethcott - St.Michael. Woolstaston - St.Michael. September 29th.

Pulverbatch - St.Edith. September 17th. St Edith, daughter of King Edgar, died at the age of twenty three on September 16th. She had been a nun and an honorary abbess of Wilton. An annual three-day fair was established on the feast of St.Edith in 1254, and this was on September 17th; it was held until 1914.

Myndtown - St.John the Baptist. June 24th is the day commemorating the birth of St.John the Baptist. John prepared people for the coming of Jesus, baptizing many and later baptizing Jesus. August 29th commemorates the beheading of John.

Church Stretton - St.Lawrence. August 10th. St.Lawrence was a Spaniard who became a deacon to the Pope and was martyred three days after him in 258. He was bound on a hot, glowing gridiron and roasted. The gridiron is represented twice in the church; a carving of St.Lawrence, holding a small gridiron, stands at the south corner of the tower outside. More poignant is the gridiron represented inside with copper flames which is a memorial to three young brothers who died in a hotel fire in Stretton. Little Stretton held wakes on the Sunday after August 21st which was apparently St.Lawrence's day in the old calendar (pre 1582).

Wentnor - St.Michael and All Angels. September 29th. St Michael (with or without all the angels) was often chosen for churches on or close to a hill, presumably because they are felt to be nearer the angels.

Ratlinghope - St.Margaret. There are several St.Margarets and it is not known which one Ratlinghope is dedicated to. The St.Margaret listed in the calendar of the Book of Common Prayer is remembered on July 20th. She was the daughter of a pagan priest and underwent much torture for her Christian beliefs before she was finally beheaded. Another St.Margaret was Queen of Scotland, renowned for her charity and remembered on November 16th.

Wistanstow - Church of the Holy Trinity.

Lydbury North - St.Michael. Cwm Head - St.Michael. September 29th.

Minton - Wakes were held on the Sunday after October 15th. It has been suggested that the chapel that once existed at Minton may have been dedicated to St.Thecla and that the wake continued long after the chapel was lost. My references put St. Thecla's day on September 23rd and not on October 15th.

All Stretton - St.Michael and All Angels.

Little Stretton - All Saints. November 1st is the day when all the saints are remembered. The preceding day is All Souls Day (otherwise known as Halloween) when all those who have died are remembered.

Plowden (Catholic church) - St.Walburga. February 25th. St.Walburga was the daughter of a West Saxon chief in the eighth century. As a nun, she went to Germany and was in charge of nuns in a monastery built by her brother. After his death she was put in charge of the monks too.

BIBLIOGRAPHY

The Victoria County History of Shropshire, all available volumes.
The Tithe Maps of the 1840s and Ordnance Survey Maps.
The Foxhall Field Maps.
Documents in the Local Studies Library relating to relevant villages.
Maps of the Long Mynd in the Earl of Powis collection, Shire Hall.
The Geology of Shropshire by P.Toghill. 1990.
Landscape of the Welsh Marches by T.Rowley. 1986.
Archaeology of the Welsh Marches by S.C.Stanford. 1991.
Domesday Book, Sciropescire edited by F. and C.Thorn. 1986.
The Old Roads of England by Sir W.Addison. 1980.
The Drovers (Shire Album) by S.Toulson. 1980.
Mediaeval Roads (Shire Album) by B.Hindle. 1989.
Turnpike Roads (Shire Album) by G.Wright. 1992.
Mediaeval Fields (Shire Archaeology) by D.Hall. 1982.
Shropshire Field Names by H.Foxhall. 1980.
The Farmer Feeds Us All by P.Stamper. 1989.
Some Water Mills of South Shropshire by G.Tucker. 1991.
Place Names of the Welsh borderlands by A.Lias. 1991.
Shropshire Place Names by M.Gelling. 1990.
Words and Places by Rev.I.Taylor. 1873.
Shropshire Folk Lore edited by C.Burne. 1883, reprinted 1974.
Herefordshire Folk Lore by E.M.Leather. 1912.
Kelly's Directories.
The Ecological Flora of Shropshire. 1985.
The Oxford Book of Trees by A.R.Clapham. 1975.
Woodlands by W.Condry. 1974.
The Trees of Shropshire by A.Morton. 1986.
The Wild Boglands by David Bellamy. 1987.
Wild Orchids of Britain by V.S.Summerhayes. 1951/1976.
The Atlas of Breeding Birds in Britain and N.Ireland by J.T.R.Sharrock. 1976.
Field Guide to Birds of Britain. Reader's Digest.
An Atlas of the Breeding Birds of Shropshire. 1992.
The Birds of the British Isles by T.A.Coward. 1920/1945.
Butterflies and Moths of Shropshire by A.M.Riley. 1970.
Dragonflies of Shropshire by Stephen Butler. 1982.
Casting for Gold by J.Bailey. 1991.
Waterside Guide by J.Goddard. 1988.
Oxford Book of Insects by J.Burton. 1968.
Field Guide to the Water Life of Britain. Reader's Digest. 1985.
Oxford Book of Invertebrates by D.Nichols and J.Cooke. 1971.
The Complete Carp Angler by Andy Little. 1992.
Mushrooms and other Fungi of G.B. and Europe by R.Phillips. 1981.
The Shropshire Naturalist, articles from.
Field Guide to the Animals of Britain. Reader's Digest. 1985.
Animal Tracks and Signs. Collins Guide. 1990.
A Calendar of Saints by J.Bentley. 1986.
The Book of Common Prayer.
The English Missal for the Laity. 1958.
The Parson's Handbook by P.Dearmer. 1931.
Bells and Bellringing by J.Camp. 1968, reprinted 1984.
Walcot Hall, a brief history. 1991.
Leaflets from many of the relevant churches.
A Night in the Snow by Rev.E.D.Carr. 1865, reprinted 1990.

BIBLIOGRAPHY

Through the Highlands of Shropshire on Horseback by M.Weale. 1935.
The Oxford Reference Dictionary edited by J.M.Hawkins. 1986, reprinted 1989.
The New Standard Dictionary of the English Language, Volumes 1 and 2. 1914.
The Great Civil War in Shropshire by W.J.Farrow. 1926.
A Civil War Trail through S.W. Shropshire by T.Bryan.
Welsh Dictionary. Collins-Spurrell. 1980.
Mysterious Wales by C.Barber. 1982.
Church Stretton by D.Bilbey. 1985.
Railways of Shropshire by R.Morris. 1991.

A MILESTONE AT THE BRIDGES

INDEX

INDEX

INDEX

Ordnance survey maps covering the area in this book:-
Landranger 126 and 137.
Pathfinder SJ 40/50, SO 29/39, SO 49/59, SO 28/38, SO 48/58.